*Oracle Press*™

Oracle Developer/2000 Handbook

Robert J. Muller

Osborne **McGraw-Hill**

Berkeley New York St. Louis
San Francisco Auckland Bogotá Hamburg London Madrid
Mexico City Milan Montreal New Delhi Panama City
Paris São Paulo Singapore Sydney Tokyo Toronto

Osborne **McGraw-Hill**
2600 Tenth Street
Berkeley, California 94710
U.S.A.

For information on translations or book distributors outside the U.S.A., or to
arrange bulk purchase discounts for sales promotions, premiums, or fundraisers,
please contact Osborne **McGraw-Hill** at the above address.

Oracle Developer/2000 Handbook

  34567890 DOC 99876

ISBN 0-07-882180-0

Acquisitions Editor Scott Rogers	**Computer Designer** Roberta Steele
Project Editor Bob Myren	**Illustrator** Lance Ravella
Copy Editor Ann Spivack	**Series Design** Jani Beckwith
Proofreader Linda Medoff	**Quality Control Specialist** Joe Scuderi

About the Author

Robert J. Muller, Ph.D., is a San Francisco consultant specializing in project management and software engineering with a focus on database and object-oriented technologies. He has worked with the ORACLE database management system since version 3 in 1983. He has a Ph.D. from the Massachusetts Institute of Technology and has published several papers on relational database and CASE applications as well as a book on testing object-oriented software.

Contents

PART II
Prototyping and Design

PART III
Implementing, Testing, and Debugging

PART IV
Deploying Forms with Other Tools

Acknowledgments

I want to thank several people from Oracle Corporation, where I first learned how to use the Interactive Application Facility. Larry Ellison, of course, was always inspirational; my real thanks to him are for guiding Oracle and its products to become the terrific success that it has become. Jenny Overstreet always helped to get things done. Kathryn Daugherty and Mary Winslow taught me most of what I learned at Oracle. Bill Friend, the inventor of Forms, was always helpful, as were Sohaib Abbassi and Peter Clare. Gary Berlind let me go beyond Forms to understanding the bigger picture. For this book, I would like to specifically thank Paul Zola, my technical editor, for finding all the flaws and muddy thinking. I also want to thank Mark Herring, a Developer/2000 product manager, for providing terrific support for the product. I could not have completed this book without their help. I would also like to thank Niall Wall for helping me get the CD-ROM that is included with this book.

I want to thank George Koch for giving me the opportunity to become a writer. Revising his first edition of *ORACLE: The Complete Reference* was a key experience in developing my confidence. I also want to thank George and the crew at KOCH Systems Corporation (especially Ann Steele, Baxter Madden, and Lynn Healy) for showing me what ORACLE could do in the real world.

At Osborne/McGraw-Hill, I'd like to thank my editors, Brad Shimmin and Scott Rogers, who had faith in the book's ideas and market; Bob Myren, project editor, and Ann Spivack, copy editor, who sharpened the prose wonderfully; and last but not least Heidi Poulin, who made sure everything got to the right people at the right time. I'd also like to thank Jani Beckwith, Roberta Steele, Richard Whitaker, and Peter Hancik, who had the Herculean task of integrating and arranging the massive bitmap illustration load that this book required. The Augean stables have nothing on this book.

It is customary to apologize to one's family for taking time on weekends and vacations to do the book. I cannot do that, since I am now a full-time writer and consultant. I will say that the weekends and vacations with my family, M'Linn Swanson and Theo Muller, provided me with the stamina I needed to finish the book while learning about the perils of a home office and running a business. I could not have done the book without them.

Preface

It is not really very hard to write a book like this, but as with writing software, the writing of the book is a pebble on the tip of the iceberg. I would like to draw a small, metaphorical picture in the hopes of conveying a deeper understanding of the architectural underpinnings of this book.

Everyone should read the article in a recent issue of *IEEE Software* magazine, "Architectural Mismatch: Why Reuse Is So Hard," by David Garlan, Robert Allen, and John Ockerbloom (*IEEE Software,* Volume 12 Number 6, November 1995, pages 17-26). This article makes explicit some of the things that have formed my way of thinking about using tools such as Developer/2000 to develop applications. Reuse, of course, is the Holy Grail of software architecture, and as yet there are no Galahads capable of finding that grail. The article details some of the reasons why this is so, the main one being that so-called reusable systems simply do not match the situations in which designers try to use them.

While it may seem logical to many to pursue the grail, I am convinced that most of us in the software industry are not Galahads, pure of heart and soul and ready to leave this vale of tears once we find perfection. Most of us simply need to get our jobs done and to contribute as much value to our customers as possible in the process. As a purely practical matter, it makes perfect sense to construct software that is as reusable as possible—but *not more so.*

We design tools for specific purposes. If you go to any large hardware store, you will find a plethora of saws designed for every possible situation. You have different saws for different kinds of wood. You have different saws for cutting wood in different directions. You have different saws for different locations of wood (cutting wood that is attached to something, as in being part of a wall, requires a special saw: you cannot move the wall to the table saw). You have different saws for different power sources. You even have different saws that vary purely in an economic sense (competing brands, international trade, local preferences). And the world is not static; new situations (new building materials, new locations, new vendors) arise every day, adding to the need for new tools. To choose the right saw for the right job is a skill requiring years of direct experience with tools, building materials, and situations, not to mention a largish cash flow.

The practical builder does not choose the tool solely by its intended use. By experience, he or she has learned how to apply tools to situations beyond those envisioned by their designers. The art of *using* tools (as opposed to *designing* them) requires just as much knowledge and creativity. But there are limits, and you cannot press a design into use beyond its intentended limits.

Developer/2000 is also a tool, like a saw. Over the twelve or so years of its existence, it has grown to be an extraordinarily capable, broad-ranging tool for developing applications. As with any tool, Developer/2000 has its limits and shortcomings, and it makes specific assumptions that are basic to its design intentions—go beyond these assumptions at your peril.

NOTE
This book covers Developer/2000 versions 1.0, 1.1 and 1.2. The examples use the following product versions:

Forms	4.5.6.0.7
Reports	2.5.3.1.16
Graphs	2.5.5.1.0

My contention has always been that software tools need to be extensible and easy to use to allow them to fit the very different situations they must confront. Developer/2000 is such a system. When you find yourself, however, spending hours trying to get that very capable tool to do something that it was not intended to do, you are wasting your time. In writing this book, I have tried repeatedly to clarify the whys of Developer/2000, so that you understand what it does. The reverse of this is to understand, clearly, what it does not do. The best way to use this tool is to build applications in a straightforward, competent manner that accomplishes your requirements and adds value to your customer's lives.

—Bob Muller
San Francisco, California, November, 1995

PART 1

Building Applications

CHAPTER 1

Introducing
Developer/2000

Since you are reading this book, the chances are good that you either have or want to have an ORACLE7 database with data to support some task. That task probably involves displaying and managing the data in some way. Welcome to Developer/2000, the product from Oracle that makes it easy to build database applications. This book will show you how to develop applications with Developer/2000 that not only satisfy your requirements but that do so with elegance and precision. Developer/2000 is a powerful product; this book will empower you to use it to create quality applications with minimal effort.

An Overview of Building Applications

An *application* is a computer program that does some task. A *database application* is a program that uses data from a database management system such as ORACLE7. Most database applications have to do with displaying data in useful ways or with entering and updating the data in the database.

There are many ways to build applications. You can use a full-scale programming language such as COBOL, C, or C++. There are many such languages, each with its advantages and disadvantages. Programming with these languages gives you a great deal of flexibility and performance, but you work hard to use that flexibility or to get that performance. It is quite easy to make errors or to inadvertently program in such a way that you crash or slow the program down rather than speed it up.

This is particularly true with database applications. Database applications have their own requirements, interfaces, and languages, which makes programming even more difficult. This is one of the reasons why database companies and others have developed application generators and report writers such as Oracle's Developer/2000 that make it much easier to develop database applications. It is also the reason for this book, which tells you what you need to know to develop database applications effectively with Developer/2000.

An *application generator* is a tool that builds applications mainly through declarative specification of the application rather than through procedural programming. In their pure form, application generators are very powerful. With just a few statements or filled-in fields in a form, you can generate very capable applications. As application generators have matured over the years, they increasingly have added back procedural capabilities, giving them flexibility, as well as power.

A report writer is an application generator that builds *reports,* applications that generate formatted output based on data from a database. Report writers tend to be powerful because they target very specific kinds of output and generate it with a minimal set of instructions.

Modern applications generally consist of a graphical user interface with menus, tool bars, dialog boxes, and windows that display the application objects, whatever they might be. The two kinds of objects of interest are forms and reports.

Form Applications

In the early days, Oracle's tools generated "applications." The first version of the Forms component of Developer/2000 was the Interactive Application Generator, IAG. As more and more developers used the tool, the culture around it began to refer to the kind of application it produced as a "form" because they strongly resembled the standard business form. Oracle then began to use the term "form" as part of the product name: SQL*Forms.

A *form* application is thus an application that presents data in an online format consisting of a series of fields laid out in one or more windows. Figure 1-1 shows a sample form application from the Developer/2000 examples.

As you can see, the form provides a good way to view the information that the application shows you. Forms also provide a way of entering and changing that information. You can type data into the form fields or change the data that is in them, depending on what the form designer lets you do.

A form application can have one form, or it can have many forms, depending on the tasks it has to accomplish. Form design, as with paper forms, is an art: you have to get just the right format and information or the form becomes difficult to use and error prone. Breaking a form into multiple parts is a common way to reduce the complexity of a very large and complicated form. The same thing works with an online application. Simple forms correspond to a *record*, which is a series of data fields—a single row of data. The form can display a single record at a time, or it can display several at once, as in Figure 1-1. The tools in a form let you manage the records (query, insert, update, delete, scroll, and so on).

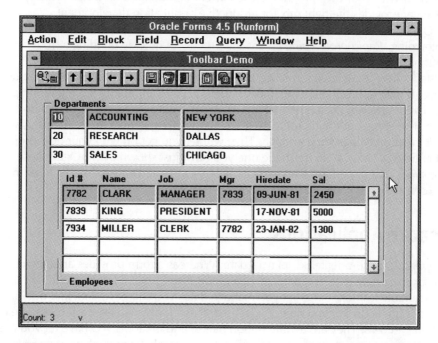

FIGURE 1-1. *A form application*

There is a particular kind of form called a *master-detail* form that divides the form into a master record and several detail records. This organization is so common that most sophisticated generators handle it as a specific option for building the form (along with the more common single-record option). Figure 1-1 is also an example of the master-detail form. The Departments section of the form is the master record. When you select a department, the form displays the employee records that correspond to that department: the department details.

Application generators such as Developer/2000 Forms let you build applications without diving into the depths of a programming language and the accompanying graphical user interface (GUI) frameworks. By abstracting the most important parts of application building into powerful commands and data structures, application generators can quickly build applications that would take days or weeks to build in a programming language. These applications use already debugged code (more or less) that does what it should do. So, you do not need to worry about the design, care, and feeding of those parts of the application unless you want to do so.

The first generation of application builders was quite limited in functionality and power. Most now have powerful and flexible programming languages and other features that let you do whatever you need to do. Many let you extend the generator with your own programs. The current combination of power, safety, and flexibility provides the right mix for productive application development.

One aspect of such development that is important to mention is rapid prototyping. *Rapid prototyping* means the process of quickly building a "rough draft" of the application, perhaps with several features missing but with substantially complete performance of its basic functionality. Because you can do so much with application generators so quickly, you can rapidly build a running application against a database that lets users see what you are proposing to do for them. The danger in rapid prototyping with application generators is that users will think the prototype is good enough. They will let you get on with your next project rather than paying you to finish the one you have just shown them! Often these prototypes do not perform well and can lack security and ease-of-use features that the users may not know they need.

Report Applications

A *report* is a page-oriented display of data. Whereas a form provides an interactive tool for managing data, the purpose of a report is to format a large amount of data in a readable fashion, not to let you manage data. You still have data laid out in records and fields, but you do not have interactive tools such as scroll bars to deal with the records. They are all laid out on pages, and the tools you have let you deal with the pages—print them, scroll through them, or whatever the format permits.

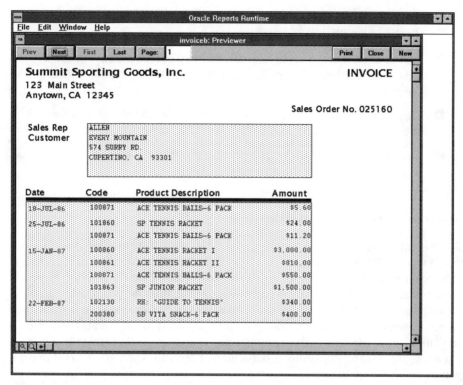

FIGURE 1-2.   *An invoice report*

Developer/2000 has a Reports tool that gives you very powerful report generation capabilities.

Figure 1-2 shows a report that represents a master-detail invoice. It closely resembles what you would see in the invoice form; if you had more invoice items on the report, you would have multiple pages with footers, headers, and all the other accoutrements of a page-oriented report.

Developer/2000 provides you with many different kinds of reports.

- *Tabular:* A simple table of data

- *Mailing label:* A series of regularly repeating records formatted on each page in a certain area (mailing labels, get it?)

- *Form letter:* Boilerplate text surrounding data from a record that fills in blanks in the text

- *Master-master:* Two groups of unrelated records displayed together

■ *Master-detail:* A master record with two or more related detail records displayed together

■ *Matrix or crosstab:* A cross-tabulation of two columns showing some aggregate or other value for the combination of each value from each column

■ *Data file:* A comma-separated or other variety of delimited data file; you use this to transfer data into other tools (there are easier ways, usually)

■ *Graph:* A report that includes a chart or graph of the data in addition to or in place of displaying the data itself

Graphics Applications

Graphics are pictorial representations of data. The term *chart* also refers to this kind of data representation. Developer/2000 gives you a sophisticated set of tools for both creating standalone graphics applications and for including graphics in your forms and reports. Figure 1-3 shows a graphics application depicting a bar graph.

You can even make the graphs react interactively. For example, in a graph that represents some kind of aggregation, you can drill down to see a graph with the detail for a single element of the aggregate or summarize a set of individual items into an aggregate. This capability is particularly powerful when you embed the graphic in a form application.

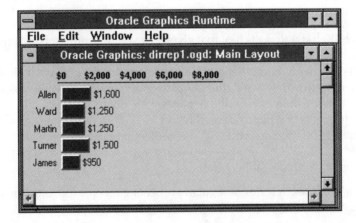

FIGURE 1-3. *A graphics application*

Applications and Development

Applications, of course, go far beyond the standard concepts of form, report, and graph. These are building blocks, not the sum of what you can do in applications. You can add things like menus and menu items, toolbars and buttons, icons, and any kind of graphic background you want. You can use any amount of free text and fonts of any description. Depending on your tools, you can do almost anything you want to do. Developer/2000 tools are more limited than a programming language in this respect, but not by much, as you will see from the demonstration programs that come with Developer/2000. The definitions of form and report tend to merge; you can make your reports somewhat interactive, and you can mimic many report-formatting features in forms.

And that brings up the final aspect of building applications: choice. You have to make many choices and decisions in the process of deciding what to do in your applications. Look at the Table of Contents of this book and compare it to the tables of contents in the Developer/2000 documentation. You will see that many of the chapters in this book are about choices you make, not about how to insert an iconic button or how to use 20 different Windows fonts in the same application.

The philosophy of application building in this book centers on the user, not the developer. Instead of developing applications just for the fun of developing, focus on giving the user of the application the value he or she expects from it. That kind of quality is what really delivers on the promise of tools such as Developer/2000. If flashy graphics and fancy layouts help the user, then by all means spend time on them. However, you should spend ample time on requirements, design, and testing to create the value in your application from a clear understanding of what the user wants and of the best way to deliver that with your tools.

This book will help you understand both the process of using Developer/2000 and the fundamentals of the tools themselves. It will give you the background you need to expand your knowledge and creativity into the infinite world of creating applications.

What Is Different About Database Applications?

What makes a database application so special? How does it differ from the ordinary, everyday application?

A *database manager* is a software system that lets you query, manipulate, and control data through the database language SQL. When you use a database manager with your application, you create a *database* application rather than just an application.

Real database managers provide data protection against the vicissitudes of life (*recovery*); support multiple users (*concurrency*), multiple applications, and *referential integrity;* protect you from unauthorized use of your data (*security*); and isolate you from the details of managing data on a particular platform (*portability*).

Good ones do a lot more than that, particularly in the area of making the data more easily accessible. SQL and relational data modeling give you a strong, reliable paradigm for data access. The best database managers provide a level of performance that scales up with your hardware. Finally, the database manager provides interfaces and tools that let you use all these features and maintain your database.

Before getting into details, a warning: Developer/2000 handles most of the following issues elegantly and well, using the features of ORACLE7 or another database manager. The following sections tell you what you need to know to understand why certain things happen in Developer/2000 applications; but in general, it is solely for your information—not because you need to do anything. That is why you use an application generator such as Developer/2000, to avoid having to design and code all this complexity.

Another warning: this is just an overview—if you want to know the details on these issues, look in the ORACLE7 documentation or a book on ORACLE7 database administration and programming, such as *Oracle: The Complete Reference, Third Edition,* by George Koch and Kevin Loney (Osborne/McGraw-Hill, 1995), or *Oracle DBA Handbook,* by Kevin Loney (Osborne/McGraw-Hill, 1994).

Recovery

Recovery is the ability of the database manager to recover from transaction, application, system, and media failures. If you write an application that depends on a file system and direct file access, you totally expose yourself to any failure at any level. Your software has to take such failures into account. Usually it deals with transaction failures, but other kinds of failure often damage the underlying data. Between Developer/2000 and the underlying database manager, you do not need to worry at all about recovery. You may occasionally need your database administrator to restore a damaged database file somewhere—as with any software, back up early and often.

Part of the reason behind the appearance of database management software was the perception that things did not have to be this way. With a little abstraction and a little technology, it should be possible to deal with all of these failures.

The abstraction comes from the concept of the transaction. A *transaction* is a logical unit of work. The transaction begins with a data-related action and ends with a successful termination command (*commit*) or an unsuccessful termination *command (rollback)*. These limits essentially set up a sequence of data operations that you can undo if needed by rolling back.

Now, adding some technology, the database manager can figure out what to do when a failure occurs. If the error is not fatal, the transaction rolls back and that is the end of it. If the error is fatal to the application, the database manager rolls back the current transaction. If the error is fatal to the database, the process of restarting the database rolls back all the active transactions. This all happens through the process of logging.

Logging

With *logging,* every data-related operation goes into a log; alternatively, the state of the database that the operation changed goes into a log. Either way, when a failure occurs, the database manager uses the log to restore the database to where it was before the problem happened. Using the log, the database manager can even roll changes forward to some well-defined point rather than leaving you back at the beginning of a transaction. This permits restoring from backup followed by rolling forward a transaction log to a known point. Your application does not need to worry about the results, and it does not need any code to recover the database.

Committing or Rolling Back

The one thing your application does need to worry about is signaling to the database manager when your transaction ends, usually with the SQL COMMIT WORK statement or the ROLLBACK WORK statement. This has some implications for application design.

The first choice you must make is whether to make the decision to commit or rollback accessible to your end user. You do this with a menu choice, keypress, or tool button. This gives the user total control over the progress of the work in the database. He or she can perform one small change or many large changes—whatever is appropriate.

The next choice is to decide what constitutes a logical unit of work. Even if you give the user control over commit and rollback, your application will still need to offer those choices at appropriate points. For example, you might allow commits or rollbacks after accomplishing both the deletion of a row and of the rows that depend on the row. If you allowed the user to commit after the deletion but before the dependent deletion, you would violate referential integrity (discussed shortly). Ask yourself what should the database manager restore if there is a disk crash? If this involves more than one operation, package all the operations involved into one transaction.

You also generally need to decide what to do if the user exits the application without explicitly committing or rolling back. Most applications tend to commit the changes or to ask what to do; very few roll back silently. Interestingly, if the user crashes the application, it is exactly the opposite: the database manager will always roll back the outstanding transaction. The assumption is that you can exit normally from an application only at the end of a logical unit of work. You should design your application and your transactions to reflect this assumption.

You may also have to put in some logic to deal with redoing your work, if that is appropriate under the circumstances.

Now, the good thing about Developer/2000 as an application generator is that it fully understands all of these issues and automatically takes care of them for you. It automatically handles commit and rollback requests from the user at appropriate points in the application logic. It automatically generates the commit and rollback commands in your interface. It gives you ways to include supporting operations in each transaction as part of its basic application structure.

Concurrency

Concurrency is the ability for multiple processes to access the database at the same time. These can be clients on different machines or separate processes on the same machine. There are as many ways to handle concurrent data access as there are academics who write about it. Again, Developer/2000 and ORACLE7 between them handle these issues automatically, so you do not need to worry about it. You may need to write the occasional error handler, but this will be infrequent.

Because the logic of concurrency relates strongly to that of recovery, it uses the same mechanism: the transaction. The database manager needs to interleave the transactions so that each process sees the data as though the transactions had proceeded separately in sequence; the academic term for this is *serializability*. And even that is not sacred for some kinds of transaction management.

ORACLE7 handles concurrency by locking tables and rows in different ways. Locking prevents other processes from starting some operation that would violate the concurrency rules. The bad part is the complexity of the locking mechanism; the good part is how well it works. It gives you a very high level of concurrency and does so automatically. If you are interested in the specifics of locking, see the *ORACLE7 Server Concepts Manual,* Chapter 10, "Data Concurrency." This should tell you all you need to know about how ORACLE7 deals with multiple users.

In any system that handles concurrency by locking, you risk the occasional deadlock. *Deadlock* occurs when each transaction in a set of transactions blocks (waits) on another transaction on the set; they all indefinitely wait for one another to do something. You can avoid deadlocks by arranging your SQL statements to access tables in the same order in all your competing applications, as Oracle's *ORACLE7 Server Concepts Manual* (Chapter 10, "Data Concurrency," the section on Deadlock Detection) recommends. A good way to do this is to centralize access to multiple tables in reusable forms or procedures that the applications can share. If that is not possible, you should experiment with application structure and test thoroughly to make sure that deadlock will not be a problem for your end users.

Data Independence

One of the central reasons for database management is the need for a central database to support multiple applications, as well as multiple users of one application. Database theorists divided their architecture into three parts: the physical aspects of database management (the *internal model*), the logical aspects (the *conceptual model*), and the logical aspects of the shared application views of the data (the *external model*). Figure 1-4 presents this three-level architecture.

This architecture leads to two major consequences for database applications. The first is that you can change the database data model without affecting the applications that use it. If you provide views of the data (SQL views, for example), you will not have to change your applications at all. The second is that you can structure different applications without having to share intermediate data structures based on the conceptual model.

For example, some applications use databases by retrieving tables into memory, then drawing data out of them. This is a poor architecture because it makes your data structure dependent. Your application data structures should reflect the needs of your application, not the structure of your database. You use SQL to recast the data into the form you want it in your application.

The internal model is the physical layout of the data: the access method structure, B-trees, file structures, secondary indexes, and so on. The conceptual

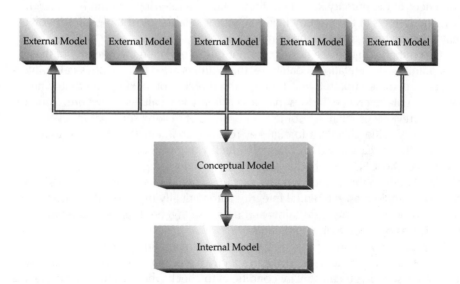

FIGURE 1-4.   *Three-level database management architecture*

model is the centralized, logical data model: the tables with their rows and columns. The external model is the *application views*: the data structures within the applications into which you query data from the database.

The key to all of this theory is *data independence.* You now can distinguish the physical data, central logical tables, and application data structures; they do not all have to be the same. In particular, this means that you can code different application data structures to use the same conceptual model in the central database. The physical data is independent of the conceptual model; the application data is independent of the conceptual model.

Referential Integrity

Referential integrity is the ability of the database to make sure that when a row refers to another row, that second row exists. You should remove your concerns about referential integrity into database construction as much as possible, getting it out of the individual application. You will be much better off. You are also much better off moving simple domain constraints (ranges of numbers, specific strings, enumerated constants, and so on) into the database, though this has nothing to do with referential integrity.

Every table has or should have a primary key. The *primary key* is one or more columns with values that uniquely identify each row of the table. The nature of relational databases represents logical relationships between tables through data references to the primary key of another table. The referring column is a *foreign key,* and it refers to the primary key of the foreign table. Most table joins involve matching the foreign key to the primary key.

Given that, you can see how important it is to maintain the integrity of these data pointers. In a relational database, the pointers are data, not physical pointers that can get fouled up. But you still have the problem of making sure that, when there is a data reference, it does map to a primary key value somewhere. You also have the reverse problem for some relationships of making sure that for every primary key value, there is a foreign key referring to it. Finally, you need to make sure that the primary key does uniquely identify the rows of the table.

Before ORACLE7, you had to enforce these rules using *application triggers,* blocks of code in the application that execute when a specific event occurs. You can now handle most referential integrity automatically in the database using a combination of integrity constraints and *database triggers* (blocks of code in the *database,* as opposed to the application).

SQL gives you many of the tools you need to maintain referential integrity in the CREATE TABLE statement. You can specify the primary key, you can specify foreign keys, and you can specify conditions to check whenever data changes in a row. Standard SQL simply prevents you from violating integrity; ORACLE7 goes one step further with DELETE CASCADE, letting you tell the database manager to propagate deletions through the foreign keys.

You should always express primary and foreign key relationships in your CREATE TABLE statements, even at the cost of the minimal performance hit it implies. The lost productivity and chances for application programming errors are so great that they far outweigh the performance improvement.

There are occasions, however, when the action you want to take because of a data change is too complex for the simple constraints to handle. You can code more complex sequences of actions in your application, or you can code the same sequences in CREATE TRIGGER statements in the database. The trade-off is again performance versus productivity, and this book would usually recommend creating database triggers rather than application triggers if you have a choice. Only in the case of severely slow triggers that affect other applications without giving them the benefits of the trigger, or when only a single application needs the procedure in the trigger, would you put the trigger in the application. You would also do this if you need database portability for your application, because databases other than ORACLE7 may not support database triggers.

You also need to make sure that your complex constraint really does reflect a complete logical constraint. Is there really a need for all the actions to occur in a single transaction? That is what you are implying with a trigger, either in the application or in the database. For example, you may be able to think of situations where you do want to delete records related to a deleted record and situations where you do not. This is not a good thing to put into the CREATE TABLE statement, nor into a trigger. You will need to code this at the application level.

Security

Security is the protection of the database against unauthorized access or change. (This definition assumes that authorized access is secure and will not damage the data, but that is another issue.) In any event, because you separate the data from the application, and because you allow multiple users access to the data, you must also take security needs into account. Different users have different needs, and not all users should have access to all data. Developer/2000 and ORACLE7 combine to provide a high level of security for your applications.

The database management system provides various kinds of security, as does your application. ORACLE7 has an extensive security model that goes well beyond the SQL model in protecting access.

The First Level of Security: Passwords
The first level of security is the ORACLE7 user. Every user has a password. ORACLE7 gives you a way to eliminate password protection for users, but this book strongly advises against using this feature; it is not a good idea to depend on

application security in a client/server environment. The implication for your application is this: you must have a way of logging on to the database with the user name and password that gives your application the right level of access. Developer/2000 handles this requirement for first-level security by providing a dialog box for connecting to the database and by handling logon user names and passwords you supply on the run-time command line. You do not have to write any code to provide this level of security; it all happens automatically in a Developer/2000 application.

The Second Level of Security: Privileges

The second level of security is the schema authorization system. Standard SQL lets you grant access to tables (though, interestingly, it does not let you revoke such access). ORACLE7 extends this system (along with adding revocation) by letting you grant many specific privileges on many specific objects. ORACLE7 also adds a level of indirection with the concept of a role. A *role* is a grouping of users. You can grant a privilege for an object to a role, and all the users assigned that role have that privilege. This provides a powerful and complete mechanism for controlling access to your database down to a very fine level of detail. See the *ORACLE7 Server Concepts Manual,* Part Number A12713-1, Chapters 17 and 18, for details on ORACLE7 security mechanisms.

Because the database manager provides such a strong security model, there is little need to provide data security mechanisms in your application. But the database manager manages its central data, not your application data. If there are additional security needs that your application imposes on the data, you need to apply them. For example, if you store data that you encrypt in your application using a special encryption mechanism, you need to protect that mechanism in your application, not in the database. Others can gain access to the data in the database with tools that do not use your application code. Never put anything into the database that requires more security than the database manager alone can provide.

Portability

Portability is the capability of running on different systems. It applies to operating systems; it also applies to windowing systems, application frameworks, and any other platform of services. This includes the database management platform. Most applications have to deal with portability in several different ways. Your requirements for a Developer/2000 application may include running the same application on different database managers or on different operating systems.

Developer/2000 is itself a portable application developer. You can develop the application and run it on any operating system platform that supports the runtime programs; Oracle Corporation tries to port these tools to as many operating systems as possible. Also, ORACLE7 is itself available on virtually every operating system you are likely to want to use.

Database Portability

Database portability refers to how independent the application is of its underlying database manager. Preceding sections have mentioned various issues regarding SQL standards versus vendor implementations of the language. Another issue is the *interface* or set of interfaces—the specific method(s) by which you access the database manager (see "Database Manager Interfaces," later in this chapter). The decision you must make here is the extent to which your application must run against more than one database manager platform. Does your client require the application to run on both ORACLE7 and Informix? Microsoft Access? SQL Server? If so, you immediately drastically limit yourself to the standard SQL, which is a *minimal* standard to say the least.

ODBC helps somewhat with this, but its main contribution is to standardize the interface to different database managers. *ODBC* (the *Open Data Base Connectivity standard*) is a Microsoft product that provides a uniform SQL language and programming interface for any database manager that cares to write a driver for it. There are vendor or third-party ODBC drivers for every database manager of any interest (see Chapter 15 for details on using the ODBC interface with Developer/2000). By using ODBC, you can switch database managers at run time without recompiling your code.

If you do need to be portable to different database managers, you will also need to decide whether you can take advantage of specific extensions. Can you use the conditional capabilities of your programming language to use different SQL statements depending on the different database managers? As with any kind of exception-based programming, this is a lot more trouble—sometimes more than it is worth in the end. You should experiment and test a good deal if you decide to take this approach.

Operating System Portability

Operating system (OS) portability is the portability of the tools and database manager itself. If you want to run your application on different platforms (Windows, Macintosh, and UNIX, for example, a common combination these days), either you must port the application to different database managers, or your database manager and tools must be able to run on different operating systems using the same interfaces. Increasingly, ODBC plays this role as ODBC drivers become available on different operating systems, as well as for different database managers.

Another way to achieve portability is to use client/server technology. By separating the application and the server, you can run the application on one operating system and the database manager on another. See the "Clients and Servers" section later in this chapter for more details.

SQL

SQL (Structured Query Language) provides a unified language that lets you *query* (ask for), *manipulate* (insert, update, or delete data), or *control* (structure and make secure) data.

If you do not already know SQL, you should get training or read one of the many good books on the language (such as *ORACLE7: The Complete Reference,* by Koch, Muller, and Loney, Osborne/McGraw-Hill, 1995; or the *LAN Times Guide to SQL* by Groff and Weinberg, Osborne/McGraw-Hill, 1994). You will not be able to do much with Developer/2000 unless you understand SQL.

The strongest differentiator between database and other applications is the use of SQL. Programming with SQL instead of navigating through links, pointers, records, and other low-level structures is a totally different way of building applications. Often, using SQL is the greatest leap for programmers new to database application programming.

For example, some programmers use basic SQL to move data from a table into the application in its entirety, then they do sorting, filtering, and other operations on the data in memory. That is what application programming is all about, right? Sorts, searches, and transformations. Well, not anymore. SQL does that for you. By creatively using WHERE, GROUP BY, ORDER BY, and joins, you can do things in three or four lines of SQL code that would take hundreds of lines of program code. Ignoring the power of SQL is the worst mistake you can make in a database application.

Having said that, you should go back and reread the preceding sections to see how the different issues limit your use of SQL. Depending on your needs, you may not be able to take advantage of all the features of SQL, especially those added on by vendors as extensions to the SQL standard.

Developer/2000 makes it easy to take advantage of SQL. First, Developer/2000 automatically generates much of the SQL you need, customizing your SQL to the needs of your forms and reports. Second, Developer/2000 understands SQL and its requirements thoroughly, letting you enter SQL wherever it is useful to do so to accomplish your needs. Third, Developer/2000 does not limit you to SQL; you also have a complete programming language, PL/SQL, that provides the full range of programming capabilities you would expect from a major programming environment. You should, at the application design stage, think about whether you can achieve your intended results better by using SQL or the more complex PL/SQL constructs. Using SQL is more productive and will usually result in fewer faults in your application; using PL/SQL will be more difficult but may give you better performance or better conformance to your requirements. Value comes from making the right choices, not from any specific technology.

There are several variations on SQL that you need to know about to use Developer/2000 effectively. The ORACLE7 dialect of SQL has loads of extensions that make the language more useful. The downside of this is that you cannot use those extensions with any other database. Why is that important?

Developer/2000 does not limit you to working with ORACLE7; you can work with any database manager that supports ODBC. You may want your applications to move readily from one database manager to another, and you do not want to have to recode all your SQL and generate new applications to do that. (See the previous section on portability.)

ODBC is in turn based on the ANSI/ISO standard for SQL (ANSI X3.135-1989, *Database Language—SQL with Integrity Enhancement,* American National Standards Institute, Inc., 1989; or see *A Guide to the SQL Standard, Second Edition,* by C. J. Date, Addison-Wesley, 1989). ODBC drivers that conform to the Minimal level of SQL support, ODBC's basic SQL conformance level, must conform to the ANSI 1989 standard. Many but not all drivers conform to the higher levels of SQL support, Core and Extended. These levels give you some additional SQL statements and data types (ALTER TABLE, for example, or date data types) that nearly every database manager supports. If you want strong portability—the ability to use any ODBC driver—you must use only ANSI SQL.

The ANSI standard, although flawed, provides the basic capabilities of SQL. See C. J. Date's critique of SQL, "A Critique of the SQL Database Language," in his book *Relational Database: Selected Writings* (Addison-Wesley, 1986, pages 269–311) for an excellent discussion of the limitations of SQL. ORACLE7 adheres to this standard, as does ODBC, but goes far beyond it in capability.

The 1992 version of the SQL standard (ANSI X3.135-1992, or see Groff and Weinberg or *Understanding the New SQL: A Complete Guide,* by Melton and Simon, Morgan Kaufman, 1993) greatly expanded the SQL language and fixed many of the problems with the standard, but few vendors (including Oracle) fully support the 1992 standard at this point.

Using only ANSI SQL is hard to do in real-world database applications. You will find it quite constraining. You can get great productivity benefits from using Core and Extended features of ODBC, even though it may limit you somewhat in using particular database managers. In the end, you may find that your customer requirements prevent you from building highly portable applications. This is a judgment call on your part.

You should also note that PL/SQL, the language in which you write Developer/2000 triggers, is an Oracle proprietary language that is not a part of the SQL standard (at least, not *yet;* the next SQL standard may include it). This book uses the term "SQL" to refer only to the SQL language, not to PL/SQL.

Developer/2000 will let you embed different dialects of SQL in PL/SQL code, but you must use the Oracle PL/SQL language in your application triggers.

There are, of course, other kinds of databases: hierarchical databases, network databases, object-oriented databases, and hybrid databases. None of them (other than ones with ODBC interfaces) work with Developer/2000.

Data Models

A *data model* is the particular set of structures you use to construct your view of the data, whether it is the application view or the central conceptual model in the database. The central issue to concern yourself with is the mapping between different data models: the arrows in Figure 1-4. With Developer/2000, you do not need to worry about varying character string comparison semantics or whether your application integers are two bytes, four bytes, or whatever. The data types in Developer/2000 are the SQL data types. There are some additional ones, but the system automatically handles the mapping to SQL. SQL has a simple, well-defined data model based on several specific data types and on the table structure or record as the basic data structure.

The mapping between the models may be more or less difficult depending on the differences between the models. In programming languages, you have very specific data models involving bits and bytes, byte ordering, and all kinds of structural issues. Moving to an application generator or report writer, the tools generally hide these issues.

If you use ODBC rather than connecting directly to ORACLE7, you may have some additional issues to consider; see Chapter 15 for details.

Performance

Inevitably, a programmer's thoughts turn to performance. When a programmer becomes a database application programmer, this fever seems to intensify beyond the bounds of rationality. For some reason, programmers often assume that using a database manager automatically means their applications will perform like slugs on a warm summer night.

Performance is just another requirement. If you can state your performance requirement (see Chapter 4), you can spend time in your application development worrying about satisfying that requirement. Otherwise, you should get on with it and not worry so much. When it becomes time to worry, tune your SQL and your database infrastructure to gain performance improvements. See Chapter 5 of the *ORACLE7 Server Application Developer's Guide*, Part Number 12716-1, for a detailed tutorial on tuning SQL statements. *Tuning Oracle*, by Michael J. Corey,

Michael Abbey, and Daniel Dechichio (Osborne/McGraw-Hill, 1995), is also an excellent guide.

Some application performance issues come from poorly administered databases: lack of appropriate indexes, poor allocation of space, poor organization of the physical data files on the network, or even poor network implementation. Sometimes even the choice of operating system, hardware, or database management software is the problem. The problems with the platform are endless.

Spend some time with the *ORACLE7 Server Administrator's Guide,* Part Number A12522-1, Part VII, "Database and Instance Tuning." You might also look at the myriad books on ORACLE7 database administration for clues here.

After tuning the database manager, the database structure is next. See Chapter 4 of this book for some guidelines on basic database design, or see any of the many books on the subject (including the chapters in *ORACLE7: The Complete Reference, Third Edition,* by Koch, Muller, and Loney). You can modify the design, for example, to support specific joins by "pre-joining" the data. You should not do this, however, unless it satisfies a specific requirement, as it makes the data model less flexible and less capable of supporting multiple applications in a useful way. You can also index and cluster the data to create more efficient access paths.

Having laid all that out, one last piece of advice: never believe everything you read (including this). Benchmark your application before your optimizations, and verify that the optimizations have the desired effect. You may well find that a given technique is a waste of time. You also may find that your application satisfies requirements without optimization at all. A little benchmark work up front may pay dramatic returns in productivity, if not in performance improvement.

Database Manager Interfaces

Another major difference in database applications, as with any application based on a complex software platform, is the interface or set of interfaces to that platform. Such interfaces always impose constraints on what you can do and structure how you do it. Developer/2000 uses the native interface to provide database connections, to provide extensive error-handling mechanisms, and to provide extensive interface options.

First, as the "Security" section discusses, you have to connect to the database, usually with a user name and password. Your application has to gather this information and supply it through the appropriate connection interface. If you are in a networked, client/server environment, the connection string that identifies the server is an important part of this interface, and getting that string right is often a major hassle. The best advice is to work with someone who knows what they are doing—preferably someone who has done it before in the same environment. Developer/2000 provides the basic connection mechanism, but many aspects of connection are outside its control, and it cannot help you much with dealing with these things.

Second, you need to handle errors from the database manager. These can range from server connection errors through SQL parsing errors to data retrieval errors. Looking at the ORACLE7 error codes manual, you can see the problem: anything can happen! Fortunately, it usually does not; there are only a relatively few errors you need to pay serious attention to, such as an unavailable database or a transaction deadlock. ODBC adds an extra layer here by not only supplying its own errors and error handling but by passing through the native database manager's errors as well. Developer/2000 provides extensive mechanisms for handling errors, and handles many errors automatically.

Third, you need to set various options when using the interfaces. Most application generators make the right assumptions and supply the options automatically, as does Developer/2000. You will find yourself faced with some minor decisions about how to use some aspect of the database manager at some point, though, especially if you use ODBC.

Clients and Servers

Client/server computing is now all the rage in the corporate data processing world. As the Internet and other links between computers grow, even home computers are beginning to act as clients to foreign computers. Rumors fly that even your TV may someday be a client to an ORACLE server somewhere.

So what is a client/server application, and why should you need to know anything about it?

A *client/server application* is an application that you divide into at least two parts, one of which requests things from the other. The requester is the client, and the other is the server. This is pretty general; it does not even mention data. Clients can request anything from a server, behavior or data. The only important thing about the relationship is that it is a relationship: there are two parts. The essence of client/server computing is the distribution of work over two or more computers.

Alternatives to client/server architectures include the following options:

- A standalone computer

- A host-based setup that connects terminals to a single processor running the application

- A master-slave setup that connects terminals to slave processors that access the host running the application

- A peer-to-peer setup that enables any computer to request or to service requests

Client/server applications have several advantages over the standalone and host-based options:

- Lower cost (well, maybe not; the jury is still out on the true cost of client/server computing and converting to it; the fat client has not yet sung)
- Better distribution of computing load
- Better user interfaces than is possible with dumb terminals
- Ability to adapt to changing technology, both hardware and software

A key facility of client/server computing is the ability to *partition* your application between client and server. Using Developer/2000 with ORACLE7, for example, you can not only move the database access operations to the server, but you can move chunks of your application code into database procedures or triggers. Another term for this is a *two-tiered* application architecture. A *three-tiered* architecture puts other parts of the application on another server, such as a transaction processing monitor or other middleware. There are application generators coming on the market that support such architectures, but they are very new at this point. A *fully distributed* architecture may place arbitrary parts of the application on an arbitrary server; the new component technologies such as OLE and CORBA are moving in this direction.

There is also a distinction between a fat client and a thin client. A *fat client* puts virtually all the application processing on the client; a *thin client* moves much of it to the server. Developer/2000 can be either kind of client, depending on where your procedure code appears—in the application triggers or in database triggers and procedures.

Your main benefit in using client/server technology is dividing the application code between the workstation and a high-powered server. The Developer/2000 runtime system handles display processing and some logic on the client; the database manager handles data processing and the rest of the logic on the server. You lose some independence, but you gain both performance and flexibility, particularly with many users of many applications using the database.

As you scale upward, you will find that Developer/2000 applications tend to scale well because they are client/server, whereas unified or peer-to-peer applications do not. Also, if you want to distribute your data across a wide area network, using Developer/2000 and ORACLE7 makes it much more likely to scale than having your application do all the work. The main reason for this is the way ORACLE7 works in a client/server environment. It requests data and behavior using SQL rather than requesting the data records. This means the ORACLE7 server does more of the work—a lot more of it. This reduces network traffic and takes better advantage of the higher power of the server.

Also, you can run the Developer/2000 runtime program on one operating system and connect to an ORACLE7 server running a different (and potentially much better performing) operating system. This provides additional flexibility and performance.

Developer/2000 provides you with all the tools you need to develop robust, scalable, and fast applications in a client/server environment, especially when you use it with ORACLE7.

CHAPTER 2

Fitting the Pieces Together

What are the specific tools you get with Developer/2000? This chapter gives you an overview of the tools and the objects with which you can create your applications. With this summary, you will have a basis for the more detailed chapters that follow.

A Road Map to Applications Development

The applications development process encompasses a development life cycle, a series of project documents and products, and a set of tools working together in a development environment. Figure 2-1 shows the structure of applications development using Developer/2000.

The *development life cycle* is a standard process through which you develop your applications. Chapter 3 goes into development life cycles and their structure in some detail.

The *project document* is a product of the life cycle that describes some aspect of the applications you are building, such as the requirements, project and test plans, architecture, or low-level design. Chapter 4 shows you some of the more important project documents.

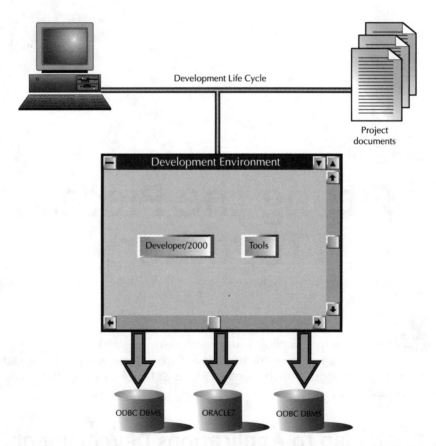

FIGURE 2-1. *The structure of applications development using Developer/2000*

The *development environment* is the set of tools and the framework you use to develop your applications. For this book, we focus on a development environment consisting of Developer/2000, ORACLE7 (or an ODBC-compliant database manager), and the tools that support these products. The development framework consists of the objects that Developer/2000 gives you: forms, blocks and block items, lists of values and record groups, PL/SQL program units and libraries, menu modules, report modules, report data models and layouts, and graphics queries and layouts—to name just a few.

This chapter introduces all these objects and more, to show you the big picture of the Developer/2000 environment. The following sections summarize the objects in the three main components of Developer/2000: Forms, Reports, and Graphics. Each of these components lets you develop one or more types of *module,* a major component of your application that is the basis for storage and object ownership. A module owns the rest of the objects in the system, and the runtime programs generally run a module. You store an entire module in a single file if you store your modules in the file system rather than in the database. Each module contains a different set of objects (some overlap), and each object has *properties* that define its behavior. Most objects allow comments and display lists of any other objects that reference that object.

NOTE

These sections do not discuss every property of the objects, only the ones you are likely to use. Use the online help or the *Forms Reference Manual* (Part Number A32509-1), *Reports Reference Manual* (Part Number A32489-1), or the *Graphics Reference Manual* (Part Number A32483-1) for complete reference information on objects and their properties.

The "Nuts and Bolts" section at the end of this chapter shows how the Developer/2000 environment joins these parts together into a working system. This final section summarizes how your applications work together with each other and with other tools to provide a complete, connected system of applications. Parts Two through Four of this book pull all these objects together to show you how to rapidly build effective, powerful, and robust applications with the Developer/2000 environment framework and tool set.

Forms

The Forms component of Developer/2000 is the environmental component in which you develop, not surprisingly, form modules. It also provides the development framework for developing menu and PL/SQL library modules.

The Form Module

The form module is the main component of your interactive applications. It is also the most complex module in terms of internal structure, containing many separate kinds of objects. Figure 2-2 shows the hierarchy of objects that make up a form module. The block labeled "Programming Objects" summarizes a group of objects; you'll see what these are in the "Programming Objects" sections later in this chapter.

Triggers

A trigger is a block of PL/SQL code you attach to another object: a form, a block, or a block item. You can also have triggers on property classes (you'll learn more

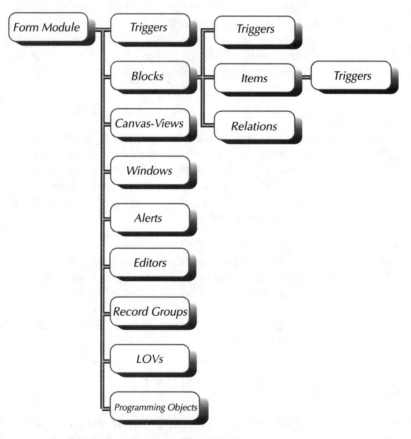

FIGURE 2-2. *The object hierarchy for a form module*

about this in the "Programming Objects" section, later in the chapter). The trigger "fires," or executes, when certain events occur: the event triggers the code.

Triggers in a form application contain the working code that you add to the application, apart from the code you put into separate program units or libraries. Triggers and their structure and processing logic are the biggest part of form design and coding. Chapter 6 contains detailed flow charts showing the structure of the different Forms processes and how triggers fire in those processes. Examples of triggers and the PL/SQL that appears in them are shown in most of the following chapters.

Most triggers you use are *built-in triggers,* triggers that the Developer/2000 framework supplies. These triggers come in several categories, as Chapter 6 details. Each trigger has a specific name—When-Button-Pressed, Post-Query, On-Delete, Key-Help, Pre-Update, for example—that you choose from a list of trigger names. If you define the same name at different levels—block and item, for example—Developer/2000 executes the one at the lowest level by default. For example, you can define a trigger in two of the 20 items in a block and the same trigger at the block level. For events on the two triggered items, the item trigger executes; otherwise, the block trigger executes. You can change this behavior with the Execution Style property of the trigger. The default behavior is Override; you can change this to Before or After in a higher-level trigger to have the trigger fire before or after the lower-level one. You can thus combine behavior in several triggers, as well as replacing behavior.

You can also add your own *user-defined triggers* and fire them explicitly. This feature was more useful in previous versions of Forms; now, with the flexibility of PL/SQL, it is somewhat of an inessential element.

Forms has two main modes: Normal mode and Enter Query mode. Some triggers are not available in Enter Query mode (see the following section, "Blocks") because the actions they take make no sense in that mode.

A certain class of triggers, *key triggers,* fire when you press a key combination in the user interface. Adding key triggers lets you reprogram your keyboard to take actions different from the standard keypress definitions. Because these are nonstandard, the trigger definition lets you display a description of the key in the list of keys available through the Help menu in the standard menu bar.

Blocks

The *block* is the intermediate building unit for forms. You can think of a block in two ways, as a collection of items (as depicted in Figure 2-2) or as a collection of records, each of which has the same structure of items. You specify the number of records to display at once, and you specify whether to display the records horizontally or vertically.

There are two kinds of block. A *base-table block* corresponds to a table or view in the database and manages some number of records corresponding to rows in the table or view. A *control block* does not correspond to a table or view, and its records do not correspond to database rows. Usually, control blocks represent a collection of single-valued items, effectively having only a single record.

The block display has two special characteristics relating to being a container of records. The block can have a *scroll bar* that lets the user manage a set of records larger than what the canvas-view can display. It can also have a special set of visual attributes (which will be covered in the "Programming Objects" section later in this chapter) that define a different display for the *current record,* the record on which the cursor currently rests.

Navigation within the block normally proceeds in the order in which you define the items in a record. The runtime system has functions to move from record to record, from item to item, and from block to block. When you navigate out of the last item in a record, you normally return to the first item in the same record. Forms lets you redefine this behavior so that you go to the next record (or previous record if you back up from the first item). It also lets you navigate to the next or previous block when you navigate out of the last or first item, respectively. You can set specific blocks to be the next block or previous block, creating a linked list of blocks. You can also tell Forms to enter the block name in the block menu, which lets you navigate to a block by choosing its name from a list.

The primary function of the base-table block is to provide an interface to a table in the database. Developer/2000 manages data in the database automatically by constructing SQL statements based on blocks and their structure. The block thus has several properties that manage the construction of these SQL statements:

- *Primary Key and Key Mode:* By default, Forms uses the rowid, a unique internal identifier, to identify the row in SQL statements that it generates. The Primary Key property tells Forms to use instead items and their values to identify the row, corresponding to the columns that comprise the primary key in the database table. The Key Mode property tells Forms whether to include primary key values in the UPDATE statement; some database managers do not permit you to update primary key values. See Chapter 15 for details.

- *<Operation> Allowed:* You can disable specific SQL statements—SELECT, INSERT, UPDATE, or DELETE—for the block.

- *WHERE Clause:* A SQL fragment that Forms adds to the SELECT statement it generates for a query.

- *ORDER BY Clause:* A SQL fragment that Forms uses as the ORDER BY clause in the SELECT statement it generates for a query.

■ *Optimizer Hint:* An ORACLE7 SQL fragment that Forms appends to the SELECT statement to use the special optimization features of ORACLE7 (see the *ORACLE7 Server Concepts Manual*).

■ *Changed Columns:* Forms includes only changed columns in the UPDATE statement it generates if this property is True; otherwise, it updates all columns in the row whether the values have changed or not.

■ *Locking Mode:* Whether to lock a row immediately when you change a value in the row, or to lock it only when you commit the changes you make to the database; see Chapter 15 for details.

Blocks also provide the interface for the query-by-example features of the form. You can place the block in Enter Query mode, then enter data into the fields of the special example record. When you execute the query, Forms then builds a SQL SELECT statement from these values. In combination with the WHERE Clause and ORDER BY Clause properties, this gives you a comprehensive query facility. You can also enter your own additional SQL for the WHERE clause while in Enter Query mode.

Items   A block *item* is the primary building unit of the form. An item has many properties, too many to even summarize here. This section thus provides a summary of the functions of an item without going into gory detail on its specific properties. You can refer to item values using a special, dot-separated syntax: *<block>.<name>*, where *<block>* is the name of the block that owns the item and *<name>* is the name of the item. The item's name is unique within the block.

Table 2-1 describes the different types of items. The description mentions any special properties relevant only to the particular type of item.

Each specific type has a set of properties. For example, text items may have scroll bars. Radio groups may have an Other Values property, which lets you define what happens when the value is not one of the radio button values on querying the database.

Because items are data values, several properties relate to the properties of the data the item holds. Table 2-2 lists the different data types that Developer/2000 Forms supports.

You can specify a format mask from a wide variety of such masks to either format the output to display or to validate the input. You can specify a default value for the item, or you can specify the name of another item from which to copy the initial value. You can specify the maximum length or range of the data. You can specify whether the user must enter the value. You can associate a list of values

Item Type	Description
Text Item	Displays text in a single- or multiple-line display field.
Display Item	Gives "read only" text items that display data without allowing changes by the user.
Button	Lets the user execute a trigger you associate with the button (When-Button-Pressed).
Check Box	Lets the user turn a Boolean value on or off.
Radio Group	Lets the user turn on one of a series of buttons while turning all other buttons off; this object owns a set of radio button items that all work together, each representing a particular value for the radio group item, which in turn represents a column in the database.
List Item	A list of text lines you can display as a pop-up list, a fixed-size list, or a combo box.
Image	Displays a bitmap or vector image.
VBX Control	Displays a VBX control; see Chapter 15.
OLE Container	Displays an OLE object; see Chapter 15.
User Area	Displays anything under the sun that you can fit into the space with a program.

TABLE 2-1. *Item Types and Descriptions in Forms*

Data Type	Description
Alpha	Any alphabetic character—uppercase, lowercase, or mixed case
Char	Any alphabetic or numeric character (corresponds to VARCHAR2 type in ORACLE7)
DateTime	A valid date and time; corresponds to an ORACLE7 DATE type)
Int	Any integer value, signed or unsigned
Long	Any integer value, signed or unsigned
Number	Fixed or floating-point numbers, signed or unsigned, with or without exponential/scientific notation; corresponds to an ORACLE7 NUMBER column

TABLE 2-2. *Item Data Types in Forms*

(LOV) with the item. The LOV constrains the item to come only from the values in the list (see the section "Alerts, Editors, Record Groups, and LOVs," later in this chapter). You can also specify an editor to use for the item value.

Items have all kinds of display attributes: fonts, colors, fills, whether to bevel the edges, and so on. A key one is whether to display the item at all: you can have an item that doesn't appear anywhere but that holds a value. You can use these items as variables in your PL/SQL code. A specific use lets you retrieve values into these items from the database, then compute other, displayed items from those values.

Another key display property for the item is the name of the canvas-view on which to display the item (see the "Canvas-Views and Windows" section below). By changing the canvas-view name, you have complete control over where and how the item appears on your display.

You can disallow navigation into an item, either disabling it completely or just allowing navigation by mouse click, not by going from item to item. You can also link the item to other items to force navigation to occur in an order different from the order of definition of the items.

There are a series of properties that affect the way Developer/2000 Forms uses the item in building SQL statements. The most important one is whether the item corresponds to a column in the block's base table. Other properties let you control query behavior, data manipulation behavior, and locking behavior.

Relations   A *relation* is a special object that Forms uses to structure master-detail forms. The relation object, which belongs to the master block, expresses the relationship of the master record to its detail records. The main properties of the relation are the name of the detail block and the join condition that Forms uses to manage the relationship.

You can also specify some special behavior regarding deletion of master records (whether to delete detail records) or the insertion or update of detail records when there is no master record. Chapter 7 discusses these properties and settings related to the automatic display of detail records.

Canvas-Views and Windows

A *canvas-view* is the background on which you place boilerplate text and items. Each item refers to exactly one canvas-view in its property sheet. You can divide a block's items between different canvas-views. The "canvas" part of this name is obvious; why the "view"?

A canvas-view does not stand alone as an interface object. To see it and its items, you must display the canvas-view in a *window,* a rectangular area of the application display surrounded by a frame and maintained by the GUI platform. Developer/2000 makes these separate objects and lets you build windows that provide a *view* of the canvas: a rectangle within the window that covers part or all of the canvas. The part of the canvas that you can see through the window is the view. The window may have horizontal and vertical scroll bars that let you scroll around the canvas to see different views.

There are four types of canvas-view:

- *Content:* Displays the basic content of a window.

- *Stacked:* Displays over other canvas-views to show conditional or separable contents; you can specify whether to display the stacked canvas-view immediately on displaying its window or to leave it invisible until you need it.

- *Vertical Toolbar:* Holds tool icons for display in a vertical toolbar along the left side of a window; the window specifies the canvas-view to use in its toolbar by name.

- *Horizontal Toolbar:* Holds tool icons for display in a horizontal toolbar along the top of a window; the window specifies the canvas-view to use in its toolbar by name.

Windows can be modal or modeless. A *modal window* requires the user to respond and dismiss the window before doing anything in any other window in the application. A *modeless window* lets you move to another window without dismissing the first one. Often, modal windows have distinguishing characteristics such as lack of scroll bars, fixed size, and an inability to be minimized to an icon.

You can also tell Developer/2000 to hide a modeless window when you navigate to an item in another window. Developer/2000, however, defines its two window types not in terms of modality but by what they do:

- *Document:* A generally modeless window that displays an application "document" object, usually a content canvas-view related to a major part of the application

- *Dialog box:* A generally modal window that displays options or other ways to control application operation

Usually dialog boxes are modal by their nature, although you can have modeless dialog boxes that continue to exist while you are doing other things in the application.

The canvas-view specifies by name the window that displays it. The window specifies by name its primary content view, which it tries to display when you first open the window. If there is more than one canvas-view in the window, you can tell Developer/2000 to raise a particular canvas-view to display on top of the others when the user gives the window the focus. You can set the height and width settings of the canvas-view rectangle to accommodate the different items and stacked canvas-views that you want to display in interaction with a window and its scroll bars.

You have all the standard visual attributes available for the canvas-view and the window. You can iconify or *minimize* a window, which results in displaying the window as an icon, and you can specify the icon to display. You can also specify whether to display horizontal and/or vertical scroll bars for windows (although usually only for modeless windows).

Chapter 7 gives a complete discussion of windows and canvas-views.

Alerts, Editors, Record Groups, and LOVs

There are several minor objects that Developer/2000 gives you to address specific needs.

An *alert* is a special dialog box that displays a message with an icon and up to three buttons, such as OK and Cancel, Yes and No, or whatever. You can also specify one of these three buttons as the default button. You could build this as a window with a canvas-view, but the alert object lets you quickly put the dialog box together without going through all the fuss. There are three types of alert: Stop, Caution, and Note. These are the usual categories of simple messages that applications display.

An *editor* is a simple text-editor dialog box that lets you enter lines of text into a text item. The editor object lets you specify the window size, visual attributes, editor title, and other properties of the window. This lets you create editors with different appearances for different text fields.

A *record group* is a special data structure that resembles a table, with rows and columns. A record group can be a query record group or a static record group. You define a query record group with a SQL SELECT statement. The SELECT list of the query gives the record group its column structure. You define a static record group with a column specification you enter through a special dialog box. There are several built-in subprograms that let you manipulate record groups at runtime. You can use record groups for LOVs (see the following paragraph and Chapter 5), for data parameters to pass records to reports or graphics displays (see Chapter 15), or as PL/SQL data structures.

An *LOV* (list of values) is a special dialog box that displays a record group and lets you choose a row of the group, returning a single value. You use an LOV as a way to choose from a specific set of values. You can, for example, associate an LOV with a text item to both provide an easier way to input values and to provide a list of values against which to validate the user's data entry. Again, you could build this dialog box using standard windows and canvas-views, but the LOV object gives you a shortcut and a way to get LOV behavior in fields automatically without any programming. Chapter 5 shows you how to use LOVs in forms.

Programming Objects

Under the rubric of "programming objects," this section summarizes several objects that you use to structure your programs (Figure 2-3). These objects apply equally to form and menu modules, and some of them (Attached Libraries and Program Units) apply to library modules as well.

A *named visual attribute* is a collection of display properties that you can refer to from another object. If you do so, the properties of the visual attribute override the properties of the object. If you change a property in the visual attribute, the property changes in all the objects that inherit the property from the visual attribute. If you change a property in an object, however, the object loses the reference to the visual attribute.

The *property class* is an object belonging to a module that contains a set of properties, *any* properties. Just as with a visual attribute, when you base an object on a property class, you get all the properties of that class that make sense for the kind of object you are defining. Again, when you change the class, you change the properties of all the objects based on that class. You can override specific properties, however, without losing the connection to the property class.

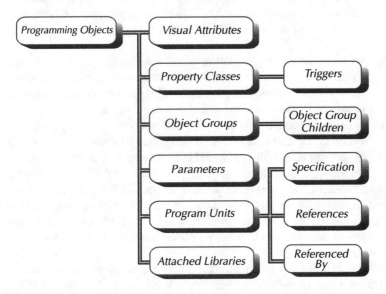

FIGURE 2-3. *The object hierarchy for programming objects*

The *object group* lets you package up your reusable objects for later copying or referring. It collects a set of objects in the module under a single heading. By copying or referring to the object group, you get all the objects it contains. You can group any objects down to the block level, but you cannot group items within a block. You have to include the entire block in the object group.

Chapter 9 explains the details of named visual attributes, property classes, and object groups. It also shows you how to use them effectively to build reusable components and to impose standard sets of properties on your applications.

A *parameter* is a form, menu, report, or display data object that you define at the level of the module. You can use the parameter as a variable in any PL/SQL program unit in the scope of the module. A parameter has a data type, a default initial value, and a maximum length. You can set a parameter by passing in a value when you start up the form, either by putting the parameter on the command line (PARAM="value") or by passing the parameter in a parameter list (see Chapter 15).

The *program units* of a module are the PL/SQL packages, procedures, and functions you define in the scope of that module. All the Developer/2000 modules permit you to define program units as part of the module. The library module is somewhat special; it packages the program units as a module and makes them available to other modules through the *attached-library* object. This is a reference to a library you have defined as a module. You can call any program unit the module defines from PL/SQL in that module; you can also call any program unit in a library you have attached to the module. You cannot call any program unit defined in other modules or libraries that you have not attached.

Each subprogram program unit shows its *specification* (the procedure or function parameters, or function return type). Each package program unit shows its *subprograms* (the package subprograms). Each program unit also shows what program units the unit refers to (References objects), and which program units refer to the current one (Referenced By objects). Chapter 11 explains the details of program units (packages, procedures, and functions).

The Menu Module

The *menu module* is much simpler than the form module, as Figure 2-4 shows. It consists of a set of programming objects (the same ones the preceding section describes) and a set of menus. Each menu in turn consists of a set of items. Chapter 7 shows you how to customize menus in detail.

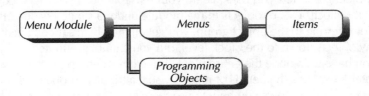

FIGURE 2-4. *The object hierarchy for the menu module*

Menu items can be plain items or they can be one of several special menu item formats:

- *Check:* A menu item with a check mark beside it; these items let you enable and disable options through menus instead of through dialog boxes.

- *Radio:* A menu item that is one of a group of mutually exclusive options; if you select one, you deselect the others.

- *Separator:* A do-nothing menu item that separates other items, usually a space or a line on the menu.

- *Magic:* A special menu item that the platform requires, such as Cut, Copy, Paste, Undo, or Help.

Each menu item has a command that Developer/2000 executes when you choose the item. This can be one of several things:

- *Null:* Does nothing; a separator must have a null command.

- *Menu:* The menu displays a submenu.

- *PL/SQL:* The menu executes a PL/SQL block, including Run_Product and Host to execute other Developer/2000 programs or operating system commands.

You can also associate a menu item with one or more security roles. Chapter 8 gives details on security and menus.

The Library Module, Built-In Packages, and Database Objects

Several of the objects you see in Developer/2000 appear in all the components: library modules, built-in packages, and database objects.

The *library module* is quite simple compared to other modules (Figure 2-5), consisting only of a set of program units and a set of attached libraries. See Chapter 11 for details on libraries and on the program units they contain. You can store libraries in the file system or in the database, as with any module.

All the Developer/2000 Designers have access to a series of *built-in PL/SQL packages*, though the packages differ with each product. These packages give you a broad array of tools for manipulating the modules and other objects in that product component (Forms, Reports, or Graphics). Each package has a package specification that lists the subprograms in the package along with their specification (parameters and function returns). Each package has extensive documentation in the product reference manual, and you should consult that documentation to see packaged types and exceptions, as well as the details of using the different subprograms.

Also, all the Designers let you access the objects in the database to which you connect. Figure 2-6 shows the object hierarchy for the *database objects*. The Designers list all the users in the database. For each user, you can see the

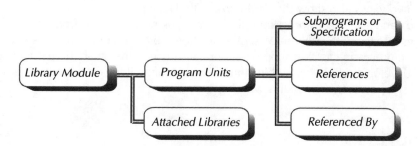

FIGURE 2-5.   *The object hierarchy for the library module*

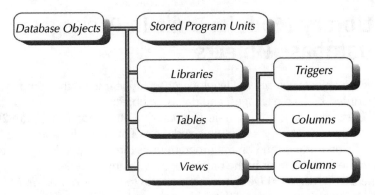

FIGURE 2-6. *The object hierarchy for database objects*

accessible stored program units, libraries, tables, and views. You only see the ones that you can access through the user name with which you logged on. If you do not have privileges to use a particular table in another user, for example, you will not see it among the database objects. Libraries are library modules you store in the database as opposed to the file system.

Tables also show the *database triggers* for the table. These triggers are PL/SQL blocks that execute when a particular event occurs in the database, such as an INSERT or DELETE. Although similar to the triggers in Developer/2000 code, database triggers respond to database events rather than to application events. Tables and views also show their columns, with data types.

You can create stored program units by dragging program units from other modules into the database objects section for stored program units. This lets you move the processing for that subprogram or package into the database, permitting you to develop multiple-tier architectures. You can often improve performance or reliability by moving code in this way.

Reports

The Reports component of Developer/2000 is the environmental component in which you develop reports modules. You can refer to external query objects, and you can set and store debugging objects in this environment. The Report Designer also includes libraries and database objects.

A *report module* has a quite involved structure, as Figure 2-7 shows. The basic components of a report are its data model, layout, parameter form, and report triggers. It can also have program units and attached libraries, which are identical to those discussed in the section "Programming Objects," earlier in this chapter.

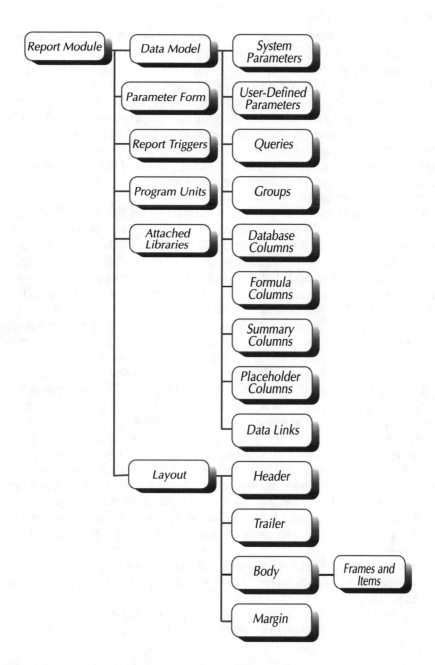

FIGURE 2-7.   *The object hierarchy for a report module*

The report *data model* is the structure of data and its different representations in the report. You create the data model in a special graphical editor.

Parameter objects are module variables that you can refer to in PL/SQL code and anywhere else that accepts data values as input. *System parameters* are the parameters that Reports defines automatically; *user-defined parameters* are those you define. You have a default form for setting parameters at runtime, or you can create a completely different one as a *parameter form* object in the report. The Reports runtime program runs this form when you run the report to prompt the user to set the parameters you specify. Chapter 9 goes into detail on report parameters, default parameter forms, user-defined parameter forms, and all the ways you can use parameters to make your report reusable.

A *query* is a SQL statement that returns the data values that are the basis for the report. You can embed the query in the report, or you can use an *external query* object; this is simply SQL text in a separate file that you can share between applications. The *group* identifies the records the queries return as a repeating group of records in the report, and there is a hierarchy of groups that represents the nesting of records within each other. The *database columns* are the columns from the query SELECT list. The *formula columns* are special columns you compute using PL/SQL blocks. The *summary columns* are special columns that accumulate summary information for multiple records in the report, such as subtotals or grand totals. These columns go in a group at a higher level than the records they summarize. The *placeholder columns* are columns you define to fill in from a trigger, formula, or user exit instead of from data or standard summarization. For example, you can derive special report fields that report the region with the highest sales among a set of regional rows. The *data links* are links you use in master-detail reports (see Table 2-3) to link one group of rows to another group of rows.

The *layout* of the report is the graphical structure of the report. Every report has a *header* and a *trailer,* and a *body* sandwiched in between them. The report *margin* is the area on the page outside the text boundaries of the header, trailer, and body. The body contains all the repeating frames and report items that graphically structure the data model into a formatted report. The header and trailer contain whatever data elements or boilerplate make sense preceding and following the body, respectively.

There are several varieties of report layout. Each layout may have specific requirements for the accompanying data model. Table 2-3 summarizes the different kinds of reports.

Chapter 5 gives an introduction to creating data models and layouts for reports. For details on the specific kinds of reports, consult the *Building Reports Manual*

Report Layout Type	Description
Tabular	A tabular report, the default type, structures a series of rows of data with a repeating column heading on each page.
Master-detail	A master-detail report structures two or more groups into related, nested sets of rows; the purpose is to display a set of rows for each row of the outer group.
Form	A form report structures data like a form, with one row of data formatted onto several lines with labels to the left of the individual fields.
Form letter	A form letter report combines boilerplate text with fields of data, with each row from the data model repeating the boilerplate; the purpose is to generate multiple copies of the form, one for each row.
Mailing label	A mailing label report is, well, a mailing label report; the purpose is to print repeating groups of fields in fixed-size boxes on each page.
Matrix	A matrix report, better known as a cross-tab report, displays a grid of data with row and column headings.

TABLE 2-3.　*Report Layouts in Developer/2000*

(Part Number A32488-1) and the *Reports Reference Manual* (Part Number A32489-1). Each layout has options that let you do an amazing number of things with the relatively few basic report layouts.

The *report triggers* are blocks of PL/SQL code that execute at well-defined points: before the report, after the report, between the pages, before the parameter form, and after the parameter form. There are other triggers in reports, but these are not separate, named objects the way they are in forms. You access these triggers through the items that own them. Chapter 6 details the way report triggers fire and the specifics of how to write them.

The Reports Designer also integrates debugging information into the objects available. It lets you create debug actions (breakpoints that you can set in your

PL/SQL code) that persist between debugging sessions. It also contains a representation of the calling stack you see at runtime. See Chapter 13 for details on debugging reports and using these objects in the PL/SQL debugger.

Graphics

The Graphics component of Developer/2000 is the environmental component in which you develop display modules. A *display module* may be one or more charts you derive from database data, or it may contain any combination of graphic elements with or without reference to the database. You can use display modules strictly for business graphics display of data, or you can use it as a graphics drawing tool, or both.

The structure of a graphics display is simple in object terms (Figure 2-8). A display module contains a layout; sets of templates, queries, parameters, sounds, and timers; and the same program units and attached library objects that the other modules contain.

The layout contains the graphic elements of the display in a hierarchy that represents their relationships. It also relates those elements to the columns of a query. There are several specific types of chart available as part of the Graphics product, as Table 2-4 shows.

A *chart template* is a customized set of options that lets you build several charts that all have identical formatting, possibly in the same display. For example, you could build a series of pie charts, all using one template to make them consistent. Chapter 9 has details on how to build templates that let you reuse chart definitions.

A *query*, as in a report module, is a SQL SELECT statement that defines a set of data to display formatted as a chart. You construct the query to return the data in exactly the format you want to chart. For example, the pie chart does not summarize the data for the slices; you must use a GROUP BY and a SUM function to do this. Chapter 5 shows you how to build a query of this kind.

The parameters, as for reports, are module variables that you define and use throughout the module in PL/SQL code. You can set the parameters on the command line or through passing a parameter list from another program such as Forms or Reports. Chapter 9 has the details.

Besides visual elements, your displays can also integrate sound objects to create full multimedia displays.

There is a special timer object in Graphics displays that acts as a kind of alarm clock for the display. You specify an interval of time at the end of which the timer wakes up and executes some PL/SQL code. You can achieve all kinds of special

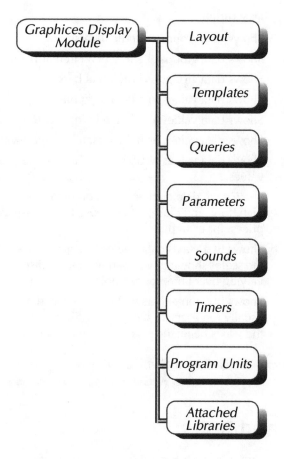

FIGURE 2-8.   *The object hierarchy for the Graphics display module in Developer/2000*

effects with timers; see the *Graphics Developer's Guide* (Part Number A32482-1) and the *Graphics Reference Manual* (Part Number A32483-1) for details.

The Graphics Designer also integrates the same kind of debugging information as does the Reports Designer. It lets you create debug actions, breakpoints that you can set in your PL/SQL code, that persist between debugging sessions. It also contains a representation of the calling stack you see at runtime. Chapter 13 gives details on debugging graphics displays and using these objects in the PL/SQL debugger.

Chart Type	Description
Column	Shows data groups as vertical bars.
Pie	Shows data groups as slices of a circular pie.
Bar	Shows data groups as horizontal bars.
Table	Shows data values in a tabular format.
Line	Shows data values as a line relating x and y values.
Scatter	Shows data values as points relating x and y values.
Mixed	Shows data values as both points and a line relating x and y values.
High-Low	Show each data element as a combination of three values: high, low, and close; you can use this to display stock-market prices, for example.
Double-Y	Shows two y-axis data values for each x-axis value, with both the scales showing; you can use this to display two variables varying over time, for example.
Gantt	Shows horizontal bars that represent start and end values; usually represents a schedule, with the x axis being time and the y axis being the set of tasks in the schedule.

TABLE 2-4.   *Types of Charts for a Graphics Display*

The Nuts and Bolts

Each object, taken by itself, is a powerful contribution to building your applications. Developer/2000 is more than just the objects that comprise it, however. It is a *system* that glues together all of these objects into a working whole. Not only do all these objects work together, but you can also work with objects from other applications and with data from database managers other than ORACLE7.

The primary glue for Developer/2000 is PL/SQL, the programming language you use in triggers, program units, and other program objects in Developer/2000. By accessing items and parameters (or even global data), PL/SQL is what makes things happen, tying together all the objects. Using the built-in subprograms for each component of Developer/2000, you can manipulate the objects in the other components: embedding graphics displays in reports and forms, passing form or report data to them; producing reports from graphics displays or forms; reading parameter values from graphics displays into a form; and so on.

Specific subprograms in each product component let you interact with things outside the standard ORACLE7 and Developer/2000 environment. You can use the Host procedure to call operating system commands. On the Windows platform, you can use OLE2, VBX controls, and DDE to manipulate objects from other applications. You can also use the Open Client Adapter to access database managers other than ORACLE7 using ODBC drivers for those database managers. You can use these to replace ORACLE7 entirely, both in the design environment and in the runtime environment. Or you can develop under ORACLE7 but use another database manager in your runtime environment, letting your users keep their data in a SQL Server, Sybase, or Informix database, for example.

All of these options make Developer/2000 a strong environment for developing well-structured, robust, and open applications. Chapter 3 discusses the development life cycle, which is a process by which you develop applications using the objects this chapter has summarized. Parts Two and Three of this book then go into detail on how to prototype, design, code, test, debug, and deploy applications to your end users.

CHAPTER 3

The Development Process

Once you understand the basic components of Developer/2000, what is the next step? Coding? Not likely. The first thing you need to understand is not so much how to glue the pieces together, but how to structure the process of gluing the pieces together. How do you actually go about building a real-world database application?

Life Cycles

You have many options for choosing a development process. Most are project-oriented and take the form of a development *life cycle,* the set of processes that take an idea for a software system and make it real. A project life cycle imitates the dynamic aspects of a living being: it is born, it lives and consumes and produces, and then it dies.

There are many varieties of development life cycles, possibly as many as there are project organizations building software products. Even the two main types discussed in the following sections overlap to some degree but differ radically in details. Some differences can depend on how you define software or application.

The term *software* includes all the results of the development processes, including documentation or training, if that makes sense. Your application does not stand alone; it comes with documentation, online help, training, and whatever else you want to package with it to satisfy the customer.

The arrangement of processes has a definite logic, though it varies in detail. Some restrictions come from the physical qualities of the inputs and outputs: coding follows design, testing follows coding, deployment follows testing (usually, anyway).

A life cycle *phase* divides the process into major subprocesses such as requirements analysis, design, coding, and testing. Often, the process requires a phase *commitment*: making one result of a phase the signature of one or more persons with authority and making this signoff the required input to another phase. This kind of commitment requirement creates a sequence of phases with intermediate approvals by Those In Charge. More sophisticated versions of commitment, such as the spiral model (discussed later), add a risk analysis for each phase.

Often, a life cycle also includes a set of *standard objects.* It can require that you create standard development documents, hold specific reviews, or test suites.

Some life cycles and their objects are better than others for the kind of application development you will do with Developer/2000. The style of design and programming it encourages definitely works better with iterative life cycles, especially those involving prototyping. In that respect, if you confront a situation where you think having others look at the product of a process before it is "done" is useless, *rethink*. The purpose is in keeping people in the loop, communicating, and building credibility as much as in getting feedback on the technology.

If you have an interest in learning more about the different ways of approaching software development, try these two books: *Wicked Problems, Righteous Solutions,* by Peter DeGrace and Leslie Hulet Stahl (Yourdon Press, 1990), and *Project Management Made Simple: A Guide to Successful Management of Computer Systems Projects,* by David King (Yourdon Press, 1992).

Defining the Processes

You should be clear on the meaning of the various processes that are part of every life cycle, such as analysis, prototyping, design, coding, testing, and deployment. Although this book does not assume any details about a development life cycle, it refers to the various phases when appropriate.

Feasability analysis is showing that you can solve the problem with software.

Requirements analysis, or just plain *analysis,* is the stating of the problem that you want to solve through software. The term "requirement" refers to a particular need of the end user of the software. Requirements can be as varied as the different aspects of software:

- A need for a specific feature, such as handling a particular kind of account or printing a particular statistic

- A need to follow a specific standard, such as ANSI SQL or corporate typography standards for fonts

- A need for a specific set of user-interface controls arranged in a specific way for ease of use

- A need for a certain level of performance

- A need for a certain level or model of security (protecting specific columns from update, for example, or implementing full access-level security based on security clearances)

- A need to allow end-user reconfiguration of the environment

The key to stating requirements is to focus on the problem, not the solution. When you phrase a requirement, phrase it as what the user needs, not as how you intend to address those needs. Say "Enter a date value in the format 'mm/dd/yy'", not "provide a date entry field with eight characters required input and a format mask 'mm/dd/yy'."

More sophisticated kinds of analysis use special methods to arrange and validate systems of requirements. You can build models that represent requirements as processes; you can even build formal mathematical models of your problems.

Design is the process of inventing a solution to the problem. Design overlaps with prototyping in that a large part of prototyping is a kind of design. Other kinds of designs model the solution on paper or through other means rather than building working models. *Architectural design* is design-in-the-large, inventing and specifying the main interfaces of the interacting systems of the overall system.

Prototyping is the design process of building a working model of your solution to the problem. The model generally is much less complicated than the finished product, either in the contents or in the process used to build it. Prototyping also includes usability testing. See the previous section for details and Chapters 5 and 6 for examples of prototyping and usability testing. *Detailed design* specifies the detailed interfaces of the interacting objects within the systems and their interactions with other objects.

Coding is the process of implementing the solution in working, finished-quality software. Some amount of coding may go on during prototyping, but a transition from prototyping to coding implies working on the finished product rather than on an intermediate, disposable version. Coding may involve unit testing and debugging. *Unit testing* is the low-level testing of the units of code, such as Developer/2000 blocks, records, items, and triggers. *Debugging* is the process of tracking down implementation problems with code.

Integration is the process of combining units of code into systems of code. When you finish a unit of code, you check it into your *configuration management* or *source control* system, integrating the code into your *product repository*, which is a set of files or a database that contains your source and perhaps the executables you compile from your source. An *integration test* is a test of several units working together as a system. *System integration* is the process of integrating all the intermediate systems into a working application. *System test* is the testing of the application working as a whole system (as opposed to a collection of parts), including the following kinds of test:

- *Validation test:* Testing that the application meets all its requirements

- *Regression test:* Testing that the application runs all tests that it successfully ran in previous versions (including unit and integration tests)

- *Performance test:* Testing specific performance requirements

- *Stress test:* Testing the application under differing loads that exceed the normal end-user environment

- *Security test:* Testing how well the security measures prevent unauthorized access to the application

Deployment is the distribution of the application software to its end users. Other terms for this include *conversion* (because you are converting users from an old system) or *implementation* (because you are implementing the solution for the user). Deploying internal, IS applications may be a matter of putting the finished application on the network or installing it on user workstations. Deploying commercial products may mean lining up distribution channels, shrink-wrapping floppy disk sets or CD-ROMs, and selling the software package to end users or their companies.

Maintenance is the process of keeping the software system running over time. Despite your best efforts at risk management, you will find that the system will always fail in some way. Maintenance is the process of fixing problems that come up, usually through upgrades to the software system. Maintenance is pure risk management: making sure your customer will keep coming back for more. You can generate incredibly ornate ways of deploying maintenance upgrades, such as automated, worldwide deployment over wide-area networks or complex pricing schemes for squeezing the last dollar out of the customer. The process for generating the upgraded software system, however, remains a microcosm of the entire development life cycle. A large microcosm: for most software, maintenance occupies by far the largest amount of effort and time of any of the life cycle phases.

As you go through the rest of the book, think about how to best organize your development life cycle. This book strongly recommends the prototyping approach using risk management techniques as an organizing principle. The following chapters all build on the basic approach this chapter introduces.

The Waterfall Life Cycle

Out of all proportion to its actual success, the waterfall life cycle has dominated software development for a long while. This brief overview should present a project landscape that is familiar to most developers; it also serves to build a straw figure that the next section will dutifully demolish. The waterfall model is not the best way to build Developer/2000 projects, but you need to know about it because many development projects seem to assume its necessity.

Figure 3-1 shows a fanciful model of the waterfall approach. The fundamental idea is to divide the development process into a series of phases or stages, each of which finishes before the next one starts. Work and work products flow down the waterfall, with the occasional salmon working its way back up to revise a design or add a requirement here and there, but generally getting eaten for lunch.

Here is a summary of the processes and their goals:

- *Feasibility:* Defining the concept and whether it makes sense to do it

- *Requirements:* Specifying what the software needs to do

- *Architectural design:* Designing the broad outlines and interfaces of the systems that make up the software

- *Detailed design:* Designing specific components with control and data structures and key algorithms and heuristics

- *Coding:* Building the components

- *Integration:* Combining the components into systems

■ *Implementation:* Combining the systems into the total software system

■ *Maintenance:* Updating the system to keep it functioning over time

The central purpose of the waterfall model is to structure the development process into an optimally ordered series of goal-directed processes. All of these goals (requirements, design, and so on) need to be met at some point in any project; meeting the goals in order minimizes the costs of production. That is, if you do the processes in the order shown in Figure 3-1, you spend less time and money fixing problems because you fix them before they become large. For example, fixing a bad requirement is a lot easier if you do it before you do any

FIGURE 3-1. *The waterfall software development life cycle*

design, coding, or testing, because all you need to do is to change the requirements document, not the design and code.

In practice, these two conclusions (you need to achieve all the goals and you need to do them in this order) apply only to very large or very formal projects (see Barry Boehm's *Software Engineering Economics,* Prentice-Hall, 1981, pages 38–41). In particular, if the requirements for the project are necessarily and largely vague, finalizing requirements at the beginning of the process may lead to disaster.

As most practitioners of the waterfall model will acknowledge, very few waterfall projects adhere to the pure model of Figure 3-1. Even the most formal project will benefit from some amount of feedback and rework based on that feedback. But the principles behind the model remain: to perform certain processes and to minimize costs by doing them in a specific order. DeGrace and Stahl summarize the problems with the waterfall model:

■ Requirement specifications that are incomplete play havoc with the waterfall's assumptions. Every step beyond requirements involves activities that excel at generating more requirements, such as thinking about algorithms and error conditions!

■ There are cheaper and better ways to avoid problems than putting them in straightjackets—a more flexible process may end up costing less.

■ There is no useful output and no feedback until late in the project, leading to all kinds of credibility, management, and quality problems.

■ Not everyone agrees on the usefulness of the process goals; in particular, not everyone thinks the statement of the problem is necessarily separate or isolated from its solution.

■ Team communications are fragmented at best and nonexistent at worst.

There are many proposals for different ways of managing software development. The next section focuses on using prototyping and risk analysis as ways to structure the development process.

Prototyping and the Spiral Life Cycle

The spiral life cycle is a variant of the waterfall model that adds *prototyping* and *risk management* to the waterfall processes. It assumes that you still need all the waterfall processes, but that doing them singly, in order, is not required. This life cycle, or variations on it, is much more appropriate for Developer/2000 projects than is the waterfall model of the last section.

Prototypes

Designers, architects, and engineers have produced models of their intended development efforts since the beginning of recorded history. Models tell you things directly that you can only guess at through abstract thinking about a product. But software products are in themselves abstract, so what is a model of a software system?

You can, with reasonably little effort, build a software system that looks, walks, and talks like the duck you eventually want to produce but which is not really the duck. It does not have the extensive help systems, the complicated date-time or statistical algorithms, or the details that the real product requires. You have not extensively validated and verified and tested the software. It does have enough to look like the product. What is the purpose of this model?

The purpose of a prototype is twofold:

■ To get feedback from users and architects on the feasibility and utility of a requirement or design, and to improve knowledge of requirements with that feedback

■ To see whether a design works in practice or whether a proposed solution sufficiently addresses a stated need

This model is a *prototype* of the working system: a model of the system you build *before* you build the real system. You can show the prototype to users and designers and ask them what they think. You can let them use the prototype software (to a point) to get a feel for how it would work in practice. You can try different ways of doing things to see which is most practical or effective.

There are many different ways of doing prototypes, including component software, simulation, video, and dozens of other techniques. This book focuses on using the powerful Developer/2000 tools as prototyping tools as well as full development tools. This dual nature of the Developer/2000 system makes it a natural fit for prototyping software development life cycles.

Risk

Risk has to do with failure. You cannot have risk without the possibility of failure. In the context of software development, there are three kinds of risk:

■ *Technical risk:* The risk of failing to meet requirements through technological failure

■ *Schedule risk:* The risk of failing to produce deliverables according to the production schedule

■   *Cost risk:* The risk of failing to produce deliverables according to the budget for such production

Risk is the combination of the *probability* of failure and the *impact* of the failure. For example, if the probability of failing to meet a requirement is very small and the impact is also very small, the risk is very low. High risks are easy to see: a high probability of failure combined with a high impact, such as using an untested application for multimillion-dollar international banking transactions. Moderate risks, where you have high probability of failure and low impact or vice versa, are harder to evaluate. For example, you may risk many typographical errors in an application, but the impact is low, merely annoying the good spellers among us and perhaps appearing less "professional." Another scenario: you discover that a certain routine can crash and destroy all the data on your system, but that it could happen only under the most bizarre set of circumstances imaginable.

Risk analysis is the process of studying your processes and deliverables to identify technical, schedule, and cost risks. Does a particular module tend to use bleeding-edge technology to achieve its requirements? Is it likely that you will discover more requirements later in the process, making you miss your deadline? Are your developers completely inexperienced with a particular tool and thus likely to take longer than estimated for a task, exceeding the budget for the component?

Risk management is the process of determining approaches to development that will bring the overall risk of the project down to an acceptable level. After identifying the major risks, you decide how best to go about reducing their impact or probability of failure. You can also decide to live with the risk, of course; the amount of risk you and your development organization are willing to live with is your *risk tolerance.*

Stepping back from all this abstract failure, consider for a moment the things you do in a software project. Think about *why* you do them. Only some of them directly produce the working software you need. Why do you do the others, such as prototypes? Internal documentation? Testing? Reviews? Approvals? Marketing? Competitive analysis? Why not just build tools and use them to build software and leave it at that?

All of these "extra" tasks and things are *risk management* techniques. They are all ways to prevent failure or to ameliorate the impact of failure. If you look at your life cycle in this way, much of what software development is about is risk and managing risk, even though you may not think of it that way. If you make your risk analysis and management explicit in your life cycle, you will find it much easier to assess your success in developing software. You will find yourself understanding exactly why you are doing what you do. Risk analysis lets you focus on doing what is truly important rather than wasting your time on things that will not happen or that will have little effect on your project. It also gives you a way to measure how well you are doing at focusing on the important things.

The Spiral Life Cycle

How do you develop a life cycle that takes risk into account with a prototyping approach? Any such life cycle needs to have feedback loops to improve quality and productivity. Feedback is meaningless without the ability to change anything, and to change you need to go back and revisit things. The life cycle thus uses prototyping and risk analysis in an open system with as much feedback as possible.

One well-defined life cycle of this kind is the spiral life cycle that Barry Boehm developed (Barry Boehm, "A spiral model of software development and enhancement," in *Proceedings of an International Workshop on the Software Process and Software Environments,* March 27–29, 1985). Figure 3-2 shows a high-level version of a spiral life cycle. Its essence is controlled feedback based on prototyping and risk analysis followed by commitment to full development.

The spiral starts out with a risk analysis and prototype, which leads to a concept document. Another risk analysis and prototype precedes full requirements, and another precedes a high-level design. The final iteration follows a final risk analysis and operational prototype with detailed design, coding, and the other parts of the waterfall life cycle, much reduced in scope.

You can even dispense with much of the design and coding with a conversion effort to turn the prototype into a complete system. The difference depends on how well your prototype satisfies your customers. For example, most Developer/2000 projects wind up moving directly from a prototype into a working system, though with quite a bit of Developer/2000 coding. Other systems take Developer/2000 prototypes and design, code, and test them in another environment such as C or COBOL for speed and quality. Many database applications do not need this much work, letting you stay entirely with Developer/2000 or a hybrid approach for your production software.

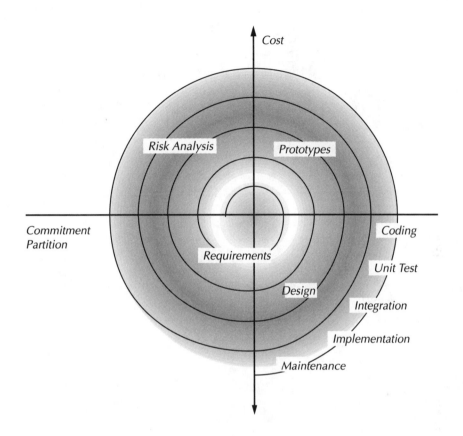

FIGURE 3-2.   *The spiral software development life cycle*

PART 2

Prototyping and Design

CHAPTER 4

What You See Is
What You Get

This first chapter in Part Two prepares the way for the prototyping and design information you will find through the next several chapters. It shows you how to start thinking about a system and the sorts of issues you must consider in sketching out the system with broad strokes.

What To Do First

What is the first thing to do when you confront the task of application development? Find out what the customer needs. Better yet, find out who the customer *is*. You will not succeed in your project without understanding for whom you're developing the application and why.

This section introduces some techniques for gathering requirements and puts them into the Developer/2000 perspective. Remember, Developer/2000 is a database application development system, not a general programming language. It is good at some things and not so good at other things. You need to make sure that you fully understand the requirements so you can decide which tasks are appropriate to do with Developer/2000 and which tasks require other tools.

To think about constructing a Developer/2000 application from its component objects (forms, blocks, items, displays, reports, libraries, and so on), you need to understand the structure of the problem you are trying to solve. How do you determine whether you need a form or a report? What kind of graphics do you need? Pie charts or line charts? You cannot decide such questions if you do not have a clear idea about the problem the application is meant to solve.

The Requirements Jungle

The first step to understanding what your requirements are is to understand whether the project as a whole is feasible. Given the general idea of the application or system of applications, is the technology there to produce them? Is the general scale of the project feasible given the available resources and time? There is no point in exploring the dark jungle of requirements without assessing the probable worth of the result and the likelihood of emerging from the jungle at the end of the project.

Once you have established the basic feasibility of what you would like to do, you need to define the problem more clearly. The objective of exploring requirements is not to determine conclusively the exact nature of the application you intend to produce. Chapter 3 has already made clear that, although it is important to understand where you are going in some detail, you should use a development process that is open and responsive to change rather than assuming that nothing will change. Things change; it is not so much that it *happens* as what you *do* about it that counts. Think of requirements as a basis for interpreting the effects and risk of changes as they occur.

Exploring Requirements

This section uses concepts for exploring requirements derived from the excellent book by Donald C. Gause and Gerald M. Weinberg, *Exploring Requirements: Quality Before Design* (Dorset House, 1989).

As with any jungle, exploring the requirements jungle is an exercise in resolving ambiguity. The purpose of developing requirements is to remove enough of the ambiguity of the problem to be able to know that your solution will work. Ambiguities can include missing requirements, words that mean different things to different people, and solutions masquerading as problems.

An interesting way to define ambiguity is to do it operationally from your own experience. Look back over the last few projects you have completed, especially the ones that failed in some sense. First, think about the customers. Did the application satisfy them? If not, why not? What was the requirement that led to the feature (or failed to lead to the feature) that the users wanted or did not want?

Once you can recognize ambiguity, you have to learn how to find its source. There are at least two main sources of ambiguity: the complexity of the situation and the questions you ask about it. The situation is often inherently ambiguous— certainly so if more than one customer is involved. Each customer has a different set of needs and preferences that, when taken as a whole, lead to uncertainties and contradictions. But your own interpretation of the situation can in turn lead to further ambiguities. If you phrase your questions about the problem in a certain way, you will get a certain response. You are likely to get a different response if you phrase your question differently.

A key trait of explorers is their expertise at *probing* the situation. A good explorer does not assume he or she understands the situation completely but asks or looks deeper. The issue becomes how deep you need to explore, not the completeness of your understanding. You need to unearth possible sources of ambiguity so that you can state the problem clearly. A good example of this probing ability in software requirements is the very common situation where a client says they want a particular feature. Your job is not to say, "OK" or "No, we can't do that," but rather to ask "Why?" Your response to that simple question will expand the meaning of the situation. It will include all kinds of things you were not aware of, and possibly that the customer was not aware of.

Probing, however, is not just asking why and crashing into the jungle from there. You need to be sure you are asking why about the right situation. In other words, because often the space you are exploring is quite complex, you must explore all paths leading into the jungle. If you focus too much on one issue, or are too inflexible in the path you follow, you get trapped in that issue rather than broadening your thinking to include side issues that may have a bigger impact on the success of your application. For example, after finding out why the customer wants a particular feature, you might ask what similar features the customer has used in the past. You might ask when the customer thinks he or she needs this particular feature, or what other ways the customer has tried to solve same problem or perform the same task that have failed (and why). You should ask the same question using different words to make sure the customer is interpreting the question correctly. In any event, you should always attempt to refocus your exploration on the problem and away from particular solutions to the problem. Solutions are not requirements, they are responses to requirements.

You should also probe by asking different customers similar questions. Make sure you are asking the *right* people: the people who are going to be using the application. Otherwise, you are getting hearsay, not probing. You should also carefully identify the people you do *not* want to be able to use your software; Chapter 8, which covers security, focuses on this in more detail.

Using the prototyping approach, you will find it possible to get different answers to probing questions if you can show the customer a working prototype. As Chapters 5 and 6 illustrate, finding out whether the prototype meets expectations is useful. But you should also use the results as feedback to further resolution of ambiguity. If something fails, use that failure to return to probing into the problem. Perhaps you can find some way of looking at the problem that changes the failure into a success, or perhaps you must throw away your first attempt entirely because it came from a completely mistaken interpretation of the requirements.

Of course, you must also consider whether the fundamental assumption you are making is still true: does a solution to this problem exist, or can you only approximate the solution? You should also work to get feedback from the customer about the process itself. That is, ask whether your questions seem relevant, and always ask if there are any questions you have not asked that you should have asked.

The Explorer's Equipage

Some specific techniques for exploring requirements include the following:

- *Brainstorming:* Meeting with others to develop as many ideas as possible about the problem

- *Sketching:* Drawing pictures of forms, reports, graphics, and the like to help visualize the problem

- *Mind-mapping:* Brainstorming by yourself on paper, dumping your thoughts, and connecting them up

Creating a Requirements Document

Once you have the problem stated as unambiguously as possible, you need to state the requirements in a way that is useful to the designers and others interested in the details of what your application is supposed to do. This requirements document can take many forms: a user manual, a reference manual, a data flow diagram (or a system of these), an object-oriented analysis diagram (or a system of these), an entity-relationship diagram, or any of the other methods for representing requirements. These methods all produce formal or informal statements that let you identify specific things:

- *Functions:* What the product is to accomplish; functions can be visible to the user, hidden from the user as much as possible, or frills that the customer can do without

- *Attributes:* Characteristics of the application that the customer wants, such as ease of use or high performance in certain situations; attributes can be essential, desirable, or ignorable

- *Constraints:* A mandatory condition on an essential attribute; the things that you must do to *be* successful

- *Preferences:* A desirable condition on an attribute; the things you can do to be *more* successful and that you can trade off with one another to adjust the cost of developing the application

- *Expectations:* Statements of what the customer expects from the system and how the customer prioritizes those expectations

Breaking Eggs

As the saying goes, "You can't make an omelet without breaking eggs." This section breaks the eggs for the rest of the book by telling you all about Talbot's farm, a historic and not necessarily apocryphal venture in New Hampshire that serves to illustrate the rest of the book.

From the Jungle to the Farm

Before we enter the jungle, let's look at some history. This section tells you about Talbot's farm, which we'll reference throughout the book. A previous book (*ORACLE7: The Complete Reference, Third Edition*, by George Koch, Robert Muller, and Kevin Loney, Osborne/McGraw-Hill, 1995) used Talbot's farm as part of its set of examples. The example suits the needs of this book very well.

The Talbot example comes from an old ledger book with entries dating from 1896 through 1905 (Figure 4-1). This book was the general ledger for Dora Talbot's farm, kept by (possibly) her son, George B. Talbot. The farm was in a rural area of southwestern New Hampshire near the towns of Keene and Edmeston.

This ledger contained sales and purchases, laborers paid, and materials bought: all the transactions of a working business in serial form. It also contained other useful information, such as a list of the addresses of the casual laborers who worked on the farm.

This ledger struck George Koch as a fine example of how people kept books before there were relational databases—and as an illustration of the similarities

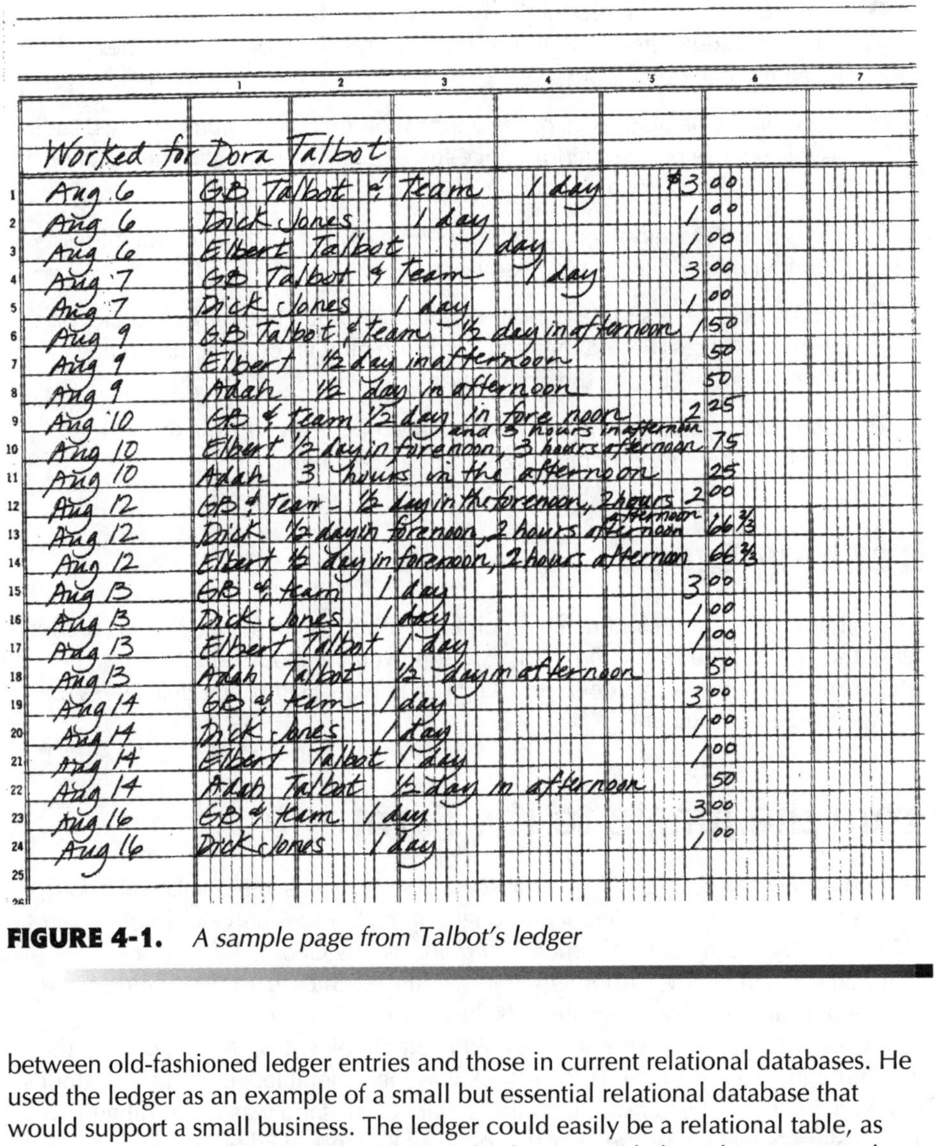

Worked for Dora Talbot

Aug 6	GB Talbot & Team 1 day	$3 00
Aug 6	Dick Jones 1 day	1 00
Aug 6	Elbert Talbot 1 day	1 00
Aug 7	GB Talbot & Team 1 day	3 00
Aug 7	Dick Jones 1 day	1 00
Aug 9	GB Talbot & team ½ day in afternoon	1 50
Aug 9	Elbert ½ day in afternoon	50
Aug 9	Adah ½ day in afternoon	50
Aug 10	GB & team ½ day in fore noon and 3 hours in afternoon	2 25
Aug 10	Elbert ½ day in forenoon, 3 hours afternoon	75
Aug 10	Adah 3 hours in the afternoon	25
Aug 12	GB & Team – ½ day in the forenoon, 2 hours afternoon	2 00
Aug 12	Dick ½ day in forenoon, 2 hours afternoon	66 ⅔
Aug 12	Elbert ½ day in forenoon, 2 hours afternoon	66 ⅔
Aug 13	GB & team 1 day	3 00
Aug 13	Dick Jones 1 day	1 00
Aug 13	Elbert Talbot 1 day	1 00
Aug 13	Adah Talbot ½ day in afternoon	50
Aug 14	GB & team 1 day	3 00
Aug 14	Dick Jones 1 day	1 00
Aug 14	Elbert Talbot 1 day	1 00
Aug 14	Adah Talbot ½ day in afternoon	50
Aug 16	GB & team 1 day	3 00
Aug 16	Dick Jones 1 day	1 00

FIGURE 4-1. *A sample page from Talbot's ledger*

between old-fashioned ledger entries and those in current relational databases. He used the ledger as an example of a small but essential relational database that would support a small business. The ledger could easily be a relational table, as could the table of addresses. The original database provided a coherent example for how to write SQL; this book takes this idea a step further and uses Talbot's ledger to develop applications with Developer/2000.

ORACLE7: The Complete Reference was not really concerned with the tasks of developing applications, just with teaching SQL and ORACLE7. The example in that book, although perfectly useful, did not adhere to the process and design suggestions the present book advocates. So, this book provides a more complete version of the Talbot database, with full integrity constraints, that will serve as a comprehensive example for the suggestions in this book.

This book also takes the liberty of extending the anachronism to make something out of Talbot's farm that it was not: an expanding, modern business with expanding, modern data processing needs. Talbot's may deal in cows and hire people to dig graves or shoe horses, but this book sees it as an example of a modern corporate farm looking toward the next century—whatever century that might be. So, suspend historical disbelief and let Talbot's illustrate how to use Developer/2000 effectively in your own business; with any luck, it will survive. (Just make sure to hide away at least one of your Developer/2000 applications for discovery in 2095 for use as an example for organic databases, or whatever technology they'll have then.)

A Proposed Life Cycle for Talbot's Systems

Talbot's data processing organization needs to have a software development life cycle to follow. The developers at Talbot's are very much aware of the need to have quality and productivity in the software process. In searching for the best way to organize their work, they decided that the best life cycle is the rapid-prototyping style (see Chapter 3). Having hired a management consultant, they adopt her recommendations:

- Take a *component approach* by identifying components of the overall system and building them to a given level of quality and risk as systems, then integrate them into a whole. This takes advantage of the component and open architecture of Developer/2000.

- *Prototype* the components in *two-week baselines,* with each baseline delivering a working version of the component as a basis for review and further work. This will yield high system quality because of increased exposure to and communication from the user community.

- Use *risk analysis and management* to decide where to focus effort for high system quality.

- *Automate* design, coding, testing, integration, and deployment where possible to get high productivity.

Talbot's Requirements

Talbot's requirements center on two clusters of query and maintenance functions: the ledger and the list of people who work at Talbot's along with their addresses and skills.

In the real world, the requirements process would uncover many, many possible requirements beyond these. For simplicity, this book limits requirements to these areas.

The first step is to assess the feasibility of the project. With the limited set of requirements and the focus of the requirements on a central database, there is every reason to believe that a straightforward Developer/2000 database application system will fully satisfy Talbot's requirements. Developing such a system should be possible, given the current budget and resources at Talbot's.

The next step is to get a problem statement. The short answer to this need is the ledger book containing the material developed during several years of keeping Talbot's books. Though the technology is different, this book represents what Talbot's sees as its current requirements for information processing.

Talbot's needs to maintain and use a database that contains cash transactions: amounts of goods bought and sold, hours of labor paid for, and amounts received. Talbot's needs to maintain and use a database that lists the people who work at Talbot's and their addresses and skills. How does this translate into functions? This section gives you some idea of the kind of requirements that a company such as Talbot's would have and what kind of information you need to get. The process followed here is not as exhaustive as a real requirements analysis.

An initial guess might be that ledger transactions are central to the database. In a way, that's true; Talbot's cares very much about keeping track of amounts spent and received. However, if you probe more deeply, you begin to realize the importance of the people involved in both the transactions and the personnel applications. People tie together the financial and human resource sides of the system. An early decision was to represent people in a central way, joining into a single table laborers with people that entered into transactions with Talbot's.

First let's list the functions our software application will need to address.

Function: To represent all the people and organizations with which Talbot's interacts in a central list available to accounting and personnel for query and maintenance.

For this function, it is essential for this list to be available to both accounting and personnel. It also is essential that anyone with which Talbot's does monetary business be on the list. It is desirable that the application make it easy to correct mistakes in the list.

Function: To track all monetary transactions that involve Talbot's, including the kind of transaction (bought, sold, paid, received), description of the item, the number of units, the rate for each unit, and the amount of the transaction. This information must be available for query and must be available for auditing.

To enable auditing, it is essential that all transactions exist in the database and that corrections are separate transactions. It is essential that no transaction change or disappear at any time for any reason. It is desirable for the application to calculate the amount of the transaction automatically from the quantity and rate. It is desirable for the user to be able to sort queried transactions by any data element.

Function: To maintain a list of the addresses of the laborers for contact and payment purposes.

It is essential that addresses be current and correct. It is desirable to be able to produce mailing labels for all laborers.

Function: To maintain a list of the skills and competencies of the laborers for work assignment purposes.

It is desirable that all laborers have skill entries and that each entry evaluates their competence at that skill.

Given these requirements, the following sections outline the kind of paper prototypes that Chapter 5 will use to work up your first working Developer/2000 prototypes.

A Little Database

You will find that the first design step after requirements analysis is almost always prototyping the database design. Without a database design, you will find it difficult to visualize the forms, reports, and graphics, because they all reflect the basic purpose of Developer/2000: presenting the database to the user. It may seem slightly anomalous to do design before prototyping, but database applications are different than other kinds of applications and require a more complex set of life cycle phases. Do not focus too much on analysis versus design versus coding; focus on what you need to do to state the problem and to formulate the initial solution. A database design states the problem in a clear, formal statement that you will find essential in defining your forms, reports, and graphics. Having a database also makes developing a working prototype much easier.

Appendix A has the complete database with data definition statements and all the data. This section explains the database design and gives you what you need to interpret the SQL and data in the following chapters.

Figure 4-2 shows the entity-relationship diagram that defines the Talbot database. If you have never seen an entity-relationship diagram before, here are the graphical conventions:

- *Entities* (the rectangles) represent the objects of the database.

- *Relationships* (the diamonds) represent the relationships between objects.

- *Attributes* (the circles) represent the data attributes of the objects; primary key attributes are marked with an asterisk.

- *Roles* (lines between entities and relationships) represent the role the entity plays in the relationship.

- Role *degree* (the 1 and M labels) represent the number of entities, one or many, that relate to the other entity in the relationship.

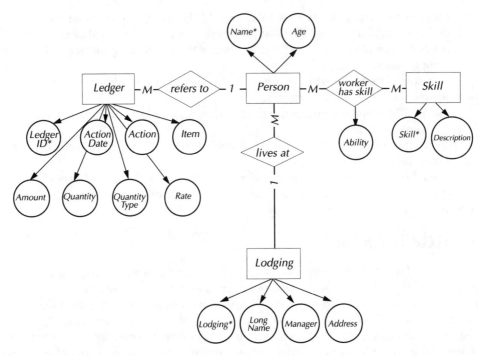

FIGURE 4-2. *An entity-relationship model of Talbot's database*

Figure 4-2 has four entities:

- *Ledger:* The entries in the ledger, each object referring to a single transaction of some kind, identified by a unique number (the Ledger ID)

- *Person:* The people that Talbot deals with; identified by name

- *Lodging:* The place where certain people live; identified by lodging name

- *Skill:* A person's skill, identified by skill name

There are three relationships in the model:

- *refers to:* Relates a ledger entry to a person; the ledger entry refers to the person as the seller or buyer or payee or payor

- *lives at:* Relates a person to a lodging; the person lives at the lodging

■ *worker has skill:* relates a person to one or more skills and a skill to one or more people; has a single attribute, Ability, that represents the ability of the worker with respect to the skill, a *relationship attribute*

The first two relationships are optional, one-to-many relationships. A ledger entry refers to exactly one person, and you can refer to a person by more than one ledger entry. A person lives at a single lodging, and a lodging may have more than one person living at it.

The third relationship is an optional, many-to-many relationship. A person may have several skills, and a skill may apply to more than one person. The skills apply only to people who are workers, a fact that this particular database does not represent because it detracts from the clarity of the example.

Transforming this to a relational database requires the following steps:

1. Create one table for each entity (Ledger, Person, Lodging, and Skill tables), creating the columns from the attributes and giving them the primary key columns (Ledger ID, Name, Lodging, and Skill, respectively).

2. Create one table for each many-to-many relationship (Worker Has Skill), creating any columns (Ability) and giving the table the primary key of the two primary keys of the entities that participate in the relationship (Name and Skill from Person and Skill, respectively).

3. Add a column for each one-to-many relationship to the table on the many side of the relationship that refers to the primary key on the one side (Person in the Ledger table referring to the Person table, Lodging in the Person table referring to the Lodging table).

In this little database, these rules are sufficient to create the relational database. In a more complex database, there are some additional things to worry about, such as relationships with more than two entities, one-to-one relationships, and one-to-many relationships with attributes. There are also more constraints to worry about, and the data types to consider, as well.

If you look at the SQL in Appendix A, you will see that it creates an additional object: a sequence. ORACLE7 provides the ability to declare a *sequence*, which is a tool that generates a unique integer in series. The Talbot database uses this sequence to generate the Ledger IDs in the INSERT statements for the Ledger table. If it were a requirement for Talbot's to be portable to other database managers, the database would not contain this sequence, as it is nonstandard. You could not depend on having the CREATE SEQUENCE statement or the NEXTVAL function to return the current sequence number. Fortunately, Talbot's has made a major commitment to use only ORACLE7, so it can take full advantage of the many nonstandard features of the ORACLE7 database manager.

Developing Forms

This section shows the development of two forms in paper sketch format with some standards that will prove necessary in developing the form prototypes. The main concern in this section is roughing out the user interface for the query and maintenance functions as the input for prototyping. Some understanding of the kinds of things that Developer/2000 can do will help in formulating the paper sketches, but generally at this stage you should avoid being constrained by technology. Focus on the requirements, not the detailed solutions. The prototypes will help to resolve many solution-oriented issues.

The first form is the Ledger form, which addresses the ledger-related functionality. This form will serve the accounting department (G. Talbot) as the main interface to the ledger table. Figure 4-3 shows the Ledger table and its connections in the database design.

This form must accomplish the following tasks:

■ The form must permit a bookkeeper to enter transactions. Each transaction must have a date, an item description, an action, a quantity and its unit type, a rate, and an amount.

■ The form must generate Ledger IDs to identify each transaction.

■ The transaction must link to a person already present in the database through the Name of the Person.

■ The form must calculate the value of the amount as the quantity multiplied by the rate.

■ The form must prevent anyone from updating or deleting transactions in the database.

■ The form must allow an accountant to retrieve the transactions using a query-by-example functionality.

■ The form should allow ad hoc sorting of the transactions by the different data elements.

The fields in the form represent the structure of the Ledger table in an accessible format. The first choice to make is whether to lay out the form to handle one transaction at a time or several. The maintenance requirements would indicate one transaction, whereas the query requirements would indicate multiple transactions. The single-transaction screen would have the fields distributed around the form window; the multiple-transaction screen would have a spreadsheet-style grid of fields and rows. In this case, the choice is to go with the multiple-transaction screen. This accommodates both query and maintenance in one form,

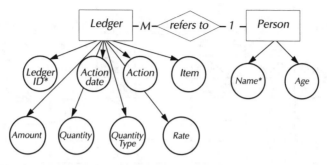

FIGURE 4-3.   *The database design for the Ledger table*

because the size and shape of the spreadsheet can fit into the required window size. If there were more fields, or if the fields needed to be bigger, it might make sense to build two forms, one for query and one for maintenance.

Figure 4-4 shows a sketch of the first pass at designing the layout for the form.

You can satisfy the requirement for linking to people by creating a list-of-values dialog box or drop-down list on the Person field in the entry table.

The second form is the Enter Worker Skills form. This form shows the second major kind of form, the master-detail form.

The function of this form is to maintain the database of laborer skills and to give managers a way to query those skills for individual workers. A reference report could also perform the latter part of the task; the following section gives an example in the Ledger Summary report. Figure 4-5 shows the structure of the skill-related tables in the database.

This database design is typical of the variety that requires a master-detail form. The many-to-many relationship makes it a little more complex, however, because you have two tables that perform roles in the relationship. The master-detail relationship is really a one-to-many relationship that lets you maintain one master and one set of detail records for each master record. The extended requirements for skill requires maintaining both employees and skills in separate tables, as well as the relationship between them.

Because of the diversity of requirements, the best solution is to maintain each table (Person, WorkerHasSkill, and Skill) in a separate form. The Person form will have the Person columns, the Skill form will have the Skill columns, and the WorkerSkill form will have the relationship columns (the keys from Person and Skill and the Ability column). In the WorkerSkill form, there is no need to include the person's age. Looking at the Skill and Description column values, the primary key is descriptive enough to serve as a short description for the WorkerSkill form. You probably do not need to display the Skill Description either. That leaves the Person Name, the Ability, and the Skill as the three fields to display on the form.

I.D.	Action Date	Action	Item	Quantity	Type	Amount	Person
1	01 Apr 01	Paid	Plowing	1	Day	$3.00	G.B. Talbot
2	02 May 01	Paid	Work	1	Day	3.00	Dick Jones
3	03 Jun 01	Paid	Work	1	Day	1.00	Elbert Talbot
4							
5							
6							
7							
8							
9							
10							
11							
12							
13							
14							
15							

FIGURE 4-4.   *A sketch of the layout of the Ledger form*

Because the form represents a relationship, you use the master-detail relationship to create a natural hierarchy for entry. The master record is read-only; you query it to find the person to whom you want to assign a skill. The detail records then link multiple skills to the person. You could also do this by having two list-of-values dialog boxes or drop-down lists on the fields. That would mean

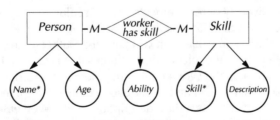

FIGURE 4-5.   *The database design for the Skill table*

displaying the same person multiple times, as well as allowing multiple people to get skills assigned at the same time, which seems confusing. The hierarchical arrangement is more natural, less confusing, and less complex to implement. It also looks simpler to the user, because the person field by itself and associated two-column table of skill information looks less complicated than a spreadsheet-style table of people and skill information would. Figure 4-6 shows the sketched layout of the WorkerSkill form.

Other forms might include the Person form with a master-detail relationship to the Lodging table and the Skill form with a simple table for entering skills.

In the process of creating these forms, you begin to realize that you require standards to ensure that all the forms present a consistent interface to the users. Here are some examples:

- Each form represents a basic function. Use the form title to summarize this function, and put the title in the window title.

- Place scroll bars for record groups on the right side of the group to conform to the usual format for scrolling windows.

- Use lists-of-values rather than drop-down lists to represent choice selection in multiple-row tables.

- Use the Helvetica 10-point bold font or the local equivalent font for column labels and Helvetica 10-point regular for data.

- Use the Helvetica 14-point bold font or the local equivalent font for captions, such as for grouped fields or graphics embedded in the form.

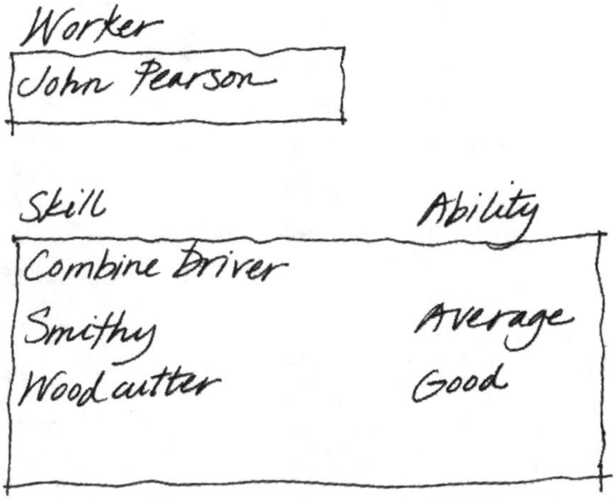

FIGURE 4-6. *A sketch of the layout of the WorkerSkill form*

Developing Reports

Although the Ledger form is adequate for ad hoc querying of transaction data, the different users of the ledger information need a more accessible report that summarizes the information in the ledger. This calls for a report rather than a form, although the distinction is a fine one.

Looking at the current accounting reports done by Talbot's outside accountants, the Talbot designers can easily produce similar reports automatically without spending any more money on the yearly accounting audit than is necessary for verification of the numbers. Their accountants will no longer need to produce the reports (and to charge for producing the reports) that they need to do their work.

These reports summarize the ledger by the person affected by the transaction. The auditing accountants need to see the individual transactions by person, listed in date order, and a total for each person. Figure 4-7 shows a sketch of the Ledger Summary report.

The accounts payable department pays workers at their home address. This is another requirement that indicates a need for a report. Personnel also wants the ability to mail company newsletters and other information to workers' home addresses. To do this, Talbot's needs to generate mailing labels from the Person and Lodging tables. Figure 4-8 shows the preliminary design for the Lodging table.

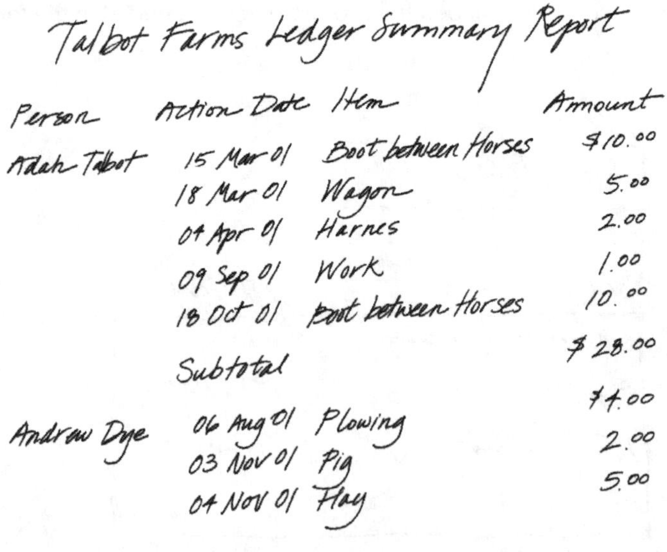

FIGURE 4-7. *A sketch of the Ledger Summary report*

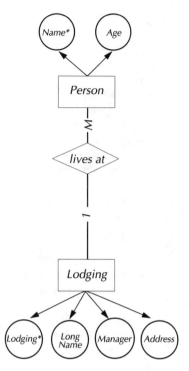

FIGURE 4-8.   *The database design for the Lodging table*

The only major decision you need to make for a mailing label report is the label size. Mailing labels now come in laser-printer sheets that contain a uniform layout of labels, usually in two or three columns per page. The Talbot Lodging Mailing Label report thus needs a layout showing how Personnel wants the names and lodging addresses to appear on the label pages. Figure 4-9 is a sketch of this report.

Some Rules for Setting Up Forms and Reports

Forms and reports seem as natural to anyone in business as a book is to a reader. Anyone who has tried to write a book will tell you it is not quite so simple to write one as to read one. Form and report design is an art that requires much experience and thought about how people use these things. This section outlines some of the major principles and issues in designing Developer/2000 forms and reports.

Adah Talbot
Papa King Rooming
127 Main, Edmeston

Andrew Dye
Rose Hill for Men
RFD 3, N. Edmeston

Bart Sarjeant
Cranmer Retreat House
Hill St, Berkeley

Dick Jones
Rose Hill for Men
RFD 3, N. Edmeston

Donald Rollo
Matts Long Bunk House
3 Mile Rd., Keene

Elbert Talbot
Weitbrocht Rooming
320 Geneva, Keene

FIGURE 4-9. *A sketch of the Lodging Mailing Label report*

There are five essential principles of design relevant to forms and reports:

- A form or report must convey information or *communicate* to the user in as efficient a manner as possible.

- A form or report must be *flexible* enough to adapt to the different needs, levels of experience, and levels of knowledge of its intended users.

- A form or report must be as *simple* as possible, but no simpler (attributed to Albert Einstein in a slightly different context).

- A form or report must *perform* to match the flow and speed of human response.

- A form or report must provide *assistance* to its users through feedback at the appropriate level, help as necessary, and the ability to undo errors.

Most of these principles apply as much to paper forms and reports as they do to online forms and reports. Reference to a tax form (*any* tax form except perhaps for the ones with which you enclose a check) will demonstrate that the state of the art is nowhere near its acme. The following suggestions for design may help you see how to make your forms better. The best way to learn this sort of design is by doing it and observing how easy it is for your clients to use the results.

These three elements sum up form and report design: *understanding, learning,* and *cohesion.* The ability to understand the form or report promotes the passing of information and derives from the innate simplicity of the form or report. The ability to learn how to use a form or report stems from its flexibility, its simplicity, and the way the form or report renders assistance. How the report or form hangs together promotes information flow and performance, particularly by letting the user enter information quickly and reliably. These elements are all aspects of the interlocking design principles, each of which contributes its part in a broad system of user interaction.

Forms and reports are of course different in many ways, but the logic of their layout and design is quite similar. They differ in that forms are by nature interactive whereas reports have a repetitive page structure but, otherwise, they are the same. The design elements here that pertain to data entry apply only to forms; the other elements apply both to reports and forms.

Communication

To effectively communicate, a form or report needs to present just the information required—no more and no less. To do this, you must first decide what exactly that information is and how the user will use it. You will sometimes find that by breaking up a requirement into two parts, you lose nothing in communication and gain in simplicity. This in turn improves communication by making it easier for the user to understand the information you are conveying.

There are several techniques for effective communication.

Minimize Jargon
First, minimize jargon. Avoid code words, acronyms, and malapropisms. Use plain English (or whatever your native language is) in both your form or report and in the data in your database. If you allow anyone to input data to the database, you will probably have to provide some kind of editing to render the input data into something that communicates well.

Use Graphics
Second, use pictures and graphics instead of text and tables if they communicate the right amount of information at the right level of presentation. The upcoming "Effectively Using Graphics" section provides a more detailed discussion of this.

Use Labels

Third, use captions or labels to give meaning to the data in your form or report. Some data or graphics may stand alone and communicate well, but this is rare. More often, you will find a few words in a caption will immediately communicate the purpose and nature of the picture or data to the user.

Minimize Redundancy

Fourth, minimize redundancy and the paths that a user must follow to get data into or out of a form or report. Redundancy improves communication when it ensures the receipt of the whole picture; it obscures communication when it makes it difficult to absorb the information in a message. The length and complexity of the paths you must take to move data into a database or to understand the content of your report will often determine the level of communication. If you have to leave a trail of bread crumbs behind you, go back to the drawing board.

Add Variety Sparingly

Fifth, use difference sparingly to emphasize important data or instructions. Using a different font (boldface, for example, or a different point size or typeface) can distinguish a caption or label from the associated data, as can the graphical layout (beveled, three-dimensional fields, for example). However, too much difference leads to increased complexity and a diminished ability to absorb information or learn relationships. Having many different typefaces, colors all over the place, or funny symbols and icons bouncing around the screen may entertain the user (briefly) but does not communicate effectively.

Flexibility

Flexibility is the degree to which users with different needs can adapt your application to their intended use. Requirements do not constrain a *truly* flexible system. That is, it really does not matter what you intended a user to be able to do; they can do whatever they want.

In the real world of the database application, things are too complex to permit true flexibility. You only get true flexibility with programming languages or other, similar levels of complexity that are not options for most users. If you are willing to use C or COBOL, you can do anything you want, within certain limits. But an end user cannot do this because the skills are beyond his or her knowledge and capabilities.

The form or report provides a carefully structured, much less flexible interface for the end user. Within the limits of this careful structuring, however, you should try to give the user the ability to use the application flexibly.

The primary flexibility issue to consider is *experience.* What level of knowledge does your target user have, and does the application scale in usability as the user learns more about using it? Often, the levels of simplicity and helpfulness appropriate to less experienced or less knowledgeable users just gets in the way of the experienced user. You should offer methods of helping the experienced user, such as the ability to turn off features, direct entry as opposed to entry through accessing lists of possibilities, special keypresses, and so on. If you cannot do this through a single application, build more than one for the different levels of knowledge. Make them consistent so that when a new user becomes more experienced, he or she can quickly adapt to the experienced-user application.

The Potential for Different Paths

The other major flexibility issue to consider is the potential for *different paths* through the network of possibilities. People view things differently, and you should try not to constrain people where it is not necessary to do so. If the order of entering information is unimportant, you should make it possible to enter data in any order. If there are several ways to enter a value (for example, a date in any of its multifarious formats), do not constrain the user to a single format just because you can easily check it for accuracy. Provide options so that different users can do things the way they want instead of the way you want.

Simplicity

By reducing complexity, you increase simplicity, and vice versa. There are many different principles that you can apply to reduce complexity:

- ■ You can *hide* levels of complexity from the user in hierarchies of windows and dialog boxes.

- ■ You can make the *common things* that the user needs to do simple and easy, even at the expense of making less common things hard.

- ■ You can *limit* the number of elements in your interface using the limits on human cognitive ability as a guide (seven elements plus-or-minus two).

- ■ You can make interface elements as *consistent* as possible to improve the ability of the user to perceive those elements.

- ■ You can make the interface elements *cohesive,* grouping elements by consistent principles and keeping all data the user needs in one place.

- ■ You can minimize *redundancy* and the *complexity* of paths, which also improves communication.

- ■ You can use *standards* for layout and formatting to guide users to the right place, making it seem a natural process.

■ You can automate data entry to improve reliability through validation and structured entry techniques (list of values, defaults, and intelligent triggers, for example).

Layout Standards

Your forms and reports should follow the natural layout conventions of the language and culture of the user. For English-speaking cultures, this means positioning the fields beginning at the upper left of the page or screen and continuing from left to right, top to bottom.

Forms should follow the layout standards that apply to the platform. For example, most graphical user interfaces place the form title in the top center of the window. Most platforms have a standard location for a scroll bar and a status bar, as well.

You should settle on a few major conventions for emphasis and use them sparingly in your layout. Remember that the more you emphasize, the less important your emphasized text will seem. Also, use different layout options to distinguish different elements of the form or report. Make captions and labels differ from data, and distinguish summaries and totals from the data they summarize.

Use mixed case (normal capitalization, just as you see in this sentence) in text; it is easier to read. You can use uppercase text in captions or labels, but this book advises against it. Keep text on one line in captions and titles. Avoid abbreviations and contractions.

Cohesion and Consistency

Keep your form and report layout cohesive by grouping elements and by balancing them on the screen or page.

Grouping elements lets you bind the elements together according to some principle. Choose your principle carefully, then adhere to it consistently throughout your groupings to make your layout easily understandable:

■ *Frequency:* Group your items by the frequency with which the user refers to them or enters them. Put the most frequently used items in the "first" location, such as the upper left for layouts in English.

■ *Sequence:* If the items form a natural sequence of some kind, lay them out in the natural order according to the cultural sequence layout (left-to-right in English, for example).

■ *Importance:* Place the more important items together.

■ *Function:* Place the items that relate to a specific function together.

Balancing elements is a graphical device for making the user feel comfortable with the layout. Align fields and other items with one another for a regular, even appearance. Make fields of similar sizes despite varying requirements for actual text length. Having many fields of different sizes tends to distract the user by drawing the eye to different locations, diminishing the value of your grouping strategy. The exception to this is to use ragged text justification in multiple-line text fields if you have them. Having a ragged right margin is more readable with most computer text layouts. Imperfections in the use of proportional fonts can make justified text look silly, and the ragged-right appearance leaves more white space for the user's eye. Finally, make the center of your form or page the center of gravity of your fields and boilerplate text. This makes the layout more comfortable for the eye.

Automated Data Entry in Forms

You can automate form data entry almost endlessly with Developer/2000, but there are some specific techniques that you should consider.

First, try to arrange your data entry fields in forms to promote reliability. You can use grouping strategies (see the previous section, "Cohesion and Consistency") to make entry a more natural process. You can also use validation (see Chapter 6) to provide immediate feedback on entered data.

Second, where possible, provide default values. Having the user press the ENTER key to accept a value is a lot more reliable and faster than any other kind of data entry. If you choose the defaults wisely, the user might need to enter just a few items, then save the entry.

Third, use lists of values to provide acceptable entries for inexperienced users. Developer/2000 makes it easy to associate a list dialog box with a field or to provide a drop-down list or combo box for entering values.

Fourth, use item triggers to make your fields more intelligent. One technique is to fill out different fields based on an entry in one field that precedes them. This works well with field-grouping strategies, for example. Another technique is to provide experienced users with shortcuts to entering values through intelligently interpreting the entry. For example, you can write reasonably generic code in PL/SQL that will take a few characters and look up a value in a table or record group. This kind of "quick-pick" approach appears increasingly in user interfaces and is not hard to do with elementary SQL WHERE clauses. You can extend this kind of thinking in many inventive ways to improve the speed and reliability of your data entry capabilities.

Performance

The basic standard for performance in a form or report is to match the speed and flow of the form or report with the human response.

Data entry in forms is a critical performance component. If you add much PL/SQL code in triggers that fire during navigation or validation events, make sure your performance matches human response. If someone navigates out of a field, they should see results of validation in reasonably quick order. If you have performance issues with such triggers, try to move the offending code to commit processing or to a trigger that fires on explicit demand rather than automatically. Most users have lower performance expectations for the commit stage, and you can set expectations appropriately for on-demand actions through feedback messages. Considering the application as a whole, you should generally make delays predictable to the user. Making slight delays consistent is better than having many variable delays that the user cannot predict.

Query in forms is not really an issue because you can set the user's expectations. You should avoid certain situations if possible, however:

- When the user presses [Execute Query] to query all the data instead of entering a query by example, the application should not go away for a long time. This is an easy thing to do because of keypress queues. Construct your default query for a form so that it will retrieve a small set of data if possible. You can also use a pre-query trigger to add a query term to the query if it has none.

- Try to ensure that your ad hoc query capabilities provide reasonable response under most circumstances. Think about what will happen if the user adds a specific field to a query. Use a pre-query trigger to warn the user if there might be slow response to the query.

Reports come in three varieties: interactive, ad hoc, and batch. *Interactive reports* use buttons to provide drill-down behavior that lets you make an interactive application out of a report. The performance of the navigation and display of the drill-down reports should match response expectations. *Ad hoc reports* are reports that you generate when you need them; again, performance on these reports should match expectations, generally requiring reasonably quick response. *Batch reports* are things you fire off before you go home for the evening or through timer mechanisms available in your operating system. The only performance requirements for batch reports are that it not take longer than the period over which you repeat the reports. In other words, if you have a daily batch report, the report had better format and print in less than a day. Make sure you understand your requirements.

Assistance

Giving the user a helping hand is always welcome in an application. You have several ways to do this. Most of the layout techniques in previous sections help the user by making it easier or more natural for the user to work with the form or report. But there are more specific things you can do to help out.

Giving Feedback

One of the most important things you can do in interactive forms is to give the user immediate *feedback* on the results of his or her actions. This means that there should be as little time as possible between the user action and a message or response. Developer/2000 usually provides basic feedback, telling you when it is working or doing something with the database. You can go far beyond this default behavior. Two specific areas that you should consider are validation and performance feedback.

If the user takes some action that results in an error condition, you should inform the user of the error immediately. Sometimes this is harder than it might appear. For example, if the user violates security by changing data without privileges to do so, Developer/2000 will not automatically catch the error until you commit and send the data to the server. You can use various options and techniques to move the feedback closer to the action; Chapter 8 describes this in more detail. Make sure that your application always confirms or invalidates the result of a user's action to the user. You can rely on Developer/2000 to do this for the most part, but you may need to go further in certain cases.

You should always provide as much information as you can to the user online. Developer/2000 gives you extensive *help* capabilities on almost every object you can think of. Make use of them. If you can, interpret common errors for the user rather than just giving them the raw error messages. Provide online documentation for your application using any of the commonly available help or interactive document tools.

Finally, you need to understand clearly how the user can undo mistakes. The best techniques for dealing with mistakes prevent them in the first place—that is the purpose of validation and reliability techniques. However, few applications achieve the peak of never permitting the user to make a mistake. If they did, they would probably be unusable. In any case, make sure you understand how the user can correct an error, then make sure the user understands that.

Developer/2000 applications use transaction management to finalize changes in the database. Up to the point of committing data, you can correct any problems; after committing, you need to change the data in the database. Provide the user with tools for identifying and correcting problems in the database if there are any necessary holes in your consistency and integrity strategy.

Effectively Using Graphics

Everyone likes to see the flash of an application that makes heavy use of graphics and visual objects. A deeper understanding of their true contribution and the structure by which they contribute their value can help you build objects you will want to reuse.

Graphics in applications are part of what you are *communicating,* not just decoration. A graphic, just as the written word, communicates well only if it communicates clearly. Most people get at least minimal training in language skills and writing at some point in their careers, but few get any training in graphics and graphic construction. This section gives you a few pointers and several references in case you want to learn more.

First, what about pictures? A picture is worth a thousand words, right? Only if you want to communicate the thousand words, unfortunately. If your concern is communicating a simple fact, showing a picture will almost always be overkill and will obscure what you wish to communicate. Use a picture in an application only if the picture represents real information: a picture of a house or apartment in a real-estate query system, a picture of a person in a personnel database, or a picture of a product in a sales application, for example.

Next, what about bitmap logos and icons? A classic use for bitmaps is to display the corporate logo. This is fine, as long as the people with whom you're communicating need to know graphically what company they should associate with the application. In an in-house application, for example, these logos are probably superfluous. On memos, for example, corporate logos establish the "official" nature of the communication. In an application, this will hardly ever be true.

Another major use for icons is to represent buttons that initiate some action, display another window, and so on. Using icons in tool bars, for example, has become extremely popular. If you build a lot of control bitmaps into your application, make sure they do not get in the way of the information the application communicates by making them small and unobtrusive, or separate them into their own window (a toolbar is a good place for these icons). Do spend some time designing and testing the icons for usability. Everyone hates those little icons that look like toilet seats, for example, instead of printers.

Now, on to the more complicated realm of graphic displays. The first decision you must make is what kind of graphic is appropriate to your application. To do that, you must first determine what exactly you want to communicate through the graphic. Just as you want to clearly state your conclusion in a piece of writing, you want your graphic to show as clearly as possible the main point. If you do not know what that main point is, you should not be using a graphic. You should also try to sum up the main point in the graphic title or caption that tells the reader what the graphic contains.

Once you have the main point, you next must determine how many components of information you need to convey. Are you comparing one thing with another? Two things compared by date? If you have more than three components, you probably will need more than one chart to show the information.

Now, for each component, you must determine whether the information is qualitative or quantitative. Qualitative data comes in categories; for example, the names of the people from whom Talbot bought goods. Quantitative data comes in numbers, such as dates or amounts. Some qualitative data can have an implicit order, such as names in alphabetical order or age groups or economic classes.

Given all this information, you can now decide what kind of graphic to use. For example, to show a two-component graphic with one qualitative component and one quantitative component, you should construct a pie chart, bar chart, or histogram. The pie slices and bars in these graphics directly represent categories in a nice way. If there is more than one quantitative component, you cannot use a pie chart but must use a double-barred chart or histogram. Stack the bars if the amounts are additive, put them next to one another if you want to compare them.

If you are comparing two quantitative components, use a line or scatter graph to show trends or a table to show exact values. Use shaded areas in a line chart to emphasize the size of total amounts, as opposed to the changes or trends in amounts.

As far as the graphics details go, the principle is to keep it simple. The point is the data, so make sure the details do not obscure the data. If there are too many labels, or you need a complicated legend, or you have too many components, simplify or you will not communicate your point. Make the data elements the prominent elements of the graphic. Surround the data area with scale lines, where appropriate, or with tick marks outside the data area to show gradations. Do not use too many tick marks; these will obscure the message. Use a reference line through the graphic to show an important value (a change point, a particular event date, and so on). Label individual data elements only if necessary to make your point. When possible, use graphical means to distinguish components rather than labels.

To facilitate their understanding, always include a legend that tells readers what the components are in the data area. Put the legend outside the data area. If you use special graphics, use a legend that tells the reader what the graphics represent. Use a scale that makes your point, but try to avoid fooling people with unusual scales. If you have more than one chart, use the same scale if the reader is going to compare them. And do not include zero on the scale just because it is there; only include it if it is meaningful and useful.

There are also a couple of practical issues you must consider. First, proofread or test your graphic displays to ensure they achieve your goals without obvious errors. Second, consider what might happen if someone needs to print a black-and-white copy of the graphic. Careers have fallen victim to the chart that looks great on the monitor but turns into a black smudge coming out of the printer. Not everyone enjoys getting their information from computers.

To learn more about how to produce effective graphic displays, consult *The Visual Display of Quantitative Information* by Edward R. Tufte (Graphics Press, 1983) and *The Elements of Graphing Data* by William S. Cleveland (Wadsworth Advanced Books and Software, 1985). To explore the depths of the possibilities in this field, consult the massive *Semiology of Graphics: Diagrams, Networks, Maps* by Jacques Bertin (University of Wisconsin Press, 1983).

This chapter has taken you from exploring what to do through giving you some basic guidelines about what works and what does not. It also introduced you to the Talbot example and used it to illustrate the first steps in building your application. The next chapter moves you from paper into the world of the working prototype.

CHAPTER 5

Prototyping

You are now in the first prototyping phase of the application development life cycle. If you are taking the risk-based approach to organizing your life cycle, your prototype will show you how to limit the risk of various kinds of technical failures. If you are taking the evolutionary approach, your prototype will provide customer feedback, giving you the basis for additional prototyping or for production development. In either case, using Developer/2000 for prototyping gives you strong tools for creating your form and report prototypes quickly and efficiently from your database.

Having set up your forms and reports on paper, you now can create a prototype model of the application using Developer/2000. Using the layout editors in conjunction with the database that Chapter 4 created (see Appendix A), you can generate the obvious forms and rearrange them quickly to look like the paper ones. After creating the forms, you can then create some prototype reports with the report layout editor. Then you can add some graphs to illustrate the forms and reports.

How far can you go with a prototype? Remember the purpose of a prototype: to get feedback to limit risks or to see what works and what does not. The sooner you get feedback, the sooner you can make progress toward a final product. Therefore, you want to focus your prototyping on quickly getting the application to the point where a customer can use it and give you feedback. Using Developer/2000 for prototyping makes this easy; the hard part is knowing when to stop. Usually, the best place to stop is when you face a significant effort that does not add much to the feedback possibilities, and that in turn depends on how easy Developer/2000 makes the task.

It is simple to create forms and reports with reasonably standard and even flashy backgrounds and structure or to create forms applications that let you display and manipulate data from the database with full data integrity. You can very easily create standard reports. You can create menus and connect them to forms, dialog boxes, and reports, and easily add basic graphs and charts to your application.

It is harder to mold the initial prototypes into easier-to-use, less complex applications, because that takes a lot of trigger programming, or to add user-interface features that are not automatic in Developer/2000. Creating well-organized, informative reports that combine data from multiple tables with complex SQL statements takes some real effort, as does getting the graphs to look just right for the specific situation. There are a lot of options you have to change. Also, adding those really spectacular application features hidden behind clicking a button or other interface item requires some serious programming.

However, let's put "harder" into perspective: getting even the simplest C or C++ program to do anything that you can do in Developer/2000 takes much more work. To bring in a cooking metaphor, this is the difference between cooking your basic meal (easy) versus cooking a gourmet meal (harder) versus raising the animals and growing the vegetables yourself, transforming them into food products (including documenting all the ways you did that), and then supervising the 16 line chefs needed to produce the meal in a restaurant (C++ programming—and that's *with* CASE tools!). If you have programmed with a programming language, you probably understand the point; if you have not, try it.

All this is not to say that there is no place for low-level programming in database application development. You won't find the really complicated financial or scientific applications being done with Developer/2000, at least not without a lot of pain and work. But unless you are a commercial software developer with a marketing department that won't quit, or you have invented a wonderful algorithm for analyzing the effects of relativity on multiple planetary elliptics, most of your applications will be everyday ones that just need to work and do so quickly. That's what Developer/2000 does well, especially the "quickly" part. That brings us back to the prototyping.

NOTE
The Forms tool in particular makes many assumptions about what a database application looks like. If you want to *lower* your productivity and *create work* for your development team, use different assumptions, whether from an aesthetic judgment or from a desire for increased performance or whatever. For example, trying to build forms that violate the way Forms handles transactions in its blocks; or building reports that look like spreadsheets, grid and all; or trying to develop a complicated, graphical application using Forms and Graphs: all of these are just likely to get you into trouble. Use Developer/2000 the way Oracle intended it and you can reap large rewards in value and productivity.

The following sections show you how to develop some of the Chapter 4 prototypes quickly as working applications. Remember, the purpose is to quickly get feedback from the customers to limit your risks or to figure out what you need to do next.

Developing Form Prototypes

To show you how to develop a quick prototype with some complexity, this section develops the Worker-Skill application from Chapter 4 that lets you associate skills with workers. There are a lot of figures in this section that introduce the various tools; you should familiarize yourself with those tools by experimenting with them as you go.

NOTE
This chapter is not a substitute for the tutorials that come with the Developer/2000 components. The sections give enough detail for you to re-create the prototypes, but the intent is to show you how to do prototypes, not to show you how to use the Developer/2000 tools in terms of menus, buttons, and dialog boxes. The screen shots illustrate the individual items, not every possible detail of Developer/2000; this is not documentation, but a book on developing applications. As the prototype progresses, the description assumes that you have become familiar with the interface and so provides less detail about the specific things you have to do. As with any software product, you learn by doing and by experimenting, not by reading. Use the Oracle tutorials and user guides to explore the user interface. Also, the example assumes that you are using ORACLE7, since Talbot's has decided to use that DBMS exclusively. Certain elements of the user interface do not work with other database managers; see the Developer/2000 documentation for details.

Launch the Forms Designer by clicking on the icon. When the Designer window displays the Object Navigator window, you will see a default form, MODULE1, as the only form in the window, as shown in Figure 5-1. Select the name by dragging the mouse over the current name, then type in the new name: WorkerSkill. Notice that Designer translates everything you type to uppercase. You now have a WorkerSkill form module! However, it doesn't do anything yet, so let your breath out.

To finish the form, you will go through these steps:

1. Create the Worker block that displays a single person from the Person table.

2. Create the WorkerHasSkill block that displays several skills from the WorkerHasSkill table and make it a detail block linked to the master Worker block.

3. Add a List of Values (LOV) dialog box to provide the possible skills from the Skill table so that you do not have to type in the skill, just choose it from the list.

4. Clean up the appearance of the form to make it look like the paper prototype from Chapter 4.

5. Save and run the application to verify that it will serve as a prototype.

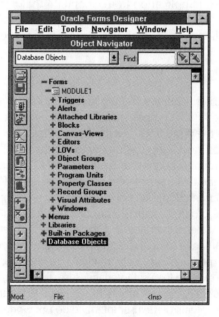

FIGURE 5-1. *The Oracle Forms Designer window*

Create the Worker Block

The Worker block corresponds to the Person table in the database. By querying the records in this block, you can scroll through all the people in the database. The Worker-Skill application lets you assign a particular skill to a person. The first thing you have to do is find the person to which you want to assign a skill.

The paper prototype from Chapter 4 shows the person's name in a single-record field labeled Worker. That's the entire block: just the one field that directly corresponds to the Name column in the Person table.

Pull down the Tools menu and select the New Block item. Designer displays the New Block Options dialog box for the WorkerSkill form (Figure 5-2).

The Select button on the right side of the Base Table field lets you get the name of the *base table* (the table to which the block corresponds) from the database. Click on it. Designer now has to connect you to your database, so it displays the Connect dialog that prompts you for your user name, password, and the database connect string. For the Talbot system, the user name is Talbot, the password is George, and the database is whatever the system administrator says it is (in this case, ORACLE7). Figure 5-3 illustrates this dialog box.

Not content with connecting you, Designer now wants to give you more choices, so it displays the Tables dialog box (Figure 5-4), which asks what kind of tables you want to see. The default (which is fine in this case) is to see the tables for the current user. You might also want to see tables from other users to which you have access, and you might want to see views and synonyms, as well as just the tables.

Now the Designer gathers all the tables and displays them in a standard Find dialog box (Figure 5-5). The Find dialog box lets you search among a set of text

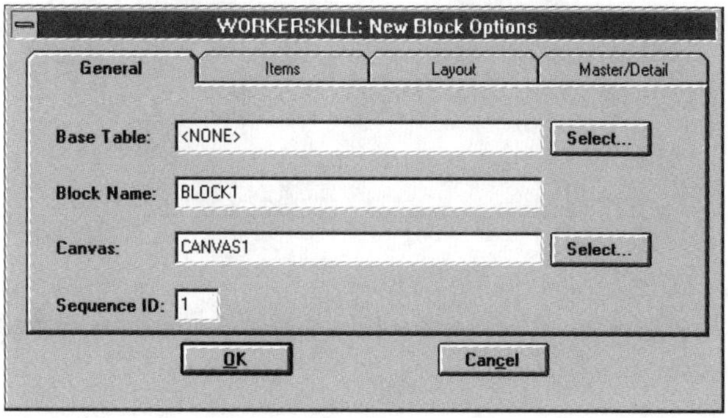

FIGURE 5-2.   *The initial New Block Options dialog box*

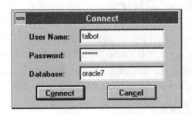

FIGURE 5-3. *The Connect dialog box for Talbot*

strings to select one for some purpose. In this case, you select the table name you want to enter into the Base Table field, "Person". Just click on that row and click OK. In the future, if you have a significant number of strings, you can enter a pattern at the top of the dialog (use the LIKE operator pattern strings from ORACLE7 SQL) to filter out strings you do not want to see. In this case, you can see all the strings in the dialog, so you just have to pick the one you want.

Now you are back in the New Block Options dialog, having entered the Person table as the Base table. Make the block name Worker and the canvas name Worker_Canvas, as shown in Figure 5-6. There are some additional options you need to set, so do not click on the OK button just yet.

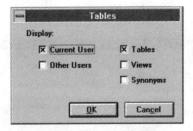

FIGURE 5-4. *The Tables dialog box*

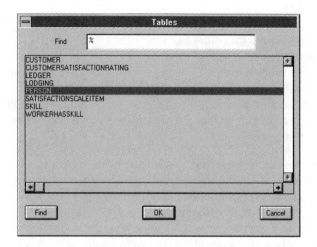

FIGURE 5-5. *The Find dialog box with Talbot table names*

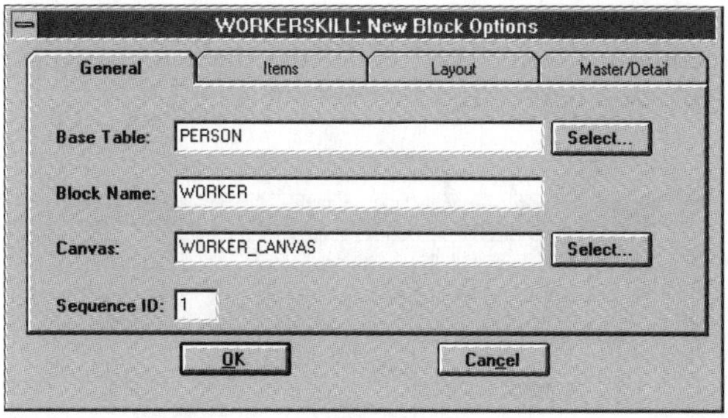

FIGURE 5-6. *The completed General tab*

NOTE
Your application data model (the external model in Figure 1-4) may
have names that differ from the central tables in the database. You
should make every effort to create consistent names, so generally
your block names will be the same as the corresponding base tables.
In the case we just saw, Talbot intends to later restrict the rows the
application sees to just workers; hence, he names the block Worker
instead of Person. For the prototype, there is no restriction; but
there will be.

Click on the Items tab in the dialog box. You need to choose which columns
from the Person table to put into the block (Figure 5-7). To see the available
columns, click on the Select Columns button. In this case, you want only the Name
column, so double-click on the other two columns (Age and Lodging) to remove
them; notice the "+" sign changes to a "–" sign. You can also select the column and
click in the small Include check box at the bottom of the dialog box to do the same thing.

Click the OK button to finalize the block. The Worker block now appears in the
Object Navigator under the WorkerSkill form. You have your first block!

Create the WorkerHasSkill Block

To finish the heart of the form prototype, you now create the WorkerHasSkill
block. Go through the same process in the General tab, as shown in Figure 5-8.

Leave the Items tab alone, but click on the Layout tab and do two things: set
the number of records to 6 instead of 1 and check the Scrollbar check box to get a
scroll bar on the block of 6 records, as shown in Figure 5-9.

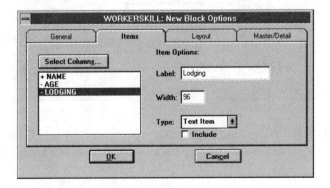

FIGURE 5-7. *The Items tab with excluded columns*

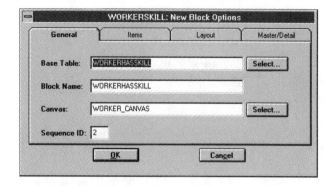

FIGURE 5-8.   *The General tab for the WorkerHasSkill block*

Finally, click on the Master/Detail tab and click the Select button to select the master block (Worker) from a Find dialog box. You see the join condition that links the two forms appear automatically in the Join Condition box, as Figure 5-10 shows. Click OK. You now have your second block!

Figure 5-11 shows the Object Navigator with the two blocks in your new form.

The Skills List

Now, you need to finish off the prototype by putting a List of Values (LOV) dialog box into the WorkerHasSkill block to give you a way of helping users to enter

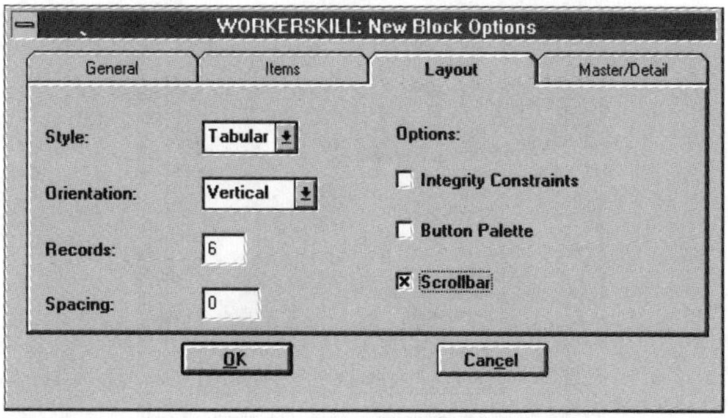

FIGURE 5-9.   *The Layout tab for WorkerHasSkill block with records and scroll bar settings*

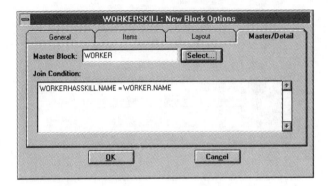

FIGURE 5-10. *The Master/Detail tab for WorkerHasSkill block with master block and join condition*

skills. There are several different ways to do this, but the easiest is to create a List of Values dialog box and link it to the Skill field in the WorkerHasSkill block. For prototyping purposes, this is good enough.

You have already seen an LOV dialog box in Figure 5-5. The Tables dialog box that displays the database tables available is an LOV dialog box. The Designer uses

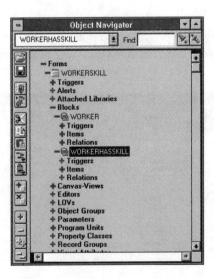

FIGURE 5-11. *The Object Navigator with two blocks defined*

LOV dialog boxes whenever it needs to display a set of values for a choice. The LOV dialog box lets you "auto-type" or enter a pattern and use the Find button to filter the values. Auto-typing lets you enter a letter or letters that become part of the pattern automatically, and the LOV then displays just the entries that match the letters you have entered. Once you have built an LOV, experiment with it; you will soon understand how it works.

Start out by creating the LOV dialog boxes. In the Object Navigator, find the LOVs header under the WorkerSkill form (the headers are in alphabetical order). Double-click on the header to create a new LOV. The Designer now displays the New LOV dialog box, as shown in Figure 5-12.

Click in the Query Text box to enter a SQL statement that will retrieve the skills from the database. For now, just enter the simple SQL statement

```
SELECT Skill FROM Skill
```

Figure 5-12 shows this SQL statement. Click OK, and you have an LOV, which appears in the LOV group with the name LOV0. A record group with the same name appears in the Record Groups group. For readability, rename the LOV and the record group to SKILLS by selecting the object, then clicking on the name in the Object Navigator, then typing over the name.

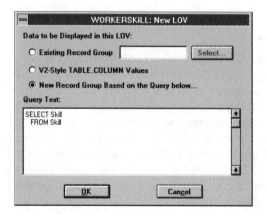

FIGURE 5-12. *The New LOV dialog box*

NOTE
You can do some fairly fancy things with SQL in these statements, such as using text functions to transform things from the database, ORDER BY, DISTINCT, and GROUP BY to sort and group the data into the list, and so on. This may or may not be appropriate for your prototype. If you have standards for prototypes, such as "lists must display in alphabetical order," then you might want to do more SQL coding here. For example, you could add the clause ORDER BY Skill to put the skills into alphabetical order. Obviously, you will have to write more code if you are constructing the list from data not already in that format: for example, by joining or unioning two tables or by transforming data in some way.

Now that you have a basic LOV, you need to take care of a few minor things before it is complete and workable. First, you need to associate the LOV with your Skill text field. Find the Skill item in the Object Navigator (Forms¦WORKERSKILL¦Blocks¦WORKERHASSKILL¦Items¦SKILL) and double-click its icon. The Designer displays the Properties window for the item. In that window, find the Miscellaneous property group at the bottom of the window, scrolling down if necessary. The first property in this group is the LOV group. Double-click on the blank space, and the Designer puts in SKILLS as your LOV for the SKILL item. Also double-click on the LOV For Validation property to set it to True; this uses the list to check any data you enter in the Skill field. Figure 5-13 shows what all this looks like in the Object Navigator.

NOTE
Double-clicking the blank space for the LOV name is a user-interface shortcut. Each time you double-click, the interface cycles to the next LOV name in the set of such names. If you have multiple names, you can just keep double-clicking until you find the right one. An alternative is to use the drop-down combo box at the top of the Properties window. When you select the LOV property, the data entry bar at the top of the window becomes a drop-down combo box, as Figure 5-13 shows. Click on the arrow to see a list of LOV names; in this case, there is only one, so choose it and continue setting up the LOV.

Having set up the field, you now need to connect up the LOV. Click on the SKILLS LOV in the Object Navigator. The Properties window now displays the properties for the LOV. Find the Functional group and double-click on the Auto Display property to make it True; this choice automatically displays the LOV whenever you click into the field. Now, find the Column Mapping property and double-click on it. The Designer displays the Column Mapping dialog box (Figure 5-14).

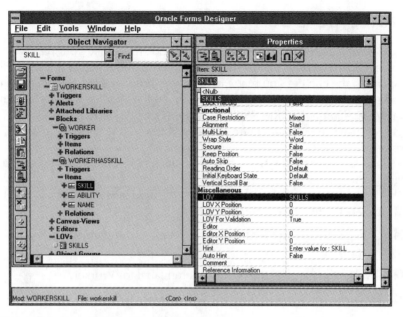

FIGURE 5-13. *The Skill item LOV choices*

The Designer has already filled in the Column Names, Display Width, and Column Title text boxes. All you need to do is to fill in the Return Item text box, which is the name of the block and field into which to put the value when the user presses OK. This connects up the LOV to the field. Finally, find the Display group and set the dialog box Title to "Choose Skill." Click on OK, and you are done.

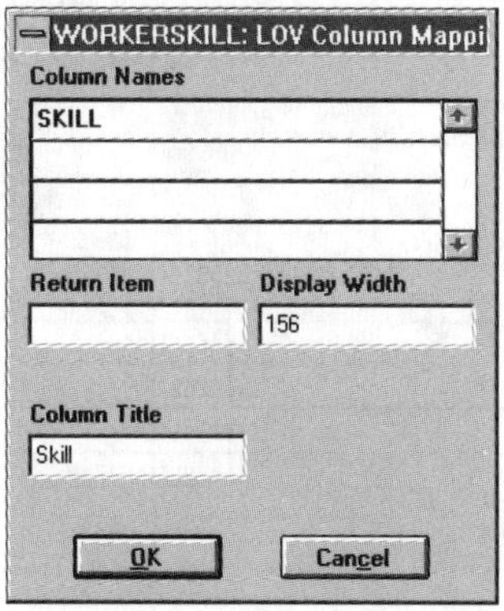

FIGURE 5-14. *The Column Mapping dialog box filled out for the Skill field*

A Prototype Is Born

You now have a prototype, but it still does not look much like your paper prototype. ORACLE Forms makes some assumptions about appearance that do not correspond to the choices you made in the paper prototype. To see what the form looks like, open the canvas by double-clicking on the Worker_Canvas icon under Canvas-Views (Forms¦WORKERSKILL¦Canvas-Views¦WORKER_CANVAS). The Designer displays the Layout Editor, showing you what the canvas looks like, as in Figure 5-15.

To complete your prototype, you need to accomplish the following formatting changes in the canvas:

- Delete the line boxes and block titles.

- Change the text font for the column labels to the standard font you want to apply.

- Change the name of the Name column label to "Worker."

- Move the scroll bar to the right side of the skills records.

- Move the fields and labels up to tighten up the space.

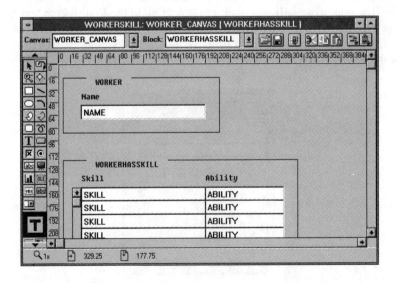

FIGURE 5-15. *The default Layout Editor for Worker_Canvas*

To delete the line boxes and titles, select each title by clicking on it, then delete it with the Edit¦Clear menu item or the keypress alternative.

To change the fonts, select all the text labels by shift-clicking (*multiselecting*) them, then choose the Format¦Fonts menu item to get a standard Font dialog box. Choose Arial, Helvetica, or your favorite sans serif font and make the style Bold.

To change the Name column, click on the Text button (see Figure 5-15), then double-click on the Name label. Type over the "Name" text with the text "Worker". Click anywhere on the canvas not over text to turn off the text tool.

NOTE

Before moving the components around, it is probably a good idea to turn on the snap-to-grid feature of the Layout editor. The Layout Editor assumes that a grid underlies the canvas, and it displays two rulers at the top and left sides of the canvas. You can display the grid with the View¦Grid menu item, though the background fill obscures it. You can tell the Editor to align components along the grid lines with the View¦Grid Snap menu item. Having selected this item, when you move the various components, you can easily line them up to the pixel by looking at the rulers.

NOTE

You can change the units of the grid with the Ruler Settings dialog box (View¦Settings¦Ruler menu item).

Now, move the individual components (the scroll bar, the fields, and the labels) by clicking on them and dragging them to a spot that resembles what you drew in your paper prototype. At the end of the process, the canvas should look like the one in Figure 5-16.

Now you are almost done. It is time to save your work and run the application to see what it looks like in practice and to verify that it works as you think it should.

You can save a form module either in a module file or in the central application's database on your server. I recommend that you take the former course. Here is an outline of some of the main issues you should consider when making this decision:

■ *Module accessibility:* If you have a relatively complex and large application environment, and you want to share your modules with other developers, saving the modules in a database accessible to all developers scales up better than saving them in files. Shared files on a network are a possibility but can involve more complexity, especially in a wide-area network.

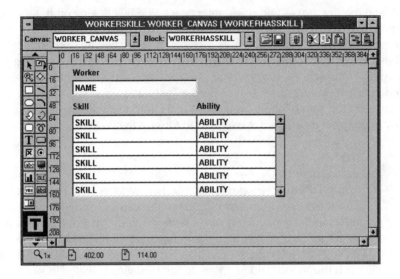

FIGURE 5-16. *The Modified Worker_Canvas in Layout Editor*

■ *Integrity:* As with any data, you have the basic issue of data integrity—that is, if there is a media failure or some other kind of data-corrupting event, you can lose your application module. Since a database provides strong integrity mechanisms, there is less risk if you store the modules in a database. Either way, you need to back up your files or database regularly to be able to restore lost data. *Always back up your system regularly,* whichever decision you make.

■ *Performance:* Saving to the database is slower than saving to files, and retrieving is also slower.

■ *Configuration management:* If you want to use a commercial version or source control system to manage your applications, you have to use files, since those systems do not work with the database.

■ *Convenience:* You can use standard file system utilities to manipulate your files, whereas the database tables and tools are much less flexible. You can use names of up to 30 characters for modules in the database (Windows/DOS limits you to eight characters; other operating systems allow longer names).

■ *Portability:* You can store modules only in an ORACLE7 database. If you are developing on another database, you must use files to store the modules.

Because this book strongly recommends using configuration management as part of your risk management process, and because of various convenience and performance issues, it recommends using the file approach rather than saving in the database. Again, *you should always back up your files regularly.*

For now, if you want to save to the database, you need to enable saving to the database, because the Designer does not do that automatically. Display the Options dialog, shown in Figure 5-17, by choosing the Tool¦Options menu item. In the Module Access section on the lower left of the Designer Options tab, change the radio button from File to File/Database or Database. File/Database lets you decide when you first save an item where to save it. You can always change your mind by retrieving the file and using Save As to save the file to the other storage format.

Now choose the File¦Save menu item to save your work. If you chose File/Database, the Designer pops up a small dialog box called Filter that gives you the choice of Database or File System (Figure 5-18). Choose the File System radio button and click OK.

Designer will work for a few moments saving the form module to your database or file. Now, you really are done, so run your form with the File¦Run menu item or

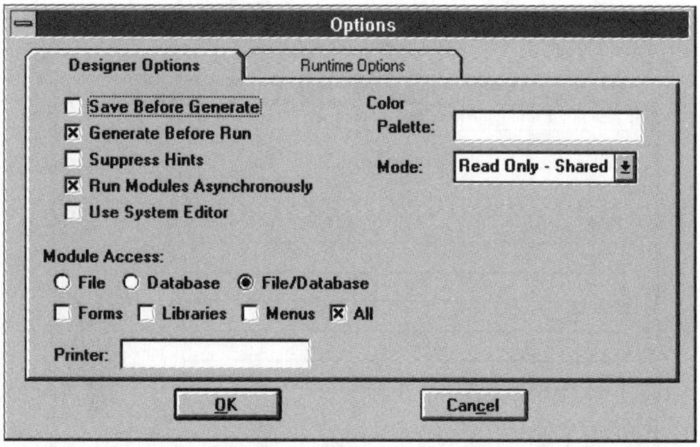

FIGURE 5-17. *The Options dialog box for module access settings*

FIGURE 5-18. *The Filter dialog box for choosing between database and file system saving*

the Run button. Designer compiles the form, runs the RUNFORM program, and tells it to run the form. Figure 5-19 shows the resulting application.

To verify the application, try some operations. Query all the workers with the Query¦Execute menu item. Use Record¦Next to move down the list of people. Notice how, when you get to a person with skills, the form automatically fills out the Skill and Ability fields.

Now click on a Skill field. Immediately, the form displays the Choose Skill LOV dialog box shown in Figure 5-20. You can select a skill, click OK, and fill in the

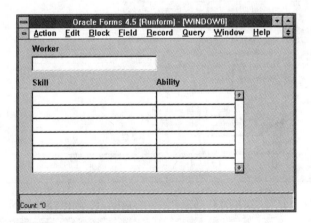

FIGURE 5-19. *RUNFORM and the Set Worker Skills window*

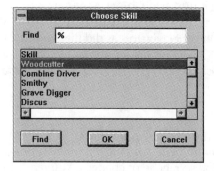

FIGURE 5-20. *The Choose Skill LOV dialog box*

Skill field. Try canceling the dialog box and typing in a skill that is not in the list; you should get an error message saying the skill is not valid.

You now have a complete, working prototype that looks just like the paper prototype from Chapter 4. You can use the prototype to query, including queries of subsets of the data through query-by-example. You can use it to manipulate the data by adding new records, deleting records, or typing over values to change the data already in the database. The prototype guarantees integrity of the data, because either the integrity constraints are in the database or the form enforces them through automatic validation such as the LOV dialog box. And you did all this in just a few minutes of work!

Developing Report Prototypes

Report prototypes are not much harder to set up than forms. The hardest part is formatting the report to your chosen look, because the ones that the Form Designer assigns by default are a bit extreme. This section develops two different report prototypes to show you how easy it is to do different kinds of reports.

A Summary Tabular Report Prototype

A *tabular* report prints out a table of data from a single SQL SELECT statement. A *summary tabular* report adds subtotals and other aggregation. In building the Talbot Ledger Summary Report, this section shows you how to quickly generate a summary report.

Open the Report Designer and Object Navigator

Open the Report Designer by clicking on the program icon. When the Designer opens, it displays the Object Navigator, as did the Forms Designer. In this case, as Figure 5-21 shows, the Object Navigator displays Reports and report-related objects instead of Forms. The Designer displays a single, default report called UNTITLED.

> **NOTE**
> Unlike forms objects, you cannot change the name in the Object Navigator until you save the report; this comes later, after going through the sequence of changes. You may also want to connect to the database at this point, although the Designer will prompt you when you need information from the database. Connecting uses the same Connect dialog box that you saw in Figure 5-3.

Design the Report Data Model

The first step in developing the report is to build the data model. Recall from Chapter 1 the distinction between the conceptual model (the server database) and

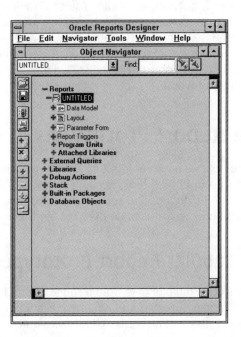

FIGURE 5-21. *The initial Report Designer window*

the external model (the application view). When you build the Reports data model, you build the application view as a formal data model that defines a set of records for the report. But the Reports data model is more extensive; it also includes a *group* hierarchy that lets you control the way the records repeat and the way to order the records. Grouping also lets you put summary fields at different points in the report logic, so you can add up subtotals, totals, and other fields that repeat less often than the records in the report.

Recall from the paper prototypes in Chapter 4 the summary ledger report. The report shows the data from the Ledger table, sorted by person, with the action date, item description, and total amount spent or received. Each person also has a subtotal showing the total amount bought or sold to that person in the ledger.

Figure 5-22 shows the query on which you will base the data model. Create a new data model by double-clicking the Data Model icon under the Untitled report in the Object Navigator. The Designer then displays a Data Model editor.

To create the query, click the SQL button. Then click in the drawing area of the Data Model editor, and the editor creates the new query, naming it Q_1. Double-click on the rounded rectangle to display the Query dialog box.

Change the name to LedgerQuery and enter the SQL statement in the text field as Figure 5-22 shows.

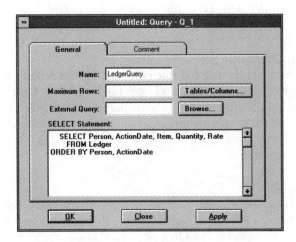

FIGURE 5-22. *The Ledger Query dialog box with a SELECT statement for data model*

NOTE
You may notice some name inconsistencies in this chapter. First, you're building a prototype, not a final application, so you do not have to cross all of your t's until later. The point is to get the prototype out as quickly as possible. Second, the naming convention that Developer/2000 assumes (prefixing names with letters indicating the type of object) is just one such convention. I prefer using standard, meaningful English to using abbreviations, such as LedgerQuery instead of Q_Ledger. The use of underscores reflects the inability to deal with mixed case, long a problem in mainframe and minicomputer environments that are no longer a concern with modern programming environments. In any case, naming conventions, like all standards, are there for a reason—productivity, reducing the risk of making errors in typing names, or whatever. Your naming convention should contain its justification, and you should choose it based on the problems you have to solve in your environment, not just to have a naming standard. Blindly accepting one imposed by your tools is often not the best choice, although there is one reason to do it: it makes life easier in that you do not have to change the names the tools create for you. It would be nice if Developer/2000 had consistent naming throughout its tools, but it does not.

When you click OK or Apply, the dialog checks the SELECT statement against the database and creates the group based on the query, as shown in Figure 5-23. Each of the columns in the SELECT appears in the group, which the editor names G_LedgerQuery.

Create Formula Columns
This data model has the quantity and rate columns, but the prototype report calls for the total amount, not the quantity and rate. The base table, Ledger, has the amount in a separate column; but for didactic purposes, the prototype here adds a formula column that calculates the amount from the quantity and rate. A *formula column* is a column in a report that gets its value from a function rather than directly from the database.

NOTE
You can do all kinds of fancy things with the PL/SQL that define the value of a formula column. Most of this you can do with SQL as well, or with database PL/SQL functions. You generally use PL/SQL when you want to do something that you cannot easily do with SQL, such as a calculation that requires a conditional (if-then-else) decision. If that is not true, why do it in report functions? There are two reasons.

First, you will generally want to compute values of interest only to
this application in the application itself. If the value is useful in
several different applications, you may want to move the calculation
to the server to share it instead of writing the code over and over. If
you can calculate the value with ORACLE SQL, though, you do not
need a function to do it, you just put the calculation directly into the
query. However, second, if you want your report to be independent
of ORACLE7, you cannot use most of the advanced features of SQL
that ORACLE7 supports by extending the ANSI standard. Putting the
calculation into PL/SQL functions in the report makes it possible
for even very sophisticated reports to use ODBC to access
databases other than ORACLE7. Third, moving the calculation to
the server may improve client performance under some
circumstances; benchmark, if this is your reason for putting the
PL/SQL in the database.

To add the Amount formula, click on the Formula Column button in the Data
Model editor, then click in the group box under the Rate column. You may want to
enlarge the box a bit by selecting it and pulling down on the lower sizing handle.
Then double-click on the resulting column CF_1 to see the Formula Column
property sheet shown in Figure 5-24.

FIGURE 5-23.   *The initial data model for the Ledger Summary report*

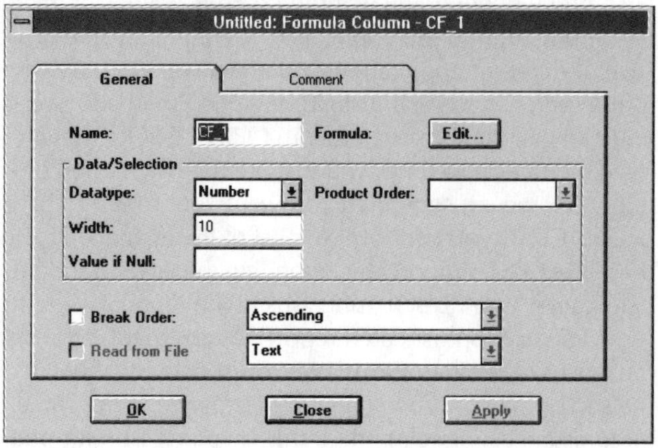

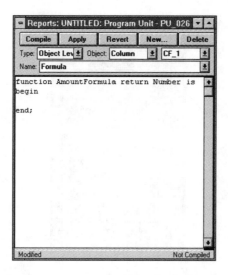

FIGURE 5-24. *The Formula Column property sheet for the Amount column*

Change the name to Amount in the General tab, then click on the Edit button to display the Program Unit editor for the PL/SQL function that computes the value, as shown in Figure 5-25.

FIGURE 5-25. *The Program Unit editor for the Amount formula column*

To create the function, add a single statement to compute the amount:

```
return :Quantity * :Rate;
```

The colons indicate references to report items. Click on Compile and deal with any errors, then click on Close.

When you click on OK in the property sheet, you see the data model shown in Figure 5-26 with the new column Amount. The editor displays the column in italics so that you know it is a formula column.

Now, you are ready to generate the default layout for the report. You generate the layout every time you make a change in the report that affects the layout by clicking on the Default Layout button in the Data Model editor. The Designer displays the Default Layout property sheet (Figure 5-27), which allows you to define the characteristics of the report. In the Style tab, leave the Tabular radio button selected (you want a tabular report). Also, click in the Options box to set the Use Current Layout Settings check box. Checking this check box tells Reports to use the current settings of the Layout Editor instead of using the defaults. In any case, Reports uses the current Format menu settings for font, size, weight, and style.

Select the Data/Selection tab to modify the report columns. You see the two groups, one for the report as a whole plus the one you have defined, G_LedgerQuery, which defaults to Repeat: Down (the standard report format). On the right, you see the columns from the data model. In this case, you want the

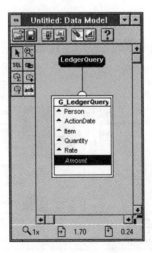

FIGURE 5-26. *The data model with formula column Amount*

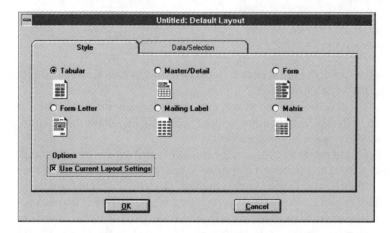

FIGURE 5-27. *The Style tab in the Default Layout property sheet*

report to print the Person, ActionDate, Item, and Amount columns; but you do not want to see the Quantity and Rate in the report. You need these two columns for the computation of Amount, so you cannot just remove them from the data model. To hide them, just click on the names in the Data/Selection tab. You can also change any labels you want to change at this point; for example, change "Actiondate" to "Action Date". Figure 5-28 shows the result.

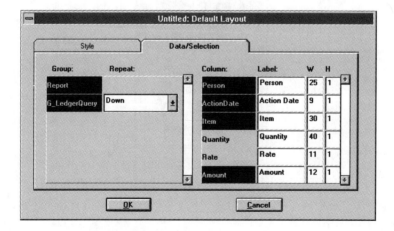

FIGURE 5-28. *The Data/Selection tab in the Default Layout property sheet*

When you click OK, the Designer opens the Default Layout editor with the report structure you specify. Figure 5-29 shows the simple, default layout for the Talbot Summary report, which contains a single table of repeating fields and a set of header fields.

This is a good time to save your report. Make sure that you have set the File/Database option as you did in your form prototype, then save the report definition. If you save to the database, the designer displays the Database Dialog window (Figure 5-30), which lets you name the report in the Save field at the bottom of the dialog box (in this case, with the name LedgerSummary). Otherwise, the Designer uses the filename as the report name. When you click Save, the Designer saves the various parts of the report and updates the Object Navigator with the name you give to the report (in this case, LEDGER.RDF).

You can run the report to see what it looks like; click on the Run button and accept the following dialog box to preview the report on screen. Details of this process come later; for now, just look at the report to get an idea of what you have.

Create the Break Groups for Summaries

The next step in the prototyping process is to create the break on Person, which will remove the duplicate display of the names in the first column of the report. Go to the Data Model for the report and rearrange the boxes by dragging the G_LedgerQuery box down a bit to make room for an intermediate group. Now click on the Person column in that box and drag it out of the box to a spot between the box and the LedgerQuery rounded rectangle. The Data Model editor creates a new group box with the Person column, as in Figure 5-31. You can leave it with the default name or rename it (as in the figure) to PersonBreak by double-clicking on the name and entering the new one in the resulting property sheet. Finally, redo

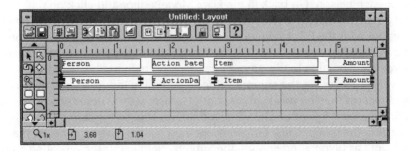

FIGURE 5-29.   *The default Layout editor for the Ledger Summary report*

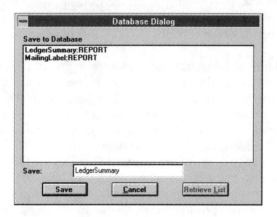

FIGURE 5-30. *Database dialog box for saving report*

the default layout by clicking on the Default Layout button again and accepting the default layout property sheet. You get a dialog box reminding you that you are replacing the previous layout. Click OK. You now have the layout that is shown in Figure 5-31; notice that the F_Person field now has only one box around it compared to two in Figure 5-29.

If you run the report again, you will see that the name now appears only once where before it appeared once per row.

Create the Summary Columns

Now you need to add the repeating subtotal field that sums the amounts from the ledger for each person. Go back to the Data Model editor and click on the Summary Column button. Click below Person in the PersonBreak group. The Data Model editor adds the CS_1 column. Double-click on this name to display the Summary Column property sheet (Figure 5-32). Name the column Subtotal and set the Source and Function to the Amount column and to Sum (the default), respectively. This creates the column value by summing the Amount column over the set of records that the break group controls. Also, set the Reset At field to the PersonBreak group; this resets the value for each group, so the sum only applies to the records in the group. Click OK to accept these values, then regenerate the default layout as before, and you see the Subtotal field under the repeating records fields in the Layout Editor.

You may want to experiment a bit with the margins and the positioning of the columns in the report. If you run the report, you will see that the default maximums

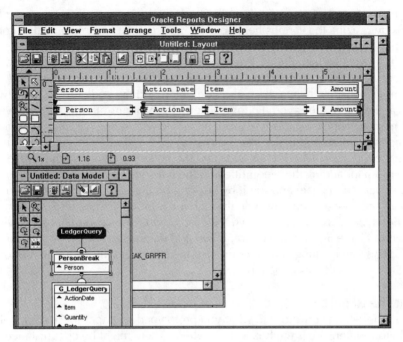

FIGURE 5-31. *The revised Ledger Summary data model and layout*

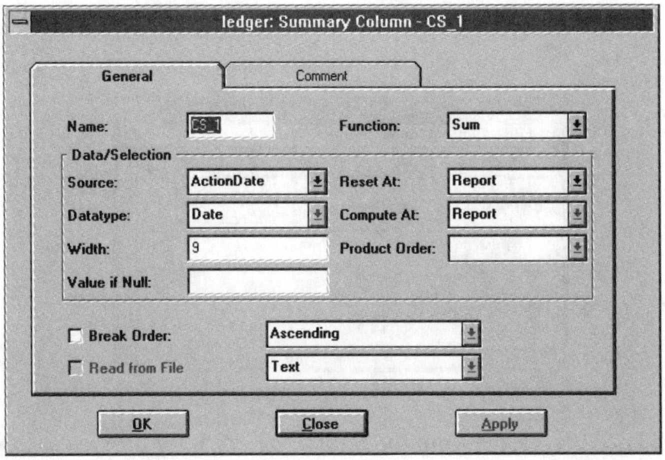

FIGURE 5-32. *The Summary Column dialog box for the Subtotal column*

are a bit large for what the report actually displays, so you can close up some of the columns by resizing the various field boxes. This is definitely something that comes with experience, so just play around with the sizes of the boxes until you are comfortable with the techniques. You can use the Arrange menu items to good effect here; read about them using Help or the Reports documentation.

To move between the margin part of the report and the body text, use the two buttons at the top of the Layout Editor. Click on the Margins button, and you will see the margins appear as a heavy, black rectangle with sizing handles. You can move the margins around in the usual way with the handles. In this case, you need to make the top margin 1.5 inches wide and the bottom margin 1 inch wide to provide room for adding the report title and the date and page number later.

Save your report again and run it by clicking on the Run button. When you run the report, the Designer prompts you through the Runtime Parameter Form for a destination type. This time, pull down the drop-down list box and choose Preview, as shown in Figure 5-33. In the future, if you add parameters to your report, this form displays them, letting you enter the parameter values when you run the report. Figure 5-34 shows the resulting report.

Format the Report

This report is getting very close to what you prototyped on paper in Chapter 4. The most obvious difference is the boxes everywhere. There might be circumstances under which all the lines make the report attractive; this is not one of those circumstances. All the lines do in this case is obscure the content of the report. If you can see them (look carefully), there are also underlines under the column headings.

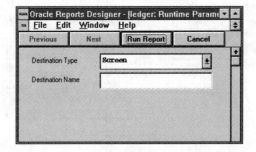

FIGURE 5-33. *The Report Runtime Parameter Form for preview of the report*

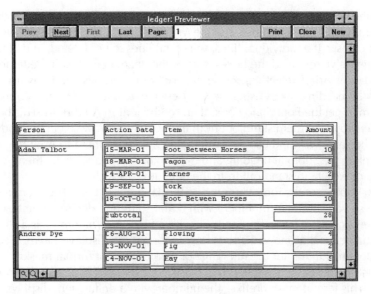

FIGURE 5-34. *The initial Ledger Summary report*

NOTE

At this point, you are going to make changes in the default layout. If you now go back and regenerate the layout again with the Default Layout button, you will lose changes such as removing the lines or changing fonts.

So, moving on to the formatting stage of building the prototype, get rid of the boxes. Close the preview screen and click on the Layout Editor to set the focus to it. First, you need to decide what to do with the underlines under the headings. You have the choice of deleting them or making them invisible. For various reasons, if you want to get rid of them entirely, you should delete them (they prevent resizing of the heading box later, for example).

Use the Edit|Select All menu item to select all the components of the layout. Now click on the Line Color button in the tool palette in the Layout Editor. The button displays a color palette.

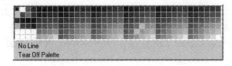

Click on the No Line choice below the colors in the palette. This removes all the lines.

To remove only certain lines, use the Magnify button to blow up the picture until you can see the individual lines, select the lines to be deleted, and clear them.

When you've removed the boxes, format the header and text in better fonts. The standard is Arial/Helvetica, so use that for both headings and body text. First, select all the heading boxes using the SHIFT-click mechanism. Use the Format¦Font menu item to get the Font dialog box, then set the font to Arial Bold. This boldfaces the headers to make them stand out from the body text. Now select the body text fields in the same way and use the Font dialog box to set them to Arial Regular. Finally, select the Subtotal heading and the Subtotal field and make them Arial Bold; this makes them stand out from the body text, as well.

When you've set the font, you need to format the numbers. These are money amounts, so you should format them with dollar signs and decimal points. ORACLE Reports lets you associate a format mask with a field. A *format mask* is a string of special characters that shows Reports how to format the displayed item. (See the Reports documentation for the full range of possibilities for format mask characters.) In this case, use the format mask "$N,NN0.00" to format the money amounts. This format mask prefixes the number with a dollar sign, displays a comma-separated thousands value, and always displays two digits after the decimal point. Zero values become "$0.00". To set the mask, select the two money fields (Amount and Subtotal). Now select the Tools¦Common Properties menu item. Figure 5-35 shows the Common Properties property sheet. Choose the Field tab and type in the format mask, as shown in Figure 5-35.

That is really all the formatting you need to do of the body text and headings. To complete the report, you just need to add the title, the date, and the page number to the margins of the report.

To create the report title, click on the Text button in the Layout Editor palette. Click somewhere above the top margin to insert a text field and type the report title, **Talbot Farms Ledger Summary Report**. Select the text box and change the font to Arial Bold 18 using the Format¦Font menu item. Resize the box to fit around the text, and center the text in the box with the Format¦Alignment¦Centered menu item. Finally, remove the box lines around the text with the Line Color button by choosing the No Line area as before. This title will appear on every page as a running header.

Although this report does not use it, there is also a way to put material before and after the repeating part of the report. The header and footer buttons next to the body text and margins buttons control this. For an example of how to use report headers see "Adding Graphics to Your Forms and Reports," later in this chapter.

The final bit of formatting is to add the page number and current date to the bottom margin of the report as a footer. Both of these items are variable text items that get their values from special variables. Developer/2000 calls these *fields*. You

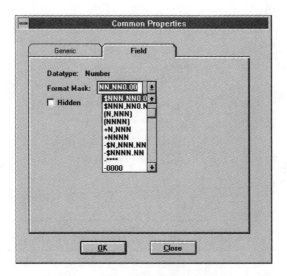

FIGURE 5-35.   *The Common Properties property sheet with format mask*

will need to experiment with positioning these fields; turning on the snap-to-grid option should help you position the fields correctly.

To create the date field, click on the Field button in the tool palette of the Layout Editor, then click under the lower-left margin corner. Double-clicking pops up the Layout Field dialog box, which you use to set the characteristics of the field. In this case, in the Object tab, pull down the Source list and choose &Current Date, as shown in Figure 5-36. Set the format mask to an appropriate date format, such as "DD-MON-YY". In the General Layout tab, set the Sizing group's Horizontal and Vertical fields to "Variable"; this tells Reports to size the field to the current date. Accept the property sheet. Set the font to Arial 9 Regular. Move the field around until the left side of the field more or less aligns with the left margin.

Do the same thing to create the page number, except place it below the right corner, make the Source "&Physical Page Number," make the Format Mask "NNN" (or something similar), and set the Sizing options to "Fixed." Figure 5-37 shows the Object tab setup. It is necessary to use fixed sizing because the page number varies on each page, unlike the current date. You will need to resize the field to fit the largest page number you are likely to have in your report. You can also add a text field with the word "Page" and put it next to the page number field. Again, set the font to Arial 9 Regular.

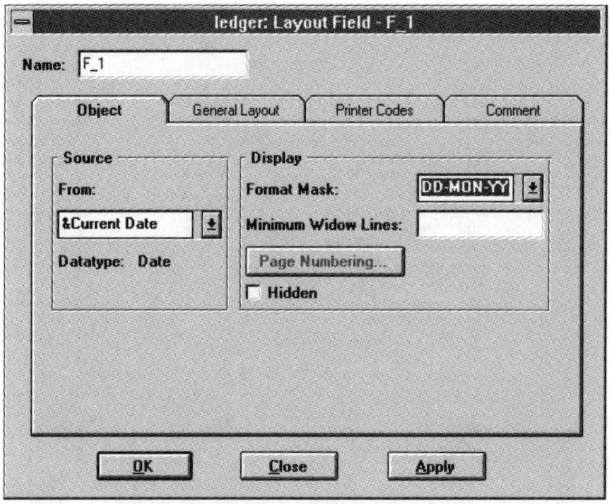

FIGURE 5-36. *The Layout Field dialog box for the date field*

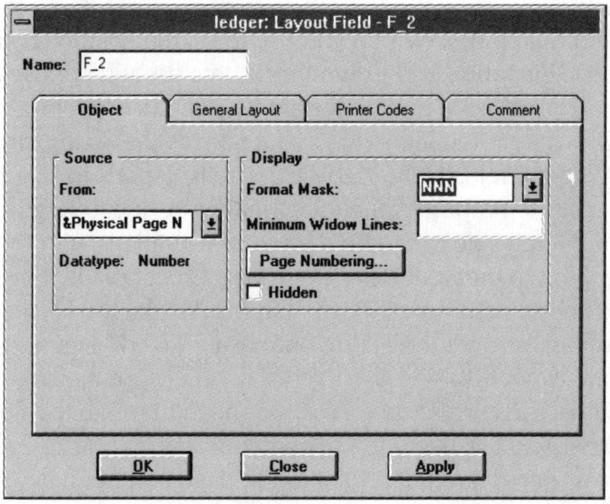

FIGURE 5-37. *The Layout Field dialog box for the page field*

Save and run the report. Figure 5-38 shows the report fully formatted in the Previewer. You can print the report directly from this screen if you so desire. Close the report when you have finished.

A Mailing-Label Report Prototype

This section builds a simple mailing-label report. The prototypes from Chapter 4 specify such a report for the people at Talbot's Farm with lodgings in the Lodging table. Talbot's can use this report to generate labels for paychecks or mailings to its employees.

A mailing-label report prints its repeating records in identically spaced chunks down a page. When you print the report, you generally do so on special adhesive mailing-label paper from which you peel off the labels after printing. This section shows you how to generate a speedy, simple prototype of such a report.

First, create a new report and build the data model. Figure 5-39 shows the SQL that defines the data model. It is slightly more complex than the previous example because it involves two joined tables instead of a single one. This gives you the name from the Person table and the LongName and Address of the lodging for the person from the Lodging table. The SQL also orders the result by the person's name.

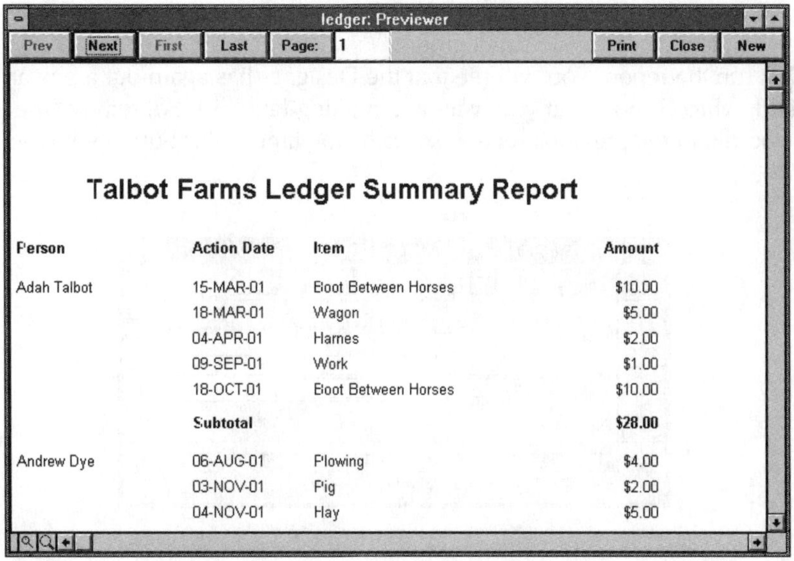

FIGURE 5-38. *The Talbot Farms Ledger Summary Report*

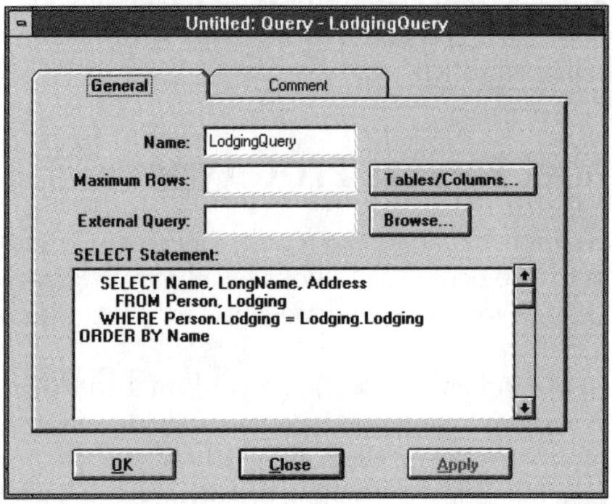

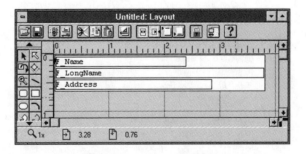

FIGURE 5-39. *The mailing-label report data model*

Now build the layout by clicking the Default Layout button. In the layout property sheet Style tab (see Figure 5-27), choose Mailing Label instead of the default Tabular style. Otherwise, accept the default layout. Figure 5-40 shows the resulting layout: the three columns, with no headers, stacked above one another, with the whole block in a repeating group.

If you run the report, you will see that the Designer has again put a box around each field, which is not what you want in a mailing-label list. So, remove the boxes just as you did in the previous section by using the Line Color button with the No

FIGURE 5-40. *The mailing-label report default layout*

Line selection and widen the surrounding box downward to leave a space between each label. Save and run the report. Figure 5-41 shows the result.

Adding Graphics to Your Forms and Reports

The Ledger Summary report gives you summary information about each person with whom Talbot Farms does business. To make that report more useful to the customers of the report (probably Talbot executives), you can add simple graphics at the beginning of the report that displays the distribution of the "Bought" or "Sold" ledger entries by person. The prototype from Chapter 4 shows this as two pie charts on the first pages of the report. You can also display this chart in your Ledger Entry form as a pop-up display.

Graphics are a full component of Developer/2000, and you can run them separately if you want to do so. You can provide graphics as standalone applications running through the Developer/2000 Graphics Runtime module. For most applications, however, you will want to embed the graphics and charts into forms and reports, and that is the route this section takes.

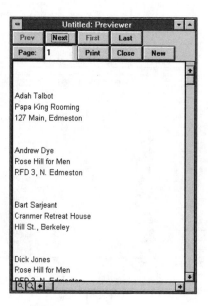

FIGURE 5-41.   *The mailing-label report*

Designing the Graphics

To design a graphic, run the Graphics Designer by clicking on the icon. Figure 5-42 shows the initial display of the Object Navigator and the Layout Editor for graphics. The Layout Editor is much the same as editors in the Forms and Reports Designers.

Before generating the graphics, it is a good idea to set up some number formats to use in the graphic labels. Display the Tools Options dialog box using the Tools¦Tools Options menu item, as shown in Figure 5-43.

Choose the Number button to enter the number formats in the Number Format dialog box. The two most common number formats are 999,999,990 and $999,999,990.00, as Figure 5-44 shows. Type the format into the Format entry box and click the Add button to add the format to the list of formats. Click OK when you have finished.

To build a chart, you need to specify the data to graph, much as for a report. The graph data model will usually, but not always, involve data aggregation through a SQL GROUP BY clause and the aggregation operators (SUM, AVG, COUNT, and so on). If you are not completely familiar with the logic of GROUP BY aggregation, you should review it in a SQL textbook before proceeding.

The data model for a graph is a SQL statement that provides the data to graph. The exact nature and type of the data depends on the kind of graph you want to

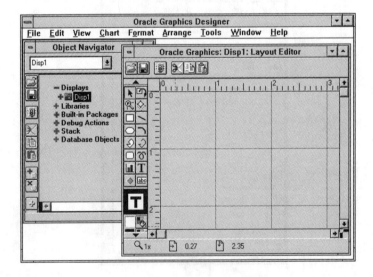

FIGURE 5-42. *The initial Graphics Designer window*

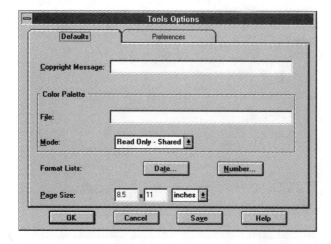

FIGURE 5-43. *The Tools Options dialog box for Graphics Designer*

build. The pie charts this section builds require a category string and a numeric value to size the pie slices. There are other graphics that require different data structures; see the Developer/2000 documentation for details on specific kinds of charts.

Click on the Chart button in the Layout Editor tool palette, then click in the Layout Editor drawing area to create a chart. Figure 5-45 shows the query for the Amount Bought pie chart. It retrieves the person and the amount sum, grouping by

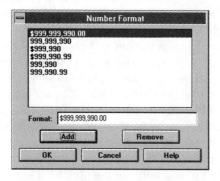

FIGURE 5-44. *The Number Format dialog box*

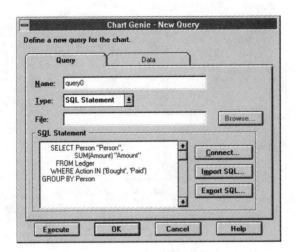

FIGURE 5-45. *The Chart Genie - New Query dialog box with initial Bought Query*

person (that is, one row per person with the sum of amounts bought by that person). Please note the aliases in double quotes after each element of the SELECT list. The Graphics Designer uses these aliases as the names for the data columns in various charts, and it is a good idea to make them meaningful and presentable.

Click on the Execute button. The Graphics Designer now does something slightly different than Reports; it actually runs the query and retrieves the data to graph when you press the Execute button. The Data tab now contains the actual data from the SELECT statement, as shown in Figure 5-46. Using this data, the Graphics Designer can present the chart as it will actually appear. As you will see, this can be a terrific time saver in developing the chart for embedding in other applications and for debugging the chart.

Click the OK button to accept the query. Now the Designer pops up the Chart Properties property sheet, as shown in Figure 5-47. In this case, you need only rename the chart ("BoughtFile"), provide a title ("Amount Bought from Person"), and choose the type of graph (the pie chart). Click OK to accept the chart.

The initial version of the chart is very close to what you want, except that in this case the pie labels obscure the heading, which needs to be in a different font anyway. Locate and select the heading just above the pie and move it above the text of the labels to the upper-left corner. Change the font to Arial 18 Bold. It is also a good idea to move the entire graphic to the upper-left corner, because this eliminates unnecessary space when you embed the graphic in other applications. Just click once anywhere on the chart background and drag it until the upper

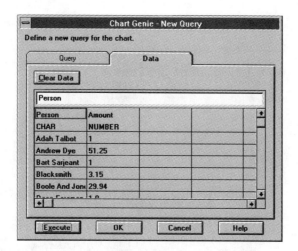

FIGURE 5-46.   *The Chart Genie - New Query dialog box with initial data*

corner is at coordinate 0,0. You could also change the font for the labels if you desired by clicking once on the graphic, then once on any label to select all the labels. Figure 5-48 shows the result of the reformatting.

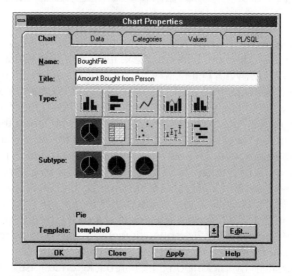

FIGURE 5-47.   *The Chart Properties property sheet Chart tab*

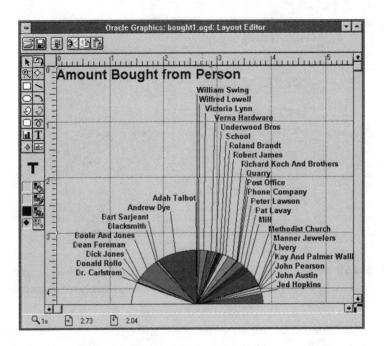

FIGURE 5-48.   *The Graphics Layout Editor with initial Bought pie chart*

As you can see from the graph, Developer/2000 does a fine job in doing exactly what you asked it to do. Unfortunately, the graphic does not really tell you what you need to know. With charts, as Chapter 4 discussed in some detail, you must be very aware of what information you are trying to convey. You must design the graphic to transmit that information directly and without clutter. In the case of Figure 5-48, although all the information about amounts bought is there, it is very difficult to pull out the specifics. In particular, you want to know who the largest contributors to Talbot expense are, not just the general distribution per person. Edward Johnson and a few others stand out, but from there it gets more and more difficult. Figure 5-49 shows a query that better models the relationships you want to see. It adds an ORDER BY clause to sort the values by the summed amount (the number "2" item in the SELECT list). Figure 5-50 shows the result. Now you can clearly see where Talbot spends its money. It would be even better to collect the small items and call them "Other," and Graphics gives you an easy way to do this.

Select the pie slices by clicking on the chart background to select the chart then clicking on the pie slice area to select all the slices. Choose the Chart⌐Frame menu

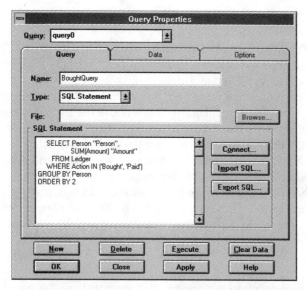

FIGURE 5-49. *The BoughtQuery Query Properties dialog box Query tab*

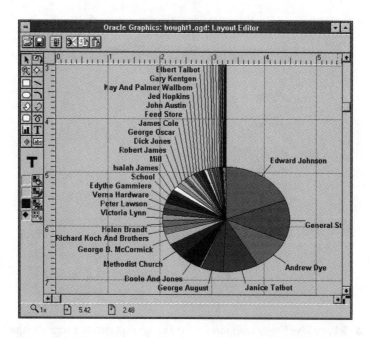

FIGURE 5-50. *The Graphics Layout Editor with revised Bought pie chart*

item to display the Frame Properties property sheet, and click on the Pie Frame tab (Figure 5-51).

Check the Put Slices Smaller Than check box and enter 1.5 into the percentage field. This will combine all values less than 1.5 percent of the total into a single pie slice; Figure 5-52 shows the result.

When you finish experimenting and formatting the chart, you need to prepare it for embedding. First, move the heading to just above the pie slice labels, then move the whole graphic to the upper-left corner by clicking on it and dragging. Second, resize the graphic to tightly enclose the view you want to see. Choose the View ¦ View Options ¦ Layout menu item to set the horizontal and vertical sizes. Leave as little white space as possible around the graphic, because you generally will not have that much space to spare in your embedding forms and reports. Also, keep track of the size (6 inches by 3.75 inches in the example), because you will need to know it later on in the chapter. Now, save the chart into an OGD file (File ¦ Save).

To build the Sold pie chart, use the query in Figure 5-53 to produce the graphic shown in Figure 5-54. Only the WHERE clause is different. Again, make sure you set the size to tightly enclose the graphic, and keep track of the size; you will need it later in the chapter.

You can now add the graphics to your prototype forms and reports.

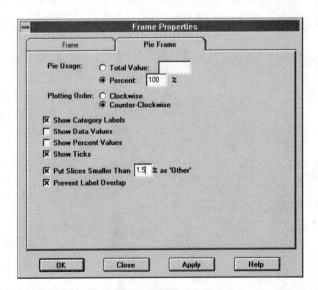

FIGURE 5-51. *The Pie Frame tab in the Frame Properties property sheet*

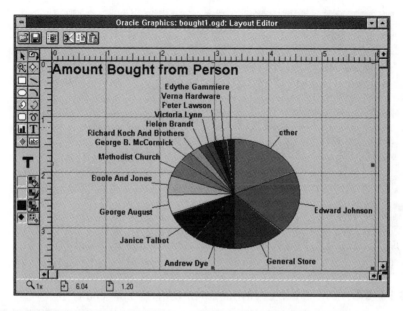

FIGURE 5-52. *The Graphics Layout Editor with "other" slice*

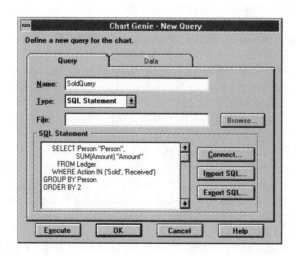

FIGURE 5-53. *The Chart Genie - New Query dialog box with initial Sold Query*

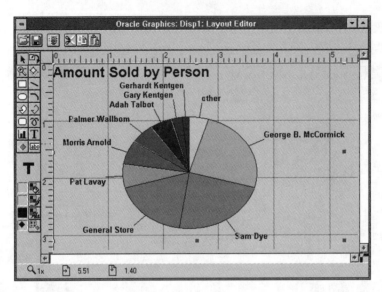

FIGURE 5-54. *The Graphics Layout Editor with Sold pie chart*

Integrating Graphics with Forms and Reports

You first must decide where to position the graphic in your report. Unless the graphic relates to some repeating element, you will most likely place it either before your main report body or after it. You can do innovative placements as well, but generally this involves PL/SQL coding, placing it outside the scope of a prototype.

To put the graphic into the header, thus displaying the graphic before the main body of the report, go to the Layout Editor for your report (Ledger) and click the Header button. You see a blank page.

Click the Graphics button from the tool palette, then drag out a region to the size of the graphics display (you should have this from the earlier resizing of the page you did in the Graphics Layout Editor). Figure 5-55 shows the resulting Graphics Display pop-up property sheet, which you can see by double-clicking the item in the Object Navigator. Enter a name if you wish, then enter the path and name of the Graphics Display (OGD) file containing the Bought graphic. You can use the List button to get the File Open dialog box to search for the file.

Click OK to accept this set of properties; you want to use the query that the graphic owns, and you do not need to pass in parameters or get back results. Now preview the report by running it with the Run button. Figure 5-56 shows what the first page of the report looks like.

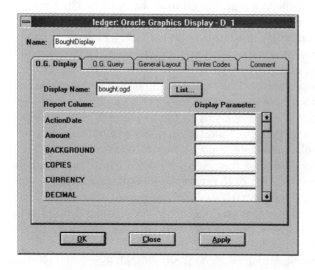

FIGURE 5-55. *The Oracle Graphics Display property sheet for a report*

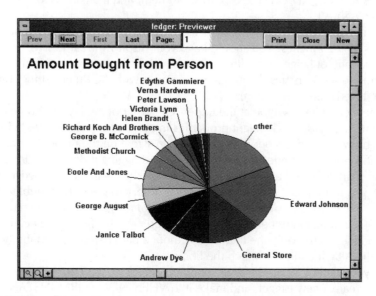

FIGURE 5-56. *Using Previewer for the graphic header in the Ledger Summary report*

Adding a graphic to a form is a bit more complicated, but not by much. As with the report, you need to figure out where to put the graphic. You need a place with enough room to display the whole chart with a readable font size. Forms will scale the chart to fit whatever size you tell it; but if you make it too small, you will find that you cannot read the labels.

As an example, this section builds the Sold pie chart into the Ledger form. The Ledger form is a simple tabular form for entering and querying ledger information; you can generate it very quickly using the techniques in the previous section on Forms prototyping. With the following sequence of operations, you will position the pie chart below the table scaled at about 100 percent.

To get Forms to display the chart, you must now arrange everything so that a trigger runs Oracle Graphics to produce the chart. First, create a control block. Select the Blocks header in the Object Navigator. Using the Navigator Create menu item, create a new block as you did before and name it Control, leaving the base table as <None>. Make sure the canvas is LEDGER_CANVAS, then accept the block by clicking on OK. Now open the LEDGER_CANVAS.

Creating the chart item is a little more difficult than usual because you must create it in a different block than the one naturally associated with the canvas. If you just create it on the canvas, you will create the item in the Ledger block instead of in the Control block. So instead, select the Forms¦LEDGER¦Blocks¦CONTROL¦Items group in the Object Navigator and create an item with the Create menu item. Double-click on the item to display the property sheet. Change the name to SOLD_PIE_CHART, the type to Chart Item, and the canvas to LEDGER_CANVAS.

Look up the size of the graphic from the previous example; it should be around 5.5 inches by 3.25 inches. You should keep your display the same size, or at least at the same ratio of height to width, or Forms will distort it. You may want to change ruler units to inches if you have it in points with the Ruler Settings dialog (View¦Settings¦Ruler menu item).

The new chart item will be at the upper-left corner of the layout. You can put the size into the Width and Height properties in the property sheet (396 Width and 234 Height, with 72 pixels per inch), or you can size it on the layout by dragging. Position the chart item under the table of data by dragging it down. Figure 5-57 shows the chart item for the Sold pie chart positioned below the table of ledger data.

Next, you must attach the Oracle Graphics library to the form. Double-click on the Forms¦Attached Libraries header in the Object Navigator. Enter the name of the library, OG, in the Library field (Figure 5-58). You can also find the specific file, but it is a good idea to use only the filename without a path name for portability. Now click on the Attach button to attach the library.

Now you need to set up the triggers. Double-click on the Forms¦Triggers header to create a new trigger, and make it a WHEN-NEW-FORM-INSTANCE trigger. This trigger fires when you open the form. In the PL/SQL Editor, enter a call

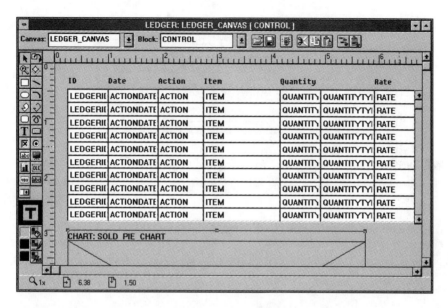

FIGURE 5-57. *The Ledger canvas Layout Editor with chart item*

to OG.OPEN to open the sold graphic, as shown in Figure 5-59. Repeat all this to add a POST-FORM trigger with a call to OG.CLOSE:

```
OG.Close('sold.ogd', 'control.sold_pie_chart');
```

Save the form and run it. You should get a running form that looks like Figure 5-60. When the RUNFORMS program opens the form, it starts the ORACLE Graphics batch program and produces the graph, then displays the form and the

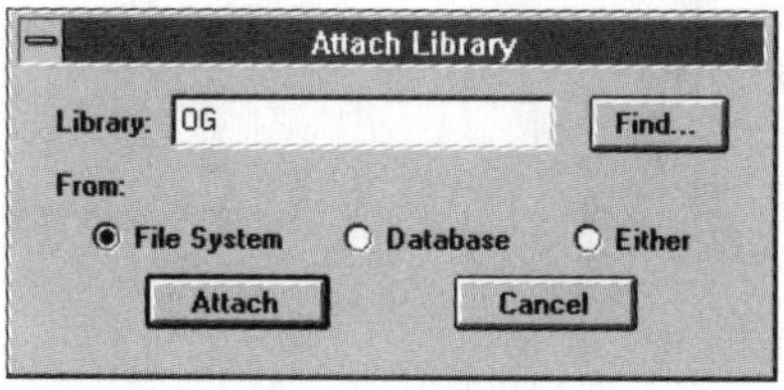

FIGURE 5-58. *The Attach Library dialog box*

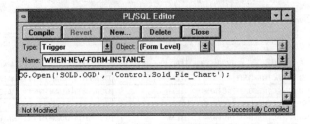

FIGURE 5-59. *The PL/SQL Editor for a graphic trigger*

graph. To get the ledger data, you need to execute a query (the Query⎮Execute menu item).

You now have a complete, working prototype with forms, reports, and graphics!

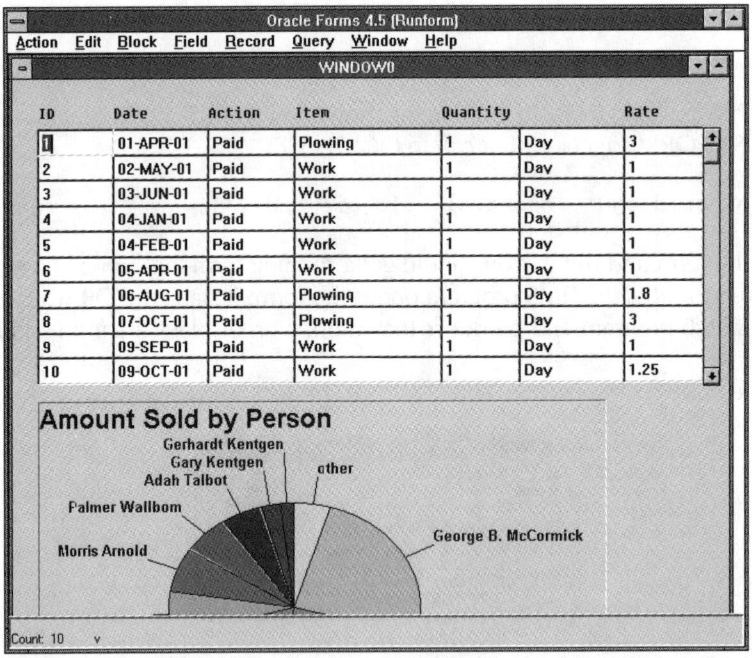

FIGURE 5-60. *The running Ledger form with graphic display*

CHAPTER 6

Taking It to the Next Level

Not everything works the first time. Most things do not work the first time—or the second. One of the strongest reasons for taking a prototyping approach to applications is to learn from history and from people who look at your work how to improve that work. This chapter builds on the prototypes you developed in the last chapter to show you how to leverage the feedback from your customers into a design that really works.

You will find that fields do not quite fit into the space that customers want them to, or that you forgot to consider alternatives in arranging screens. You might find that customers miss a connection to some tool they want to use for business analysis, or that they prefer line graphs to pie charts, being on a diet. In any event, now that you have an actual working version of your application, you can find these things out in a direct way, by asking people.

Usability testing is a key means of getting early feedback on your design. It works best when the user believes he or she is using something real, and Developer/2000 prototypes fit that bill.

Once you have developed a better understanding of requirements and how your design meets them, you can take advantage of the more advanced features of Developer/2000. This chapter shows you how to redesign your prototypes to use these features, and how they work to produce the effects you want.

Finally, you need to consider *platform portability*—how to get your application to run on more than one target computer platform. This chapter describes the issues associated with cross-platform application development in Developer/2000. It shows you how to design your forms, reports, and graphics for maximum portability. It also shows you when to design for *platform specificity*; sometimes full portability is a holy grail that gets in the way of completing your job. It may be better to take full advantage of a platform and recode the application for other platforms if it contributes to the value of your application to your customers.

Usability Testing and Feedback

A classic book on software quality, *The Frozen Keyboard: Living with Bad Software* by Boris Beizer (TAB Books, 1988), refers to "software perpetrators" instead of to software developers. *Software abuse* is the intentional infliction of pain on unsuspecting users of software systems. The issue of bugs, or defects, or faults, or whatever you might call problems with software is a large one; however, as Beizer notes, it is far overshadowed by the simple unusability of many software systems. They *do not do what the customers want done.*

How can you tell whether your application is usable or not? Ask a random sample of potential customers a simple question: "Do you need to refer to a manual when you use this application?" If you have a really well-designed system, the customer should be able to just start using the application because it does what the customer expects it to.

Most applications cannot meet this simple criterion because software is not yet at a point where you have the tools that would permit you to design such clear and easy-to-use systems. Your customers must therefore judge your applications based on specific expectations that you can reasonably meet. Certain problems tend to crop up repeatedly with applications that do not meet expectations:

■ *Hard to use*: The software slows the user down and makes the user error prone.

- *Hard to learn:* The software requires more knowledge than the user can easily acquire.

- *Unsuitable:* The software requires more thinking than the user can easily provide.

- *Slow:* The software runs too slowly for the user's patience to handle.

- *Incapable:* The software does not do what the user wants done.

NOTE

Unusability is definitely not the same thing as running slowly. Slowness is one possible cause of unusability, but only one of many. You can benchmark it until the cows come home and tune it like a concert piano and still get very poor satisfaction ratings for your application.

Chapter 4 discussed the process of gathering requirements and setting expectations by paper prototyping. Now that you have taken this one step further and have a working software prototype, you can start to evaluate how well that prototype meets user requirements. You do that by usability testing.

Usability testing is the repeated rating of your application by its intended users on a set of criteria related to their satisfaction with the application. The criteria relate directly to the requirements you gathered before developing the prototype. The objective of usability testing is to determine whether your application design process is improving satisfaction with the product.

If you have read the definition above carefully, you should have already realized that usability testing is not a one-time event. It is a series of tests with values that you compare over time. The objective is not to prove that your system is perfect (the acid-test question above can do that), but to tell you whether you are on the right track. Is your work improving customer satisfaction or not?

To test for usability, you need to expose customers to the prototype, then administer a short survey to measure their satisfaction with the prototype on several criteria.

You can be very sophisticated about customer interaction with your prototype, or you can just have a few people try it out. You can get a random sample or not, you can use a usability testing laboratory or not, you can have hierarchically stratified user group samples, and so on. The point is to get feedback in a way that maximizes your confidence in the results of the survey. If you do not have enough resources to do even a small focus group with some real customers, you can pretty much abandon any hope of improving customer satisfaction in any systematic way. You could be lucky—but never confuse luck with good development practices.

User Satisfaction Surveys

Don Gause and Gerald Weinberg's book *Exploring Requirements: Quality Before Design* (Dorset House, 1989) has an excellent chapter on user satisfaction testing. The following suggestions for constructing a user satisfaction survey come from a summary of that chapter.

You want to create a very short survey that tells you numerically how users feel about your prototype. The survey should be cheap to produce, easy to fill out, nonintrusive, educational, and enticing—in short, a survey that users don't mind filling out and that your boss can afford. You want to pinpoint ambiguities, areas of dissatisfaction, and specific user communities with problems. You also want the test to be statistically reliable. Here is a good way to generate such a survey:

1. Make a list of the major requirements for your application.

2. Talk to your customer (preferably the people who came up with the requirements), and ask them to choose six to ten areas on which to evaluate the system.

3. For each area, create a *bipolar adjective pair*. This is two adjectives, one representing the most favorable condition for the area, the other representing the least favorable, for example, "performs well" and "performs poorly."

4. Organize these into seven-point scales, with the least favorable on the left and the most favorable on the right. Create a table with the rows representing the areas and the columns representing the scales.

5. Finally, add a large area for freehand comments. Figure 6-1 shows an example for the Talbot prototype.

Each time you complete a prototype and want feedback, give the prototype to a group of users (preferably randomly selected) and let them use it for a while. If you can, videotape them or observe how they interact with the product. After a set length of time appropriate to the complexity of the prototype, administer the survey. Score each box from one to seven and take the arithmetic mean (sum the scores and divide by the number of items). This is your overall satisfaction rating. Now graph this over time to show how satisfaction changes. Figure 6-2 shows one graph charting increasing satisfaction over time and another graph showing a system with some problems.

If you see a drop in satisfaction, analyze the results and figure out which criteria seem to contribute to the drop. Question the users to get more details.

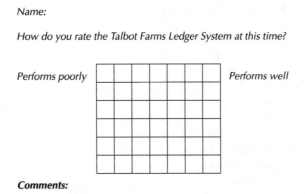

Name:

How do you rate the Talbot Farms Ledger System at this time?

Performs poorly   *Performs well*

Comments:

FIGURE 6-1. *A user satisfaction survey for the Talbot prototype*

If you get many additional comments, it could be that you are not evaluating the right criteria. You should probe the users to decide whether you need to go back to the drawing board for requirements, to change the survey, or to give up the project as impossible.

If you get many weird comments ("terrible survey," "I hate this product," or "did anyone run this before showing it to us?"), listen hard—and go back and probe into why users expressed their feelings that way. You will learn a lot if you want to.

You might also consider constructing a small database, form, report, and graph application in Developer/2000 to gather all the data instead of paper forms. For

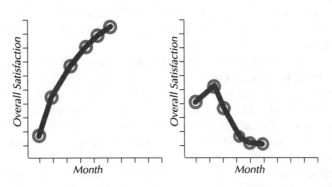

FIGURE 6-2. *User satisfaction charts*

example, Talbot could create the following schema in his ORACLE7 account TALBOT:

```
CREATE SCHEMA AUTHORIZATION Talbot
CREATE TABLE Customer (
    Name VARCHAR(50) PRIMARY KEY,
    Address VARCHAR(200),
    Phone VARCHAR(20))
CREATE TABLE SatisfactionScaleItem (
    Project VARCHAR (25),
    LowAdjective VARCHAR (50),
    HighAdjective VARCHAR (50),
    PRIMARY KEY (Project, LowAdjective, HighAdjective))
CREATE TABLE CustomerSatisfactionRating (
    Name VARCHAR(50) REFERENCES Customer,
    Project VARCHAR(25),
    LowAdjective VARCHAR (50),
    HighAdjective VARCHAR (50),
    PRIMARY KEY (Name, Project, LowAdjective, HighAdjective),
    FOREIGN KEY (Project, LowAdjective, HighAdjective)
            REFERENCES SatisfactionScaleItem (Project,
            LowAdjective, HighAdjective));
```

Developer/2000 Processes and Triggers: How It All Works

This section gives you an overview of how Developer/2000 performs its magic. Prior sections have introduced you to some of the basic concepts of database applications and the objects in Developer/2000. Now, you will see how these objects interact to behave as a system.

The most practical of all your low-level design decisions in a Developer/2000 application is *where* to put your code. Because you are not developing the application logic from scratch, you must fit your additions into the Developer/2000 logic. To do that, you need to understand where Developer/2000 runs your code, and what happens before and after your code executes. This section gives you a clear picture of where you can intervene in the Developer/2000 processes by showing you what the processes are and where the triggers fire within those processes.

Developer/2000 applications are event-driven. When you run an application, you interact with the runtime system to cause *events*, which in turn start various *processes*. The processes contain the preprogrammed *default behavior* for forms, reports, and graphs. As various internal events occur during this processing, the runtime system handles them by running the code you write in PL/SQL: it *fires triggers*.

See Chapter 10 for an extensive discussion of PL/SQL programming. This chapter tells you how Developer/2000 fires triggers; Chapter 10 and later chapters tell you what you can do in those triggers.

Forms Processes and Triggers

Of the three parts of Developer/2000, Forms has the most complicated logic. This section gives you an overview of the different processes and triggers in Forms; for details, you should consult the Developer/2000 *Forms Reference Manual,* Part Number A32509-1. Chapter 2 of that manual details the triggers, Chapter 7 describes default processing, and Chapter 8 describes the individual processes in great detail.

The following sections outline the main Forms processes at a high level. The diagrams use standard flow chart notation (boxes for processes, diamonds for decision points, with lines between boxes and diamonds representing the flow of logic through the process). These diagrams leave out many minor options and error handling to give you the big picture of the process; again, see the *Forms Reference Manual,* Chapter 8, for detailed charts.

Trigger Scope

You can define triggers in Developer/2000 forms at the item, block, or form levels in the Object Navigator hierarchy. The *trigger scope* is the set of objects that fire the trigger; it consists of the object that owns that trigger and any objects belonging to the object. For example, if you attach a trigger to a block, events in all the items in that block fire that trigger.

If there is more than one trigger with the same name in a particular scope, by default Developer/2000 fires the one attached to the object lowest in the hierarchy. For example, if you put a When-New-Item trigger on both an item and that item's block, Developer/2000 fires the trigger on the item and ignores the one on the block. You can change this behavior for a particular trigger by changing the Execution Style property of the trigger in the trigger's property sheet. The default is Override, but you can also choose Before or After. Before specifies that the trigger fire before any higher-level trigger, and After that it fire after a higher-level trigger. The next-higher-level trigger fires with either choice along with the current trigger. You can set the properties in higher scoping levels to cause all the different triggers at those levels to fire before or after the item trigger.

Some triggers only make sense when defined at a specific level. When-Validate-Record, for example, does not apply to individual items, so you can define it only at the block and form levels.

You can also inherit triggers through property classes, and you can include triggers by referring to an object group that has the trigger defined. The same rules apply to these triggers; only one trigger executes. If you override the Property-Class trigger with a trigger on the item, the item trigger executes. Object groups can only define form-level triggers; block and item triggers come along with their blocks and items. See Chapter 9 for more details.

Transaction Processing

A forms transaction is a sequence of events, processes, and triggers that ultimately results in either committing data to the database or rolling back changes. This section describes the processing that underlies your actual work in transactions (see the following sections for those processes).

Posting to the Database   *Posting* to the database means writing any pending changes in a form to the database through a series of INSERT, UPDATE, and DELETE statements. Developer/2000 generates these statements as part of its default processing. Posting does not commit the changes, but it is usually followed by a commit or rollback as part of the default processing.

By default, there is one post to the database followed by a commit or rollback to end the transaction. You can use the POST built-in procedure to post the changes without committing, however. This can speed processing under certain circumstances; this book does not recommend this practice because it increases the complexity of the code you must write. It also dramatically increases the complexity of the testing required to validate your application.

Figure 6-3 is the simplified flow chart for the posting process. First, Developer/2000 navigates to the form level, then validates the form. If there are no changes that require posting, the process stops right there.

Developer/2000 then issues a savepoint before posting. The *savepoint* is a feature of ORACLE7 that marks a point in a transaction to which you can roll back if necessary without rolling back the entire transaction. This permits Developer/2000 to post multiple times without rolling back all the posts—just the one that failed.

NOTE
The SAVEPOINT statement may not be available with database managers other than ORACLE7, so if you have a database portability requirement, you should not use the POST procedure. Also, Developer/2000 uses the SAVEPOINT when you call another form using the CALL_FORM built-in function, so that if a commit fails in the called form, it rolls back only to the savepoint.

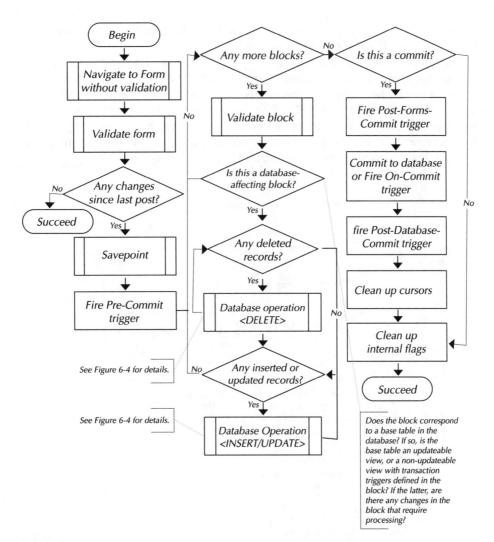

FIGURE 6-3. *A simplified flow chart for the posting process*

After issuing the savepoint, Developer/2000 fires the Pre-Commit trigger, then loops through the blocks. For each block, it validates the block, then determines whether the block has any changes that affect the database. If the block is a control block, it has no such changes. If the block's base table is a *non-updateable view* (one with a join or other disqualifying condition), Developer/2000 only processes the block if there are transaction triggers defined in it. Finally, if the block has no changed records, Developer/2000 skips the block.

Block processing then proceeds in two parts: dealing with deleted rows and dealing with inserts and updates by looping through the records in the block. Figure 6-4 shows the details of database operation processing. Database operations consist of DELETE, INSERT, or UPDATE statements and include the Pre- and Post-operation triggers. You can replace the default operation with an On-<Operation> trigger if you need to control database operations (for example, in using database managers other than ORACLE7 with differing syntaxes).

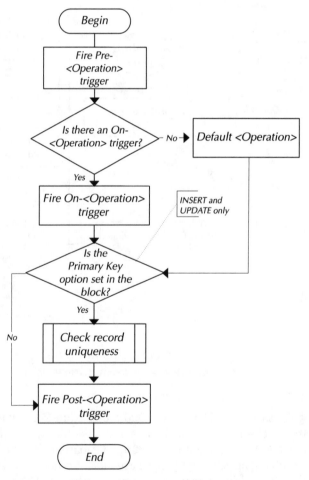

FIGURE 6-4. *A flow chart for database operations*

After processing all the blocks, if the process is a commit, not just a post, Developer/2000 fires the Post-Forms-Commit trigger, commits the changes (or fires the On-Commit trigger if there is one), and fires the Post-Database-Commit trigger. It then cleans up SQL cursors as required. In any case, Developer/2000 then cleans up the internal flags, including marking all the inserted records as database records and marking any changed items as Valid.

NOTE
If you use any of the Pre- or Post-operation triggers to change database-related data in the form, it is possible for Developer/2000 to commit these changes to the database without validating them.

Locking   Chapter 1 introduced the concept of transaction and described how the database manager makes transactions serializable through locking resources such as tables and rows. Developer/2000 uses the exclusive row lock, which is a lock on a specific row that prevents other transactions from updating or deleting the row by preventing them from acquiring locks on the row. SQL lets you acquire such locks using the SELECT...FOR UPDATE OF syntax; see the *ORACLE7 Server SQL Language Reference* for details. See the *ORACLE7 Server Concepts Manual* for details on transaction management and locking in general.

By default, Developer/2000 acquires row locks under any of the following conditions:

■ When the operator changes the value of a base table item in a database row

■ When the operator requests an explicit row lock for the current record through the Record¦Lock menu item

■ When a trigger makes a change to the database through an UPDATE or DELETE statement

■ When a trigger calls the DELETE_RECORD, ENTER_QUERY(FOR_UPDATE), EXECUTE_QUERY(FOR_UPDATE), or LOCK_RECORD built-in functions

■ When a trigger contains an explicit SQL LOCK TABLE statement; this will usually seriously impact transaction performance in your application, and you should not do it without an overwhelmingly good reason and several design reviews with people who understand the transaction behavior of the application

If Developer/2000 cannot obtain a lock immediately, it tries to obtain the lock repeatedly for a fixed number of times, then asks you whether to proceed. If this happens a lot, you should have your database administrator monitor the database to figure out why the resources are unavailable. Often, this is a result of using explicit, exclusive table locks, which you should avoid when possible.

As with any transaction, when the transaction commits or rolls back, the database manager releases all the locks. Because Developer/2000 uses savepoints, it is possible to retain some locks after a rollback, permitting you to redo the commit after making necessary changes.

NOTE
If you explicitly lock queried rows in a trigger, you will need to query those rows again to reestablish the locks on the rows after a commit or rollback. Clearing a block or record does not release any row locks on rows that correspond to the record(s).

If you define an On-Lock trigger at any level, Developer/2000 fires that trigger whenever it tries to obtain a lock at that level. You can use this trigger to replace the default locking mechanism (if you have sufficient justification to do so).

You can, if you wish, change the Locking Mode property on the block to Delayed instead of the default Immediate. Delaying locking means that Developer/2000 waits until just before committing to acquire the locks. Under some circumstances, this can improve transaction performance; the risk is that there will be conflicts that invalidate the user's changes, causing an error that requires additional work unexpectedly. You should only use the Delayed setting if your benchmarks show its superior performance.

Validation

Validation is the process of making sure that an object satisfies all the constraints you put on it in defining the form. Developer/2000 automatically validates items, records, blocks, and forms. You can add additional constraints in triggers, either as part of the validation process (validation triggers) or as part of the transaction process (see the previous section). Validation happens when you navigate out of the object or when you press the [Enter] key or call the ENTER built-in procedure. Also, the posting process automatically validates the form.

Validation Units and States
You can validate item, record, block, or form objects. The automatic validation by default validates items, meaning that automatic validation fires off every time you navigate out of an item. You can set the validation unit to record, block, or form to suppress automatic validation to a certain level. Generally, you should leave the validation unit at item level for best results.

Before getting into detail about dynamics, you need to understand the different trigger-related states of items and records in a Developer/2000 Forms application. An *object state* is the configuration of properties of the object at some point in the object's life cycle. Most Developer/2000 objects have many different properties, such as screen location, width, height, and so on. *Trigger-related* object state does not refer explicitly to these properties, only to the properties relevant to trigger behavior. This simplifies the object state considerably.

The following subsections build from the individual item all the way up to form. Each object refers to the state of other objects, usually down the hierarchy. For the gory details on the processes and triggers, see Chapters 7 and 8 of the *Developer/2000 Forms Reference Manual* (Part No. A32509-1).

Item State and Validation   The state of items has to do with the value of the item and what you have done to that value. An item can be New, Changed, or Valid. Figure 6-5 shows the flow chart for the item validation process.

NOTE
For simplicity, the flow charts do not show triggers with their decisions, but every trigger results in either a success or failure. If the trigger succeeds, the process continues as the diagram shows; if the trigger fails, the process stops with a failure return.

You can create an item in any of three ways: by creating a record, by duplicating a record, or by fetching a record from the database.

Creating a record creates the items in the record as New. Developer/2000 can fill in the value with a default value or copy it from another item in the process, but the item is still New.

Duplicating a record—copying the values from the previous record into a New record—puts the items in the New record into any of the three substates New, Changed, or Valid. The exact state duplicates the state of the item in the previous record, from which Developer/2000 copies the item.

Fetching the record immediately makes the items in the record Valid and executes the On-Fetch and Post-Change triggers for each item (the latter exists for compatibility; you should not use it).

When you modify an item in any way, Developer/2000 marks the item Changed.

Item validation happens only for New and Changed items. When you have a New or Changed item and the Validate Item process results in True, Developer/2000 runs the On-Change and When-Validate-Item triggers, then marks the item Valid. When the Validate Item process results in False, the item remains as it was, and the cursor remains on the item.

Records own items, so the only way to get rid of a particular value is to clear the record; this can happen in any item state.

When you validate an item, the process checks the following properties (Figure 6-5):

- *Format mask:* The format of the item value for a text item (status can be Valid or Invalid)

- *Required and input allowed:* Whether the item value must exist

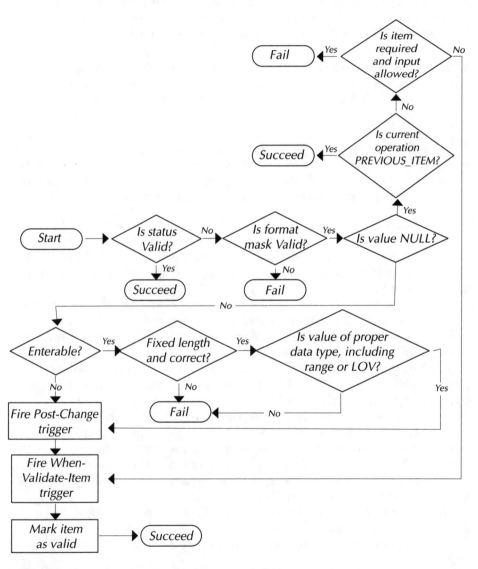

FIGURE 6-5. *The flow chart for the item validation process*

- *Fixed length:* Whether the item value must be a certain length and is that length

- *Data type:* The basic type of value

- *Range:* The possible minimum and maximum values

- *List of values:* Check the value against a list of possible values in a list-of-values object (LOV)

If everything validates, the process fires the Post-Change and When-Validate-Item triggers for the item to do any additional validation. The process marks the item as Valid if these triggers succeed.

Record State   A record has three validation states:

- *New:* When you Create Record, the record object is New

- *Changed:* When you change any item (see the previous section for how this happens) in the record, the record becomes Changed

- *Valid:* A record becomes Valid after Developer/2000 validates all the Changed or New items in a record and validates the record or after it fetches the record from the database or commits the record to the database

Duplicating a record copies the state of the source record.

Record validation and posting proceed only for Changed records. Figure 6-6 shows the flow chart for the record validation process; see the previous section for post processing.

The record validation process iterates through all the items in the record, validating them. If any item fails validation, the process stops. After validating all the items, the process marks any items changed through triggers to be valid without revalidating them. Then, if you have updated the record, the process locks the row (see the earlier section, "Locking," for details). The process then fires the When-Validate-Record trigger and marks the record as Valid.

Form and Block Validation   Validating a block means validating all the records in the block. Validating a form means validating all the blocks in the form.

Query Processing
A query is a request for data from the database. A Developer/2000 forms application has a built-in query process that gives you tremendous power and flexibility without writing a line of code. This section helps you understand the logic of the different parts of the query process.

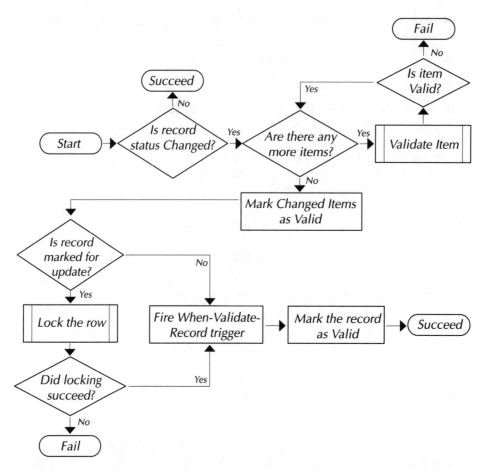

FIGURE 6-6. *The flow chart for the record validation process*

Figure 6-7 is a summary flow chart of the query processing in a form. The idea is to create an example record in a block (that is, *enter a query*) that lets you enter conditions to attach to the default query. This query in turn contains a set of conditions and a default ordering specification. You can, if you wish, enter more complex SQL conditions through a special dialog box. You then *execute the query* and *fetch the records*, displaying them in the block. These are the three main processes this section discusses; each has some subprocesses that it shares with other processes.

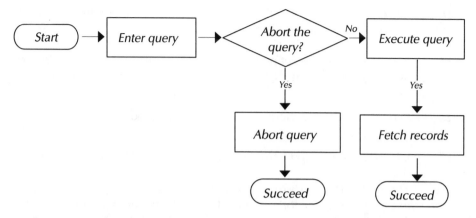

FIGURE 6-7.   *A summary flow chart for query processing*

Also, you have the following processes:

■ *Count the query:* This process prepares the query and requests the server to tell you how many records the query will return in an informational message; the process fires the On-Count trigger, if there is one, replacing the counting process.

■ *Abort and close the query:* While entering the query, you may want to end it without executing it; the process fires the On-Close trigger, if there is one, which replaces the close process.

Entering a Query   Recall from your basic SQL training the structure of the SQL SELECT statement:

```
SELECT select-list
   FROM table
  WHERE query-condition
ORDER BY order-by-list
```

When you enter a query in a Developer/2000 Forms application by pressing the [Enter Query] key or calling the ENTER_QUERY built-in procedure, you are building a SELECT statement. The *select-list* is the set of column names that correspond to your record items. The *table* is the base table that corresponds to the block. The *order-by-list* is a list of the columns in the select-list that specifies the order for the queried records. You specify the order-by-list through the ORDER BY clause block property or interactively through the Where dialog box.

The *query-condition* is the set of SQL expressions that specifies which records to return. This set of expressions has three parts:

- *Default conditions:* The set of conditions you specify as the default WHERE clause as a block property, which you can also change at runtime through a trigger

- *Column conditions:* Conditions you enter by filling out columns in the example record

- *Special conditions:* Conditions you enter through the Where dialog box

See the *Forms Developer's Reference* (Part Number A32509-1), Chapter 6, the *Querying the Database* section, for a detailed look at the query-by-example features of Developer/2000 Forms applications. You can use relational operators (>, <, =, !=, and so on) and other SQL features as part of the column conditions, for example.

When you are entering a query, Developer/2000 does not validate items or records, uses standard key definitions rather than executing key triggers, and disables various function keys (mainly record navigation and commit processing functions).

NOTE
You can set the "Fire in Enter Query Mode" property of a key trigger to True if you want to be able to override a particular key. This is probably going to confuse you, however; be careful when you do it to test your form carefully both in regular and Enter Query modes.

Figure 6-8 is the flow chart for the process of entering a query.

The decision about whether the block allows queries depends on two block properties. The Query Allowed property (see the Block property sheet) lets you disable a query for a block. You can specify a block to be a *control block* by leaving the base table blank. Either of these two conditions prevents you from entering a query for the block. Also, you must have at least one item in the block that comes from the base table in the database.

The preceding paragraphs have summarized the process for entering the query conditions into the example record.

Executing a Query   Once you have entered your query conditions, you then execute the query by pressing the [Execute Query] key or calling the EXECUTE_QUERY built-in procedure. It is not quite that simple, of course. You can execute a query without having entered a query first; this means you want to retrieve all the rows using only the default WHERE clause. You can execute a query while there are changed records in the block; Developer/2000 asks you whether to commit the changes. There are also some complexities relating to the number of rows fetched that the following section discusses.

Figure 6-9 is the flow chart for the process of executing a query. For the sake of simplicity, the flow chart does not illustrate the process of putting the cursor on the first records (or the error return if the fetch returns no records).

When you execute the query, Developer/2000 first checks whether the block allows queries (see the previous section). If so, it navigates to the block, validating any records not already validated. If there are Changed records in the block, it prompts whether to commit, and posts or clears the changes as appropriate.

Developer/2000 then fires the Pre-Query trigger for the block, another place to specify WHERE column conditions, and checks whether there is a base table for this block. Although this duplicates the first check of the block, you can get to this point in the process from other places, such as counting query rows, without having done that previous check. If the check succeeds, Developer/2000 builds the SELECT statement and fires the Pre-Select trigger. If there is an On-Select trigger, it executes it; otherwise, it executes the SELECT statement. It fires the Post-Select and When-Clear-Block triggers and flushes the example record from the block, then fetches the records.

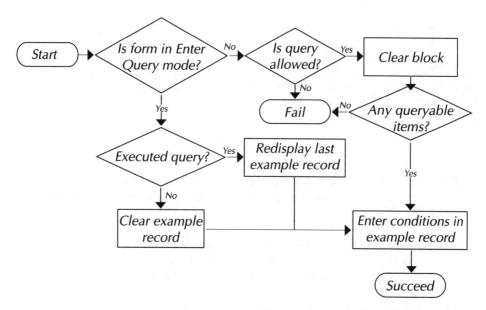

FIGURE 6-8. *A flow chart showing the process of entering a query*

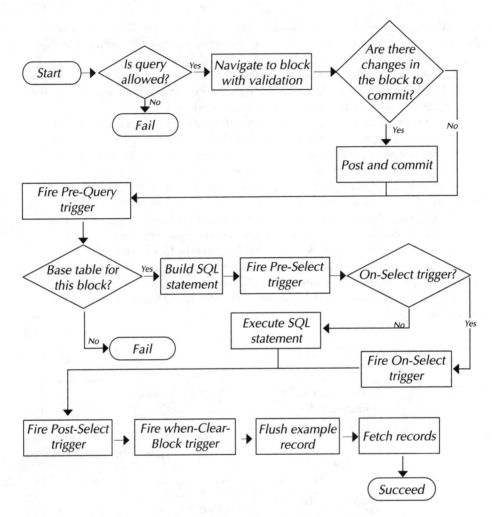

FIGURE 6-9. *A flow chart showing the process of executing a query*

Fetching Records   After completing the process of executing the SQL query, Developer/2000 organizes the fetching of records. This is a complex process that retrieves rows from the database based on several variables:

- Whether you have turned on array processing
- The number of rows the query selects from the database

- The number of rows that are visible at once in the block

- The number of rows that the block stores in memory

- The operation causing the fetch (deleting records, scrolling, or any number of other candidates are possible)

If there is an On-Fetch trigger, Developer/2000 fires that trigger rather than fetching a row from the database into the record buffer.

See the *Forms Developer's Reference* (Part Number A32509-1), Chapter 8, *Open the Query* section and *Fetch Records* section for the full logic of fetching records.

Navigational Processing

There are several triggers that you can use for special effects when the user moves around the application. The trigger-firing processes contain various ways of creating defaults, such as creating a default New record when you enter a block for the first time. Again, see the details in Chapter 8 of the *Forms Developer's Reference* (Part Number A32509-1).

Entering an object fires the Pre-navigational trigger for that object (Pre-Form, Pre-Block, Pre-Record, Pre-Text-Item). Leaving an object fires the Post-navigational trigger (Post-Form, Post-Block, Post-Record, Post-Text-Item). Creating an instance of the object fires the When-New-Object-Instance trigger (When-New-Form-Instance, When-New-Block-Instance, When-New-Record-Instance, and When-New-Item-Instance).

Logon Processing

Logging in and out of a Developer/2000 Forms application fires triggers at several points. Logging into a Forms application sets various options, connects you to the database, and sets column security for all blocks in the current form. Figure 6-10 is the flow chart for the logon process. The process checks whether you have already logged on and only proceeds if you have not. After firing the Pre-Logon trigger, the process checks for a valid connection. If there is no connection, it fires an On-Logon trigger if one exists. If no such trigger exists, it attempts to connect to the server, failing after three attempts.

If you are connecting to ORACLE or SQL*Connect, as opposed to some other database manager, Developer/2000 sets up the ORACLE-specific client-side objects (savepoints, column security, shared cursors, and SQL tracing).

After resetting the savepoint counter, the logon process goes through all the blocks in the form, checking the columns for security restrictions. You enable this by setting the Column Security property to True for the blocks you want to restrict. In any such block, the operator must have column-level update privileges in the data dictionary on the server, or the logon process dynamically sets the Update

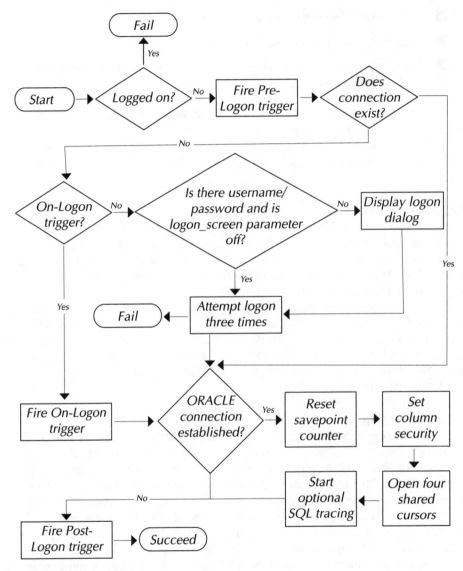

FIGURE 6-10. *A flow chart for logging on*

Allowed property for the item off. You can define your own security process by defining an On-Column-Security trigger.

After enforcing security, the process opens four shared cursors, starts tracing if you requested it, and fires the Post-Logon trigger.

Logging out of a forms application cleans up the database-related memory and logs out of the database. First, it fires the Pre-Logout trigger. It then closes the ORACLE7 shared cursors. If there is an On-Logout trigger, the process executes that instead of logging off the server and firing the Post-Logout trigger.

Block Processing

The block is at the center of much of what happens in a form. A *block* is an object that is the parent of a set of items. Most blocks map to a single base table on the server, but you can also have *control blocks,* blocks that do not map to a database table. You use control blocks to add items to your form that do not come from the database and do not fit into database-linked blocks. In any case, the block is the basic structure that contains items, and it provides a level of aggregation for the group of items it contains. You use this level for many different actions and effects.

Besides the extensive block query facilities that the previous section discussed, there are some basic block processes that drive major parts of your application.

Creating a record is a fundamental process, though a simple one. Figure 6-11 shows the flow chart for the process. After navigating to the block level with validation, the process creates and initializes a new record (if the block allows creation of new records). The process then fires the When-Create-Record trigger and positions the cursor to the new record.

The process of *marking items and records changed* can happen in various ways; see the previous section on validation for some of them. This process is central to understanding how records relate to transaction processing. Figure 6-12

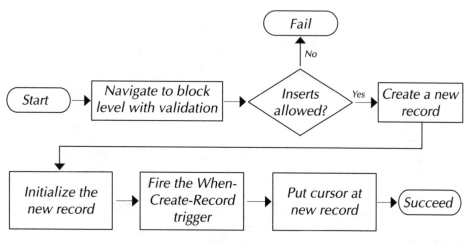

FIGURE 6-11. *A flow chart for creating a new record*

shows the flow chart for this process. After marking the item as Changed, if the record is New, the process marks all the items as Changed. It then checks for any database field marked as Changed without the record having been marked as an Insert or Update and marks the record after firing the When-Database-Record trigger. Updates are records that correspond to a row in the database, while Inserts are records that do not.

Clearing a block validates the block and prompts you if there are changes to commit. If you wish, it posts and commits, then it fires the When-Clear-Block trigger, flushes the current block, and puts the cursor at the current block.

Clearing a record has a relatively complex logic relating to rearranging the remaining records in the block and on the display. The main process of interest here is the firing of the When-Remove-Record trigger.

Interface and Key Event Processing

There are dozens of interface events in a Developer/2000 Forms application. Fortunately, there is little complex logic surrounding these events and their processes in the application. Usually, all that happens is that you raise the event

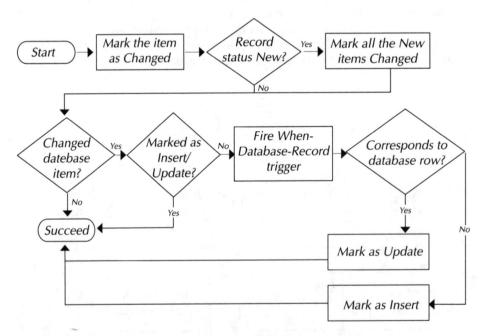

FIGURE 6-12.   *A flow chart for the record-marking process*

(click the mouse, press the button, check the check box, close the window, or whatever) and the trigger you associate with the event fires.

See the *Forms Developer's Reference* (Part Number A32509-1), Chapter 2 for details of these triggers, and Chapter 8 for details of the various processes.

Using these triggers, you can define what happens for most interface events in a Forms application:

- *User interface controls:* You can define what happens for the different items in your block, such as images, buttons, check boxes, radio buttons, and lists.

- *Mouse events:* You can define the logic behind clicks, double-clicks, mouse-down, mouse-up, and so on.

- *Key events:* You can define what happens for the various function keys ([Clear Block], [Insert Record], [Previous Block], [Enter Query], and so on), and keyboard function keys (F0-F9).

Master-Detail Coordination

A *coordination-causing event* is any event in a master block (of a master-detail pair) that makes a different record the current record in the master block. Developer/2000 handles all actual processing of the event through triggers that it generates by default: On-Clear-Details, On-Populate-Details, and On-Check-Delete-Master. Developer/2000 stacks the triggers and processes them as part of the stacked sequence of processes before the next event. This behavior is somewhat unusual compared to the rest of the logic in the forms application. If you intend to modify the triggers to handle the coordination yourself, be prepared to experiment with the logic until you fully understand it.

Forms creates the On-Clear-Details trigger when you define the master-detail relationship. It automatically clears the detail block when a coordination-causing event occurs, if the Auto-Query property of the relation is False.

Forms creates the On-Populate-Details trigger when you define the master-detail relationship. It automatically populates the detail block when a coordination-causing event occurs.

Forms creates the On-Check-Delete-Master trigger when you set the property Master Deletes to Non-Isolated in the relationship property sheet. This means that you want to prevent deletion of the master record if there are details associated with it.

There is also some logic having to do with the Auto-Query setting, which permits you to defer populating the details until you navigate into the detail block.

See the *Forms Developer's Reference* (Part Number A32509-1), Chapter 8, section on the *Master-Detail Coordination* process for details.

Message Handling

There are two triggers that affect message handling in a Developer/2000 Forms application: On-Error and On-Message. The former fires when Developer/2000 tries to display an error message; the latter when it tries to display an informational message. You can use these triggers to handle errors and messages. In the trigger code, you can access built-in functions that return various parts of the message:

■ *ERROR_CODE or MESSAGE_CODE:* The error number

■ *ERROR_TEXT or MESSAGE_TEXT:* The text message

■ *ERROR_TYPE or MESSAGE_TYPE:* The kind of message

■ *DBMS_ERROR_CODE or DBMS_MESSAGE_CODE:* The server error number, which may differ from the forms error number

■ *DBMS_ERROR_TEXT or DBMS_MESSAGE_TEXT:* The server message, which may differ from the forms error message

With sufficient motivation, you can thus extract any element of a message and use it in further processing, or you can provide your own error handling.

Reports Process and Triggers

The Developer/2000 report process is much simpler than the form processes the previous section discusses. Most of what you do with reports, and in particular the repetitive looping, you specify with a combination of data model group, repeating frame, and report type. There are some special effects, particularly those involving conditional decisions, that you must do in custom programming in report triggers. Figure 6-13 shows the report process, which contains several trigger points.

The report process starts with the command line arguments you give the report runtime system. If there are any, Developer/2000 fires the Validation trigger you have entered through the Parameter property sheet to check and/or change the parameters for the report instance. The Runtime Parameter Form lets the user enter runtime options for the report. Developer/2000 fires a Before Form and After Form trigger, as well as potentially firing the Validation trigger again.

After setting up the parameters, Developer/2000 compiles the report and fires the Before Report trigger. The logic of executing the report is more complex than the figure shows, but the places you can intervene are in Format triggers you associate with any object in the report and in Between Page triggers that fire after printing each page except the last one.

After printing the last page, the report commits to end the transaction, then fires the After Report trigger.

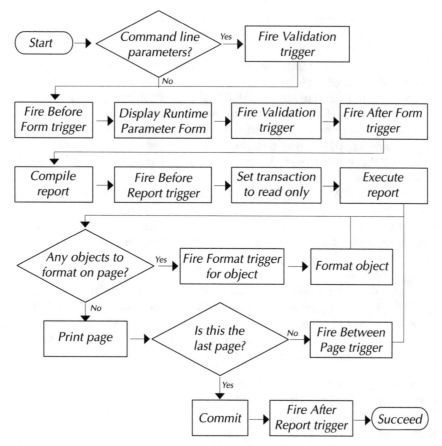

FIGURE 6-13. *A flow chart showing the report process*

You can run a report in the Previewer or just send the results to a destination. If you choose to preview the report, you have interactive access to the report, and you can use certain triggers to do interactive things, particularly the Action triggers (see the upcoming section). You can treat a report as an interactive application through this mechanism. You should realize that things such as forward references can cause triggers to fire in unexpected ways in the Previewer.

Report Triggers

The Report triggers (Before and After Report, Between Pages, and Before and After Form) give you procedural access to report processing at the report and page levels.

The Before Report trigger fires before any formatting of the report objects but after querying the data for the report. You can initialize things with this trigger. If the trigger fails, Developer/2000 displays an error message and returns.

The After Report trigger fires after printing the report or exiting the Previewer. You can use this trigger to clean up anything you do not want left around after running the report. Even if triggers fail during the report, this trigger always fires. You have to explicitly display any error messages; the trigger does nothing if it fails.

You can use the Between Pages trigger for custom page formatting. In the Previewer, Developer/2000 fires this trigger only the first time you display the report page. If the trigger fails, Developer/2000 stops formatting pages and displays an error message.

Before Form and After Form let you manipulate the parameters of the report. You cannot manipulate data model objects such as columns from these triggers. After Form always fires, regardless of whether you suppress the Runtime Parameter Form. If these triggers fail, Developer/2000 stops and returns.

NOTE
You should avoid DDL and DML statements in Before and After Report triggers and in Between Page triggers. Developer/2000 takes a snapshot of tables during report compilation. It also executes queries in arbitrary ways, so you cannot count on DML statements having the desired effects in your transaction.

For various warnings and exceptions to using these triggers, see the *Reports Reference Manual* (Part Number A32489-1), Chapter 13.

Format Trigger

When it formats an instance of the object, Developer/2000 calls a Format trigger you have associated with any object in a report. You can change borders, format masks, or any other aspect of the object you can access through the SRW PL/SQL library package. You can skip processing within an object based on variable values.

You should avoid DML and DDL statements in these triggers, as the firing of these triggers can be unpredictable. The triggers can fire many times during the formatting of a single object.

You can format cells in a matrix by putting a frame object around the field and associating a Format trigger with the frame.

Action Trigger

You can put buttons on reports in order to be able to do something interactive when you run the report in the Previewer. An Action trigger runs when you push the button. You can use this trigger to run another report in a separate Previewer, letting you "drill down" based on the current report values. See the *Building Reports*

Manual (Part Number A32488-1), Chapter 7, on using the new drill-down feature of Developer/2000 Reports.

Graphics Process and Triggers

The Developer/2000 graphics process is also much simpler than the form processes. Most of what you do with graphics, and in particular the basic display object formatting and association with database data, you specify with a combination of layout editor, query, and chart type. There are some special effects, particularly those involving conditional decisions, that you must do in custom programming in graphics triggers. Figure 6-14 shows the graphics process, which contains several trigger points.

When you open a graphics display using the runtime graphics system, it fires the Open Display trigger for the display. The process then executes the query and fires the Post-Execution trigger, then fires the Filter trigger. The process then updates the chart, firing any Format triggers associated with the objects in the chart. If there is a timer, the timer fires the Timer trigger after a set time period passes. If there is a mouse event on an object that acts as a button (for a drill-down relationship, for example), the process fires the Button trigger.

You can build your own chart templates as a way to program a specific format and use it in multiple charts. You can use the various triggers to add special effects to a particular graphics display.

Graphics Triggers

Graphics triggers are all PL/SQL procedures (not anonymous blocks as for forms). You can link any procedure to a trigger in the Object Navigator through the property sheet for the object that owns the trigger. You have a special library package, OG, that contains functions for obtaining internal elements (the display, the query, the timer, and so on), for formatting objects, and for executing the different Graphics processes. See the *Graphics Reference Manual* (Part Number A32483-1) for details of this library package.

If you need to initialize anything in the chart, such as setting up display layers, starting timers, or executing special queries, you can do that in the Open Display trigger. Both the Open Display and Close Display triggers are entries in the Display Object property sheet.

If you want to process query data in some way or set up something that depends on having done the query, you can use the Post-Execution trigger. You can create this in the Query property sheet.

If you want to format individual chart elements based on other elements or queried data relationships, you can do that with the Format trigger you associate with the chart element. Developer/2000 executes the Format trigger just before

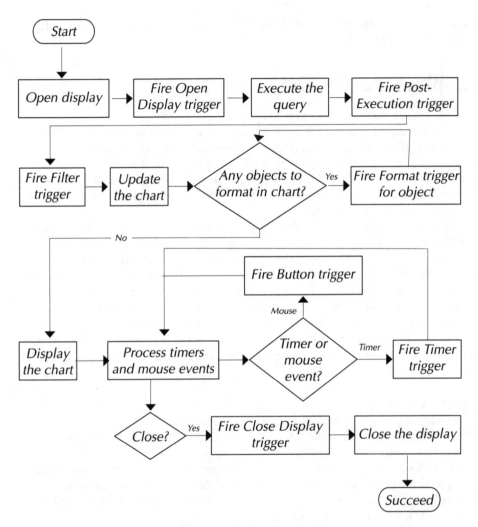

FIGURE 6-14. *A flow chart showing the graphics process*

updating the display for the element. You can create the Format trigger from the object's property sheet.

Timers handle situations where you want to update a display after some time interval. A common example is querying real-time transaction data to get a completely up-to-date graphic that shows the changes that occurred during the period. Timers are a bit complex; see the *Graphics Developer's Guide* (Part Number A32482-1) and the *Graphics Reference Manual* (Part Number A32483-1) for details on timers, associated queries, and the Timer trigger. You can automatically execute a query and/or execute the Timer trigger, for example. You associate a Timer trigger with a query or a timer object.

Button procedures are yet more complex. Developer/2000 automatically sets up the appropriate events and processing for drill-down for you; but if you want more complex events and graphics changes, you will need to associate Button triggers with chart objects. Developer/2000 Graphics handles the mouse events down, up, move down, and move up; and you can set the object to receive these events. You can then test for the events in the trigger procedure. For example, you could set up a button procedure on a button graphic that turns off the timer that automatically updates the display. You can set up event reception and create the button procedure through the object's property sheet.

Finally, you can use the Close Display trigger to clean up anything that needs cleaning up. You can commit changes to the database here if you have programmed other parts of the graphic to make such changes.

Cross-Platform Redesign

Having done your basic work, what do you need to do to make your application portable across several platforms? There are several issues with cross-platform portability:

- *Control and menu standards:* What are the standards for controls such as buttons and menus on the target platform? Do you want to absolutely conform to all such standards?

- *Colors and patterns:* How do colors and patterns translate between different platforms?

- *Fonts:* How do fonts translate to different platforms?

- *Platform-specific functionality:* Do you use any icons, user exits, or specific features of a platform, such as OLE or Apple Events?

NOTE
If you need to run with character mode applications, you are in a different world from these considerations. You may need to worry about fonts, because everything in character mode uses only monospace fonts. Also, you may find that aligning the boilerplate with snap points to the fields will help with portability to character mode displays.

You will find it easier to deal with these issues through planning and standardization than by dealing with the issues as they arise.

Control and Menu Standards

Each platform has specific graphical user interface guidelines that all applications should follow. Developer/2000 automatically translates the standard control objects (buttons, check boxes, radio buttons, and the like) to the appropriate format for the platform on which you design the application.

Please see the following references for the specific guidelines for each platform:

- *Windows 3:* Microsoft Corporation, *The Windows Interface: An Application Design Guide,* Microsoft Press, 1992.

- *Macintosh:* Apple Computer, *Macintosh Human Interface Guidelines,* Addison-Wesley, 1992.

- *Motif:* Open Software Foundation, *The Motif Style Guide Release 1.2,* Prentice-Hall, 1992.

Other platforms may have their own style guides, which you should obtain and use as references.

Colors and Patterns

Color, even a splash, can make your applications come alive. Use too much or the wrong kind, and it will kill it. Application developers regularly get bug reports these days about the color combinations of the applications they develop. This is especially true when the applications run on monochrome monitors or when documentation people try to print pictures of the screens and key parts come out black, not that nice, dark blue they saw on the screen.

Unless you are a color expert, you should restrain your use of color to three or four basic colors that work well together and that work in their monochrome, gray-scale equivalents. Put these in your named visual attributes and templates to make sure all your applications start with the right effects. You should test the color combinations on all the target systems to make sure they work.

The same rules apply to patterns; use them sparingly, as they can differ dramatically on different displays.

Finally, although Developer/2000 gives you a 256-color palette, the actual colors that you see on a particular display may differ, sometimes greatly. Again, you should limit your range of colors, and test them on your target displays to identify any problems.

Fonts

It is still quite difficult to translate fonts between platforms. Developer/2000 does all it can, but in the end it relies upon your specifying translations explicitly for portability.

The first thing you need to do is to choose a font palette: what typefaces do you want to use, in what type sizes and weights? A typeface is a particular style of type, such as Times Roman or Helvetica. Because of intellectual property issues, different systems and vendors provide essentially the same font with different names. For example, Apple Computer and Adobe Systems Adobe Type Manager provide the Helvetica font, while Windows 3.1 provides the system font Helv and the TrueType font Arial. There are minor differences in the typefaces, but generally this issue is not important in developing database applications. Typefaces become more important for applications such as World Wide Web pages that need to express individuality and creativity—unlike database applications, right? Well, if you want to develop some creative applications, try a book such as *Stop Stealing Sheep* by Erik Spiekermann and E. M. Ginger (Mountain View, CA: Adobe Press, 1993). But be aware that "creative" and "portable" may be mutually exclusive terms, at least with respect to font technology.

You should also decide where and how to use font characteristics such as boldface, italics, and underlining. You should standardize the type size of different display text objects, making all labels 10 points, for example. This will help if you need to translate a font on a different platform.

You may find that a given font differs across platforms due to differences in the font technology. As with color, you should test your standard fonts on all your target platforms.

You can set your default font for boilerplate text in Forms applications with the variable FORM45_DEFAULT_FONT in the ORACLE initialization file (ORACLE.INI on Windows, for example). You should implement your standards decisions in named visual attributes and property classes to ensure that your applications conform to the standards.

If you need to translate fonts between platforms, you need to use the Developer/2000 font alias files. These files simply map one font by name into another font. See the *Installation Guide* for the target platform for details on font specification for the platform.

Platform-Specific Functionality

There are several things you can do in Developer/2000 that limit you to a single platform.

Icons come from icon files in a platform-dependent format, so you need to have a complete set of icon files for each platform in the format appropriate to that platform.

User exits get compiled separately on each platform into the executable library format of the platform. If your application depends on user exits, you will need to port your code from platform to platform.

Finally, there are specific things you can use on each platform that are not available on other platforms:

■ *Windows:* DDE, OLE, and VBX

■ *Macintosh:* AppleEvents

■ *All:* Anything you call through the HOST built-in procedure

Standards and Planning

The one essential thing you must do to be portable is to specify what platforms you intend to support. If you can avoid certain very different platforms, such as character-mode terminals, you will find your portability much easier to achieve. If you can limit certain issues to certain applications, this can help too. For example, if your mobile sales force uses laptops for lead tracking and sales management applications, but everyone else uses 17-inch SVGA terminals, you can save yourself much pain by restricting the window size of only the two critical laptop applications. In any case, knowing the window size variations is essential in designing the layout of fixed forms and graphics. You can also use scrolling judiciously to accommodate smaller screens in some cases.

Once you are clear on your platforms, you should put together a set of standards for user interface objects and properties that takes portability into account. If you make full use of named visual attributes, property classes, and graphics templates to make your standards easy to implement in working applications, you will find it much easier to move those applications to the different platforms. See Chapter 9 for details on increasing reusability of your code through named visual attributes and property classes (and other methods).

One trick you can use in your trigger code is to refer to the application properties that determine portability issues. You can thus choose what property values to use at runtime by checking the values of these properties using the GET_APPLICATION_PROPERTY built-in function:

■ *DISPLAY_HEIGHT and DISPLAY_WIDTH:* These variables tell you how big the current display is. The unit depends on how you have set up the form coordinate system, a property of the form module.

- *OPERATING_SYSTEM:* This variable tells you the name of the platform on which the application currently is running (MSWINDOWS, MACINTOSH, SunOS, VMS, UNIX, or HP-UX).

- *USER_INTERFACE:* This variable tells you the name of the user interface technology on which the application currently is running (MOTIF, MACINTOSH, MSWINDOWS, PM, X, CHARMODE, BLOCKMODE, or UNKNOWN).

To summarize the portability issues, it is relatively easy to build portable applications using Developer/2000, but it does take some planning and standardization to do it effectively and efficiently.

Now you are ready to take your prototype to the next stage by using the advanced programming and development features of Developer/2000. The next two chapters delve into even more advanced issues that will add dramatically to your productivity in generating safe and solid applications.

CHAPTER 7

Doing Windows

U nderstanding the processes of the Forms component of Developer/2000
gives you a structure in which you can begin to expand the horizons of your
forms application. Two additional topics will round out your ability to design
full-scale, complete applications with Developer/2000: windows and menus. You
can use these Forms features as design features with little or no programming.

In Chapter 5, the prototype form presented a single canvas-view in a single
window. This chapter shows you how to expand your application into multiple
windows using multiple canvas-views. These features give you the ability to build
dialog boxes, toolbars, and alerts.

The default menu of the application in Chapter 5 is not the extent of what you
can do with menus, either. You can build your own custom menu to integrate
forms with reports and graphics or whatever else you want to call from a form.

Windows

The topic of using windows in Developer/2000 is really two topics: how to create the contents of the window and how to create and manage the window itself. The following discussion expands on the prototype of Chapter 5 to show you how to make full use of Developer/2000 canvas-views and windows as design features of your application.

Painting Canvas-Views

Recall from Chapter 5 that a canvas-view is the way you display your blocks and items. You edit the canvas-view in the Layout Editor, and it becomes the basis for much of the work you do in building your forms. What, then, exactly is a canvas-view?

A *canvas-view* is the background on which you place boilerplate text and items. Each item refers to exactly one canvas-view in its property sheet. You can divide a block's items between different canvas-views. But what is the origin of the "view" part of this object?

A canvas-view does not stand alone as an interface object. To see it and its items, you must display the canvas-view in a window. It might be possible to make the canvas-view and the window the same, but this is not the most flexible architecture. Developer/2000 makes these separate objects and lets you build windows that provide a *view* of the canvas: a rectangle that covers part or all of the canvas. For example, in Figure 7-1, the Ledger form shows a window that reveals a little more than half of the underlying canvas. The part of the canvas that you can see through the window is the view. The window has horizontal and vertical scroll bars that let you scroll through the canvas to see different views.

This separate-but-equal division of labor between display and content lets you build your forms without regard to the window size that will display them. This widens your horizons but narrows your interface, literally. You may find that users who constantly need to scroll through their canvases express a dissatisfaction with the interface. Your best interface will show all the fields and other items on a canvas all the time. But, as with most aspects of life, sometimes you need to have more than you can show at once. Windows and canvas-views give you that flexibility.

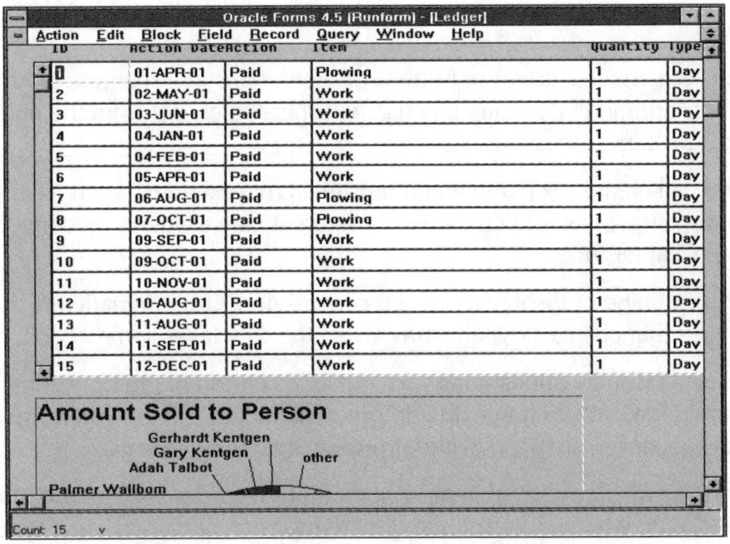

FIGURE 7-1. *A view of the Ledger canvas through the Ledger window*

Choosing the Right Background

Building on this flexibility, however, certain kinds of canvas-view can do more for you than just letting you scroll around within a window. There are three kinds of canvas-views:

- *Content:* A canvas-view that contains the "contents" of a window; every window has at least one content canvas-view, and usually just one.

- *Stacked:* A canvas-view you display on top of another canvas view, usually containing some items in a group separate from the items in the underlying content canvas-view.

- *Toolbar:* A canvas-view containing tool icon buttons that the window displays in horizontal and vertical bars at the top of or to the left side of a window, respectively.

You can use the stacked canvas-view to create special effects:

■ You can create a group of buttons or other items in a separate cluster with a background that graphically distinguishes the cluster from the underlying content canvas-view.

■ You can create a separable and reusable group of items, such as a button array, that you can reuse in different canvas-views by copying (see Chapter 9).

■ You can hide or display a stacked canvas-view programmatically to create a view that changes dynamically when the user takes some action.

■ You can display unchanging text and fields on top of multiple content canvas-views that change in and out dynamically, giving you a way to have recurring elements without producing multiple items.

■ You can display a set of items in a multiple-record display that remains on the screen while you scroll the underlying content canvas-view to see other items. For example, you can display the primary key in an unchanging column while you view the rest of the columns by scrolling, so you always see the primary key no matter where you are in the canvas. This trick behaves like a multiple-display view in a spreadsheet.

Although all of these tricks are interesting, the details of stacked canvas-view design are too extensive for the scope of this book. See Chapter 11 of the *Forms Developer's Guide* (Part Number A32505-1) for a complete guide to using stacked canvas-views. The rest of this section focuses on the more central issues of the content and toolbar canvas-views.

Filling Up the Canvas

To get a canvas-view to work with, you can just create a block, as in Chapter 6. Developer/2000 automatically creates a content canvas-view with the name you specify in the New Block window. You can also start up the Layout Editor in a new form to get a default content canvas-view. Otherwise, you must create a canvas-view in the usual way in the Object Navigator, by selecting the Canvas-View header and clicking on the Create button. You can set the view type (default Content) and the window that displays the canvas-view in the property sheet (Figure 7-2).

To see the canvas-view in the Layout Editor, double-click on the Object Navigator icon for the object. You have already seen in Chapter 5 how to use the Layout Editor to put items and boilerplate text on the canvas. The only difference here is that you are building the canvas from scratch rather than working with a canvas-view with a set of items that Developer/2000 generates when you create a

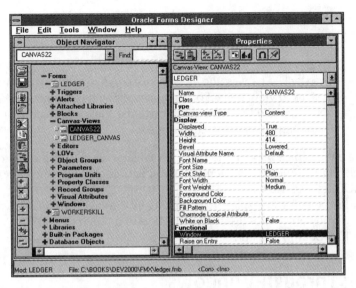

FIGURE 7-2. *Creating a canvas-view*

block. You can create an item in the Object Navigator, then set the item's Canvas property to be the new canvas-view. You can also create the item in the Layout Editor and change the properties of the item through its property sheet. You can create a second canvas-view and move items to it from the base view by changing the Canvas property in the items that already exist. If you set this property to NULL, the item appears in no canvas-view. This lets you define items that do not display their values.

You can control the display of the canvas background through the View¦Show Canvas menu item, available when the Layout Editor is active. If you set this item off, you will see the background grid directly under the items. If you turn it back on, you will see the canvas with no grid. This menu item serves two purposes. First, when you are placing the items, you may want to see the grid. Second, if you want to resize the canvas-view itself, you can do so by dragging the selection handle in the lower-right corner of the canvas. To see this, turn on the Show Canvas menu item, then click on the right or bottom edge of the canvas. You can also change the Width and Height attributes in the canvas-view property sheet.

The View¦Show View menu item lets you see the view. That is, if you displayed the canvas in its window, the view is the area of the canvas you would see. The Layout Editor displays the view as a 1-point black rectangle with size handles that you can use to resize the default window. You can also change this size by changing the window's Width and Height in its property sheet. You can move the view by dragging the rectangle or by changing the X/Y Position properties of the canvas-view.

NOTE
For a stacked canvas, the view is independent of the window (hence the stacked view's effect of not changing with the window). You control the width and height through the View Width and View Height properties of the canvas-view.

You delete the canvas view in the Object Navigator by selecting it and clicking on the Delete button. This sets the items that you had displayed in the canvas-view to have a NULL canvas-view.

The window, when you display it, automatically displays the base canvas-view for a window. You can control display of other views through the SHOW_VIEW and HIDE_VIEW built-in functions in triggers.

Viewing Through Windows

The canvas-view structures the contents of your form; the window lets you see it. By adding windows and their canvas-views to your forms, you can create forms that are easy to understand and to use. Each window has at least one content canvas-view that defines the contents of the window.

Using Multiple Documents

The Microsoft Windows platform introduced an architecture called the Multiple Document Interface (MDI) that structures the use of multiple windows in an application. Developer/2000 adopts the MDI architecture and extends it to other platforms by making specific assumptions and facilities available.

An MDI application has an *application window* that owns all the other windows in the application. The application window has no canvas-view but rather displays the other windows. The main menu belongs to the application window, and that window is always open. The form windows are children of this window and can be either document or dialog windows.

A *document window* is a window contained entirely within the application window. If you move the document window beyond the application window, that window clips the document window. Usually, you display the document windows in an overlapping or tiled group in the application-window display area. You can also *maximize* a document window to take up the entire display area of the application window, or you can *minimize* the document window into an icon. The document window usually displays the central content of the application, such as the database table data and graphics.

A *dialog box* is a window that is independent of the application window. You can move the dialog window outside the application window (if its properties allow this) without having the application window clip the dialog window. The dialog window typically contains fields that let the application interact with the user, such as collections of options or parameters for the application.

Another way to categorize windows is as modal or modeless. A *modal window* requires the user to respond and dismiss the window before doing anything in any other window in the application. Usually, only dialog boxes are modal, by their nature, although you can have modeless dialog boxes that continue to exist while you are doing other things in the application. A *modeless window* lets you move to another window without dismissing the first one. Often, modal windows have distinguishing characteristics such as lack of scroll bars, fixed size, and an inability to be minimized to an icon. On some platforms, the modality extends to other applications. That is, you must respond to the window and dismiss it before doing anything else in the system, not just the application (this is called *system modal* as opposed to *application modal*).

In Developer/2000 applications, the application window corresponds to the currently executing form. The main menu for the application is the menu for the form. You can also have horizontal and vertical toolbars by specifying their canvas-views as the Horizontal MDI Toolbar or Vertical MDI Toolbar properties of the form.

You can set the application window's properties programmatically in trigger code by using the name FORMS_MDI_WINDOW in the SET_WINDOW_ PROPERTY built-in procedure.

You can create a special window by creating a window named "root_window." This *root window* serves as the application window on platforms that do not directly support the MDI architecture. You can use this root window to display the *console* (the status bar that appears in the application window in Windows), the main menu, and a canvas-view with special support for the current form. For example, on Motif you could display a toolbar and menu for the current form in this window. When you call a new form, you can set up the forms Root Window property so that the new form takes over the root window and displays its content canvas-view automatically. You can also change this content view by navigating between forms.

For more details on this special feature, see the *Forms Developer's Guide* (Part Number A32505-1), Chapter 11.

Using Windows

When you create a new form, you get a new window (WINDOW0). Your first canvas-view will use this window automatically. When you want to create more windows, use the Object Navigator in the usual way: select the Windows heading and click on the Create button.

Setting Window Properties   You determine almost everything to do with a window through the properties in the Window object property sheet (Figure 7-3).

The GUI Hints (Table 7-1) section lets you set up the basic interface capabilities of the window. These are hints because not all of them apply to all platforms.

To set up the basic structure of the window, use the settings in the Functional property group (Table 7-2).

> **NOTE**
> Developer/2000 scrolls a canvas-view in a window automatically when you navigate to an item in the canvas-view that is outside the current window. You can also control scrolling through triggers with the SCROLL_VIEW built-in procedure or by setting the X or Y Position on Canvas property of the canvas view with SET_VIEW_PROPERTY.

Developer/2000 makes it easy for you to display and close windows. It controls this automatically for you through navigation. When you navigate to an item on a

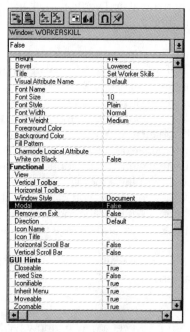

FIGURE 7-3.   *The Window property sheet*

Hint	Description
Closeable	Whether you can close the window with the platform-specific Close command
Fixed Size	Whether the height and width of the window is fixed or the user can resize the window; only valid with Zoomable set to False
Iconifiable	Whether the user can minimize the window to an icon
Inherit Menu	Whether the window displays the form menu; not valid on Microsoft Windows
Moveable	Whether the user can move the window
Zoomable	Whether the user can maximize or zoom the window with platform-specific operations; valid only if Fixed Size is False

TABLE 7-1. *GUI Hints in the Form's Window Properties*

canvas-view that is not active, Developer/2000 displays the canvas-view in its associated window. When you navigate out of the canvas-view to another canvas-view in a different window, Developer/2000 automatically closes the first one only if you have the Remove on Exit property set to True. Otherwise, the window goes to the back but still displays.

NOTE
See the following section for modal window behavior; the Remove on Exit property does not apply to modal dialogs.

You can also open and close windows in triggers by navigating with built-in navigation subprograms or with the SHOW_WINDOW and HIDE_WINDOW built-in procedures. If you do this for an inactive, displayed window behind the currently active window, Developer/2000 raises the inactive window to the top of the window stack and activates it. You can show and hide particular canvas-views in the same way, with navigation or with SHOW_VIEW and HIDE_VIEW.

Opening and Closing Modal Dialog Boxes To create a modal dialog box, set the Window Style to Dialog and set Modal to True. Create the content canvas-view and the items that constitute the dialog box, along with their block if necessary, and associate the canvas-view with the dialog box. Most dialog boxes benefit from being a fixed size, so you should also set the Fixed Size property to true and the window Width and Height properties to the size of the canvas-view. This ensures that the window displays the entire canvas-view. It is also a good idea to make the

Property	Description
View	The name of the canvas-view to display in this window as the *primary context view,* the base view that the window always displays when you open it; this is optional but can be necessary if you use SHOW_WINDOW to display the window or if you use stacked canvas-views and navigate directly to them.
Vertical Toolbar, Horizontal Toolbar	The canvas-view to display in the vertical or horizontal toolbar; see the following section, "Using Toolbars."
Window Style	The kind of window, Document or Dialog.
Modal	Whether the window is modal.
Remove on Exit	Whether to close and deactivate a modeless window when you navigate out of it to another window; valid only if Modal is False.
Direction	The direction of flow of text; the Default setting is usually what you want, as it inherits the proper direction from the NLS setup in ORACLE7; see Appendix B for details.
Icon Name, Icon Title	The name of the icon file and the title to display when the user minimizes the window; valid only if Iconifiable is true; the path and other characteristics of this icon file depend on the platform, and using icon files requires extra work to port the application to other platforms.
Horizontal Scroll Bar, Vertical Scroll Bar	Whether to display a horizontal and/or a vertical scroll bar, which lets you scroll the view over the canvas if the canvas-view is larger than the window; valid only for modeless windows.

TABLE 7-2.   *Functional Form's Window Properties*

dialog box smaller than the window or windows it will appear over; this keeps the user aware of the application's modal status.

You need to set up the displaying of the modal dialog box on the appropriate events. There are two simple ways to do this. First, you can arrange the item navigation order in such a way that the user navigates to an item on the dialog's canvas-view. You can do the navigation explicitly, without regard to navigation order, in a button trigger or menu command. In either case, Developer/2000 automatically displays the dialog box when the user navigates to the dialog item.

Second, you can call the SHOW_WINDOW built-in procedure from a button trigger or menu command. This procedure displays the window and navigates to the first item on the dialog box canvas-view.

The Modal property in Developer/2000 prevents the user from navigating out of the dialog box with the mouse. It does not, however, suspend keypresses; so the user can navigate out using the navigation keys. When you do this, Developer/2000 closes the dialog box automatically. However, this behavior is not what users expect from dialog boxes. Modal dialog boxes should remain on the screen as the active window until a positive user action to dismiss them, usually by clicking on an OK or Cancel button.

To turn off the keypress navigation keys, you have several choices:

■ You can set the Previous Navigation Block and Next Navigation Block properties for the blocks with items in the dialog box to the block itself, making navigation circular. If you do this, you should have separate blocks with all items appearing in the dialog box canvas-view.

■ You can create a Key-Others trigger to turn off all keys except those keys for which you define a key trigger. You need to minimally define Key-Next-Item and Key-Previous-Item to allow tabbing between the dialog items.

You then need to set up the triggers on the OK and Cancel buttons, or whatever alternative ways you have of instructing Developer/2000 to close the dialog box. Developer/2000 closes the dialog box automatically when you navigate out of the window with, for example, the When-Button-Pressed trigger. You must navigate to an item in a *modeless* window with its block outside the dialog canvas-view.

You can open another modal dialog box from a modal dialog box. For example, you can have an Options button that displays a second dialog box of extended options. You can also achieve some fancy effects such as having an Extended button that replaces the current dialog box with a second, larger dialog box. Experiment. Navigating to a modal dialog box item does not close the original modal dialog box item.

Using Toolbars

A toolbar is a strip of icons along the top or left side of a window. The first step is to create a toolbar canvas-view (the canvas-view types Horizontal Toolbar or Vertical Toolbar) that contains the button items and boilerplate graphics. See the preceding sections on creating canvas-views. Specify the window that will display the toolbar as the Window property for the canvas-view, and set the width and height to values that achieve the toolbar effect you want. For example, you want the width of the toolbar canvas-view for the horizontal toolbar to be the same as the window's width and the height to just encompass the icons.

The next step is to set the Horizontal Toolbar or Vertical Toolbar properties for the window object to the name of the appropriate canvas-view. This tells the window to display the toolbars in the appropriate locations.

> **NOTE**
> In Microsoft Windows, you can also display MDI application window toolbars through the Horizontal or Vertical MDI Toolbar properties of the form object. Developer/2000 ignores the Window property of the toolbar canvas-view for these toolbars.

You can have multiple toolbar canvas-views for a single window. Developer/2000 uses the standard rules for displaying these; you just navigate to the first item on the toolbar to display it instead of the original toolbar. Usually, dynamically changing toolbars are *not* a good idea, as they tend to confuse the user. You could use this feature to disable and enable tools on the toolbar by substituting a different icon for the disabled tool (dimmed, grayed, crossed out, or whatever).

Alerting

An alert is a modal window that displays a message or asks a simple question that elicits a yes-no type of response from the user. Developer/2000 has a special object for alerts to simplify programming for these very common windows.

To create an alert, select the Alerts heading in the Object Navigator and click on the Create button in the usual way.

There are three kinds of alert, which you specify with the Alert Style property in the alert's property sheet:

■ *Stop:* Displays a stop sign icon with the message

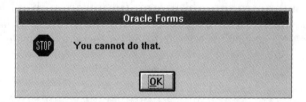

■ *Caution:* Displays an exclamation point icon with the message

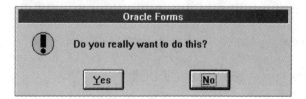

■ *Note:* Displays an information icon with the message

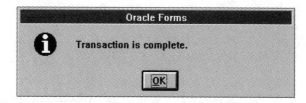

The message property lets you enter a message to display in the alert. You can enter up to 200 characters (although not all platforms can display the full number of characters).

The Button 1, Button 2, and Button 3 fields in the property sheet let you label the buttons the alert displays. If you do not enter a label, the alert does not display the button. For example, if you use the default OK and Cancel settings, you get an alert with two buttons labeled "OK" and "Cancel". If you delete the Cancel setting for Button 2, you get a single button with "OK". You must label at least one button. You also should designate one button as the default button; when the user presses [Accept], Developer/2000 selects the default button.

You display an alert from trigger code using the SHOW_ALERT function. This function returns the number ALERT_BUTTON1, ALERT_BUTTON2, or ALERT_BUTTON3 depending on which button the user selects. You can then test the returned number and take the appropriate action in your trigger code. For example, the following code prompts the user with the continue_processing_alert alert to decide whether to continue with the trigger or not. Button 1 is Yes and button 2 is No.

```
DECLARE
  alert_button NUMBER;
BEGIN
  -- Initial processing
  alert_button := Show_Alert('continue_processing_alert');
  IF alert_button = ALERT_BUTTON1 THEN
    null; -- Continue processing
  END IF;  -- do nothing for button 2
END;
```

With a bit of coding, you can create reusable alert objects and alerts that display dynamic messages that refer to specific values or objects. For example, you can create a single informational alert with just an OK button. By setting the message text at runtime, you can reuse this single object instead of creating a separate alert for each message. You could build a simple procedure in a library with this code:

```
PROCEDURE Show_Info_Alert(text VARCHAR2) IS
  alertID ALERT := Find_Alert('generic_info_alert');
  dummy NUMBER;
BEGIN
  Set_Alert_Property(alertID, ALERT_MESSAGE_TEXT, text);
  dummy := Show_Alert(alertID);
END;
```

You then just pass in a message string as the text parameter to the procedure call to display the generic_info_alert alert with that message. The procedure deliberately ignores the return code from Show_Alert.

You could also build more complex, reusable functions that accept arguments for the message, build the message text by concatenating the arguments, display the dynamic message, and return the appropriate button number. Again, you should put the function in a library for reuse in other modules.

```
FUNCTION Show_Info_Alert(text1 VARCHAR2, text2 VARCHAR2)
    RETURN NUMBER IS
  alertID ALERT := Find_Alert('generic_info_alert');
  message VARCHAR2(200);
BEGIN
  message := 'The '||text1||' is '||text2||'.';
  Set_Alert_Property(alertID, ALERT_MESSAGE_TEXT, message);
  RETURN Show_Alert(alertID);
END;
```

Menus

The menu system in Developer/2000 Forms lets you execute the different commands that make up the runtime system, such as [Next Record], [Enter Query], or [Previous Item]. Most of these commands correspond directly to keypresses, and most have built-in procedure equivalents. You can use the menu that Developer/2000 displays by default, or you can build your own custom menu to add or change commands.

Using the Default Menu

The Developer/2000 Forms system has a built-in command menu. When you execute the Runform program, if you do not define a custom menu, the system displays the default menu in Figure 7-4.

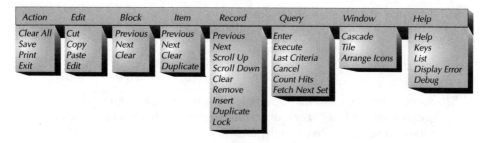

FIGURE 7-4.   *The default menu structure in Runform*

Creating Custom Menus

You cannot directly modify the default menu. If you want to customize the menu by adding some commands to the default menu items, you should copy the MENUDEF.MMB file rather than starting from scratch, as in Figure 7-5.

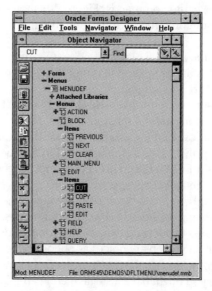

FIGURE 7-5.   *The Default Menu template file MENUDEF.MMB*

Creating Menus, Items, and Submenus

There are two kinds of objects in a menu module:

- *Menu:* The main menu, the individual menus (such as Action or Record), and submenus (hierarchical menus that pop up from a menu item).

- *Menu item:* The items on each individual menu or submenu that correspond to PL/SQL code or command text; the individual menu or submenu owns the items on the menu.

Each menu and menu item has a name that uniquely identifies it within the menu module. Menu items have, in addition, a label. The label string appears on the individual menu when you display the menu.

You should follow four guidelines in creating your menu structure.

First, any individual menu or submenu should have no more than nine separate menu items. It is a cognitive fact of life that the human brain has a hard time recognizing more than this number of things at once. Your menus will be much easier to use if you keep them short. Use submenus to gather several menu items into groups if necessary.

Second, if you do use submenus, try to keep them to one level below the individual menus on the main menu. Having deep hierarchies of nested submenus just makes it difficult to execute commands. Figure 7-6 shows the single Report submenu in the Query individual menu. It has two menu items, Ledger Summary and Mailing Labels.

Third, do not even *think* about a way to do dynamic menus that change depending on the current state of the application. This guarantees a mystified user. Menus should be stable and unchanging.

Fourth, to help the user avoid mistakes, *disable* (gray out) the menu items that do not apply given the current state of the application. For example, if you display a particular modeless window that uses some commands but not others, disable the menu items that do not apply to it or to the application as a whole. You can do this with the SET_MENU_PROPERTY built-in procedure in a trigger, specifying the menu item name and the ENABLED property.

If you find it increasingly difficult to follow these guidelines, you should move to a different kind of command interface to simplify your menus. For example, set up a group of control dialog boxes that let you execute the commands by pushing buttons, or set up dialog boxes that let you enter choices as options rather than offering each command as a separate command on the menu. Instead of listing all your reports as menu items, for example, you might have a single menu item, Query¦Run Report, and a dialog box that lets you specify which report to run with a series of radio buttons.

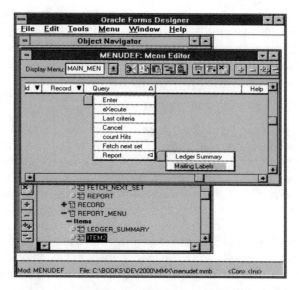

FIGURE 7-6. *The Menu Editor with one level of submenus*

You might even benefit from a graphics display that represents your command structure. Get creative to make your application easier to use.

There are three kinds of menu, only one of which this book discusses in detail:

■ *Pull-down menu:* A menu that you pull down by clicking on the individual menu name; this is the default style and the one this book uses.

■ *Full-screen menu:* A menu occupying the complete character-mode screen that lets you navigate to a command by choosing items and displaying new screens; these menus are well suited to character-mode and block-mode applications but not to GUI applications.

■ *Bar-style menu:* A menu that replaces the main menu with the individual menu items when you click on it; this kind of menu occupies only the menu bar space and never extends into the content area of the application; again, this style suits character-mode applications better than GUI ones.

If you want to know more about full-screen or bar-style menus, see the *Forms Developer's Guide* (Part Number A32505-1), Chapter 23.

Before you can use a menu, you must generate the compiled version of the menu file (an MMX file). Use the File¦Administration¦Generate menu item in the Forms Designer to generate the MMX file before attempting to run any form that uses the file. You also need to generate the MMX file after you make any changes. None of this happens automatically when you run a form.

Editing Menus

The Menu Editor shown in Figure 7-6 has several features to understand before you can fully edit your menus and menu items. The small tabs on the upper-left corner of each menu are selection tabs. Clicking on these tabs selects the menu object. You can also move a menu by clicking on the tab and dragging to the new location; control-dragging copies the menu rather than moving it. Clicking on any menu item selects that item. As with forms, you can see the properties of any object in its property sheet by choosing the Tools¦Properties menu item or by double-clicking on the object's icon in the Object Navigator. Double-clicking on a menu in the Menu Editor pulls down the menu; double-clicking on a menu item lets you edit its label. You can delete a selected object with the Delete button.

Two special buttons on the editor toolbar let you add menu items and submenus. The Create Down button lets you add a menu item to the menu under the menu item you select. The Create Right button lets you create a submenu to the right of the selected menu item. These buttons correspond to the Menu¦Create Down and Menu¦Create Right menu items.

You can change menu item names in the Object Navigator or property sheet in the usual way. (Changing the item name does not change the item label, however, and vice versa.) If you change the name, the menu looks the same in the Editor because you have not changed the label. You can change the label in the Menu Editor by double-clicking on the item or in the property sheet with the Label property.

NOTE
Interface design guidelines often tell you to place an ellipsis (three dots) after the label: "Options...", for example. You should be careful to do this only when you are displaying a dialog box that requests more information to perform the command. For example, you do not do this for submenus or for document windows that you invoke through a menu item.

There are several minor interface features that the Menu Editor adds to the preceding set. See the *Forms Developer's Guide* (Part Number A32505-1), Chapter 22, for the details.

Coding Menu Items

The Command Type property of a menu item lets you specify the kind of command you want to execute by choosing the item. See Table 7-3.

You refer to a menu item in PL/SQL using the menu name and item name in the dot-separated syntax menu_name.item_name. You can use this syntax to attach commands to menu items, initialize items, change startup code, or disable/enable menu items. Use the syntax main_menu.item_name to refer to an item on the main menu, such as Block or Query.

To create the code, double-click in the Command Text property in the property sheet for the menu item and enter the code into the resulting PL/SQL editor. Compile it and close the editor.

NOTE
If you are executing a simple, standard command that corresponds to a keypress of some kind, use the DO_KEY built-in procedure:

DO_KEY('COMMIT_FORM');

This PL/SQL code implements the Save item. Using DO_KEY lets you unify your menu items with your command keys so that you do not have to duplicate effort.

You can run an ORACLE product with the RUN_PRODUCT built-in procedure. For example, in Figure 7-7, the Ledger Summary menu item runs the Ledger Summary report. The code for this menu item would look like this:

```
RUN_PRODUCT(REPORTS, 'ledger', SYNCHRONOUS, RUNTIME, FILESYSTEM,
            NULL, NULL);
```

Value	Description
Null	Does nothing; you can use this to create a separator item or to null out a particular item for the time being.
Menu	Invokes a submenu; the command text is the submenu name.
PL/SQL	Executes a block of PL/SQL code in the command text; the code cannot directly refer to form module variables but must use NAME_IN and COPY to refer to them indirectly.
Plus, Current Forms, Macro	Do not use these compatibility choices. Use the HOST or RUN_PRODUCT PL/SQL built-in procedures to run SQL*Plus, forms, or operating system commands.

TABLE 7-3. *Menu Item Command Type Property Values*

This command runs the Runform program with the LEDGER.RDF file from the file system. It runs the report immediately (RUNTIME) instead of in batch mode, and it runs the report synchronously so that you must wait for the report to finish printing before you can continue work in the application. There are no parameters and no Graphics display.

To refer to an item value in the form to which you attach the menu, use the NAME_IN built-in function. For example, to compare the value of the WORKER block's NAME item to a specific name, you would use the following code:

```
IF Name_In('WORKER.NAME') = 'Adah Talbot' THEN
```

Similarly, use the COPY built-in procedure to assign a value:

```
COPY('Adah Talbot', 'WORKER.NAME');
```

If your PL/SQL is even moderately complex, you are better off putting the code into a separate program unit in a library that you associate with the menu module.

There is a Startup Code property for the menu module. Developer/2000 executes any code in this property when you start up the form that loads the menu. This code can do various setup tasks in the rare cases where you need to do something menu-related before displaying the form. You should rely on default property settings where you can, but sometimes you must enable different menu items depending on the platform, or something similar.

Using Special Menu Items

The Menu Item Type property lets you change the kind of menu item to display. There are five types of menu items, as shown in Table 7-4.

You can associate a command with check and radio menu items, but this produces counterintuitive effects for most uses, so you should avoid doing it.

The magic items Cut, Copy, Paste, Clear, Quit, and Window all have built-in functionality in Developer/2000, which also handles their display in the manner appropriate to the platform (position and style). You must set up command text or submenus for the other ones, such as Help, About, and Undo.

Setting Up Menus in Forms

To attach a menu to a form, generate the menu (File|Administration|Generate), select the form in the Object Navigator, then enter the menu module name in the Menu Module property of the form.

You can tell Developer/2000 when using the CALL_FORM procedure to start up a form to use the current menu instead of the menu attached to the form you are starting up. This lets different forms share a single menu in a single application.

Value	Description
Plain	The default style with just a label
Check	Displays a check mark against the label; sets the item state to TRUE or FALSE, which you can test through the GET_MENU_ITEM_PROPERTY built-in function with the CHECKED option and set through the SET_MENU_ITEM_PROPERTY procedure
Radio	Makes the item one of a set of items in a radio-button group, where choosing one item sets that item to TRUE and the rest to FALSE; again you can test the state through GET_MENU_ITEM_PROPERTY and set the state through SET_MENU_ITEM_PROPERTY
Separator	Makes the item a separator line to create visual groupings of items
Magic	One of the several special menu items: Cut, Copy, Paste, Clear, Undo, About, Help, Quit, and Window

TABLE 7-4.   *Menu Item Type Property Values*

Getting Keyed Up

There are three kinds of keypress assignments you can use in a Developer/2000 forms application: standard function keys, menu access keys, and accelerator keys.

A previous section alluded to the standard *function keys,* such as [Execute Query] or [Next Record], which you can change using the ORACLE Terminal utility (see Chapter 15). By carefully using DO_KEY in your menu PL/SQL command text, you can ensure that both a menu command and a function key have the same effects.

Most GUI platforms define a system of menu access keys. A *menu access key* is a keypress sequence (ALT-F-G, CTRL-D, COMMAND-Q, and so on) that selects a menu item without having to access the menu directly. The menu access key thus acts as a keyboard shortcut to execute the command that the menu item executes. The menu usually displays the menu access keys using a special notation that depends on the platform standards. In Windows, for example, the menu access key appears as an underlined capital letter. You execute it by a sequence of characters starting with ALT and navigating through the access keys on the menu bar and in the submenus. The Ledger Summary report menu item, for example, is ALT-Q-R-L (Query menu, Report submenu, Ledger Summary item, as shown in Figure 7-7).

You get these menu access keys without doing anything special. Developer/2000 uses the first uppercase letter, or the first letter if none is uppercase, in the label for the menu access key.

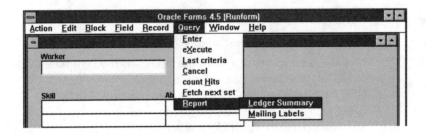

FIGURE 7-7.   *The menu hierarchy and access keys Q, R, and L*

If you have menu labels on a menu for which the above rule produces two or more menu access keys that are the same, you need to change the label to tell Developer/2000 which key to use. You can capitalize the specific letter you want to use—"rEport" instead of "Report," for example. If you do not like the funny capitalization, you can add an ampersand character in front of the letter—R&eport, for example. Developer/2000 removes the ampersand and makes the letter that follows it the menu access key. You can use a double ampersand to put a literal "&" into the menu item if you wish.

Developer/2000 also provides accelerator keys. An *accelerator key* is a key sequence you can assign to a menu item along with its menu access keys. Often, you do this to shorten the key access sequence or to attach a standard key sequence to a standard function of some kind.

Developer/2000 provides for five logical accelerator keys, [Accelerator1] through [Accelerator5], that you set up with ORACLE Terminal (Chapter 15). You can only assign five accelerator keys in any given menu module. To assign a key, find the menu item in the Object Navigator and display its property sheet. Put the logical name, such as [Accelerator3], in the Accelerator property. Then, using ORACLE Terminal, associate this logical key to a physical key sequence such as CTRL-X or SHIFT-CTRL-Y.

This chapter has completed your introduction to the advanced graphical design techniques available in Developer/2000. Using the triggers and other control features of the preceding chapter and the windows and menus you learned to customize in this chapter, you can create sophisticated GUI applications. The following chapters give you some special tools to make your design more secure, robust, and reusable.

CHAPTER 8

No Entry

Safety is one of the basic human needs. Although seemingly far removed from the realm of personal safety, a database application must provide some degree of security from harm. What you do to achieve the level of safety you desire is your application's *security policy*.

Why Be Secure?

What is the point of security? Why should you spend any time on it? Does ORACLE7 or Developer/2000 automatically guarantee the safety of your data?

Here are some things that might happen through the intentional actions of some person:

- *Unavailability:* Your system could deny service to legitimate users because someone crashes or overloads it.

- *Unaccountability:* You might become unable to account for the accuracy or legitimacy of data in an application or database because of your inability to trace the source of a data item.

- *Uncontrollability:* You might become unable to control the operation of your application, leading to an inability to guarantee the legitimacy of its results.

- *Theft:* Someone might be able to steal data or even real money or goods through forgery or fraud. This includes stealing information for intelligence.

This is not a book on computer security, a broad field with many sophisticated aspects. The point is that a lot can happen to your Developer/2000 software system if you do not protect it from harm. How can you best do that?

First, you must identify the risks that come from deliberate actions to harm your software. As with any risk, evaluate the probability of failure and its impact. For those risks you deem unacceptable, take actions that reduce the risk. This analysis lets you decide what is a security problem and what is not. You can eliminate many "security problems" by realizing that they are really not a problem. Never fall into the trap of believing that everything must be secure simply because it must.

NOTE
You should have already identified the risks that derive from unintentional acts that harm your system. An example might be the risk of an [Execute Query] that brings the system to its knees by querying huge amounts of data. Your database and application design should take such risks of technical failure into account. Security risks are a different beast.

Second, in taking action, your alternatives come down to stopping the unauthorized use of your software and stopping authorized use from leading to unauthorized use. If you believe you must ensure the safety of data through security measures, do not fool yourself: your tactics will involve preventing someone from using your software. Depending on the problem, it may even involve making your software harder to access and use for legitimate users. Again, justify the action before taking it if its consequences lower the quality of your work.

Third, you may want to extend your alternatives to forensic detection after the fact: auditing. *Auditing* is tracing events and activities in the database or in the application. Establishing an audit trail may help you simultaneously investigate and deal with any problems that arise and may prevent problems from arising by deterring intruders.

The universe of techniques for ensuring security is very broad. The following sections focus on ORACLE7 and Developer/2000, which use discretionary access control and auditing. The section following that summarizes a more secure approach—called mandatory access control—that you can use for highly secure applications.

Ultimately, the physical access that people have to your application may determine its true security. You must take physical measures as well as software measures into account in your risk analysis and management plan. For example, a security-conscious application should not be available through public telephone lines. You must limit physical access to machines running the software, including network connections.

This book does not recommend that every database application be heavily security conscious; just the reverse, in fact. A common security model is to limit access to just that necessary to doing your job (the "need-to-know approach"). Although this yields excellent security, the consequences may be chilling for ease of use. The less security overhead you impose on your users, the more usable your application will be. *You* are the ultimate judge of your security needs and how much ease of use to forfeit to meet those needs. Be as paranoid as your risk tolerance demands, but not more so.

Discretionary Access Control

Discretionary access control is the ability to control access to an application and its data through the granting of privileges to subjects (users and processes) that use the application and its data.

This section gives a summary of the different kinds of discretionary access control you have available in Developer/2000. It distinguishes standard SQL security controls from those that ORACLE7 provides in addition to the standard. It also details the different mechanisms available in Developer/2000 for imposing discretionary access control.

NOTE
Many of the security measures described in the next few sections are server based, not part of Developer/2000. The concepts are important enough, however, that this chapter deals with them in some detail. You can find more detail in books on SQL or in the ORACLE7 documentation (see the following sections for specific references).

SQL Access Control

The ANSI SQL standard provides a primitive level of access control that is the base for ORACLE7's security system. If you want to develop a database-portable application in ODBC, you may have to limit yourself to ANSI security techniques; otherwise, you should definitely use the extended facilities of ORACLE7 or whatever other database manager you want to use.

Schemas and Authorization

The ANSI security scheme starts with the schema and its accompanying authorization identifier. In ANSI SQL, the *schema* is an object that owns a specific set of tables, views, and privileges (views and privileges will be discussed presently). Any particular table, view, or privilege belongs to exactly one schema. Each schema has a name called an *authorization identifier*. This name also serves to identify a table, as different schemas can contain tables with the same name. That is, schemas provide a scope for the names of the objects they own.

In ORACLE7, these terms are equivalent to the *user* and its *user name*. ORACLE7 permits you to have a password for the schema as well (you'll learn more about this in the following section on ORACLE7 extensions).

The authorization identifier is the basic means for separating access to different parts of the database. Using this feature of SQL, you can partition the database into different schemas with differing access controls. Creative relationships between modules and schemas can produce sophisticated access control. For example, it is quite common to create the basic application data in a central schema, then create separate users for the different people who use the application, granting them the appropriate levels of access to the data.

The schema and its authorization identifier thus let you achieve the security objective of limiting access to part of the database by separating the database into sections rather than securing it as a whole.

Privileges

An ANSI *privilege* authorizes a category of action on a table or view by a specified authorization identifier. There are five actions:

- *INSERT:* Lets the grantee put new rows into the table or updateable view
- *DELETE:* Lets the grantee delete rows from the table or updateable view
- *SELECT:* Lets the grantee read rows from the table or view
- *UPDATE:* With an optional list of columns, lets the grantee change the values in the columns you specify for a table or updateable view

■ *REFERENCES:* With an optional list of columns, lets the grantee refer to the column in an integrity constraint

You define a privilege with the GRANT statement, like this:

```
GRANT <privileges> ON <table name>
TO <grantee> [{, <grantee>}...]
[WITH GRANT OPTION]
```

The ANSI security system works by associating an authorization identifier with an abstraction it calls a *module*, which contains the SQL to execute against a database. You must have granted the privileges necessary to execute the SQL statements in the module to the authorization identifier. This provides a basic level of access control for each table and view in the database.

The WITH GRANT OPTION clause lets a grantee grant the privileges to another grantee; otherwise, only the owning authorization identifier can grant privileges for an object.

ORACLE7 and the 1992 SQL standard add a REVOKE statement that drops a privilege, optionally cascading revocation from grantees of the grantee. The 1992 standard also extends privileges to all the objects it adds to the schema (domains, character sets, and so on). It adds a list of columns to the INSERT privilege along with DEFAULT values for columns. It also adds a new privilege, USAGE, for the new objects: the ability to use domains, character sets, translations, and collations.

Using schemas, you can achieve the following security objectives:

■ You can limit access to specific tables, columns, and views using privileges granted to other authorization identifiers.

■ You can limit the kind of access to those tables and views using the several types of privilege.

Views

A *view* is an object that looks like a table but is in fact a SELECT statement that defines the table. The view thus derives its data from one or more base tables or views. Certain views are not updateable—those with joins or grouping or expressions in the SELECT list, for example.

You can also use a view for security, because it can encapsulate reference to underlying tables but does not require that you have any privileges on the underlying tables when you use it. That is, you can create a base table in one schema, create a view on that base table, and grant privileges only on the view to other authorization identifiers.

With a view, you can achieve the following security objectives:

■ You can limit access to specific columns of the base table or tables through the select list of the view definition.

■ You can limit access to specific rows of the base table or tables through the WHERE clause of the view definition.

ORACLE7 Access Control

ORACLE7 extends the ANSI SQL standard in several different ways to provide a complete discretionary access control system for your database server.

See Chapters 17 and 18 of the *ORACLE7 Server Concepts Manual* (Part Number A12713-1) for a full description of the access control and auditing facilities of ORACLE7.

Authentication

Authentication is the process of confirming that the user is who he or she claims to be and hence can legitimately use the privileges granted to that user. As the previous section mentioned, ORACLE7 provides a password system along with the standard authorization identifier, which ORACLE7 calls a *user name*. ORACLE7 takes the authorization identifier one step further and adds a CREATE USER command to SQL. This command lets you create a user (and hence a schema with no objects defined in it) with a password, default and temporary tablespaces, quotas, and a profile (the following sections discuss tablespaces and profiles).

ORACLE7 provides two separate password mechanisms. The first assumes that the operating system provides a password scheme and thus disables password checking for ORACLE7 sessions.

```
CREATE USER <user name> IDENTIFIED EXTERNALLY
```

The second scheme keeps the passwords in encrypted form in the database data dictionary on the server and checks it whenever you start a session. You can use either scheme or both at once in any given database through the CREATE USER statement.

```
CREATE USER <user name> IDENTIFIED BY <password>
```

If you use EXTERNALLY, ORACLE7 uses a standard prefix, usually "OPS$", to prefix the operating system userid in ORACLE operations. You should therefore use the same prefix in the <user name> for the CREATE USER command. See the OS_AUTHENT_PREFIX initialization parameter for your particular system.

Regardless of which scheme you use, the passwords are only as good as your password-changing practices. Every user should change passwords at least once a month, if not more often. Passwords should be words or jumbles that are not

obvious (first names, and so on) and that include odd symbols ($, #, _, and so on).
Also, people should not write the passwords on yellow stickies and put them on
their terminals, and they should not tell the passwords to people passing by on the
street or post the passwords on electronic bulletin boards. Your system's
authentication security is only as good as the degree of belief (and respect) your
users put in it.

The ORACLE7 authentication scheme achieves the security objective of
authenticating the user when he or she starts up a session.

Roles

An ORACLE7 *role* is a collection of privileges. You can grant privileges directly to a
user, or you can grant a set of privileges to a role, then grant the role to the user (or
to a number of users). This object puts a level of indirection between the user and
the privilege, giving you an ability to manage very complicated privilege
combinations with many different users.

For example, Talbot could hire a new accountant and just add his or her user
name to the Accounting Role. If an application required a new table and hence
privileges on that table, Talbot would just change the privileges for the role, and all
the users for that role would get the right privileges.

To set up a role, you must first identify your security objectives. Each role
should be a coherent group of privileges that means something. For example, each
application can have a single role established for it that contains all the privileges
you need to run that application. For a complex application, you may be able to
identify several different sets of users that use an application; each of these sets of
users would get a different and perhaps overlapping set of privileges and would
thus be assigned different roles. You should really do this as part of your
application requirements analysis. If you identify different roles, you can more
easily identify the access requirements for those roles.

You can grant roles to roles, so you can combine a role with additional
privileges or other roles in a hierarchy of roles.

You can password-protect roles through an IDENTIFIED BY clause on the
CREATE ROLE statement. This permits you to require users to enable roles by
supplying the role password before they get the privileges of the role. This adds one
more layer of protection to the role but obviously doubles the difficulty of logging
on for the user. You should only password-protect roles if you have a critical risk of
some kind that justifies it.

ORACLE7 also provides a special keyword, PUBLIC, that refers to all the users
that the database currently has defined. By default, this user group provides access
to data dictionary tables. By assigning privileges to PUBLIC, you grant those
privileges to all users, which is sometimes useful. You can also create synonyms
and database links as PUBLIC synonyms or links, which means that any user can
refer to them.

The role serves the security objective of making it easier to manage a complex set of privileges, leading to a finer granularity of access control because it is much less work to maintain the security structure. This in turn satisfies the objective of limiting access to just that necessary to doing your job.

System and Object Privileges

ORACLE7 adds several different kinds of privilege to the server security system. A primary reason for the additional privileges is the extensive set of additional schema objects that ORACLE7 adds to the database besides the standard tables and views:

- *Synonym:* An alias for any object name

- *Cluster:* A storage structure for storing multiple tables together that share common information, such as tables related by a foreign key integrity constraint

- *Index:* A secondary storage structure that provides an alternative access path to data in a table

- *Sequence:* An object you can use to generate unique integers to use as primary keys

- *Procedure:* A stored PL/SQL procedure or function

- *Trigger:* A stored PL/SQL procedure you associate with a server event on a table, such as BEFORE or AFTER an UPDATE or INSERT

- *Snapshot:* A table that holds the results of a query on master tables, usually in a remote database

System privileges let you manage your schema and its operation by performing a particular action on a particular *type* of object. You may get the privilege to use the CREATE, ALTER, and DROP commands to add, change, or drop any of the different kinds of objects from your schema. Adding the keyword ANY to the privilege means that you can exercise your privilege on any schema, not just your own.

There are some specific system privileges beyond just managing schema objects. These privileges are mostly for database administration, but you may have occasion to grant them to an application role. These are explained in Table 8-1.

You can grant a system privilege only if another user has granted you that privilege with the ADMIN OPTION or if you have the GRANT ANY PRIVILEGE privilege.

An *object privilege* is the privilege to take some action on a *specific, existing object.* The matrix in Table 8-2 describes the set of privileges.

Privilege	Description
BECOME USER	Lets you import objects from any schema
BACKUP ANY TABLE	Lets you export objects from any schema
EXECUTE ANY PROCEDURE	Allows executing any function, procedure, or reference to any public package variable
FORCE [ANY] TRANSACTION	Lets you force COMMIT or ROLLBACK of your (or any) in-doubt transaction in a two-phase commit
GRANT ANY PRIVILEGE	Lets you grant any system or object privilege
GRANT ANY ROLE	Lets you grant any role to any user
SELECT/INSERT/UPDATE ANY TABLE	Lets you SELECT, INSERT, or UPDATE data in any database table
LOCK ANY TABLE	Lets you lock any database table
MANAGE TABLESPACE	Lets you take tablespaces online and offline for backups
READUP	Lets you query data with a higher access class than that of the current session (see the section "Mandatory Access Control," later in this chapter)
RESTRICTED SESSION	Lets you log on after restricting the server access mode
SELECT ANY SEQUENCE	Lets you refer to sequences
UNLIMITED TABLESPACE	Lets you override any assigned quota
WRITEDOWN	Lets you CREATE, ALTER, DROP, INSERT, UPDATE, or DELETE objects with access classes lower than the current session (see the section "Mandatory Access Control," later in this chapter)
WRITEUP	Lets you CREATE, ALTER, DROP, INSERT, UPDATE, or DELETE objects with access classes higher than the current session (see the section "Mandatory Access Control," later in this chapter)

TABLE 8-1.   *ORACLE7 System Privileges*

Privilege	Table	View	Sequence	Procedure Function Package	Snapshot
ALTER	X		X		
DELETE	X	X			
EXECUTE				X	
INDEX	X				
INSERT	X	X			
REFERENCES	X				
SELECT	X	X	X		X
UPDATE	X	X			

TABLE 8-2.   *ORACLE7 Object Privileges*

The discretionary access system works by assuming initially that no privileges exist. Therefore, you must either grant a privilege explicitly to a user or to the role of that user for that person to be able to take the action in question.

See the *ORACLE7 Server SQL Language Reference Manual* (Part Number A12714-1) or a book on ORACLE7 SQL such as Koch, Muller, and Loney's *ORACLE7: The Complete Reference* (Osborne/McGraw-Hill, 1995) for a complete discussion of the syntax of the SQL GRANT and REVOKE commands that let you assign privileges to roles and users.

Using ORACLE7 system and object privileges, you can achieve the following security objectives:

■   You can limit access to specific ORACLE7 objects of any variety using privileges granted to other users or roles.

■   You can limit the kind of access to those objects using the several types of privilege.

■   You can limit the administrative capabilities required in the practical maintenance of the database server and its databases.

Procedural Encapsulation

The EXECUTE privilege gives you an interesting alternative to granting extensive privileges to objects: *procedural encapsulation.* One limitation of the discretionary approach of users, roles, and privileges is that, being server-based, those privileges apply regardless of the mechanism by which you start a session. That is, privileges available to you when you log on through an application are just as available to you if you log on through SQL*Plus or some other program. The carefully wrought limits on visibility and execution of SQL may not apply in those environments.

If you really want to restrict the ability of users in a high-security environment, you can encapsulate the allowed behavior in a stored procedure, then grant EXECUTE privilege on the procedure to the role or user. The user does not need any privileges on the underlying objects to execute the procedure. Only you need those privileges to create the procedure itself. Thus, a user logging in through an application that runs a procedure can do the necessary things, but the same user logging in through SQL*Plus cannot do those things directly with SQL (other than running the same procedure, of course, with all the restrictions that implies).

NOTE
This discussion applies to stored triggers, as well as to procedures.

Using procedural encapsulation, you can achieve the security objective of limiting access to clearly defined behaviors encapsulated in PL/SQL procedures rather than permitting broad SQL access to the objects.

Profiles
ORACLE7 *profiles* give you a way to control the resources that a user can consume in a session. ORACLE7 establishes a default profile that applies to all users. If you set the initialization parameter RESOURCE_LIMIT to TRUE, you can then define and use additional profiles. You can use the CREATE USER statement to give a new user a specific profile, or assign profiles to existing users with the ALTER USER statement.

The CREATE PROFILE statement lets you define a profile that sets one or more limits on the resources a user can use in a session. These limits are explained in Table 8-3.

You can use the ORACLE7 auditing facilities (discussed later in this chapter in the "Auditing" section) and the SQL*DBA Monitor feature (see the *ORACLE7 Server Utilities User Guide*) to gather resource information for different kinds of users. You should then analyze the risks associated with these resources and determine what policies you need to put in place to limit your risk.

User profiles let you achieve the security objective of limiting risks associated with server interactive resource use, such as overloading or crashing applications due to resource exhaustion.

Tablespaces and Quotas
Profiles let you control interactive resources, but what about storage? The CREATE USER statement also gives you the ability to control the amount of space a user can use in the database through quotas on tablespaces.

Resource Limit	Description
SESSIONS_PER_USER	Limits the user to a specific number of concurrent sessions; you can use this, for example, to limit the number of users of a specific application if you have everyone log on to that application with the same user name
CPU_PER_SESSION	Limits the amount of CPU time a session can use
CPU_PER_CALL	Limits the amount of CPU time a particular parse, execute, or fetch call can use
CONNECT_TIME	Limits the elapsed time of a session
IDLE_TIME	Disconnects the session when the session remains idle for a specified amount of time (not counting time during execution of a query)
LOGICAL_READS_PER_SESSION	Limits the number of blocks the session can read from the database
LOGICAL_READS_PER_CALL	Limits the number of blocks the session can read from the database during a parse, execute, or fetch call
COMPOSITE_LIMIT	Limits the total cost of a session in composite units
PRIVATE_SGA	Limits the amount of space a session can allocate in the SGA as private space

TABLE 8-3. *ORACLE7 Profile Resource Limits*

A *tablespace* (CREATE TABLESPACE) is a set of operating system files and a storage specification that applies to the creation of tables, indexes, and clusters on disk.

A *quota* is a limit on the amount of space a user can create in a particular tablespace.

Using tablespaces, you can partition your data into specific parts of the physical database. Using the various CREATE statements, you can create objects belonging to users in specific tablespaces. Using quotas, you can then limit the amount of data that a particular user can create in that specific tablespace for those objects he or she creates in the tablespace.

For example, this statement creates the Talbot user with a quota on his default tablespace:

```
CREATE USER Talbot IDENTIFIED BY George
DEFAULT TABLESPACE LocalTables
QUOTA 5M ON LocalTables
PROFILE CentralAdministration;
```

Quotas let you achieve the objective of limiting risks associated with consumption of physical storage resources.

Client Security

Column update controls and menu access controls give your Developer/2000 forms some needed security. The former lets you control the updating of columns through Developer/2000. The latter uses the custom menu features to let ORACLE7 roles enable and disable menu items.

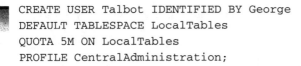

> **NOTE**
> Both of these features depend on ORACLE7. If you have a requirement for database portability, neither of these features is relevant.

Column Updating

The section on the logon process in Chapter 6 detailed the process of starting up a form. Part of that process was enforcing column security.

The Update Allowed property of a *block* lets you control whether the user can update block records. Updating a record implies querying the record, then changing one or more items. If you set Update Allowed to False, the user can query records but cannot change them.

The Update Allowed property of an *item* lets you control the updating of a particular column in a record. If you set the block property to True, you can set one or more of the item properties to False to stop the user from being able to change that item's value. The Update If Null property of an item lets you control the updating of NULL values. False means that the user cannot supply a value if the value is NULL.

These features achieve the objective of preventing changes to table rows or values through a particular block in a form. You can set these properties when you design the form. You can also change them through PL/SQL calls in triggers at runtime.

Developer/2000 can do some of this work for you through the column security feature. You can set the Column Security property of the form to True. When a user logs on to a form, Developer/2000 queries the data dictionary for the update privileges on tables and columns in the form's blocks. It sets the Update Allowed property to False for any column for which the user does not have UPDATE privilege. If you use this feature, you can take advantage of the privileges you have set up on the server.

Menu Access Controls

There is no room in this book to go into detail on the custom menu features of Developer/2000. Please see the *Forms Developer's Guide* (Part Number A32505-1), Chapter 23, for complete details on customizing menus. This section presents a summary of developing menu access controls.

If you create your own menus, you can use a special feature of Developer/2000 menu customization to disable menu items through ORACLE7 security roles. There is even a dialog box for setting up security roles and granting those roles to specific user names from within Developer/2000 (File¦Administration¦Database Roles menu item).

Once you've defined the roles, go to the menu module in the Object Navigator and select the Menu Module Roles property in the menu property sheet. Open the dialog box by clicking on the More button. You can now enter the roles that you want to control menu access for this module.

Now, select the menu item in the Object Navigator that you want a role to control. You can access the Menu Item Roles dialog box through the property sheet for the menu item. This dialog box lets you toggle the roles that enable the menu item. When you select a role, it means that a user granted that role sees the menu item enabled in his or her menu bar, but a user not granted that role sees the menu item disabled. The Display Without Privilege flag controls whether Developer/2000 disables the menu item or removes it completely.

Finally, to make everything happen, set the Use Security flag to True in the menu property sheet.

The menu access control features of Developer/2000 thus give you some additional tools with which to make your system more secure.

Auditing

Auditing is the process of investigating the activities of a database system and its users. You can monitor database activities, then trace them back to their origin or collect statistics on them. You can also record historic information to make sure you can always reconstruct a chain of events. The information you record (regardless of the type of information it is) is called the *audit trail*.

Auditing in ORACLE7

ORACLE7 provides extensive auditing facilities.

■ *Statement auditing:* The tracing of statements of a particular type for one or more users

■ *Privilege auditing:* The tracing of actions relating to specific system privileges for one or more users

■ *Object auditing:* The tracing of specific statements on a particular schema object for all users of the database

All of these options let you store the audit trail in a table, AUD$, that belongs to the SYS user. You access the information through data dictionary views. See the *ORACLE7 Server Administrator's Guide* for details on this data dictionary support for auditing.

Auditing is a way for you to check whether your security policy is having its desired effects. If you identify specific risks that you regard as sufficiently serious, you can audit the actions that might cause the system to fail. If it does fail, you can then identify the sequence of actions that caused the failure, or you can trace the failure to its possibly illegitimate source and deal with that source. You can also isolate the failures by locating them in the audit trail. You can audit only successful or unsuccessful statements, if that is appropriate. How often have you confronted a problem with little information about its context? Auditing can provide that context.

You can best understand the impact of auditing by studying the different options and experimenting with them to understand how they apply to the security problems in your particular application.

Auditing lets you achieve the overall objective of ensuring that you meet your other security objectives.

Client Audit Trails

ORACLE7 lets you audit the database activity, but it has no way to extend auditing to the meaningful events in your client application. Depending on your security issues, you may want to build additional auditing into your application.

One broad area is *application auditing.* This is the standard practice of maintaining transaction histories as part of the application data. For example, in an accounting application, you must ensure that an audit trail exists for all data changes. You must always be able to reconstruct a given value as it was at a given time, no matter what has happened to that value in the database. You must also be able to relate each object to its real-world counterpart; for example, an inventory record to the actual inventory item on a shelf. All of these requirements need to be explicit in the database design for the application.

You can also have requirements based on specific security issues; this is called *issue auditing.* For example, there may be some transactional issue that is so vital to your application that you want to verify that the transaction is legitimate and successful under all circumstances by storing traces of the transaction in separate audit trails. This is approximately what ORACLE7 does, but it applies to the meaningful events in your application, not to the server events that ORACLE7 auditing supports.

Generally, because of the sensitive nature of this kind of audit trail, you will want to encapsulate the auditing and the trace tables in separate database schemas and procedures so that clients cannot interfere with the auditing process. See the preceding sections on authorization, authentication, and procedural encapsulation.

Mandatory Access Control

Mandatory access control is a security system that puts much stronger controls on access to objects in the database by associating a security label with each object and with each session. The labels provide a classification scheme that permits the server to judge whether to grant access to the object based on the level in the classification rather than on specific privileges.

Why would such a scheme be necessary? Under discretionary access control, data is just data. If you move data somewhere else, the privileges on that data come from the place it is, not from the data itself. For example, if a user has SELECT privilege on a table without GRANT option, the user can still copy the data to another table he or she has created with the same structure, and can then grant others access to this table. There are many similar situations that limit the ability of discretionary access control to manage security risks.

Mandatory access control deals with most of these issues by associating the security constraint with the data. When you copy the data, you also copy the security constraint. You can do this with privileges, but it is much easier to handle through a security-level classification scheme.

Trusted ORACLE7

ORACLE7 provides a mandatory access control scheme that makes ORACLE7 conform to the US B1 TCSEC criteria and the E3 assurance level for the European ITSEC standard. This is an optional product called Trusted ORACLE7. It only works on operating systems that provide similar features with similar conformance to security standards. Windows and Macintosh cannot be Trusted ORACLE7 servers, for example.

See the *Trusted ORACLE7 Server Administrator's Guide* (Part Number A12851-1) for details on the mandatory access control scheme in Trusted ORACLE7. The following gives you a summary of how all this works.

Each label in this scheme has a classification component, a category component, and a marking component.

The Classification Component

A *classification* is a hierarchical level that identifies that sensitivity of the labeled information. You define the classifications and orders at the operating system level. Some examples: TOP SECRET, SECRET, SENSITIVE, and UNCLASSIFIED.

The Category Component

A *category* is a division within a classification that regionalizes the classification. This permits you to restrict access to particular areas, even within the classification scheme. For example, you could have categories for each project, breaking up classifications by project. Only those sessions with labels containing the project category could see information relating to the project.

The Marking Component

A *marking* is a further piece of information that gets associated with the data under different circumstances. You could mark a particular object as PROPRIETARY, for example, and your applications could ensure that printing always marks PROPRIETARY objects with a specific warning about dissemination.

The mandatory access control mechanism works by comparing the object label to the session label you establish through your operating system security clearance when you log on the session. This comparison works through the process of domination: one label *dominates* another if its classification is greater than or equal to that of the other label, and its categories are a superset of the other's categories. The label strictly dominates another if it dominates but does not match the other label. The label is noncomparable if neither label dominates the other due to differences in the categories and classification. Your *security clearance* is the range of labels for which you are authorized to read and write information. You can read an object only if your label dominates the label of the object, and you can write to an object only if your label *matches* that of the object.

There are several ORACLE7 system privileges that get around these constraints:

- ■ *READUP:* Lets you read data with a label that strictly dominates your label

- ■ *WRITEUP:* Lets you write data with a label that strictly dominates your label

- ■ *WRITEDOWN:* Lets you write data with a label that your label strictly dominates

See the earlier section, "Discretionary Access Control," on ORACLE7 discretionary access controls through system and object privileges for the context of these privileges.

To summarize, if you need serious security, the government or other customer will almost certainly require that your application conforms to B1 or other security standard. The combination of operating system and Trusted ORACLE7 may make it possible to use Developer/2000 to develop such applications. Note, however, that Developer/2000 must run on the Trusted operating system to conform to the security standard.

Keeping Talbot's Safe

As an example of using Developer/2000 and ORACLE7 security, this section considers the development of Talbot's security policy from start to finish. The example is very simple; a real security policy would be much more extensive.

Talbot's Security Risks

There are several possible security risks that the risk analysis of Talbot's computer operations identifies.

The major risks of system intrusion and intelligence gathering do not exist for Talbot's. Talbot's isolates its database physically with no access other than through the farm workstations, which the Talbots keep in locked offices around the farm. There is an exposure to intrusion through the local area network, as it is accessible in unsecured areas, but the impact analysis shows that even the impact of a full system failure would be minimal. The risk assessment team in this case decided that daily backups stored in a secure location and a disaster recovery policy were sufficient to handle any risk of system failure due to intrusion. They also decided that the impact of information leaked to competitors was very low and did not require extraordinary measures to protect data from unauthorized access.

Because Talbot's uses an operating system that provides no security, the risk assessment team decided to rely on database server security: ORACLE7 user names and passwords.

The risks relating to the database contents include the three following possibilities:

- Corrections or changes to ledger entries could lead to auditing problems, which could in turn lead to problems with tax audits and corporate audits.

- There is a regulatory requirement that worker's addresses be kept private; the risk is of regulatory penalty or employee lawsuit if an address becomes available through inadvertent information leakage or lack of security measures.

- Talbot's experience with maintaining a skills database suggests that giving full access to everyone will likely result in inaccuracies in the database, rendering it useless.

The risk assessment team considered two possibilities for managing corrections to the ledger. The first was to maintain an audit trail by double-recording all updates to the database ledger. The advantage to this would be that the ledger would always be as correct as possible, while auditors could reconstruct the history of changes from the audit trail. The second possibility would be to require corrections to be separate ledger entries, correcting entries. The advantage to this approach would be reduced complexity, reduced system overhead, and ease in auditing. (The second approach is a standard one in accounting practices.) The team decided to disallow updates to ledger entries and to require that all corrections be through additional ledger entries. As additional security, the team decided to separate the Ledger table from the other tables into a password-protected schema.

The risk assessment team noted that part of accounting's job was to maintain the accounts payable information in the Person table. This did not extend to managing addresses (addresses will be discussed shortly).

The risk assessment team decided to separate the Lodging table into a separate schema to make it as secure as possible from intrusion. Only authorized individuals in human resources would have access to this data.

The remaining tables (Person, Skill, WorkerHasSkill) all reside in a single schema, with human resources having manipulation access and all others having query access only.

Talbot's ORACLE7 Security Architecture

Figure 8-1 shows the original entity-relationship diagram with the additional schema constraints as dashed boxes around the tables in different schemas. Each schema corresponds to a specific ORACLE7 user name and password.

Each actual user of the system will have an ORACLE7 account with a distinct password. The security team recommended standard password maintenance procedures (changing passwords once a month, and so on).

The roles associated with these requirements are straightforward:

- *Accounting:* Needs to be able to query and insert ledger entries but not to update or delete them; needs to be able to query entries in the Person table; needs to be able to query, insert, update, and delete from the Person table, but cannot delete or update entries for individuals with addresses.

- *Address:* Owns and manages the private address table.

- *HR Skills:* Needs to be able to insert, update, and delete skills and relationships between people and skills.

- *HR Personnel:* Needs to be able to insert, update, and delete information from the Person table.

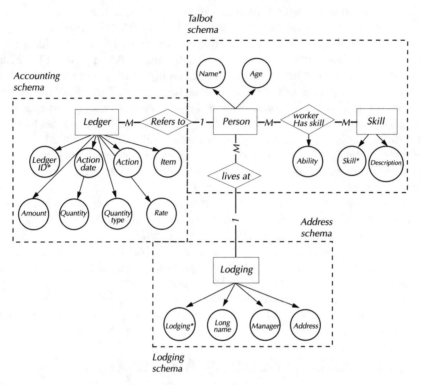

FIGURE 8-1. *Security schemas for Talbot's database*

Besides these roles, there is the standard DBA role that Talbot assumes to create the schemas, users, roles, privileges, and so on.

To set up the database, Talbot logs onto ORACLE7 through SQL*Plus as SYSTEM and executes the following six statements:

```
CREATE USER Talbot IDENTIFIED BY FT3R$27SD;
GRANT CONNECT, RESOURCE TO Talbot;
CREATE USER Accounting IDENTIFIED BY TYB##5X$5;
GRANT CONNECT, RESOURCE TO Accounting;
CREATE USER Lodging IDENTIFIED BY M45C$BHI_9Z;
GRANT CONNECT, RESOURCE TO Lodging;
```

Talbot then connects to each account and creates the schema for the account by running a script with the CREATE SCHEMA statement. To avoid complicated series of CREATE and ALTER TABLE statements, you need to create the tables in the order that permits you to refer to tables already created in another user in foreign key integrity constraints.

First, create the Lodging schema:

```
CREATE SCHEMA AUTHORIZATION Lodging
CREATE TABLE Lodging (
Lodging        VARCHAR(15) PRIMARY KEY, /* short name for lodging */
LongName       VARCHAR(40),             /* complete name */
Manager        VARCHAR(25),             /* manager's name */
Address        VARCHAR(30)              /* address of the lodging */
);
GRANT REFERENCES ON Lodging to Talbot;
```

This last statement grants the REFERENCES privilege to the Talbot user to make a foreign key reference to the Lodging table in the Person table. Now, create the Talbot schema:

```
CREATE SCHEMA AUTHORIZATION Talbot
CREATE TABLE Skill (
Skill          VARCHAR(25) PRIMARY KEY, /* name of a capability */
Description    VARCHAR(80)              /* description of the skill */
)
CREATE TABLE Person (
Name           VARCHAR(25) PRIMARY KEY,      /* worker's name */
Age            INTEGER,                      /* age in years */
Lodging        VARCHAR(15) REFERENCES Lodging.Lodging
                          /* reference to short name of lodging */
)
CREATE TABLE WorkerHasSkill (
Name           VARCHAR(25) REFERENCES Person, /* worker's name */
Skill          VARCHAR(25) REFERENCES Skill,  /* capability name */
Ability        VARCHAR(15),             /* how skilled is the worker? */
PRIMARY KEY (Name, Skill)
);
GRANT REFERENCES ON Person TO Accounting;
```

As before, this last statement allows the Accounting user to make a foreign key reference to the Person table from its Ledger table. Also, notice that the foreign key REFERENCES clause in the Person table uses the authorization identifier Lodging to prefix the name of the table Lodging. Finally, create the Accounting schema, along with the LedgerSequence for the Ledger primary key values:

```
CREATE SEQUENCE LedgerSequence /* sequence numbers for Ledger */
;
CREATE SCHEMA AUTHORIZATION Accounting
CREATE TABLE Ledger (
LedgerID        INTEGER PRIMARY KEY,/* sequence number, primary
key */
ActionDate      DATE,               /* when */
Action          VARCHAR(8),         /* bought, sold, paid,
received */
Item            VARCHAR(30),        /* what */
Quantity        INTEGER,            /* how many */
QuantityType    VARCHAR(10),        /* quantity: lbs, bushels,
etc. */
Rate            NUMERIC(9,2),       /* how much per quantity type
*/
Amount          NUMERIC(9,2),       /* rate * quantity */
Person          VARCHAR(25) REFERENCES Talbot.Person /* who */
);
```

With all the users and tables set up, you can now set up the roles with their privileges. The SYSTEM user is the DBA, which already has all the needed privileges. Connect to SYSTEM to create the roles:

```
CREATE ROLE AccountingRole;
CREATE ROLE AddressRole;
CREATE ROLE  HRSkillsRole;
CREATE ROLE HRPersonnelRole;
```

Now connect to the Accounting user to grant privileges on Ledger to the Accounting role:

```
GRANT SELECT, INSERT ON Ledger TO AccountingRole;
```

Now connect to the Talbot user to grant privileges on the Person, Skill, and WorkerHasSkill tables:

```
GRANT SELECT, INSERT, UPDATE, DELETE ON Person to AccountingRole;
GRANT SELECT, INSERT, UPDATE, DELETE ON Skill to HRSkillsRole;
GRANT SELECT, INSERT, UPDATE, DELETE ON WorkerHasSkill to
HRSkillsRole;
GRANT SELECT, INSERT, UPDATE, DELETE ON Person to HRPersonnelRole;
```

NOTE
Discretionary access control cannot use privileges to enforce the restriction of the Accounting role not being able to update users with addresses; you will have to enforce this constraint in database triggers. You could do this by creating a separate view that excludes those rows with a WHERE clause. That solution, however, does not allow the application to see those names, which violates another requirement to be able to query all the names. You could use the view for updating and the underlying table for querying, but this is hard to do given how Developer/2000 blocks work. You would have to have two separate blocks, one for query purposes and the other for query/update purposes.

Finally, connect to the Lodging user and grant privileges on the Lodging table to the Address role:

```
GRANT SELECT, INSERT, UPDATE, DELETE ON Lodging to AddressRole;
```

Now, having created all the roles with all the required privileges, you can create the individual users and grant them their roles. For example, to set up an accounting user, connect to SYSTEM in SQL*Plus and issue the following statements:

```
CREATE USER User1 IDENTIFIED BY JU8##NMY78$;
GRANT CONNECT TO User1;
GRANT AccountingRole TO User1;
```

Talbot's Application Security

The Ledger form must satisfy the requirement of not being able to update or delete rows in the Ledger table. Through the AccountingRole security role, the ORACLE7 database enforces this restriction. If you try to update a value or delete a row in Ledger, you will get an error when you save the changes to the database because the SQL statements will fail.

Although this solves the problem, it is not as well designed as it might be. One principle of a good interface is to give immediate feedback when you make a mistake. Relying on database security gives you feedback only when you save, not when you actually change a value or delete a record. To enforce this constraint with more immediacy in the interface, you need to put a little extra code in the application.

To address the first issue, updating, all you need do is turn off the Update Allowed flag in the Ledger block. This will stop users from updating any values queried from the database. Figure 8-2 shows the property sheet through which you change this value.

NOTE
You could alternatively set the Column Security flag in the module to True, but in this case the Update Allowed flag on the block seems more direct.

Having dealt with updates, what about deletes? There is no specific flag to disable deletes, so you must do it by disabling the [Delete Record] key through the Key-Delrec trigger for the block.

Create a new Key-Delrec trigger in the Object Navigator by selecting the Triggers heading and clicking on the Create button. Figure 8-3 shows the LOV dialog box with the trigger name selected.

In the trigger, you merely need to raise an alert telling the user that he or she cannot delete records from the Ledger table. First, create the alert by selecting the Forms¦LEDGER¦Alerts heading in the Object Navigator and clicking on the Create button. Enter the message as shown in Figure 8-4.

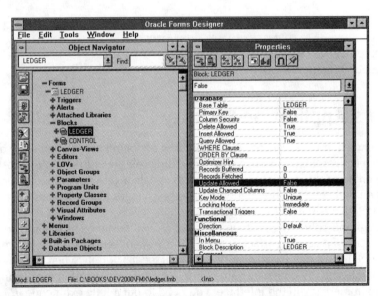

FIGURE 8-2. *The Ledger block property sheet with Update Allowed set to False*

FIGURE 8-3.   *The LOV dialog box showing the Key-Delrec trigger selected*

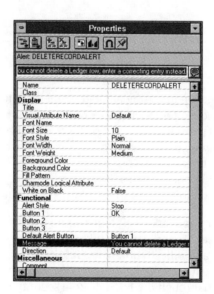

FIGURE 8-4.   *The Alert property sheet for the Delete-Record alert*

The code in the procedure editor for the Key-Delrec trigger that raises the alert is as follows:

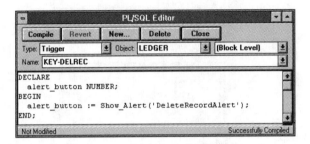

The actual alert that you'll see when you try to delete a record in the Ledger block is as follows:

NOTE

An alternative to raising an alert might be to turn off the menu and key methods of removing a record (that is, the Record￤Remove menu item and the standard keypress for [Delete Record]). This would yield a better interface by refusing to permit the action at all, but the work involved (creating custom menus and so on) seems out of proportion to the additional benefits. If you already have your own menus and keypress definitions for these items, you should change them there.

In developing other applications, Talbot's could use the menu security system to configure the menus in its applications differently based on the ORACLE7 roles. Space does not permit a full illustration here, but one example of this might be for the Skills form to have data manipulation menu items (such as Create Record or Delete Record) enabled through the HRSkillsRole security role and disabled through the other roles.

In summary, Developer/2000, working in conjunction with ORACLE7, gives you strong security tools. Using them takes some thought and careful preparation, but when you finish you will be able to sleep at night, knowing that your applications are as secure as you can make them.

CHAPTER 9

Advanced Design for Reuse

This last chapter in Part Two deals with several topics relating to advanced design of applications. When you have mastered triggers and processes and understood the basic operations of forms, reports, and graphics, you are ready to optimize your architecture. Developer/2000 provides several tools by which you can make your applications adapt more easily to changes in the environment or to the differing needs of multifarious users.

Recycling: Everyone Should Do It

Reusability is the ability to use objects in different contexts. This translates directly into increased productivity through reducing the amount of code you must build for each new requirement you undertake. The more code you can reuse in new applications, the less time, effort, and money it will take to produce the new applications.

There are three key elements in building reusable code: usefulness, compatibility, and safety.

Every Developer/2000 object provides some functionality; the degree to which that functionality is *useful* is the extent to which you will want to reuse the functionality in other applications. If you design your objects for optimum utility, you will make them more reusable by making designers and developers want to use the features. Part of this is a selling job: your objects must have the documentation and "public relations material" that will let designers and developers know what the object does for them. The rest of the job is to make the object as flexible as possible, given constraints on the way your particular system works and the cost of building and testing the object. The following sections give you some tools to increase flexibility throughout your Developer/2000 code.

One of the strongest benefits of Developer/2000 is its object-based nature. Because each application comprises a set of objects, and because the developer interface builds on the objects and makes it easy to reuse them, Developer/2000 encourages you to build compatible objects. *Compatibility* is the ability to use a given object in a context other than that for which you designed it. For example, if you can drag an object from one module to another without change and have it work, the object is compatible with the new module. As with any software system, you can find ways to make objects incompatible, and some objects are essentially incompatible for reasons often beyond your control. Developer/2000 gives you some tools that make the job of reusing compatible code much easier. If you follow the recommendations in the following sections, you should be able to optimize your ability to reuse objects in different applications.

Finally, *safety* is the degree to which you trust an object to function properly when you reuse it. Trust comes down to two things: documentation and testing. If you are not sure what an object does, you will not be sure how it will work in your application. You will not trust the object to function correctly when you reuse it. Therefore, documentation is critical to your willingness to trust an object for reuse. The flip side of this trust, once you know what the object has contracted to do, is to know that it delivers on its contract. Testing ensures that the object meets some objective criteria for correctness. See Chapter 12 for a thorough discussion of unit and integration testing for Developer/2000 objects.

The following sections summarize or introduce the elements of Developer/2000 that contribute to reuse in major ways. You should also consult Chapter 11 for approaches to packaging functions and procedures for reuse in different modules.

Modules

Developer/2000 structures its operations around a few major objects, which you have already seen in action. These are the Developer/2000 modules:

- *Form:* A module that contains blocks, records, and items that represent an interactive database application for presenting data in forms

- *Menu:* A module that contains menus and menu items that represent the interface to a set of command actions

- *Report:* A module that contains a data model and a layout for a report that you can generate from data in the database

- *Display:* A module that contains one or more charts or other graphics and one or more queries that represents a graphical display of data from the database

- *External query:* A query you build using the Reports Designer to which you can refer in other modules

- *Library:* A library of PL/SQL code you build using the Forms, Reports, or Graphics Designers, to which you can refer in other modules

Various chapters of this book thoroughly discuss the form, report, and display modules. For more information about menu modules, see the *Forms Developer's Guide* (Part Number A32505-1), Chapters 22 and 23. There is a brief discussion of this in the "External Queries" section in this chapter and an extensive introduction to libraries in Chapter 11.

As you design your modules, you should think about them as *reusable components* of applications, not just as standalone applications. If you design your components in such a way that you can use them in other applications, you will optimize reusability in your development life cycle.

The key to module reusability is to *decouple* the modules as much as possible from their environment. *Coupling* is the degree to which a module uses data and operations external to the module. Here are some guidelines for decoupling modules.

Where possible, do not use variables from outside the module, such as global variables or variables in other modules. The more you use such variables, the less likely are you to be able to reuse the module in different contexts. Also, it is hard to predict how other modules will use shared variables, so using them when interacting with other modules is likely to produce unpleasant surprises. A good alternative to using global variables is to create a package that exports a variable object. When you refer to a package attached to your module, Developer/2000 loads the package into memory for the duration of the session. This means you can use the variable from anywhere in the module, but nothing outside the module can access it. These variables are also an alternative to using the global parameters and can be faster to access under some conditions. Chapter 11 has more details on using packages.

Try to isolate application-specific or platform-specific components in procedures or libraries to decouple your module from the underlying dependencies on a specific application or platform. For example, if you only need certain text on screen in a specific application, do it in a procedure you call from an instance trigger. If you want application-specific help, put it in a PL/SQL library and switch the library for different applications.

Avoid boilerplate text (text hard-coded into the canvas-view, report, or display) that ties the object into a specific application. Minimize the use of titles and especially help text in boilerplate. Use generic terminology, and use the database table and column names where possible instead of the application version. You can always modify it if it really does not work, and you can do some things to parameterize those parts of the application that need to be application specific. See the following sections.

If you use many PL/SQL procedures and functions, cluster these procedures and functions into packages and libraries with high cohesion. Design your modules in layers and subsystems that minimize the connections between each other. The more connections you make between layers through inadequate structuring, the less likely you are to be able to decouple a module for partial reuse elsewhere. Also, the more you hide the functionality of your module in layers, the easier it will be for developers and designers to understand what your module does. The top layer will speak for the complex interactions hidden within the module.

Templates

If you cannot reuse modules because they are too application specific, you can at least get some mileage from abstracting various elements into templates. A *template* is an object that you can use to format a module with basic options or contents. If you have standards and development guidelines, build them into templates that you can reuse in building modules. You can create a form, report, or display module, for example, that has all the standard settings that represent your standards and guidelines. Then developers can copy that module as a template to start developing their own forms. Chapter 6 discusses the Graphics template, which lets you format charts within display modules.

The design of the original Talbot prototypes did not take reusability into account. By the second or third round of design, the architects should start looking at the forms, reports, and graphics to see whether they can improve the design for reusability. For example, it may be possible to build the forms so you can combine them into different applications. There may be some applications that require a form for entering ledger information and a form for entering information about buyers and sellers. There may be other applications that require the same form for entering information about people (workers) and their skills. With a little creative rearranging, you could build a form to accept information about people and use it unchanged in both applications. Another example is the graphics. You could build a set of standard displays that you could reuse in different applications as required by linking through chart items. The report and form prototypes, for example, reused the graphics prototypes.

Modules and templates are the basic building blocks of Developer/2000. The more reusable you make your modules, and the more you can use standard templates, the more productive will be your development process.

If you start using Graphics extensively, you will find yourself doing the same kind of chart over and over again. You might also find yourself building many charts that look identical, such as drill-down charts or multiple-chart displays. Instead of individually customizing each chart, you should build a custom chart template that formats all the charts with similar characteristics.

Setting up chart templates is as easy as setting up charts. Start up the Graphics Designer, open a display, and find the Templates category in the Object Navigator. (It is right under the Layout category for the display.) Select the category and click on the Create button or use the Navigator¦Create menu entry to create a new template (template0). Figure 9-1 shows the resulting Chart Template Editor.

The editor shows the frame editor with its *frame template,* which contains the title, axis labels, and legend position, set up for a column chart. Using the Type menu, you can select any of the over 50 default templates (line charts, column charts, bar charts, pie charts, Gantt charts, scatter charts, or tables, for example).

You can move around or change any of the frame elements in this editor. For example, you can select all the elements and change the font to Arial 10 Bold instead of using the system font. By double-clicking on any element, you can set various parameters to make the chart frame appear any way you want.

You can have one frame template in each chart template, but you can have multiple field templates. A *field template* is a specification for the display characteristics of a particular set of data in the chart. You can associate a different field template with different columns in the query to display the data from each column using a particular style. This lets you set up a standard set of line and fill colors, fonts, symbols, or any other characteristic of a data element display. Figure 9-2 shows the default field template for a column chart.

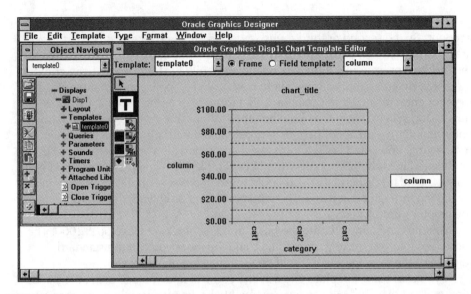

FIGURE 9-1. *The Chart Template Editor with frame template*

You can assign a particular chart template to a chart through the Chart property sheet. Double-click on the chart object in the Object Navigator. The Template field

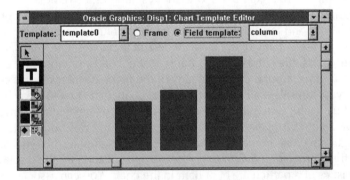

FIGURE 9-2. *The Chart Template Editor with field template*

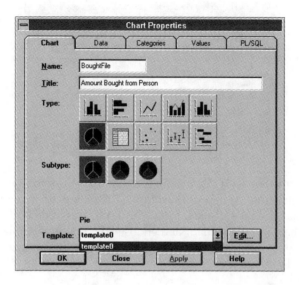

FIGURE 9-3.   *The Chart property sheet with chart template pull-down list*

at the bottom of the Chart tab (Figure 9-3) lets you pull down a list of the available chart templates, and the chart reconfigures according to the template when you click on OK.

You can assign a particular field template to a column through the Values tab of the Chart property sheet (Figure 9-4). Select the column you want to format, then pull down the list of available field templates and assign the one you want to that column.

If you experiment with the template capabilities of Developer/2000, you will find it much easier to develop large numbers of graphics using your graphics standards. Your goal in developing templates is to reduce the amount of custom work you need to do for a particular chart to just the changes that chart requires (such as the Other pie slice in the Talbot pie charts). Things such as fonts and colors should be standard, not decided on a chart-by-chart basis.

To get the maximum use from your templates, you should export them into separate template files. Select the template you want to export in the Object Navigator, then choose the Edit¦Export¦Template menu item. This displays the Export dialog box.

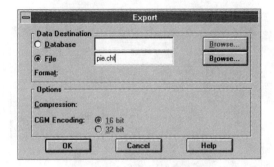

Just enter a filename (PIE.CHT, for example) and click on OK to save the template in some central directory. When you want to use the template in another display, import the template into the display. Select the Templates node under the display or display the Chart Template editor and choose Edit｜Import｜Template to display the Import dialog box, which is very similar to the Export dialog box. Find the file and click on OK to import the template.

External Queries

An *external query* is a text file that contains a SQL SELECT statement. You can refer to this external query from the data model of any report. By separating the query into a module, you are making the query reusable by different reports.

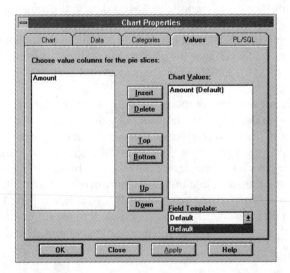

FIGURE 9-4. *The Chart property sheet with field template pull-down list*

NOTE
The Developer/2000 documentation consistently refers to this as an ANSI-standard SELECT; but Reports does not enforce this restriction on the SQL, and the presence of ORACLE7 comments and other elements seems to indicate that the query can be any SQL query.

When you build a report data model, think hard about the queries you are creating and see whether you can build them as external queries that would be useful in other applications.

Creating and Using an External Query

To create an external query, locate and select the External Query heading in the Object Navigator and click on the Create button to create an Untitled external query. Double-click on the external query icon to display the External Query Definition editor. Figure 9-5 shows the editor with the query from the ledger report from Chapter 5.

After you enter the query, close the editor and select the UNTITLED object in the Object Navigator. Save it to a file by clicking on the Save button, and giving the file the extension .SQL, such as LEDGER.SQL.

To use the query, you must enter the query name into the External Query field in the query that belongs to the data model for a report. For example, replace the internal query in the LEDGER report with the newly created LEDGER.SQL query. You do this by opening up the Query property sheet and double-clicking on the query Reports⎮LEDGER⎮Data Model⎮Queries⎮LEDGERQUERY icon. You can use the Browse button next to the External Query field to find the query you want to insert. Figure 9-6 shows the property sheet with the External Query field filled in. You should use just the filename for the query and rely on the path in the initialization variable REPORTS25_PATH to identify the directory in which you store the file. You can then move the file around to different file systems and different platforms without having to redo your Query property sheet entries.

NOTE
Once you make the query refer to an external query, you cannot edit the query in the property sheet, even though it displays it in the normal manner. You must select the external query object and edit it by double-clicking on its icon. When you click on OK to dismiss the property sheet, Developer/2000 parses the query and reports any problems.

Now that you have defined the external query, you can refer to it from any report. For example, if you wanted to create a new report based on the ledger query but with different layout, different summarization and grouping, and so on, you could build the new data model and refer to the external query in the Query property sheet just as in the previous example.

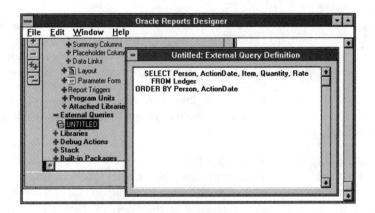

FIGURE 9-5. *The External Query Definition editor*

Lexical References and Bind Variables

Sometimes, as with any piece of code, you could make the query reusable by parameterizing it. That is, if you could specify a placeholder in the query and replace it at runtime with a value, you could use the query in more places.

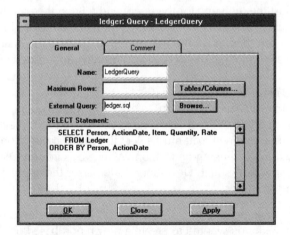

FIGURE 9-6. *The Query property sheet for LedgerQuery*

There are two ways to do this in Developer/2000. You can use lexical references to replace chunks of text in the SQL statement, or you can include bind variables in the SQL statement. A *lexical reference* is a reference to a column or parameter in your report that you prefix with an ampersand (&). Developer/2000 parses the SQL when you refer to the SQL statement and accept the property sheet or when you run the report. At this time, it substitutes the value of the variable into the SQL statement as text.

A *bind variable* is a reference to a column or parameter in your report that you prefix with a colon (:). Instead of substituting text, this construct tells Developer/2000 to substitute a value.

NOTE
The references and variables are either to data model columns or to report parameters. This book recommends that external queries refer only to parameters; if you refer to report columns, you are coupling the query too closely to the application. To reuse the external query, the other reports would need to have the same column defined in the data model, which is too constraining for good reuse. See the following section on parameters and arguments for details on using parameters. Also, you will find the rules for referring to columns at different levels in your data model quite confusing, and this is always a good way to add defects to your application.

The difference between the lexical reference and the bind variable can seem mysterious until you have used each of them. The practical difference in a report is that you can use lexical references to substitute whole chunks of the SQL as *text,* such as an entire WHERE or GROUP BY clause. But you can only use a bind variable in a situation where you could put a literal value, such as a number, string, or date. You will usually use bind variables when you want to bind some value into a SQL SELECT or WHERE clause to use as a constant for comparison purposes. You will usually use lexical substitution when you can figure out a way to make the statement more reusable by substituting pieces of the statement text on a report-by-report basis. Also, you do not have lexical substitution available in PL/SQL code, only in SQL statements.

For example, say you have a report that you want to parameterize with a specific type of ledger action, such as Bought or Sold. You might do this with lexical substitution:

```
SELECT Person, ActionDate, Item, Quantity, Rate
    FROM Ledger
&WHERE_CLAUSE
ORDER BY Person, ActionDate
```

In this case, however, you would usually just use a bind variable:

```
SELECT Person, ActionDate, Item, Quantity, Rate
  FROM Ledger
  WHERE Action = :ActionType
ORDER BY Person, ActionDate
```

The first example takes the parameter WHERE_CLAUSE and lets you substitute in the entire text of the WHERE clause: "WHERE Action = 'Bought'". The format is so specific and regular, though, it makes more sense to structure it for users rather than requiring that they understand WHERE clause syntax. In the second example, all they need do is supply the value for the ActionType parameter: 'Bought' or 'Sold', for example.

An example of a good use of lexical reference is when you want to refer to different tables in different reports but with otherwise identical SQL. You might, for example, have several different tables with various kinds of people in them, all of which share the columns in the report. You could use the following external query to represent the SQL for the report query:

```
SELECT Name, Age
  FROM &PersonTable
ORDER BY Name
```

The parameter PersonTable would contain the precise name of the table from which you want the report to get its data. You could not use a bind variable in this case because there is nowhere in the FROM clause you could put a bind variable; it just contains table names, which are identifiers. "FROM 'WorkingPerson'", for example, would yield a syntax error because of the single quotes, and with a bind variable there is no way to remove the quotes and treat the string as a table name.

The rules for using lexical substitution and bind variables are quite complex, particularly if you refer to columns at different levels in your data model. See the section "Referencing Columns and Parameters" in Appendix E of the *Reports Reference Manual* (Part Number A32489-1) for a complete discussion of these rules.

NOTE
You should define your parameters (or columns) and give them initial values before referring to them from a SQL statement. Accepting the Query property sheet parses the query and also creates variables for you, but you may want more control over the process than that.

Named Visual Attributes

A *named visual attribute* is an object in a form or menu module that contains a set of visual attribute option settings. These objects act as formatting agents for the module objects to which you apply them. When you apply the named visual attribute, the object takes on only those aspects of the attribute that make sense for that object. When you change the values in the attribute, the corresponding values also change in the objects to which you have applied the attribute.

If you carefully design your set of named visual attributes, you can copy them from module to module to apply your standard visual attributes with nothing more than setting the items to use the visual attribute object. This also lets you change a standard by just changing the named visual attributes rather than having to change all the object visual attributes throughout your modules. For example, in the form prototypes in Chapter 5, you had to constantly convert all the text to use the Arial or Helvetica font instead of the default font. You could change the default font in the initialization file, but another way to do this would be a named visual attribute that sets text to Arial 10 point bold.

You should think about the different combinations of visual attributes you are likely to use in your applications. Create a separate named visual attribute object for each combination of visual attributes you are likely to use. Put these into your form and menu templates so that developers start with the appropriate sets of attributes.

To create a named visual attribute through the Object Navigator, find the Visual Attributes heading under the module, right below the Record Groups heading, and click on the Create button. To apply the named visual attribute to an object, select the object and display its property sheet, then set the Visual Attribute Name property to the name of the named visual attribute object.

NOTE
This is an all-or-nothing proposition. If you change any visual attributes of an object in the Layout Editor or through a property sheet, you lose the connection to the named visual attribute. The Visual Attribute Name property becomes Custom. At least you start out with the right visual attributes; but you can no longer change them for the custom object by changing the properties in the named visual attribute.

Property Classes

The nature of named visual attributes limits their impact to fonts, colors, and patterns. Another kind of object provides a much more extensive level of shared property definition in form and menu modules: the property class. The *property class* is an object belonging to a module that contains a set of properties, *any* properties. Just as with a named visual attribute, when you base an object on a property class, you get all the properties of that class that make sense for the kind of object you are defining. Again, when you change the class, you change the properties of all the objects based on that class.

Inheritance and the Property Class

The property class gives Developer/2000 a form of inheritance. *Inheritance* is a relationship between objects such that the child object has all the properties of the parent object plus whatever additional ones make it different. In most object-oriented programming languages, inheritance represents a typing hierarchy: the child is *a kind of* the parent. Figure 9-7 shows a simple example of an object-oriented inheritance hierarchy.

The root class is the Object class; every object has certain characteristics that its subclasses inherit. The next class down is the Person class; every Person has a name, an address, and a home phone number, as well as the attributes that it inherits from the Object class. The next class down from that is the Employee class,

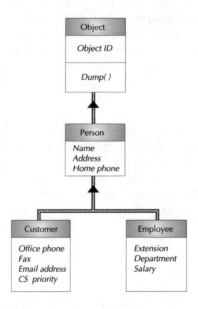

FIGURE 9-7. *An example inheritance hierarchy*

with each Employee having an extension, a department number, and a salary, as well as the attributes inherited from the Person class and the Object class. On the same level as Employee is Customer; a customer is also a kind of person (that is, inherits from the Person class). The Customer, however, has an office phone number, a fax number, an e-mail address, and a customer service priority ranking. Again, the Customer has all the attributes of a Person and an Object. All of these classes determine the structure of each object of the class. That is, you can create many different Customer and Employee objects, and each of these objects has the structure of its class of objects. The Object and Person classes are *abstract* classes, classes that do not themselves correspond to objects; their only purpose is to represent the shared properties of their subclasses.

The property class relationship to the object in Developer/2000 is somewhat different from the usual object-oriented way of doing things. In an object-oriented system, when you create an object from a class, the object gets its attributes and behavior from the class. You create different kinds of objects with different attributes and behavior by creating additional subclasses of the class. With property classes, on the other hand, when you associate an object with the property class, you take the values of the properties from the corresponding properties in the property class. Although similar to inheritance, this is in reality quite different. You do not control all attributes and behavior through the property classes, but through the objects and the values you give the properties in the objects. The property classes supply the initial values for the properties, which you can then override to customize the object to your needs. You cannot add properties to Developer/2000 objects through property classes, but just assign default property values to them. The object does not get all the properties from the property class, just the values for the ones the object already supports.

Despite these limitations, the property class is still an excellent way to build reusability into your modules. What you are doing is abstracting the property values into shared parents. As long as the values you assign in the parent class apply equally to all the children, you save yourself the coding of those properties in the child objects. Perhaps more importantly, when you change the parent, all the children pick up the change, as long as they actually share the default value and you have not overridden it in the object.

Another advantage of property classes is that you can inherit a property class in them. This lets you create parents of parents of parents in the same kind of inheritance hierarchy of abstract classes you find in object-oriented systems. You can use this hierarchical structure to get more exact combinations of properties, and this makes the property classes more reusable. For example, you could construct a huge property class with all the known attributes of all items in it. When you assigned this, the object to which you assigned it would pick up the properties that are relevant and ignore the rest. But if you had differences between objects, you would have a different, equally massive property sheet. Instead, you could abstract the properties shared between the different property classes into a higher-level property class until you reach the highest level where all objects share the properties. Then the lower level classes contain just those properties that are relevant to your object, which is much easier to understand and to deal with.

Creating a Property Class Hierarchy

You can create a property class in either of two ways: by creating a new property class object and adding properties, or by using a current object as a template in the property sheet to create a property class with all the properties and settings of the current object.

The Property Classes heading in the Object Navigator is right below Program Units for forms or menu modules. To create a new property class, select the heading and click on the Create button.

Once you have created the property class, double-click on its icon to display its property sheet (Figure 9-8). The buttons on the toolbar at the top of the property sheet control the addition and removal of properties in different ways.

Click on the Add Property button in the property sheet toolbar to display the Properties LOV dialog box (Figure 9-9). Select a property from the list, then set the property value to be what you want.

You can also copy properties into the property sheet. Select the object from which you want to copy all the properties, then click on the Copy Properties button to copy all the object's properties and their settings.

Find and select the property class object and click on the Paste Properties button to paste all the copied properties into the property class.

To remove unwanted properties, select the property you want to remove and click on the Delete Property button to delete it.

You can create a property class directly from another object. First, select the object and display its property sheet. Click on the Property Class button to create a property sheet by copying the properties and values from the object you are displaying. Developer/2000 informs you that it is creating a new property class and gives you the name of the class. You can then select that property class object in the Object Navigator and add more properties or remove ones that you know you will not want to inherit in the objects based on the property class. Usually, these removed properties will be the ones that change for each object you create, such as the horizontal or vertical position in the canvas.

The final step is creating a property class that inherits its properties from another property class. You use the same techniques as before to create a property class from an object; but the object is another property class. If you are creating your hierarchy bottom up, you can remove properties from the superclass using the Remove Property button. You then have the properties that two or more property subclasses share. For example, say you want to have two different kinds of text entry fields, one with a specific format mask and fixed text length and one with a

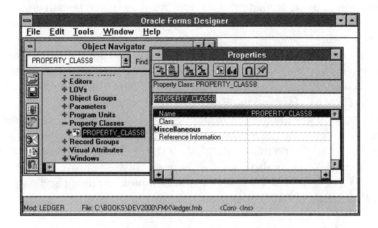

FIGURE 9-8. *The empty Property Class property sheet*

different format mask and not fixed length. Say that both shared all the other properties of a text entry item. You could create the FIXEDTEXTFORMAT property class from the fixed object, then remove all the properties that you will set for each object, such as X Position, Y Position, Primary Key, and so on. You could then do the same for VARIABLETEXTFORMAT. Finally, you could create TEXTFORMAT

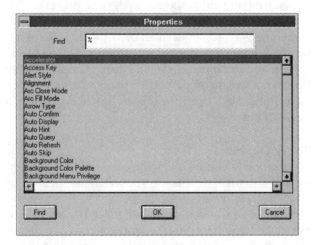

FIGURE 9-9. *Adding a property to a property class*

from either one of these property classes, removing the Fixed Length and FormatMask properties but leaving the shared ones such as Data Type and Maximum Length.

If you are creating your hierarchy top down, you can add properties using the Add Property button and the Properties LOV dialog box to create the subclass. In this case, you would first create the TEXTFORMAT class, then the FIXEDTEXTFORMAT class and the VARIABLETEXTFORMAT class.

If your property class hierarchy would be useful in more than one module, you should define it in a template module as suggested earlier in this chapter. You can base your new modules on this module by using File|Save As to save the template as a new module. You can also copy the property classes you want to use from the template into a new module by dragging and dropping or cutting and pasting them. See the following section on copying and referring to objects.

Inheriting and Overriding Properties from the Property Class

For an object to inherit the properties from a property class, you need to assign the property class to the object. Each object has a property called Class. To assign the property class, set the Class property in the usual way by selecting the object in the Object Navigator and selecting the Class property in the property sheet. The property sheet provides a drop-down list of the property class names in the module that owns the object.

When you set the Class property, Developer/2000 copies the property values from the property class into the object properties that exist for the object. It marks these properties in the object with an equal sign. If there are properties in the object that have no corresponding values in the property class, Developer/2000 leaves them unchanged. If there are properties in the property class that have no corresponding properties in the object, Developer/2000 does not copy them.

You can override inherited properties in an object with a different value, making that property a *variant* property. Just set the value in the object, and the plus sign will disappear. Variant properties do not inherit changes in the property class.

You can also convert a variant property back to an inherited property by selecting the property in the object and clicking on the Inherit button in the toolbar on the property sheet for the object.

Triggers in Property Classes

A very nice feature of property classes is that they can not only have properties in their property sheet but also triggers. This lets you inherit application behavior in your objects. The trick with using triggers in property classes is to write them to be reusable. Using bind variables can help here, but only a bit; because the names must refer to names in the form that owns the property class and trigger, thus coupling the trigger to the form. This feature works best to define behavior that does not require referring to actual values other than that in the field itself.

To create a property class trigger, expand the property class object in the Object Navigator, then create a trigger of the appropriate kind in the usual way, using the Triggers LOV dialog box and the PL/SQL editor. When you assign the property class to an object, the object (a form, block, or item) inherits the trigger and runs it when the appropriate event occurs. If the event is not an appropriate event for the kind of object you associate the class with, the object ignores the trigger (as it would ignore the trigger if you put it directly on the object).

You can override an inherited trigger by adding a trigger for the same event to the object itself. If you expand the trigger heading under the object, you will see that it does not display the inherited trigger name. You can see that only under the property class.

Copying and Referring to Objects

The Object Navigator in the Forms Designer gives you an easy way to reuse objects: copying and referring to objects elsewhere in the system. For example, you can implement a block in at least six ways:

- Create the block from scratch, as illustrated in Chapter 5.
- Copy the block from another block by dragging and dropping it.
- Copy the block from another block by copying and pasting it.
- Move the block by cutting and pasting it.
- Move the block within a module by dragging it while holding down the CTRL key.
- Refer to another block by dragging and dropping the block.

Drag-and-Drop Copying and References

When you select an object and drag it elsewhere in the Object Navigator, you are doing one of several possible things: copying the object, moving the object, or referring to the object.

Copying the object means that you are creating a new object and initializing it with most of the contents and associations of the original object. *Moving* the object means that you are removing the object from its starting location and physically moving it, with associations, to the new location in which you drop or paste it. *Referring* to the object means that you are creating a new reference object in the location you drop the object. A *reference object* inherits the properties and associations of the object to which it refers, except for a few properties you can change. When you change the original object, the reference object also changes by inheriting the changes in the object to which it refers.

The easiest way to copy or to refer to an object is to *drag and drop* it from its original location to a new location in the Object Navigator. Select the object, or several objects of the same type if you wish, and drag it while holding down the left mouse button to a location suitable for that type of object. When you do this, Developer/2000 displays a small dialog box that lets you choose to copy or to refer to the object by clicking on the appropriate button.

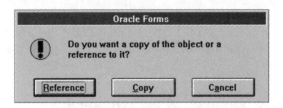

Objects you copy both own a set of objects and associate to another set of objects. For example, a block *owns* a set of items and triggers, but it *associates* with a canvas view. The associations appear as properties in the property sheet of the object, not as objects underneath the copied object in the Object Navigator. Copying always copies the objects the copied object owns but gives you the choice of copying or changing the associations.

When you copy an object, Developer/2000 attempts to resolve the associations within the module by looking for objects with the names you have in the property sheet. If it cannot resolve one or more associations, it displays the Copy Options dialog box. This lets you decide whether to copy the associations to other objects such as LOVs, editors, canvas views, or named visual attributes. For example, Figure 9-10 shows the Copy Options dialog box with the Block tab selected.

If Developer/2000 resolves all the associations, you will not see the Copy Options dialog box. When you cut or copy and paste an object, you lose all the associations, so you do not see the Copy Options dialog box there either.

The process of referring to an object is much the same. You get an additional dialog box asking whether to strip the path name from the name of the module that contains the object to which you are referring.

With a copy, you can change any property you wish in the new object. With a reference, you can make only very limited changes. If the name of the referred-to object already exists, Developer/2000 changes the name, and lets you change it again if you wish. You can change the comment property to give the reference a comment of its own. You can change the canvas view name and the X and Y positions in an item reference. You can also use the Reference Information property in the property sheet (double-click for the dialog box) for the reference object to reset the access information for the reference. Other than that, you are stuck with

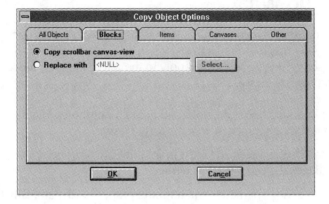

FIGURE 9-10. *The Copy Options dialog box with Block tab selected*

the original properties and contents of the object to which you refer. To change them, you must change the original object and inherit the changes.

NOTE
In a way, you *increase* coupling in the system when you reuse code by reference. For example, if you change trigger code in a module and other modules or applications refer to that code, and the code has problems, all your other modules inherit the problems with the new code. On the other hand, you only need to fix the problem in one place. Be careful when making changes to code to which you refer.

Object Groups

Another feature of Developer/2000 lets you package up your reusable objects for later copying or referring. The *object group* collects a set of objects in the module under a single heading. By copying or referring to the object group, you get all the objects it contains. You can group any objects down to the block level, but you cannot group items within a block. You have to include the entire block in the object group.

To create an object group, find the module's Object Group heading in the Object Navigator. Create the new group with the Create button. Now drag and drop all the objects you want to gather together into the group by dropping them on the Object Group Children node under the group you have created.

When to Do What

How do you choose between using named visual attributes and property classes? When should you copy these objects and when should you refer to them?

There are some specific rules that apply to the interaction of named visual attributes and property classes:

- You can define only font, color, and pattern attributes in a named visual attribute but any property in a property class.

- You can define a property class to inherit from a property class but a named visual attribute stands alone.

- You can change named visual attribute properties dynamically through PL/SQL, but you cannot change property class values in this way.

- Named visual attributes take precedence over property class settings; so if you have both, the fonts, colors, and patterns will be those of the named visual attribute, not the property class.

- You can copy any objects you wish, but you cannot update all the copies in a single operation.

- If you refer to an object, you must change its properties in the original object; you cannot change them in the reference. Also, if you make an error in the original objects, all its references pick up the error.

- Object groups make available chunks of modules, such as several blocks and triggers taken as a whole.

These points lead to the following recommendations:

- Use named visual attributes to represent visual information where possible. Include the named visual attributes in your property classes so that you can inherit them as properties.

- Use property classes to represent hierarchically related properties that you use in more than one module. That is, if you can abstract at least two levels, you should be using property classes, not just copies or references or named visual attributes.

- Use references where possible to reuse major parts of modules in other modules, and use object groups to create packaged, reusable chunks of modules.

■ Copy objects only to create an initial setup for making local changes. That is, if you intend to customize your objects a good deal in the local module, copy the objects rather than referring to them.

■ Use object groups wherever possible for clusters of objects that work as a unit, such as a series of tools for a toolbar or a series of button items for a button canvas view.

Getting into Arguments

Using parameters, you can customize forms, reports, and graphics when you run them, as well as when you code them. A *parameter* is a variable that you set when you activate the object by passing in values as *arguments* on the command line or calling procedure. Parameters let you construct objects to be flexible to external requirements by allowing the user of the object to configure the object dynamically.

Forms Parameters

A *form parameter* is a form variable to which you can assign values through arguments you pass when you start up the form. You can pass arguments to a form either through the command line (F45RUN) or through the various subprograms that start up a form from another object, such as CALL_FORM, NEW_FORM, OPEN_FORM, or RUN_PRODUCT. Each of these procedures takes a parameter list as an argument. Forms parameters can be any of three data types: CHAR, NUMBER, or DATE.

Creating Form Parameter Objects
A form parameter is an object that belongs to a form. To create one, find and select the Parameter heading in the Object Navigator, just below the Object Groups heading under the Form module, and click on the Create button. Double-clicking on the icon displays the Property sheet for the parameter (Figure 9-11).

This particular parameter accepts a string that represents the name of a named visual attribute to use to set the Current_Record_Attribute property of the form when you start up the form. This lets you start up the form with one of a set of different visual attributes. You could do this for portability reasons (different fonts on different platforms) or for different projects with different visual standards (10-point on one project but 12-point on another, for example).

You need to set the Data Type (CHAR, NUMBER, or DATE), the Length for a CHAR parameter, and the internal Name of the parameter in the property sheet. You also need to set the Default Value, which the form uses when you do not supply an argument for the parameter. Leaving this variable uninitialized is not a

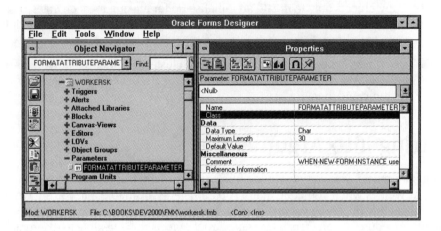

FIGURE 9-11. *The property sheet for a form parameter*

good thing to do. In this case, the default value is "Default," which means that the form will use the default named visual attribute for the form.

Using Form Parameters

You can use form parameters with bind variable syntax in PL/SQL code or in certain properties. To refer to a parameter, you prefix the name with ":PARAMETER" and a dot separator. For example, to use the parameter FormatAttributeParameter from the last section to set the form property in a WHEN-NEW-FORM-INSTANCE trigger, you would refer to :PARAMETER.FormatAttributeParameter:

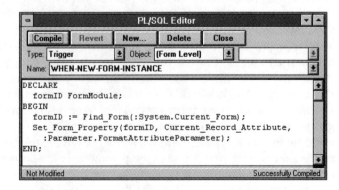

Object	Property
Block	WHERE Clause
Block	ORDER BY Clause
List of Values	Return Item (in Column Mapping dialog box)
Item	Default Value
Text Item	Range Low Value
Text Item	Range High Value

TABLE 9-1.   *This is a figure caption*

You can refer to parameters, still prefixing the name with ":PARAMETER.", in the object properties in Table 9-1.

Passing Arguments

To supply arguments to the WorkerSkill form, you could just put them on the command line that sets up the Runform environment:

```
F45RUN MODULE=workersk USERID=talbot/george
FORMATTRIBUTEPARAMETER="Windows31FormVisualAttrs"
```

MODULE and USERID are system parameters valid in any form, and FORMATTRIBUTEPARAMETER is a user-defined parameter that the WorkerSkill form defines.

Parameter Lists   If you want to run a form from within another form, and you need to supply parameter arguments to the form, you do so by building a parameter list before you call the built-in procedure to run the form. A *parameter list* is an object that contains a list of parameters with their values.

To create a parameter list, you call the Create_Parameter_List built-in function, which returns a ParamList id. You then call the Add_Parameter built-in procedure for each parameter argument you want to add to the list. The actual list gets created in form memory and persists beyond the code block, so you need to create and add a list only once for the form instance. You do this by getting the id for the id variable, then testing whether it is null. Finally, you pass the ParamList id to the call to Call_Form, New_Form, Open_Form, or Run_Product. The following anonymous PL/SQL block, for example, sets up a parameter list to pass a name, 'MotifFormVisualAttrs', to use for the FormAttributeParameter:

```
DECLARE
  listID ParamList :=
    Get_Parameter_list('WorkerSkillFormArguments');
BEGIN
  IF ID_Null(listID) THEN  -- No list yet, create it
    listID := Create_Parameter_List('WorkerSkillFormArguments');
    Add_Parameter(listID, 'FormAttributeParameter',
TEXT_PARAMETER,
                   'MotifFormVisualAttrs');
  END IF;
  Open_Form('WorkerSk', ACTIVATE, NO_SESSION, listID);
END;
```

An Alternative Way of Passing Arguments   As an alternative for passing arguments into a form, you can create a control block (a block that does not correspond to a base table) with the items being the parameters, with appropriate defaults and other settings. You can then display the parameter form as a modal dialog window with a special canvas-view for the user to enter arguments. You should include a means in your application to display this dialog box at any time to set the parameters with different arguments. See Chapter 11, Working with Windows and Canvas-Views, of the *Forms Developer's Guide* (Part Number A32505-1) for details on creating dialog windows and canvas-views for them.

Internally, you can refer to the parameters as you would any control block item. The only differences are the inability to specify the arguments on the command line and the need to prefix the item name with the control block name rather than with PARAMETER.

For a bit of extra reusability, you could structure the parameters into several control blocks that represent cohesive clusters of parameters. You could then refer to these control blocks in different forms as you needed to include the particular sort of parameter. You could structure the entry of the arguments into separate options dialog boxes or into a single dialog box if that was appropriate, and you could build an object group for all these objects.

Report Parameters

Report parameters are similar to form parameters, but you have an additional option for using them: lexical references in SQL statements. You also have a built-in way to create a form for entering parameters.

The Reports part of Developer/2000 comes with a standard set of system parameters. You have already seen the parameters in Table 9-2 on the form that Reports displays when you previewed a report in Chapter 5.

Creating Parameters

You create parameters in the Object Navigator in much the same way as for form parameters. The heading to look for is User Parameters under the Data Model heading for the report (for example, Reports¦LEDGER¦Data Model¦User Parameters). In the Parameter property sheet, you can enter a name, a data type, a width for CHAR parameters, an input mask, an initial value, a validation trigger, a comment, a list of values (LOV) dialog box, or a combo box set of values. You should always enter an initial value, and you should try to use the input mask, LOV or combo box, and/or validation trigger where possible to make sure that the input arguments are acceptable.

You can also create a parameter automatically if you refer to a parameter as a bind variable in a query.

Creating a Parameter Form

You will find the Parameter Form object under the report object, right after the Layout object. Double-clicking on the object icon displays a special Parameter Form editor that lets you add fields for the different parameters. If you do not build a form of your own, the default form comes with fields for the various system

Parameter	Description
Background	Whether to run the report in a background process
Copies	How many copies of the report to print
Currency	The symbol to indicate a monetary value, such as "$"
Decimal	The symbol to separate the decimal portion of a number, such as "," or "."
Destination Format	The format of the output device
Destination Name	Name of the output device (filename, printer name, and so on)
Destination Type	Where to send the output (screen, file, mail, printer, preview)
Mode	Bitmap or character
Orientation	Landscape or portrait
Printjob	Whether to display the Print Job dialog box
Thousands	The symbol to separate the groups of three digits in a number, such as "," or "."

TABLE 9-2.   *Report System Parameters*

parameters. When you add one of your own from scratch, it is blank, so you have to create parameter fields for any system parameters you want the user to see. You can change the form title, add a hint line text, add boilerplate text, add fields for argument entry, or break the form into two or more pages.

A better strategy is to use the Tools ¦ Default Parameter Form menu item to create a parameter form that includes the system parameters. Select the Parameter Form heading in the Object Navigator first, then choose the menu item. This displays the Default Parameter Form dialog box (Figure 9-12), which lets you choose the system parameters you want to display. The dialog box automatically selects the first two items; to select additional parameters or to deselect any selected ones, click on them. Scroll down to see the whole set of parameters. You can also enter a hint and a status bar text if you wish.

When you click on OK after making your choices, Developer/2000 generates the layout and displays it in the Parameter Form editor (Figure 9-13). You can then edit the boilerplate text and add other parameters.

The Report Properties property sheet has a Parameter Form tab (Figure 9-14) that lets you specify the number of pages in the parameter form. You can also specify the size of the pages and the title for the Previewer window.

When you add a field, you access its property sheet in the usual way by double-clicking on the field in the editor or in the Object Navigator. Here, for example, is the very simple property sheet for the field, in which you specify the

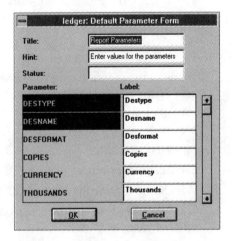

FIGURE 9-12. *The Default Parameter Form dialog box*

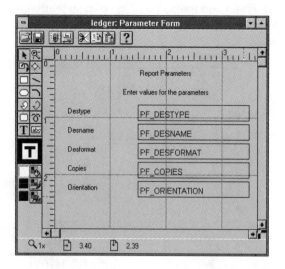

FIGURE 9-13. *The Parameter Form editor with default parameter form layout*

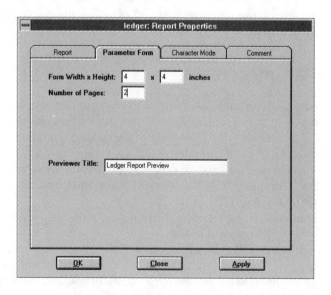

FIGURE 9-14. *The Report Properties property sheet Parameter Form tab*

name of the parameter field and the name of the parameter that is the source of the data to display in the field:

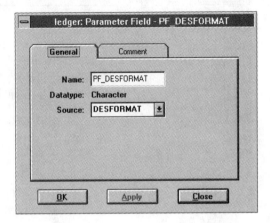

The drop-down list provides all of the parameters, both system and user defined.

Using Parameters

You can use parameters in queries either as bind variables or as lexical references. See the "External Queries" section earlier in this chapter for details on these alternatives. You can also use parameters as part of your drill-down report setup; see the *Building Reports Manual* for details.

Graphics Parameters

Graphics parameters are very similar to form and report parameters, but they have a special role to play in the Graphics product: they are the basis for drill-down behavior, passing the value of chart elements or the name of a graphic object. You can also use them through bind variables in PL/SQL code or through bind variables or lexical references in queries, as in reports. As with reports, when you refer to a parameter in PL/SQL or query code, Developer/2000 creates a parameter for you automatically if it does not already exist.

For more information about creating drill-down relationships, see the *Graphics Developer's Guide* (Part Number A32482-1).

One difference in using Graphics parameters is that, because display modules have no items or fields, you just use the parameter name without further qualification. For example, to parameterize the query of amounts bought by Talbot's so that the user can control the ordering of the pie slices:

```
SELECT Person "Person", SUM(Amount) "Amount"
   FROM Ledger
   WHERE Action IN ('Bought', 'Paid')
GROUP BY Person
&Ordering
```

The Ordering parameter appears in lexical reference form. To sort by amount, set the parameter to "ORDER BY 2"; to sort by person, set the parameter to "ORDER BY Person" or "ORDER BY 1".

The Graphics product provides no way for the end user to enter these values as parameters, although you can write code for buttons or chart elements that sets the parameters when the user clicks on them. The user can also enter the parameters directly through the G25DES and G25RUN command lines.

> **NOTE**
> For reusability and to reduce complexity and coupling, you should avoid using parameters as global variables in PL/SQL code. That is, do not pass information from one program unit to another by setting a parameter value unless you can find no other better structured way to do this. Use PL/SQL program unit parameters to move data in and out of PL/SQL code, not global variables.

In Triplicate?

When you build a form application, you often have the choice of building a large form with many blocks or a series of small forms. Although the large form may contain more functionality, it will serve a smaller range of possible applications because of its complexity. There will always be some part of the form you do not need. The smaller forms, although they are less functional, are more reusable because they offer their functions in smaller groups that you can reuse in more places.

The key to deciding how to break up form modules is to understand how the modules *cohere* as a functional unit. If you can break a module into separate modules and use them with minimal connections to other modules, the original module was less cohesive than the set of smaller modules.

Reports and graphics, by their nature, are cohesive. You may find that reports can get quite involved, however. Step back every so often and look at your data models that involve more than one query. Can you produce two or more reports that might be a clearer way to represent the information than in the master-detail, matrix, or other complex report that you have developed? Could this in turn lead to opportunities to reuse the simpler reports in different contexts? All of these considerations can lead to better and more reusable report designs.

Why Do It Six Times When You Can Do It Once?

Other chapters have briefly mentioned the possibility of building procedures, functions, and triggers in the database rather than in the application. What are the advantages of doing this for reuse?

If you are using ORACLE7 as your database server, you have the choice of running your PL/SQL code in your applications or on the server. To make this decision, you must look at two issues, code/data cohesion and performance.

How does cohesion apply to triggers and procedures? As Chapter 11 details, you can use packages and libraries to group your procedures and functions into reusable, cohesive clusters. What role can the database play in this? Unlike a standard programming language, PL/SQL by its nature is a database programming language. Although you can and do use it for purely programmatic functions such as calculations and decision logic, you also use it to maintain database relationships. When you have a cluster of procedures or functions that work together with tables in your database, you need to consider the cohesion of both the data (the tables and columns) and the code (the procedures and functions).

This issue is similar in many ways to the integrity constraint mechanism in the database. Because ORACLE7 and other ANSI-compliant database managers supply primary and foreign key constraints, you no longer need to place the code that maintains these relationships in your applications. You can define the tables with the constraints and let the database manager maintain the data. Using this feature increases the cohesion of the system by placing the constraints where they belong, with the table.

Similarly, when you have procedures and functions that interact with specific tables and columns to do specific things, you generally will want to place these procedures and functions on the server with the tables, not in your applications. You thus place the code closer to the data it uses and accrue all the benefits of the increased cohesion. You no longer have to move code around your network so that different applications can use it, and anyone with access to the database has access to the procedures. An example of this is when you use procedural encapsulation as a security measure (see Chapter 8). You could place your procedures in your applications; but because you intend for the procedures to encapsulate all references to your data, you should place it with the data and grant the appropriate privileges to it to guarantee your access control. Another example is when you have procedures that represent things that must happen when a database event happens, such as deleting a particular kind of row or some such server event. Again, you could do this in every application that initiates the event, but it is simpler and more straightforward to put the code into a database trigger.

As Chapter 8 already mentioned, if you want to prevent users from accessing data through tools other than your applications, triggers and other database procedures provide a way to encapsulate access to the data through privileges on the data and the procedures. Triggers also ensure full enforcement of the constraints they represent regardless of the tool a user uses to modify the data.

There are also performance implications. You may find that putting the code on the server can improve client performance substantially and can also reduce network traffic if there is a lot of interaction with the data in the database within the code. This leads to the concept of *application partitioning,* the breaking up of your application code into client and server portions to improve resource usage, particularly over a network.

You access database objects through the Database Objects heading in the Object Navigator. Once you connect to a database, this heading shows a list of all the user names the database defines. Each user name in turn shows the Stored Program Units, Libraries, Tables, and Views that belong to the user.

To create a stored procedure, you select the Database Objects!<USER NAME>!Stored Program Units heading in the Object Navigator and click on the Create button. This displays the New Program Unit dialog box through which you enter the procedure name and type (Procedure, Function, Package Spec, or Package Body):

When you click OK, Developer/2000 displays the Stored Program Unit editor (Figure 9-15).

You can then enter the code for your program unit and compile it by clicking on the Save button. This issues a CREATE PROCEDURE (or whatever), which compiles the program unit on the server and returns any PL/SQL compilation errors after running it. You need to have CREATE privilege for the kind of program unit you are creating.

To create a database trigger for a particular table, expand the table object in the Object Navigator to see the Trigger heading under it. Click on Create just as before to see the Database Trigger editor shown in Figure 9-16; this is very similar to the

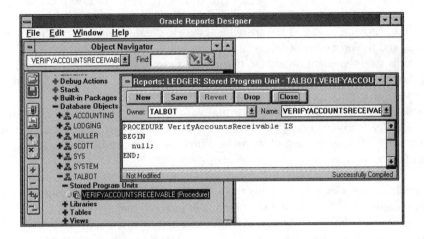

FIGURE 9-15. *The Stored Program Unit editor with Procedure*

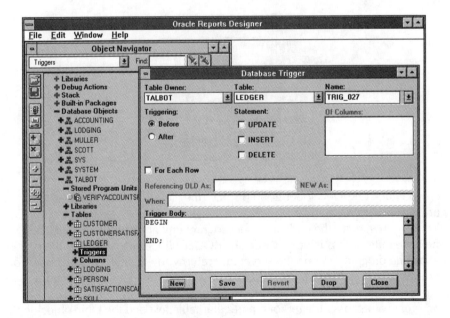

FIGURE 9-16. *The Database Trigger editor*

Stored Program Unit editor in Figure 9-15. Click on the New button to create a new trigger. The editor contains several different radio button and check box fields to specify parts of the trigger such as the trigger type (which kind of statement) and timing (Before or After the statement). As before, clicking on the Save button compiles the code by issuing a CREATE TRIGGER statement.

NOTE
You cannot refer to any form items in your stored program unit or database trigger code. That is, you cannot refer to an item in a block through a bind variable. The client-side items are not available to the server that executes the PL/SQL. Instead, you must add the variable to the parameters of the program unit to pass information in and out of the program unit. This is generally a good way to structure program units within the module as well, as it makes them more reusable. You should note that database triggers do not have parameters.

Part Two has taken you through the process of prototype and design. You are now at a point where you need to learn the details of producing a working, final application through coding, testing, and debugging techniques. If you apply what you have learned in this part, you will find that coding, testing, and debugging are less time-consuming and less likely to be rework instead of work.

PART 3

Implementing, Testing, and Debugging

CHAPTER 10

Real Programmers

The chapters in Part 3 teach you how to use Developer/2000 to build real, complete applications from your prototypes and designs. PL/SQL is Oracle's procedural extension to SQL. That is, PL/SQL gives you not only the ability to execute SQL but to embed it in control structures such as if-then-else and loops. This lets you do much more sophisticated work in your applications than you could using only SQL. The PL/SQL syntax derives from the more complex Ada programming language but is in practice much simpler to use.

This chapter teaches you the fundamentals of the PL/SQL programming language: how it organizes data, how you program with control structures, and how to use SQL as a part of the language. The next chapter expands on this one with more complex program structures that let you organize your programs into robust collections of reusable code. Chapters 12 and 13 introduce you to the discipline of testing and to the chaos of debugging in Developer/2000. When you have completed this part of the book, you will understand how to create, test, and debug your applications.

This chapter focuses on basic programming structures in PL/SQL. In Developer/2000, you place your code into two kinds of structures: triggers and program units. The material in this chapter tells you what you need to know to code basic triggers; the next chapter tells you how to produce more complex program units (procedures, functions, and packages). You can also use the knowledge gained here to develop stored program units (database triggers, procedures, and packages) in your ORACLE7 database.

NOTE
Developer/2000 uses a local version of PL/SQL to compile your program units. ORACLE7 uses the version of PL/SQL current for the ORACLE7 release to compile program units. The versions of PL/SQL may not be the same, so there may be some features available through the server PL/SQL that are not available through the Developer/2000 PL/SQL.

The basic program unit structure in PL/SQL has the following structure:

```
DECLARE
   --Data declarations
BEGIN
   null;--Program statements
EXCEPTION
   --Exception handlers
   WHEN OTHERS THEN
      null;--default handler
END;
```

A complete program with this structure is an *anonymous block,* a block of code without a name. The whole block is a single PL/SQL statement; hence, the END requires the semicolon statement terminator. If you have no data declarations, you can omit the DECLARE, BEGIN, and END keywords; and if you have no exception handlers, you can omit the EXCEPTION keyword and the WHEN clause. You usually will have a BEGIN-EXCEPTION-END sequence, not just an EXCEPTION clause. You must have at least one valid programming statement in the block; hence the use of the null statements in the preceding code listing. The code examples in this chapter always include a null statement so that the example compiles if there is no code in a block.

NOTE
A PL/SQL block is completely different from the Developer/2000 Forms block. A *PL/SQL block* is an executable program (an anonymous block, a procedure, or a function), whereas a Forms block is a collection of item definitions within a form that might or might not map to a base server table definition. You can also see a Forms block as a list of records. A PL/SQL block can contain PL/SQL blocks nested within itself to any level, with the scope of names in each block restricted to the block in which you declare the nested block. PL/SQL is thus a *block-structured programming language,* as is Ada.

Here are some practical issues you should know about:

■ Most PL/SQL expressions use the same syntax as SQL expressions, and you can use most of the ORACLE7 SQL built-in functions. If you know SQL, you already know most of PL/SQL.

■ PL/SQL is not case sensitive, so you can code using uppercase or lowercase letters, or use a mixture of the two for readability. Literals in quotes are case sensitive.

■ PL/SQL identifiers must start with a letter and may contain only letters, numbers, underscores, number signs ("#"), and dollar signs ("$"). Identifiers can have up to 30 characters and cannot be any of the reserved words of the language, such as DECLARE or END.

■ Use single quotes to embed a single quote in a quoted string literal: 'Talbot''s Farm', for example.

■ BOOLEAN type values can be TRUE, FALSE, or NULL. These are not quoted strings, they are values: IS_WINDOW_DISPLAYED := TRUE, not 'TRUE', for example.

■ You can comment lines either with an inline comment starting with two dashes or with a multiple-line comment between a /*-*/ pair:

```
null;      -- This is an inline comment terminated by the line end
/* This is
a multiple-line
comment terminated by */
```

If you do much PL/SQL programming, consult the *PL/SQL User's Guide and Reference* (Part Number A12715-1) for the full details of PL/SQL syntax and semantics. The reference contains a full list of the various built-in functions you can use.

A Brief Introduction to Data

Probably the single most important thing to understand about a programming language is how the language organizes data. Some programming languages have a tremendously complex type system, and some are quite simple. Some languages let you extend the type system, and others do not.

Data Types

A *data type* is the category of data into which a value falls, such as character, number, or date. PL/SQL unifies its programming language types with the SQL data types, extending the SQL types with special features. Because the primary purpose of PL/SQL is to embed SQL, it is logical to expect the language to map directly to SQL statements and the types of values therein. PL/SQL also adds some data types that are useful in block programming: BINARY_INTEGER, BOOLEAN, and RECORD. Using PL/SQL with Developer/2000 also adds several types corresponding to the different objects in forms, such as windows and blocks.

NOTE
CURSOR is a special data type you associate with SQL statements. See the following section on using SQL with PL/SQL for details.

SQL Types
PL/SQL provides a one-to-one mapping with the SQL type system, at least for the important SQL types. See the *ORACLE7 Server SQL Language Reference Manual* (Part Number A12714-1) for details of these types: DECIMAL, FLOAT, INTEGER, NUMBER, REAL, SMALLINT, CHAR, CHARACTER, LONG, RAW, STRING, VARCHAR, and VARCHAR2. You can use the standard ORACLE7 SQL conversion functions to handle explicit conversion of these types in PL/SQL blocks.

PL/SQL Binary Integers and Booleans
PL/SQL adds three data types to handle signed integer numbers. When you use signed integer numbers in PL/SQL calculations, it does not need to convert the data to an internal format, as it does with NUMBER or any of the other SQL types. In blocks that do heavy integer arithmetic, you can increase performance by using signed integers instead of NUMBER data.

The basic signed integer type is BINARY_INTEGER, with which you can represent numbers in the range –2147483647 to 2147483647. The two subtypes represent smaller ranges. The NATURAL type represents numbers from 0 to

2147483647, and the POSITIVE type represents numbers from 1 to 2147483647. You use these to restrict data to nonnegative values.

The BOOLEAN type lets you handle TRUE and FALSE values directly. You can also set a BOOLEAN to NULL, meaning the value is undefined. This means that PL/SQL Boolean values have three possible states: TRUE, FALSE, and NULL, and that the logic is a three-valued logic.

NOTE
Three-valued logic can be counterintuitive. For example, if you compare two Boolean variables and both are NULL, the result is NULL, not TRUE. For a full discussion of three-valued logic and its use with SQL, see Chris Date's article "Null Values in Database Management," Chapter 15 of his book *Relational Database: Selected Writings* (Addison-Wesley, 1986).

PL/SQL Records
A PL/SQL record lets you define a single variable that comprises several data elements, much like a database row. You can use the RECORD type to create structured data of any type. You can then refer to the data as a logical unit using dot notation.

To create records, you must first create the individual record type. For example, to create a type corresponding to part of the Ledger table, you could use the following statement in a DECLARE section:

```
DECLARE
  TYPE LedgerType IS RECORD (
    LedgerID VARCHAR(25) NOT NULL := 0,
    ActionDate DATE,
    Action VARCHAR(8),
    Amount NUMBER(9,2));
BEGIN
  null;
END;
```

In this case, the record represents only part of the table data. The NOT NULL clause is the same as the SQL NOT NULL, which prevents you from assigning NULL to the field. Although the obvious use for the RECORD type is to represent data that corresponds to table data, you can have fields of any type, including a RECORD type, in any combination. You can use records in packages, for example, to represent runtime objects that you do not store in the database, such as a particular time of day on the 24-hour clock. You could then package the type with

a set of functions that operate on the data in the record. This lets you call the
function Subtract with values for the time and the time interval to subtract from it.

```
PACKAGE Time24Package IS
  TYPE Time24Type IS RECORD (
    hour NATURAL NOT NULL := 0,
    minute NATURAL NOT NULL := 0,
    second NUMBER NOT NULL := 0);

FUNCTION Subtract(time Time24Type,
                  interval TimeIntervalPackage.TimeIntervalType)
    RETURN Time24Type;
END;
```

You can declare two variables of Time24Type, pass them to the function, get
back the difference, and assign it to a third variable of Time24Type. This kind of
packaging, an *abstract data type,* lets you represent more complex objects than the
simple PL/SQL types. Chapter 11 gives a complete discussion of packages and
abstract data types.

NOTE
See the following section on attributes for a way to make the field
types correspond exactly to the database column types.

Once you define the type, you can then use the type to create a variable, also
in a DECLARE section:

```
DECLARE
  TYPE LedgerType IS RECORD (
    LedgerID VARCHAR(25) NOT NULL := 0,
    ActionDate DATE,
    Action VARCHAR(8),
    Amount NUMBER(9,2));
  ledgerItem LedgerType;
BEGIN
  null;
END;
```

The resulting record has a LedgerID field with value 0 and the rest of the
fields NULL. PL/SQL creates the variable when it executes the DECLARE section
and destroys it when it reaches the END of the block in which you declared it. You

can assign values to the fields and refer to the fields using dot notation, as in this code fragment:

```
IF ledgerItem.Action = 'Sold'
THEN ledgerItem.Amount := 0.0;
END IF;
```

Notice that the comparison operator is "=" whereas the assignment operator is ":=".

Developer/2000 PL/SQL Object Types

When you use PL/SQL in Developer/2000, you also have several types available that represent the different kinds of objects in Developer/2000. Table 10-1 shows the different objects that Forms gives you.

When you call built-in subprograms with arguments, you can usually supply either the unique name of the object or the object id. The *object id* is a *handle* to the object, a value that uniquely identifies it. When you declare a variable with one of the types from Table 10-1, you are really declaring an object id handle. You

Object	Type	Lookup Function
Alert	ALERT	FIND_ALERT
Block	BLOCK	FIND_BLOCK
Canvas	CANVAS	FIND_CANVAS
Record Group Column	GROUPCOLUMN	FIND_COLUMN
Editor	EDITOR	FIND_EDITOR
Form	FORMMODULE	FIND_FORM
Record Group	RECORDGROUP	FIND_GROUP
Item	ITEM	FIND_ITEM
List of Values	LOV	FIND_LOV
Menu Item	MENUITEM	FIND_MENUITEM
Parameter List	PARAMLIST	GET_PARAMETER_LIST
Relation	RELATION	FIND_RELATION
Timer	TIMER	FIND_TIMER
View	VIEW	FIND_VIEW
Window	WINDOW	FIND_WINDOW

TABLE 10-1. *Forms PL/SQL Object Types and Lookup Functions*

get the id by calling the FIND function,which returns the id when you pass in the name. You can thus use the name to find the id, then use the id for a series of subprogram calls. This can speed up processing if you are making many references to an object, because each time you pass in a name, Developer/2000 must look up the id internally.

The parameter list object has a special id type, PARAM_LIST, which corresponds to the GET_PARAMETER_LIST function rather than to a function starting with FIND.

See the *Forms Reference Manual* (Part Number A32509-1), Chapter 3, for detailed descriptions of the FIND functions and the different subprograms that take object id arguments.

Table 10-2 shows the Graphics data types and their corresponding GET functions, which work in much the same way as the Forms types despite the different naming conventions.

See the *Graphics Reference Manual* (Part Number A32483-1), Chapter 4, for detailed descriptions of the GET functions and the different subprograms that take object id arguments.

NOTE
Reports has no object types and no object ids.

Object	Type	Lookup Function
Axis	OG_AXIS	OG_GET_AXIS
Button Procedure	OG_BUTTONPROC	OG_GET_BUTTONPROC
Chart Template	OG_TEMPLATE	OG_GET_TEMPLATE
Display	OG_DISPLAY	OG_GET_DISPLAY
Field Template	OG_FTEMP	OG_GET_FTEMP
Graphic Object	OG_OBJECT	OG_GET_OBJECT
Layer	OG_LAYER	OG_GET_LAYER
Query	OG_QUERY	OG_GET_QUERY
Reference Line	OG_REFLINE	OG_GET_REFLINE
Sound	OG_SOUND	OG_GET_SOUND
Timer	OG_TIMER	OG_GET_TIMER
Window	OG_WINDOW	OG_GET_WINDOW

TABLE 10-2. *Graphics Object Types and Lookup Functions*

Declaring Variables and Constants

You have already seen several declarations of variables earlier in this book. A variable declaration in a DECLARE section takes this form:

```
variable_name  type_name  [NOT NULL] [:= initial_value];
```

You can also declare variables in a parameter list of a subprogram (procedure or function); see Chapter 11.

The NOT NULL qualifier specifies that you cannot assign a NULL value to the variable. The assignment of an initial value sets the variable to the value you specify with a literal or an expression. If you specify NOT NULL, you must also specify the initial value. It is a good idea to initialize all variables to ensure that you have a valid value to which to refer the first time you use the identifier. You can also use the reserved word DEFAULT in place of the assignment operator: DEFAULT initial_value instead of := initial value.

You can refer to Developer/2000 objects through host variables. A *host variable* is a name from the embedding application that you reference by prefixing a colon (":") to the name. You can use these host variables anywhere you can use a PL/SQL variable, inside a SQL statement or outside.

```
BEGIN

/* Update the age in the block field and the database. */
  :Person.Age := :Person.Age+1;
  UPDATE Person SET Age = Age+1 WHERE Name = :Person.Name;
END;
```

PL/SQL has the same types as all the Developer/2000 products, so the host variables do not need a separate declaration in the PL/SQL procedure. PL/SQL treats them as though you had declared them with the type you specified in the item definition.

NOTE
Developer/2000 objects use the VARCHAR2 type to represent text values. The differences between CHAR, VARCHAR, and VARCHAR2 are important in certain cases. CHAR represents fixed-length data. If you assign a value to a CHAR variable with a length greater than the value's length, PL/SQL pads out the string to the length of the variable with blanks. VARCHAR and VARCHAR2 are the same and do not pad in this way. In the future, Oracle Corporation may change the behavior of VARCHAR, so you cannot assume that it will always be the same as VARCHAR2. You may have problems with

assignments and with comparisons. If you assign a value that is shorter than the size of the CHAR variable, PL/SQL pads the string. If you have trailing blanks in a VARCHAR2 variable and compare it to another string of any type, PL/SQL treats the blanks as valid characters and makes them part of the comparison, but it does not pad out the other string. If you compare two CHAR variables, PL/SQL pads out the shorter one to the length of the longer one before comparing. This means that if you have trailing blanks in the longer string, PL/SQL will effectively ignore them by comparing them to padded blanks in the shorter string. For a complete discussion of comparison semantics, see Appendix C of the *PL/SQL User's Guide and Reference* (Part Number A12715-1).

A *constant* is an identifier that gets a value when you declare it and to which you cannot thereafter assign any values. You declare a constant with the CONSTANT keyword:

```
constant_name   CONSTANT   type_name   := value;
```

PL/SQL requires the initialization of the constant; this value is the value of the constant for its entire life cycle.

Using Type Attributes

A PL/SQL *attribute* is a modifier that you can use to get information about an object for use in declaring other objects. The %TYPE attribute lets you get the type of a variable, a constant, or a database column. The %ROWTYPE attribute lets you get the types of all the columns in a database table or a SELECT cursor result table.

You can use %TYPE to declare variables with the same type as another variable or constant. You can also use it to declare variables with the same type as a database column, usually because you are going to store a value from that column in the variable.

The following example code retrieves a value from the database, increments the value, and assigns the result to a new variable with the same type.

```
DECLARE
   dbAge      Person.Age%TYPE;    -- database column type
   newAge     dbAge%TYPE;         -- type from dbAge
BEGIN
   SELECT Age INTO dbAge FROM Person
    WHERE Person.Name = :Person.Name;
   newAge := dbAge + 1;
END;
```

NOTE
Even when you declare a database column with the NOT NULL attribute, PL/SQL does not give the variable the NOT NULL qualifier. You must do that explicitly if you wish to prevent assignment of NULL to the variable.

You can use the %ROWTYPE attribute to create a record variable that can contain all the columns from a table. For example, say you wanted to retrieve skills and abilities from the database for further processing in a trigger. The following declarations create a record that will hold the columns of the WorkerHasSkill table:

```
DECLARE
   hasSkillRecord    WorkerHasSkill%ROWTYPE;
BEGIN
    -- Retrieve records and process; for example,
hasSkillRecord.Name := 'Gerhardt Kentgen';
END;
```

The %ROWTYPE attribute also applies to tables you create as the result of a cursor SELECT. Using %ROWTYPE, you can create a record that PL/SQL automatically formats correctly to hold whatever data the SELECT returns. If you use %ROWTYPE, you need not declare the individual variables with their types, making maintenance easier. For example, if you wanted to retrieve the sums of the amounts from the Ledger table grouped by person, you could declare the variable this way:

```
DECLARE
   CURSOR sumCursor IS SELECT Person, SUM(Amount) Total
      FROM Ledger GROUP BY Person;
   sumRecord   sumCursor%ROWTYPE;
BEGIN
   null;  -- Retrieve rows and process
END;
```

When you use %ROWTYPE this way, you *must* specify an alias for any expressions in the SELECT list, such as Total in the sumCursor SELECT. This alias becomes the variable name for the field in the record PL/SQL creates.

See the following section on using SQL with PL/SQL for more details on cursors.

You can assign one %ROWTYPE variable to another if they both come from the same table or cursor. You cannot assign the record you create with %ROWTYPE to variables you create with a RECORD type. You can use RECORD types in much the same way as %ROWTYPE declarations except with cursors. The disadvantage of a RECORD is that you cannot automatically create its structure from the data dictionary. The advantage is that you can give it whatever structure you like, including additional fields that do not correspond to database columns.

An Even Briefer Introduction to Control

The control statements in a programming language are its primary reason for existing, which is especially true for PL/SQL. Control structures differentiate a procedural programming language from a declarative programming language such as SQL. When you embed SQL in PL/SQL, you combine the best aspects of the declarative language with the added benefits of the control structures with which you surround the SQL statements.

There are three kinds of control structures: sequential, conditional, and iterative.

A *sequential structure* is the simple order of program statements. PL/SQL executes them in order, one at a time. SQL works on a statement-by-statement basis; the language understands only a single statement at a time. PL/SQL processes a series of statements and has variables that connect the statements. This gives you much more flexibility to structure your processing by letting you break it into a series of steps, including multiple SQL statements.

A *conditional structure* is a statement that branches program flow based on the truth or falsity of a logical condition. You use conditional structures to make decisions about further processing, which you cannot do easily in SQL. The DECODE function gives you a limited ability to make decisions on a row-by-row basis, but complex conditions quickly get out of hand in the declarative syntax.

An *iterative structure* is a statement that controls a looping process that repetitively executes program statements. SQL, by its nature, provides for looping in several ways as an internal mechanism. Besides the simple iteration over the multiple rows of the result table, SQL has nested subqueries that let you loop in a highly structured, powerful way using predicate calculus operators (ANY and ALL, EXISTS and IN, for example). SQL even has the correlated subquery to let you test the row of an outer query to the rows of a nested subquery on a row-by-row basis. Still, even these capabilities are not flexible enough to easily handle all the possible iterative situations you will find yourself in during database application programming. Iterative control structures give you both the ability to retrieve rows from the database and to process them using more SQL. This can be much simpler and faster than the nested selects or joins in a single SQL statement. Iteration also lets you accomplish many standard programming tasks at the application level, for which SQL is not appropriate.

NOTE
PL/SQL also provides an unconditional branching statement (GOTO with a statement label), which you should avoid unless it makes the program clearer. For example, in lengthy procedures you can sometimes get very complex conditional and iterative procedures that, if replaced with a simple GOTO, would be much easier to understand. This is rare. The standard case of simplifying error handling, for example, by branching to an ERROR label, is better done with exceptions; see Chapter 11.

Conditional Control

PL/SQL provides the IF-THEN, IF-THEN-ELSE, and IF-THEN-ELSIF-ELSE structures for conditional control of program execution. The IF-THEN structure tests a condition and, if it is true, executes a block of code. For example, the following trigger block tests the age of the current worker and displays an alert, then causes the trigger to fail by raising the FORM_TRIGGER_FAILURE exception.

```
DECLARE
  alertButton NUMBER;
BEGIN
  IF :Person.age < 16 THEN
    alertButton := Show_Alert('under_age_alert'); --Display error
    RAISE FORM_TRIGGER_FAILURE;
  END IF;
END;
```

NOTE
See the section on exceptions and exception handling in Chapter 11 for more information on the RAISE statement.

If you have two program blocks, one for the TRUE decision and one for the FALSE, you can use the IF-THEN-ELSE structure:

```
DECLARE
  alertButton NUMBER;
BEGIN
  IF :Person.age < 16 THEN
    alertButton := Show_Alert('under_age_alert'); --Display error
    RAISE FORM_TRIGGER_FAILURE;
  ELSE
```

```
    alertButton := Show_Alert('over_age_alert'); --Display error
  END IF;
END;
```

If your decision has several parts, you can use nested IF statements in your ELSE clause, but a better way is the ELSIF structure:

```
DECLARE
  alertButton NUMBER;
BEGIN
  IF :Person.age < 16 THEN
    alertButton := Show_Alert('under_age_alert'); --Display error
    RAISE FORM_TRIGGER_FAILURE;
  ELSIF :Person.age > 70 THEN
    alertButton := Show_Alert('over_age_alert'); --Display error
      RAISE FORM_TRIGGER_FAILURE;
  ELSE  -- Worker is between 16 and 70 years old, inclusive
    alertButton := Show_Alert('age_ok_alert'); --Display info alert
  END IF;
END;
```

In this control structure, the first condition identifies values under 17, the second identifies values over and including 17 but greater than 70, and the ELSE clause identifies values between 17 and 70, inclusive. The ELSIF clauses all imply that the conditions in prior IF and ELSIF clauses evaluated to FALSE.

> **NOTE**
> Rules for testing NULL values are the same as for SQL. Remember that NULL is not a value, it is the absence of a value. Therefore, you must use the IS NULL and IS NOT NULL expressions instead of equality comparisons to test whether some expression is or is not NULL, respectively.

Iteration Control

The Developer/2000 tools build in quite a bit of iteration control. Forms retrieve sets of records automatically through blocks, executing triggers at all levels. Reports loop over rows and groups with a very complex iteration structure that the report data model drives through its groups. Even Graphics fetches data into a table for translation into charts in a looping process. Before using iteration in trigger code and program units with Developer/2000, you should try to make use of what is already there. For example, you can put program statements into item or record triggers, and Forms will execute them automatically for each row in an iteration structure. You can put statements into page triggers in reports, and Reports will execute them after each page. The PL/SQL control structures give you some additional control within a particular trigger, but you should avoid the complexity if you can.

There are three kinds of iteration control statements in PL/SQL: LOOP, WHILE, and FOR.

The LOOP statement, in combination with the EXIT WHEN statement, lets you loop until a particular condition evaluates to TRUE. For example, to loop through all the records in a block, incrementing age by 1, you could use this block:

```
DECLARE
   currentPosition  VARCHAR2 := :SYSTEM.CURSOR_RECORD;
BEGIN
  FIRST_RECORD;
  LOOP
    :Person.age := :Person.age + 1;
    EXIT WHEN :SYSTEM.LAST_RECORD = 'TRUE';
    NEXT_RECORD;
  END LOOP;
  Go_Record(currentPosition);    -- Reset cursor
END;
```

This structure executes the statements at least once, as the test for EXIT WHEN comes at the end of the statements. In this case, if the first record is a New record with NULL age, the result will be NULL, with no effective change even though there was one iteration of the loop.

If you nest LOOP statements within other LOOP statements, you can label them and refer to the label in the EXIT WHEN statement to specify what loop in the nested stack to exit. See the *PL/SQL User's Guide and Reference* for more information.

The WHILE statement lets you control processing by evaluating a condition before executing the statements:

```
DECLARE
   currentPosition  VARCHAR2 := :SYSTEM.CURSOR_RECORD;
BEGIN
  FIRST_RECORD;
  WHILE :SYSTEM.LAST_RECORD != 'TRUE' LOOP
    :Person.age := :Person.age + 1;
    EXIT WHEN :SYSTEM.LAST_RECORD = 'TRUE';
    NEXT_RECORD;
  END LOOP;
```

```
   :Person.age := :Person.age + 1;
   Go_Record(currentPosition);    -- Reset cursor
END;
```

This structure need not execute the statements within the control structure at all if the condition immediately evaluates to FALSE. In this case, the example would never update the last record, so there needs to be a final update after the loop. As before, if the age is NULL, the statement evaluates to and assigns NULL to the age, resulting in no change.

Finally, the FOR statement lets you put an explicit numeric limit on the number of iterations:

```
DECLARE
   currentPosition   VARCHAR2 := :SYSTEM.CURSOR_RECORD;
   lastRecord VARCHAR2 := 0;
BEGIN
   LAST_RECORD;
   lastRecord := :SYSTEM.CURSOR_RECORD;
   FIRST_RECORD;
   FOR I IN 1..To_Number(lastRecord) LOOP
     :Person.age := :Person.age + 1;
     NEXT_RECORD;
   END LOOP;
   Go_Record(currentPosition);    -- Reset cursor
END;
```

This structure executes the loop within the range of numbers you specify. It also gives you a value to use through the counter you declare in the FOR statement. You can use this value to look up specific records, to insert values into the database with an incremented number, and so on.

You can specify the lower and upper limits of the range with an expression, as in the example. You can use this feature to tie the range to some variable outside the loop, or you can use it to determine the range dynamically at runtime. For example, you could get a count of the number of rows in a table with a SQL statement, then loop through the fetching of the rows that number of times. This is not the most efficient use of loops, however, because you can more effectively use the %NOTFOUND attribute on the cursor (see the following section on SQL) to exit a standard LOOP.

The example gets the number of the range end by setting the cursor to the last record and saving the record number. This lets you loop over the records precisely the right number of times. As in the LOOP example, if there is only one New record, it gets updated with NULL.

Looking at the three examples, none stands out from the others as being better, though perhaps the LOOP is the most straightforward. You can usually do the same thing with any of the three iteration control structures. You will usually have to judge which is better by the number of lines of code and your subjective judgment about which design is simpler. One way to make that judgment is to look at how easy the code would be to verify as correct: how many things would you need to look at? Do you have a single decision or multiple decisions? Do you have special cases you must take into account? For example, the preceding WHILE code must use a statement after the loop to update the last row, which seems like one thing too many given the alternatives.

NOTE
See the following section for a special version of the FOR loop that automatically handles cursor fetching. This structure can save you much programming if its functionality does what you need.

Using SQL in PL/SQL

There are two reasons to use PL/SQL in Developer/2000 applications: to add special-purpose code that does calculations or uses control structures, or to issue SQL statements to the server beyond what the Developer/2000 tools give you automatically.

NOTE
SQL error handling in PL/SQL uses exceptions. Chapter 11 gives details on raising and handling exceptions, and tells you how to use the SQLCODE and SQLERRM built-in functions in error handlers.

Simple SQL

The simplest way to use SQL in PL/SQL is to just use it. PL/SQL treats SQL statements as programming language statements and will accept almost any standard SQL. Many triggers will consist of a simple INSERT, UPDATE, or DELETE statement, perhaps using host variables to connect the statement to items in the application.

There are some SQL statements that you cannot use in PL/SQL:

- DDL statements such as CREATE TABLE, GRANT, or ALTER VIEW, which imply the end of a transaction
- Session control commands, such as SET ROLE

- ALTER SYSTEM

- EXPLAIN PLAN

You should avoid DML statements (INSERT, UPDATE, and DELETE) in triggers that can modify application items after committing data to the database, as this may lead to incorrect results. Refer to the trigger processing descriptions in Chapter 6.

You can use COMMIT, ROLLBACK, and SAVEPOINT statements in PL/SQL programs, but it is not a good idea for client-side code. The Developer/2000 runtime systems have very specific ideas about transaction processing, and doing a COMMIT or ROLLBACK is likely to disrupt that. Developer/2000 Forms does interpret a COMMIT as an implicit call to the procedure COMMIT_FORM, but you should use it only in very high-level code that executes at a well-defined point in your program.

There is a special SELECT syntax that lets you retrieve a single row of data: the implicit cursor or single-row select. The ANSI standard requires that the SELECT statement actually return only one row; if the statement finds more than one row that qualify, it must raise an error.

The implicit cursor adds an INTO clause after the select list, with host variables that map to the elements in the select list. You can declare these variables with %TYPE or use items that map to the data correctly.

```
SELECT Age INTO :dbAge FROM Person WHERE Name = :Person.Name;
```

Using Explicit Cursors

The serious SQL work for PL/SQL programs begins when you need to work with queries that return more than one row. To do this, you must declare and use explicit cursors. An *explicit cursor* is a PL/SQL data structure that represents the position of a query in a result table deriving from execution of a SELECT statement. PL/SQL gives you many tools to make using cursors easier.

NOTE
Remember that blocks and their records in Forms and data models in reports handle this kind of thing automatically. You can use these automatic facilities if you can develop blocks or data models that represent the iteration. Explicit cursors, although very useful in general PL/SQL programming, have less application in Developer/2000 programming. You can use them to implement more complex SQL than you can create automatically. The disadvantage is that you must rewrite all the automatic features you render useless. If you need more details than this section presents, see the *PL/SQL User's Guide and Reference*.

The basic form for an explicit cursor looks like this example:

```
DECLARE
  CURSOR skillCursor IS SELECT Skill, Description FROM Skill;
  skillRecord skillCursor%ROWTYPE;
BEGIN
  OPEN skillCursor;
  LOOP
    FETCH skillCursor INTO skillRecord;
    -- Process the row
    EXIT WHEN skillCursor%NOTFOUND;
  END LOOP;
  CLOSE skillCursor;
END;
```

The two declarations set up the basic data structures for the block. The cursor contains the SELECT statement that retrieves all the data from the Skill table. The record declaration uses the %ROWTYPE attribute to create a record with the structure of the SELECT.

The OPEN and CLOSE statements execute and terminate the query. When you OPEN the cursor, you are executing the query; you must then fetch the rows. When you CLOSE the cursor, you can no longer fetch any more rows.

NOTE
There is a limit on the number of cursors you can open set by the OPEN_CURSORS initialization parameter. Running out of available cursors can stop your program with an exception. You should carefully match OPEN and CLOSE statements to make sure that you close each cursor when you finish with it.

The LOOP shows the basic structure of fetching. This variation uses the %NOTFOUND attribute of the cursor to test for an attempt to fetch beyond the end of the results table. It is the same as the SQL message ROW NOT FOUND.

There is a shortcut way to do all this using a special option to the FOR LOOP statement:

```
DECLARE
  CURSOR skillCursor IS SELECT Skill, Description FROM Skill;
BEGIN
  FOR skillRecord IN skillCursor LOOP
    null;-- Process the row
  END LOOP;
END;
```

This block does exactly the same thing as the longer block above. You should use this shortcut syntax unless you have complex logic that requires that you have explicit control over fetching, opening the cursor, or closing the cursor.

NOTE
Remember that if you use expressions in the SELECT list, you must supply an alias that you can use as the field name in the record. Without the alias, you will not be able to refer to the field.

There are several cursor attributes that you can use to get information about the status of the cursor. Most of the attributes in Table 10-3 apply to both explicit and implicit cursors. For explicit cursors, you use the attributes by appending them to the cursor name. For implicit cursors, you use the implicit cursor name "SQL": for example, SQL%NOTFOUND or SQL%ISOPEN.

NOTE
You can use these attributes on the implicit cursors for data manipulation statements (INSERT, UPDATE, and DELETE) as well as for SELECT statements. %ROWCOUNT, for example, gives the number of rows inserted, updated, or deleted for an implicit cursor on these statements.

An important feature of cursors for reuse is the ability to parameterize cursors. You can use cursor parameters in the SELECT statement anywhere you could use a host variable or a literal value (see the section on host variables above). When

Attribute	Description
%NOTFOUND	TRUE when the last fetch failed to return a row; you use this attribute to test whether your loop has fetched the last row.
%FOUND	TRUE when the last fetch did return a row; you use this attribute to test whether there is valid data from a fetch to execute some further action, such as inserting the data into another table.
%ROWCOUNT	0 when you open the cursor, and increments by one for each row you fetch.
%ISOPEN	TRUE if the cursor is open, FALSE otherwise; you use this attribute to test whether you need to open the cursor if there was some control action that might have closed it.

TABLE 10-3. *The PL/SQL Cursor Attributes*

PL/SQL opens the cursor, it accepts the values you supply for the parameters and inserts them into the SQL statement. The scope of the parameters is the cursor; you cannot use the parameter names anywhere other than the SELECT statement in the cursor. The following code illustrates the use of a parameterized cursor:

```
DECLARE
  CURSOR skillCursor (abbrev IN VARCHAR2 DEFAULT '%') IS
    SELECT Skill, Description FROM Skill
     WHERE UPPER(Skill) LIKE UPPER(abbrev);
BEGIN
  FOR skillRecord IN skillCursor('%Horse%') LOOP
    null; -- Process the row
  END LOOP;
END;
```

This example expands the Skill query to handle subsets based on pattern lookups in the Skill table. You supply a LIKE operator expression, and the query finds those records that match the expression. In the example, the FOR LOOP passes in a pattern that tells the SELECT to look for any skill that contains the term "horse." Notice the conversions to uppercase in the SELECT; this makes it case insensitive for comparisons, making the cursor even more reusable. Also, notice the DEFAULT clause attached to the parameter; this clause supplies the obvious pattern to use when you pass no arguments, the "match any characters" pattern.

NOTE
Parameterized cursors are more useful when you declare them as part of a package specification, exporting the cursor and its parameters. This lets external programs use the cursor, supplying arguments as required for the particular purpose of the program. See Chapter 11 for details on packages.

Chapter 10 has taken you through the basic parts of PL/SQL programming. You can now declare data structures, write basic procedural code, and integrate SQL into your code in reasonably complex ways. The next chapter will expand your horizons into the different ways that PL/SQL lets you structure your code.

CHAPTER 11

Super Programmers

PL/SQL is a simple language, but as with many simple things, it is most complex when it is simplest. In particular, you can use the tools described in Chapter 10 to create an infinite structure of badly organized code, duplicated over and over throughout your chaos of applications.

To reduce the complexity, PL/SQL offers a series of tools that let you structure your system of code in seemingly simple ways. Although the structure adds complexity to your initial programming task, you will find that judicious use of these facilities will make your system much more reusable and more easily maintained over its lifetime. These tools include *exceptions* for error handling; *functions* and *procedures* for organizing chunks of code; *packages* for clustering code into abstract data types using cursors and other data structures; and *libraries* for building easily reused systems of code.

Making Exceptions

Exceptions are gradually finding their way into mainstream database applications programming after many years of languishing on the sidelines. Anyone who has ever programmed large database applications (except, perhaps, in PL/1) knows that the error-handling code in database programming often grows to obscure the code it supports. The exception is the preferred way to do error handling in modern programming languages. You can also use it to replace most of the uses of the GOTO statement, because it implements a well-understood flow of control within a block.

An *exception* is a signal of some kind that the runtime system raises when your program identifies or encounters an anomalous condition. In PL/SQL, these events have names and a system for handling the signal: the *exception handler*.

There are three kinds of exceptions you can use in your programming:

■ *Built-in PL/SQL exceptions*: Exceptions that are part of the PL/SQL programming language.

■ *Built-in runtime exceptions*: Exceptions that are part of the Developer/2000 runtime environment (Forms, Graphics, and Reports all have different exceptions).

■ *User-defined exceptions:* Exceptions you define to handle ORACLE7 error messages or other situations in your code.

Recall from Chapter 10 the basic form of a PL/SQL block:

```
DECLARE
  --Data declarations
BEGIN
  null;--Program statements
EXCEPTION
  --Exception handlers
  WHEN OTHERS THEN
    null;--default handler
END;
```

This section focuses on the last clause in the block, the EXCEPTION clause. The structure of your exception handlers within this clause looks like this:

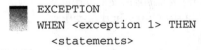

```
EXCEPTION
WHEN <exception 1> THEN
  <statements>
```

```
...  -- more exception handlers
WHEN OTHERS THEN
  <statements>
```

The EXCEPTION clause is a series of exception handlers, each of which begins with WHEN and the exception name. When the block raises an exception, PL/SQL stops executing the block and checks the EXCEPTION clause of the block for a handler for that exception. If there is one, PL/SQL jumps to the handler, executes it, and returns to the caller. If there is none, PL/SQL jumps out of the current block and goes to the exception handler in the block that encloses the first block. Either way, no further program statements in the main part of the block execute, and PL/SQL does not execute any statements between the one that raised the exception and the exception handler.

This handing off of the exception is called exception *propagation*. If the top-level subprogram does not handle the exception, control passes back to the caller's exception handler, and the exception propagates within the calling subprogram. Eventually, if nothing handles the exception, it propagates to the host environment, which handles it by some default action, usually rolling back. A Developer/2000 application will display an alert that prints a default message, then it will take the action appropriate to the exception. For example, on raising FORM_TRIGGER_FAILURE, Developer/2000 Forms will abort the trigger and the process driving it, usually leaving the cursor on the offending item or record.

NOTE
When you propagate the exception outside the subprogram, PL/SQL does not set the OUT parameters of the subprogram and automatically rolls back work done in the subprogram. If this is not what you want to happen, you should code a WHEN OTHERS clause in the outer block of the subprogram to handle the exception the way you want.

You can explicitly raise any exception with the RAISE statement:

```
RAISE <exception-name>;
```

When PL/SQL executes this, it transfers control to the exception handler in the block. If the block does not handle the exception, it propagates.

If you handle the exception, but you want the outer block or calling subprogram to see the exception, you can explicitly propagate it with just the RAISE statement:

```
RAISE;
```

This should be the last statement in your handler.

NOTE
If you raise an exception in a declarations section or in an exception section, the exception immediately propagates. You must put any exception handler for this exception in an outer block.

PL/SQL Built-in Exceptions

PL/SQL defines several exceptions as part of its STANDARD package. These are described in Table 11-1. All PL/SQL programs can raise these exceptions.

The most common built-in exceptions you need to handle in your code are the NO_DATA_FOUND and VALUE_ERROR exceptions. NO_DATA_FOUND occurs when your single-row select (SELECT ... INTO) fails to return a row. VALUE_ERROR occurs when a statement has a problem with a value (arithmetic, conversion, truncation, or constraint). The most common problem that raises VALUE_ERROR is assigning a string that is too long to a variable. For example, if you define a variable as VARCHAR2(10) and try to assign the string "George E. Talbot" to it, you will raise VALUE_ERROR. The string has 14 characters, but the variable allows only 10.

Developer/2000 Built-in Exceptions

Each of the three Developer/2000 products has a set of built-in exceptions. Reversing the usual trend, Forms is quite simple, whereas Graphics and Reports use exceptions extensively.

Forms provides a single built-in exception during normal, runtime processing: FORM_TRIGGER_FAILURE. Forms raises this exception whenever a trigger fails during one of the many Forms processes. You can use this exception in your code within a trigger to tell PL/SQL that the trigger failed:

```
RAISE FORM_TRIGGER_FAILURE;
```

Forms also provides the DEBUG.BREAK exception, with which you can explicitly embed a debugger break through a RAISE statement in a block. See Chapter 13 for details.

Exception	Description
CURSOR_ALREADY_OPEN	You tried to open an open cursor.
DUP_VAL_ON_INDEX	You tried to insert a row with a duplicate value in a column indexed with a unique index.
INVALID_CURSOR	You tried to execute a cursor operation on a closed cursor.
INVALID_NUMBER	You tried to convert a string to a number in a SQL statement, but the string had non-numeric characters in it.
LOGON_DENIED	You tried to log on to ORACLE but failed because of an invalid logon name or password
NO_DATA_FOUND	You executed a SELECT ... INTO statement, but the server did not return a row. This exception applies only to single-row selects, not to explicit cursor selects; use the %NOTFOUND attribute on the cursor to determine whether a fetch was successful.
NOT_LOGGED_ON	You tried to access the database through PL/SQL without being logged on to a database.
PROGRAM_ERROR	PL/SQL encountered some kind of internal error.
STORAGE_ERROR	PL/SQL ran out of memory while executing a statement.
TIMEOUT_ON_RESOURCE	PL/SQL timed out waiting for a resource.
TOO_MANY_ROWS	A SELECT ... INTO statement resulted in more than one row in the result table.
TRANSACTION_BACKED_OUT	A remote transaction could not complete; you need to roll back your transaction and retry it.
VALUE_ERROR	You encountered an arithmetic, conversion, truncation, or constraint error in a procedural or SQL statement. A SQL statement raises INVALID_NUMBER for a conversion error on a number instead of VALUE_ERROR.
ZERO_DIVIDE	You tried to divide a number by zero.

TABLE 11-1. *Built-in PL/SQL Exceptions*

Reports packages its exceptions in the SRW package, which defines the exceptions in Table 11-2.

The two most common exceptions you will use in Reports code are the RUN_REPORT_FAILURE exception and the PROGRAM_ABORT exception. RUN_REPORT_FAILURE indicates to Reports that a report failed, so it prints a general message and ends the report. You can code an exception handler to display your own error message, say when you are running a second report from within a report. You can raise PROGRAM_ABORT to stop report execution on some fatal error in your code with the appropriate error message.

SRW Exception	Description
SRW.CONTEXT_FAILURE	You called a packaged procedure from an invalid place.
SRW.DO_SQL_FAILURE	The DO_SQL procedure failed.
SRW.INTEGER_ERROR	You supplied a nonintegral number to a subprogram that requires an integer (SRW.MESSAGE or SRW.SET_MAXROW).
SRW.MAXROW_INERR	Reports had an internal error in SET_MAXROW.
SRW.MAXROW_UNSET	You called SET_MAXROW after completing the fetching of the report records.
SRW.NULL_ARGUMENTS	You called a procedure with missing arguments.
SRW.PROGRAM_ABORT	This is a general failure exception that you can use to stop the report from executing.
SRW.RUN_REPORT_FAILURE	A general failure in the RUN_REPORT procedure occurred.
SRW.TRUNCATED_VALUE	You tried to set a parameter or column with a value that is larger than the object's defined maximum length.
SRW.UNKNOWN_QUERY	You called SET_MAXROW with an unknown query.
SRW.UNKNOWN_USER_EXIT	Reports cannot locate the specified user exit that you want to run.
SRW.USER_EXIT_FAILURE	You returned from an exit with the SRWERB buffer containing a value.

TABLE 11-2. *Reports' Built-in SRW Exceptions*

Developer/2000 Graphics has a truly stupendous array of built-in exceptions, too many to detail here. See the *Graphics Reference Manual* (Part Number A32483-1) for a complete list. If you code extensively in Graphics, you will find yourself using many exception handlers to deal with the many exceptional situations that arise. There is a broad array of objects you can program in a Graphics display, each with a different set of possible error situations. There are about 200 such exceptions, one for each possible error you can get in programming with the OG and TOOLINT packages.

For example, Graphics raises the exception OG_DATE_OVERFLOW when you try to display a date axis with OG_UPDATE_CHART but the data extend beyond the valid range of the axis. It raises OG_INVALID_POSITION when you specify an invalid position on an axis.

User-Defined Exceptions

There are two kinds of user-defined exceptions: ORACLE7 error exceptions and user exceptions.

You can use the pragma EXCEPTION_INIT to set up a named exception for a particular ORACLE7 error message. A *pragma* is a compiler directive that tells the compiler to do something while compiling. In this case, it tells the compiler to create an exception for the ORACLE7 error code:

```
privilegesException EXCEPTION;
PRAGMA EXCEPTION_INIT(privilegesException, -1031);
```

This statement associates ORACLE7 error -1031 with the name privilegesException. When ORACLE sends that error to PL/SQL, PL/SQL raises the named exception and passes control to your exception handler. This PRAGMA saves you some code; otherwise, you would have to catch the general ORACLE7 error condition and test the error code (SQLCODE) for the error number in a complicated conditional control structure.

To define a simple user exception, all you need to do is to declare the exception in a DECLARE block. For example, if a trigger did some internal validation for a ledger record, it might have a special exception for the failure of this validation so that you can report the problem:

```
DECLARE
   validationException    EXCEPTION;
   alertButton NUMBER;
BEGIN
   null;   -- Do the validating.
EXCEPTION
```

```
WHEN validationException THEN
   alertButton := Show_Alert('LedgerValidationAlert');
   RAISE FORM_TRIGGER_FAILURE;
WHEN OTHERS THEN
   RAISE FORM_TRIGGER_FAILURE;
END;
```

Exceptions are scoped just like variables. You can define an exception as many times as you want in different scopes. You may find it better to define a given exception just once in a package (see the following section), exporting it to the subprograms that use it. You can also define exceptions with different names. This ensures that an exception handler that handles the exception will in fact handle it. If you define two exceptions with the same name, they are *two separate exceptions.* This can be very confusing when you code your error handlers, particularly in subprograms with nested blocks. It is *particularly* unwise to declare your own exception with one of the built-in exception names such as NO_DATA_FOUND.

Using Blocks to Control Exception Handling

In some situations, you will want to continue processing after handling an exception. Unfortunately, when PL/SQL raises an exception, it ends block processing and returns to the caller after executing any exception-handler code. This means that you cannot go back to the point in the block that raised the exception and continue. The usual situation is where you have several statements and you want to execute all of them even if one fails for some reason.

If you want to have full control of this sort over processing, you must divide your subprogram into nested blocks. See the following section on subprograms (functions and procedures) for more details on block nesting. What this lets you do is to put the exception handler for each "nonfatal" exception in a separate block. After the handler executes, the block exits to the enclosing block and continues executing. It only skips the code in the nested block.

For example, say you wanted to look up a data value in a table, but also to set up a default value to use in case the original data value isn't in the table. You could execute several SQL statements to determine the true state and branch accordingly, or you could have a structure like this:

```
DECLARE
   lookupValue VARCHAR2;
BEGIN
   BEGIN
      SELECT lookupValue INTO lookupValue FROM LookupTable;
```

```
EXCEPTION
  WHEN NO_DATA_FOUND THEN
    lookupValue := 'N/A';
END;
INSERT INTO AuditTable (currentDate, currentValue)
  VALUES (sysdate, lookupValue);
END;
```

This block first executes the single-row select to find the lookup value. If the server returns no data, the nested block exception handler assigns a default value, and processing continues with the first statement below the END of the nested block: the INSERT statement.

Error-Handling Functions

There are two PL/SQL built-in functions that you can use in exception handlers to deal with database errors.

The SQLCODE function returns the error code of the last error. This code will be a negative number, or it will be +100 (NOT FOUND) or +1 for errors you define with PRAGMA EXCEPTION_INIT.

The SQLERRM is the text of the error message, including the error code.

Developer/2000 Forms also provides some built-in functions for error handling, which Table 11-3 describes.

Function	Returns	Description
ERROR_TYPE	CHAR	Returns the type of error that last occurred: FRM for a Forms error or ORA for a database error
ERROR_CODE	NUMBER	Returns the code of the last Forms error
ERROR_TEXT	CHAR	Returns the text of the last Forms error
DBMS_ERROR_CODE	NUMBER	Returns the code of the last database error message that Forms detected
DBMS_ERROR_TEXT	CHAR	Returns the type and text of one or more database error messages; DBMS_ERROR_CODE is the first of these

TABLE 11-3. *Forms' Built-in Error-Handling Functions*

Making Blocks Less Anonymous

Chapter 10 used the anonymous block to great effect in showing you how to build simple chunks of code for triggers. When you get to the stage of needing to reuse code, the anonymous block becomes less useful. You need to move on to more formal organizations that name the block and parameterize it.

Subprograms

PL/SQL provides two kinds of objects that perform this organizing role in the language: procedures and functions. Together, these two kinds of code organization are *subprograms:* named, parameterized blocks of code that you call with arguments to perform some operation. A *function* is a subprogram that computes a value, whereas a *procedure* performs an action. In Developer/2000, you can code these into each module under the Program Units heading or you can add them to a library module. Either way, you must call the subprogram explicitly within trigger code or anywhere else that you refer to a subprogram name (group filters and formulas in Reports, for example, use functions). The subprogram call is a PL/SQL statement; hence, when you create a subprogram, you are *extending* the PL/SQL language by adding a new kind of statement.

You will typically program a *function* when you want to compute a single value as the result of the operation. You will program a *procedure* when you want to perform an operation rather than computing a value. However, all subprograms can have *output parameters,* which let you return a value through the parameter. Because you expect functions to return a single value, you should code functions without any OUT or IN OUT parameters. For error conditions and returns and the like, you should define and raise exceptions (see the preceding section). See the following section on parameters for more information about output parameters.

You can *overload* subprograms in a package or in another subprogram or block by having multiple subprograms with the same name. See the following section on packages for details.

Procedures

A procedure has a name, a set of parameters, and a block of code, as shown here:

```
PROCEDURE <name> [<argument list>] IS
  <declarations>
BEGIN
  <program statements>
END;
```

This syntax is similar to the anonymous block except for the replacement of the DECLARE keyword with the PROCEDURE ... IS sequence. Otherwise, the syntax is the same. The PROCEDURE ... IS sequence is the procedure *specification,* and the rest of the block is the procedure *body.* You can code the specification alone to *forward declare* a subprogram to another subprogram or block that uses it, then later code the entire subprogram.

Functions

A function has a name, a set of parameters, a return type, and a block of code. When you return from the function, the function returns to the caller a value of the type you specify. (This syntax is like the procedure's except for the RETURN clause in the specification.)

```
FUNCTION <name> [<argument list>] RETURN <type> IS
   <declarations>
BEGIN
   <program statements>
END;
```

To finish the function's processing and return a value, you use the RETURN statement with an expression that evaluates to the value to return.

NOTE

You can have as many RETURN statements as you like, but it is poor practice to have more than one. Having two or more exits from a subprogram leads to an explosion of possible control paths through the program, making unit testing difficult. When you get to integration testing, your tests must validate each return against each caller to ensure that the caller gets the correct value. Thus, saving a bit of coding with multiple returns leads to a tremendous increase in testing effort and in the potential for defects. One approach you can use is to raise internal exceptions and return from the exception handler. In general, though, it is better to structure your code to avoid the necessity. You can use nested blocks to achieve this (described in the upcoming section on nested blocks).

Parameters

To define a set of parameters to a subprogram, you have a list of declarations in parentheses:

```
( <variable> [ <mode> ] <type> [ := ¦ DEFAULT <value>, ... )
```

The <variable> is a standard PL/SQL identifier that names the parameter. The <mode> is one of three possibilities:

- *IN*: The parameter value is an input into the subprogram, and assignments to the variable do not change its value to the calling program. This is the default if you do not specify a mode. This kind of argument can be a variable, a constant, a literal, or an expression.

- *OUT*: The parameter value is an output from the subprogram, letting you assign a value to the variable that is accessible to the caller when the subprogram returns. You cannot use the variable until you assign a value to it. The variable in the caller (the argument) must be a variable you can modify; and it must be a variable, not a literal, because you assign a value to it.

- *IN OUT*: The parameter value is both an input and an output variable. You can use the input value and you can assign an output value for the caller to see. This kind of argument must be a variable because you can assign a value to it.

Again, you should avoid specifying OUT or IN OUT parameters on functions, which should return only a single value as their return value.

The <type> can be any valid PL/SQL type, including the Developer/2000 objects or types that you define. You do not constrain the types with scale or precision, such as VARCHAR2(20), you use only the type name.

The ":= ¦ DEFAULT <value>" clause means that you can use either the assignment operation := or the keyword DEFAULT to assign a default value to the parameter. This lets you call the subprogram without an argument for that parameter, in which case the subprogram assigns the default value as the argument. This works only for IN variables, not for OUT or IN OUT variables.

This sequence repeats in a comma-separated list.

If a subprogram has no parameters, it has no parentheses:

```
PROCEDURE <name>;
FUNCTION <name> RETURN <type>;
```

Calling Subprograms

A subprogram call is a PL/SQL statement, and you can put such a call anywhere you can put a PL/SQL statement. You can have the subprogram call as the only statement in the block:

```
Do_Key('NEXT RECORD');
```

You can have the subprogram call as part of an anonymous block or as part of a procedure:

```
DECLARE
   alertButton NUMBER;
BEGIN
   alertButton := Show_Alert('WarningAlert');
END;
```

When you call a function, as in the immediately preceding example, you must assign the result to a variable. If you do not, you will get an error saying that PL/SQL cannot find the procedure. The return type is part of how PL/SQL recognizes a function.

Where you define a subprogram determines where you can call that subprogram. If you define a subprogram in a module (a form, menu, report, or display), only the triggers and other subprograms you define in that module can call the subprogram. For example, if you define a procedure in a form module, only the form triggers and form subprograms can call that subprogram. If you define a function in a menu module, only the menu item commands and startup code can call that function.

If you define a subprogram in a library module, you must first attach the library to the module to be able to call the subprogram. To do this, find the Attached Libraries header in the module, click on the Create button, and choose the library to attach through the resulting dialog box.

Positional Notation   There are two ways to pass arguments to a subprogram. The first way is *positional notation*—big words that mean passing values for arguments in the same sequence as the subprogram defines the parameters. For example, say the procedure specification looks like this:

```
PROCEDURE testLedgerItem(itemID NUMBER, amount NUMBER);
```

Your procedure call might look like this:

```
testLedgerItem(456, :Ledger.Amount);
```

This passes the value "456" for itemID and the form item Ledger.Amount for the amount. Note the use of the bind variable syntax (the colon prefix) to pass the item object value.

Named Notation   The other way to pass parameters is *named notation*. Using this syntax, you can pass the values in any order by naming the parameter:

```
testLedgerItem(amount => :Ledger.Amount, itemID => 456);
```

Named notation is particularly helpful with defaults. If you use defaults with positional notation, you can leave out trailing parameters that have defaults. If you use named notation, you can leave out any parameter with a default, not just trailing ones. That means you can leave out some parameters with defaults but include others that follow the ones left out in the subprogram specification.

Report Filters and Formulas

A major use for functions in Developer/2000 reports is to implement filters and formulas.

A report *group filter* is a function returning a BOOLEAN value that Developer/2000 uses to select which records to display for the group. By setting the Filter property of the group to Condition and supplying a function, you tell Reports to display only those records in the group for which the function returns TRUE.

A report *formula* is a function you attach to a column with type property Formula that returns a value for each record in a group. You can use an expression instead of a function for this, but you cannot use the full facilities of PL/SQL without using a function. The function returns a single value with a data type corresponding to the column data type: number columns have functions that return NUMBER; date columns have functions that return DATE; and character columns return CHARACTER, VARCHAR, or VARCHAR2.

Nesting Blocks

The block-structured nature of PL/SQL gives you great control over the scope of the parts of your subprograms. The block structure of a program is the way in which you use PL/SQL blocks (DECLARE ... BEGIN ... END; sequences) to structure the availability of variables and exception handlers.

The basic idea of block structuring is that a block is a program statement. This statement executes in order, just as would any program statement. Within the statement, however, you can have an infinitely complex structure about which the outer block and its processing know nothing. This hiding, or *encapsulation*, permits you to decouple the complex workings of the internal block from the sequence of the outer block. This in turn reduces the complexity of your program and makes it easier to understand, debug, test, and maintain. For example, you can defer coding the nested block body, making it a program *stub*. You can then continue with coding and testing of the rest of the subprogram without worrying about the details of the nested block until you are ready.

The preceding section on exception handling provided an example of using nested blocks to control the flow of execution after exception handling. By putting the exception handler in an inside block, you can continue processing the outer block after handling the exception.

Block structure also lets you isolate logical clusters of code in a subprogram. For example, if you find yourself needing to have multiple returns from a subprogram, you should consider nesting the code you do not want to execute and executing that block conditionally. Then you can have a single point of exit from your subprogram. This clarifies the control structure of the program, especially for testing.

By declaring nested blocks, you can share data elements between blocks without using global variables. The nested blocks can refer to any variable you declare in the outer block.

You can nest entire subprograms within other subprograms by including them in the declarations section of the outer subprogram. You must declare nested subprograms after all other declarations (variables, types, or exceptions).

Positioning Blocks in the Navigator

Now you know how to code subprograms. The next question is where and how to do it. The introduction to this section noted two places in which you can code subprograms:

- *Program units*   Under the Program Units heading in a form, menu, display, or report module

- *Library*   In a library under the Libraries heading in Forms, Reports, or Graphics

There is a third choice as well:

- *Stored*   Stored in the database using CREATE FUNCTION and CREATE PROCEDURE statements or by creating the subprogram under the Database Objects heading

How do you decide where to define your subprogram?

Use a stored subprogram if you are using the subprogram to access data that you do not want to be generally available. This is the encapsulated procedure that Chapter 8 discusses. Use a stored subprogram if you are trying to accomplish a lot of database work in the subprogram. This will let you call the subprogram and have the (presumably) more powerful server execute everything. This also reduces network traffic. Use a stored subprogram if the operation is a general operation on a database object. This will let you share the operation among all the users of the object. This is the principle of cohesion, storing the operations near the data on which they operate. See the *ORACLE7 Server SQL Language Reference* for details of the CREATE commands you use to create stored subprograms (CREATE PROCEDURE and CREATE FUNCTION).

Use a library if you want to make the subprogram available to more than one module. This usually applies to a general operation that is applicable to different situations. Also, the subprogram should use the database in only limited ways; a stored subprogram should be used for most database-related operations. One exception would be subprograms that need to call built-in subprograms for the module. Another exception might be subprograms that need to refer to module variables. However, you should pass these values as arguments to the subprogram rather than directly referring to them. This *decoupling* of the subprogram from the data of the module is a basic tenet of good system architecture. The decoupling means you can store the subprogram in the database and pass module data to it.

The "Checking Out the Library" section at the end of the chapter shows how to create subprograms in libraries. Once you have coded your subprograms, you can then attach the library to any module to use the subprograms in that module. To attach a library, find the Attached Libraries heading in the module, select it, and click on Create. You can then choose the library through a standard Open File dialog box.

That leaves subprograms in the module. You should put subprograms in modules only if the code is so specific to the module that you cannot conceive of its being of any use in any other module. Heavy use of many module items, logic relating solely to a specialized application, or heavy use of other module objects through built-in subprograms would indicate module specificity.

To create a module program unit, find the Program Units heading under the module. Follow the same instructions used earlier for library modules. You see the New Program Unit dialog box (shown as Figure 11-1 in the "Creating a Library" section later in this chapter) and use the same PL/SQL editor to define the subprogram, but Developer/2000 stores the code with the form, menu, display, or report module.

Another situation would be the definition of an object group that included subprograms that operate on the objects in the group. This group acts as a kind of package, and it makes sense to include subprograms in that package for reuse in other modules. This is an alternative to PL/SQL packages or libraries; you'll learn more about this in the following sections.

Creative Packaging

A *package* lets you combine other PL/SQL elements into a single whole: a package of data objects, types, cursors, exceptions, and subprograms. The package has a specification and a body. A *package specification* is the public face of the package:

the specifications of the elements that the package lets you use. These elements are *public* elements. The *package body* is the implementation of the cursors and subprograms the package specifies, as well as any *private* elements you want to declare. You can replace the package body without recompiling the package specification.

Note:
You cannot nest packages within program units.

Creating a Package

Why would you create a package?

The package provides a way to combine PL/SQL elements into a cohesive system. The package is comparable to an object in an object-oriented system: it includes both state and behavior relating to some cohesive piece of the system. It provides for complete data abstraction and information hiding to improve the modularity of your program. This improved cohesion and decoupling of the data abstraction leads directly to improved understanding of the code and improved ability to maintain the software.

You can, for example, change a function in a package body without recompiling any of the callers of that function, because the interface specification does not change. You can also stub out the subprograms until you are ready to code them, or even not supply a body at all. This lets you compile and possibly unit-test program units that use the package without having to actually finish the package first.

The package also lets you define variables, constants, and cursors that persist throughout your session as either public or private elements. That gives you the ability to keep information around between procedure calls or transactions without having to rely on unstructured global variables. With a package, you have structured control of the data and operations. All such elements are NULL unless you initialize them in the declarations. You can also define subprograms entirely within the package body. You cannot access these subprograms outside the package.

Finally, PL/SQL's implementation of the package loads the entire package into memory when you use any part of it. That means that additional calls to the programs in the package do not require any additional loading of code, which increases performance. This feature also suggests that it is a good idea to keep your packages relatively simple and cohesive rather than collecting large numbers of disparate things into a single package.

There are several kinds of cohesion that indicate that you should be using a package.

- *Functional cohesion:* A set of elements that together apply to a specific function of the application, such as an object type or a cluster of related object types, represents functional cohesion.

- *Abstract cohesion:* A set of program units that work together as a layer of abstraction to provide a well-defined set of services is abstract cohesion; an application programming interface or API exhibits this kind of cohesion, and examples of it include the SRW package for Developer/2000 Reports and the OG package for Graphics.

- *Practical cohesion:* Using a set of objects and/or program units together, even though there are no service or functional aspects to such use, is practical cohesion. A specific case of practical cohesion is the packaging of a transaction and its elements, however diverse, into a single package of cursors and subprograms.

The logic for positioning packages is the same as for subprograms. (If necessary, review the "Positioning Blocks in the Navigator" section earlier in this chapter.) If you structure your packages well, you will easily distinguish database-related packages from purely client-oriented packages. For the sake of reusability, you should develop most application packages in libraries rather than in modules. The one exception to this rule is when you group a package with module objects such as blocks or charts. The process for creating your package is identical to that for subprograms. See the "Subprograms" section earlier in this chapter for details.

There are two package-related syntaxes, one for the specification and one for the body.

The Package Specification

```
PACKAGE <name> IS
  {<variable spec>|<type spec>|<cursor spec>|<exception spec>} ...
  <subprogram spec> ...
END;
```

See Chapter 10 for details on the specifications for variables and types. The specification includes a set of object specifications (variables and constants, types, cursors, and exceptions) followed by a set of subprogram specifications.

The cursor specification takes the following form:

```
CURSOR <name> <parameter list> RETURN <type>;
```

The cursor specification, because it does not include the SELECT statement, must provide the RETURN clause to identify the type of record the cursor fetches. The <type> can be any of the following types:

- *Record:* A previously defined record type
- *Variable%TYPE:* The type of a previously defined variable
- *Table.Column%TYPE:* The type of a database column
- *Table%ROWTYPE:* The record with types for all the columns in a table

If you are doing more than just selecting columns from a table, such as including a GROUP BY or an expression in the SELECT list, you must supply a record type. That type must match the type you specify in the cursor body, which you define in the package body. The objective of the cursor specification is to specify the interface of the cursor, which consists of the cursor name, parameter list, and return type.

The subprogram specification has the following syntax:

```
PROCEDURE | FUNCTION <name> <parameter list>
  [RETURN <type>];
```

See the "Parameters" section earlier in the chapter for the parameter list syntax. The RETURN clause applies only to the function. In a full subprogram definition, the statement continues with IS and the subprogram body. The objective of the subprogram specification is to export the interface of the subprogram, which consists of the name, the parameter list, and the return type. The subprogram specifications come *after* all the other declarations in the package specification.

You can *overload* subprograms in a package or in another subprogram or block by having multiple subprograms with the same name, as long as the number and/or type of the parameters differ. This lets you create alternative versions of the subprogram with different parameters. An example is the Developer/2000 built-in subprograms in the built-in packages that take either an object name or an object id as the first argument. These are really two separate, overloaded subprograms in the built-in package (Forms STANDARD, Reports SRW, or Graphics OG). Subprogram overloading lets you create a very flexible array of operations for different uses, making the package much more reusable and easy to use.

NOTE
The types must differ completely; REAL and NUMBER and FLOAT are all the same type when considering subprogram overloading. This applies to the RETURN type for functions.

The following example of a package specification is the declaration of the interface of a package for handling 24-hour time values. The package includes a record type, a set of exceptions, and arithmetic functions that operate on the record type. It refers to another package, TimeIntervalPackage, that exports a time interval type (TimeIntervalType) and the functions for dealing with that type. It overloads the arithmetic addition operator for convenience in specifying the time and interval to add in either order. Subtraction is not symmetric.

```
PACKAGE Time24Package IS
  TYPE Time24Type IS RECORD (
    hour NATURAL NOT NULL := 0,
    minute NATURAL NOT NULL := 0,
    second NUMBER NOT NULL := 0.0);
  invalidHourException EXCEPTION;
  invalidMinuteException EXCEPTION;
  invalidSecondException EXCEPTION;
  FUNCTION CurrentTime RETURN Time24Type;
  PROCEDURE SetTime(time IN OUT Time24Type, hour NUMBER,
    minute NUMBER, second NUMBER);
  FUNCTION Add(time Time24Type,
               interval TimeIntervalPackage.TimeIntervalType)
    RETURN Time24Type;
  FUNCTION Add(interval TimeIntervalPackage.TimeIntervalType,
               time Time24Type)
    RETURN Time24Type;
  FUNCTION Subtract(time Time24Type,
                    interval TimeIntervalPackage.TimeIntervalType)
    RETURN Time24Type;
  FUNCTION Format(time Time24Type) RETURN VARCHAR2;
  PROCEDURE Validate(time Time24Type);
END;
```

This is an example of a package that represents an object. The TYPE declaration does not create an actual record, it merely defines what a record looks like. The functions all take an instance of the record type, or two instances. The package itself thus contains no data. You create the data object, a variable of the record type, in the subprogram that uses the package. You then call the functions on that variable to do things to it or to create new data by returning a new object of the type. The individual elements of the record are visible to the caller as part of the specification; good practice would ignore this and use only the functions to operate on the data.

NOTE
There is only one copy of a package in memory, which means that if you define your variable as part of the package, you can have only one such variable. If that fits your needs, fine; the example above is clearly one case where it is inadequate. You have to be able to create multiple time values, not just one. That means, however, that you cannot fully encapsulate the structure of the record type within the package, at least not without a lot of programming, handle indirection, and some maintenance nightmares. This is a case where it is better to use what you have, rather than insisting on "doing it the right way." You can do what you want easily and with little effort, but you incur some risk that someone will abuse the privileges by accessing the structure directly.

The Package Body
The package body has the following syntax:

```
PACKAGE BODY <name> IS
{<variable spec>|<type spec>|<cursor body>|<exception spec>} ...
   <subprogram body> ...
[BEGIN
   <statement>; ...
[EXCEPTION
   <exception handlers> ...]]
END;
```

Only the cursor and subprogram bodies correspond to subprograms you declare in the package specification. The rest of the declarations (variables and so on) are all private to the package body; you cannot use these elements in your external code.

The cursor body syntax is just like the cursor specification syntax except for the addition of the SELECT statement:

```
CURSOR <name> <parameter list> RETURN <type> IS <SELECT
statement>;
```

The parameter list must exactly match the parameter list on the cursor specification, as must the RETURN type.

Package body initialization happens in the optional BEGIN ... END sequence at the end of the package body, after you have finished defining all the implementations of cursors and subprograms in the declarations section. This block of code executes once, when you first refer to an element of the package. You use it to initialize private or public variables in the package. The exception handlers handle any exceptions that the initialization code raises.

The following example shows the body for the package the last section specified.

```
PACKAGE BODY Time24Package IS
  separator CONSTANT CHAR(1) := ':';  -- format separator hh:mm:ss
  secondModulus CONSTANT NUMBER := 60.0;
  minuteModulus CONSTANT NATURAL := 60;
  hourModulus CONSTANT NATURAL := 24;
  secondsPerMinute CONSTANT NUMBER := 60.0;
  secondsPerHour CONSTANT NUMBER := 60*secondsPerMinute;
  secondsPerDay CONSTANT NATURAL := 24*secondsPerHour;
  secondsOverflowException EXCEPTION;  -- internal error

  -- This internal procedure validates the time record
  PROCEDURE Validate(time Time24Type) IS
  BEGIN
    IF time.hour NOT BETWEEN 0 AND 23 THEN
      RAISE invalidHourException;
    END IF;
    IF time.minute NOT BETWEEN 0 AND 59 THEN
      RAISE invalidMinuteException;
    END IF;
    IF time.second NOT BETWEEN 0 AND 59.0 THEN
      RAISE invalidSecondException;
    END IF;
  END;
  -- An internal Convert function to convert time values
  -- to and from seconds
  FUNCTION Convert(time Time24Type) RETURN NUMBER IS
    seconds NUMBER := 0;
  BEGIN
    Validate(time);
    seconds := (time.hour * secondsPerHour) +
               (time.minute * secondsPerMinute) +
                time.second;
    IF seconds NOT BETWEEN 0 AND secondsPerDay THEN
      RAISE secondsOverflowException;
    END IF;
    RETURN seconds;
  EXCEPTION
  WHEN secondsOverflowException THEN
    message('Error converting seconds, number out of range:  '||
```

```
                    TO_CHAR(secondsPerMinute));
      RETURN 0.0;
  END;
  FUNCTION Convert(seconds NUMBER) RETURN Time24Type IS
    timeBuffer Time24Type;  -- return value
    secondsBuffer NUMBER := seconds;
  BEGIN
    IF seconds > secondsPerDay THEN
      RAISE secondsOverflowException;
    END IF;
    timeBuffer.hour := FLOOR(secondsBuffer / secondsPerHour);
    secondsBuffer := MOD(secondsBuffer, secondsPerHour);
    timeBuffer.minute := FLOOR(secondsBuffer / secondsPerMinute);
    secondsBuffer := MOD(secondsBuffer, secondsPerMinute);
    timeBuffer.second := secondsBuffer;
    Validate(timeBuffer);
    return timeBuffer;
  EXCEPTION
    WHEN secondsOverflowException THEN
      message('Error converting seconds, number too large:  '||
              TO_CHAR(secondsPerMinute));
      SetTime(timeBuffer, 0, 0, 0);
      RETURN timeBuffer;
  END;
  FUNCTION Add(time Time24Type,
               interval TimeIntervalPackage.TimeIntervalType)
    RETURN Time24Type IS
    timeBuffer   Time24Type;  -- Buffer for return value
    carry  NATURAL := 0;  -- carry digits to next component
  BEGIN
    Validate(time);
    TimeIntervalPackage.Validate(interval);
    timeBuffer.second := MOD(time.second + interval.second,
                             secondModulus);
    carry := FLOOR(time.second + interval.second / secondModulus);
    timeBuffer.minute := MOD(time.minute + interval.minute +
carry,
                             minuteModulus);
    carry := FLOOR(time.minute + interval.minute + carry /
                   minuteModulus);
    timeBuffer.hour := MOD(time.hour + interval.hour + carry,
                           hourModulus);
```

```
      Validate(timeBuffer);
      RETURN timeBuffer;
   END;
   FUNCTION Add(interval TimeIntervalPackage.TimeIntervalType,
                time Time24Type)
      RETURN Time24Type IS
   BEGIN
      RETURN Add(time, interval);
   END;
   FUNCTION Subtract(time Time24Type,
                     interval TimeIntervalPackage.TimeIntervalType)
        RETURN Time24Type IS
      timeBuffer Time24Type;  -- Buffer for returned value
      seconds1 NUMBER := 0.0;
      seconds2 NUMBER := 0.0;
      resultSeconds NUMBER := 0.0;
   BEGIN
      -- Convert the time and interval to seconds to simplify
      seconds1 := Convert(time);
      seconds2 := TimeIntervalPackage.Convert(interval);
      resultSeconds := seconds1 - seconds2;
      IF resultSeconds NOT BETWEEN -secondsPerDay AND secondsPerDay
        THEN RAISE secondsOverflowException;
      ELSIF resultSeconds < 0 THEN
        -- Add negative value to total seconds per day to get the
        -- "reverse" number of seconds
        resultSeconds := secondsPerDay + resultSeconds;
      END IF;
      timeBuffer := Convert(resultSeconds);
      Validate(timeBuffer);
      RETURN timeBuffer;
   END;
   FUNCTION CurrentTime RETURN Time24Type IS
      datetime DATE := SYSDATE;
      time Time24Type;  -- return value
   BEGIN
      time.hour := TO_NUMBER(TO_CHAR(datetime, 'HH24'));
      time.minute := TO_NUMBER(TO_CHAR(datetime, 'MI'));
      time.second := TO_NUMBER(TO_CHAR(datetime, 'SS')); -- no
fraction
      Validate (time);
      return time;
```

```
    END;
    PROCEDURE SetTime(time IN OUT Time24Type, hour NUMBER, minute
NUMBER,
                        second NUMBER) IS
      timeCopy Time24Type;
    BEGIN
      time.hour := hour;
      time.minute := minute;
      time.second := second;
      timeCopy := time;
      Validate(timeCopy);
    END;
    FUNCTION Format(time Time24Type) RETURN VARCHAR2 IS
    BEGIN
      Validate(time);
      RETURN TO_CHAR(time.hour)||separator||
             TO_CHAR(time.minute)||separator||
             TO_CHAR(time.second);
    END;
    -- This internal procedure validates the time record
    PROCEDURE Validate(time time24Type) IS
    BEGIN
      IF time.hour NOT BETWEEN 0 AND 23 THEN
        RAISE invalidHourException;
      END IF;
      IF time.minute NOT BETWEEN 0 AND 59 THEN
        RAISE invalidMinuteException;
      END IF;
      IF time.second NOT BETWEEN 0 AND 59.0 THEN
        RAISE invalidSecondException;
      END IF;
    END;
END;
```

NOTE
There are some restrictions on packages. First, when you call a packaged subprogram, ORACLE7 executes an implied savepoint. If the subprogram fails with an unhandled exception, PL/SQL rolls back the transaction to this savepoint before raising the exception in the caller. Second, if you are using the package in a distributed transaction, you cannot include any transaction commands (COMMIT, ROLLBACK, or SAVEPOINT).

Using a Package

You refer to an element of a package with a dot-separated name consisting of the package name and the element name:

```
DECLARE
  time Time24Package.Time24Type;
BEGIN
  time := Time24Package.CurrentTime;
END;
```

Built-in Packages

Developer/2000 comes with several built-in packages that provide you with a very fine degree of control over your applications. Although the details of these packages are beyond the scope of this book, carefully reviewing the reference manual descriptions of the contents of these packages will pay off if you are going to do any significant amount of PL/SQL programming in your applications.

Forms provides the packages in Table 11-4. See the *Forms Reference Manual* (Part Number A32509-1), Chapter 3, for details on the contents of some packages (STANDARD Extensions, FORMS_OLE, and FORMS_VBX). The other packages you can find in online help or in the *ORACLE Procedure Builder Developer's Guide* (Part Number A32485-1), Chapter 8. The packages themselves appear in the Object Navigator under the Built-in Packages node.

The Reports product has many of the same packages as Forms, but the main package of interest is the SRW package. Chapter 13 of the *Reports Reference Manual* (Part Number A32489-1) describes SRW in great detail. The components of this package provide most of the access to report elements that you need to do special report programming.

Graphics again uses many of the same packages as Forms, but in addition has the two packages OG and TOOL_INT. The OG package provides an enormous number of components that do just about everything you can do to any element of a chart or display. The TOOL_INT package provides the tools for creating parameter lists to pass parameters to other products. See the *Graphics Reference Manual* (Part Number A32483-1), Chapters 2 to 6, for details on these packages.

Checking Out the Library

Several of the sections above have mentioned the PL/SQL library. The library exists as a way to group and store PL/SQL program units in a disk file. Ordinarily, you store PL/SQL code as database objects. With the availability of PL/SQL as a

Package	Description
DDE	Provides access to Microsoft DDE
FORMS_OLE	Provides access to Microsoft OLE
OLE2	Provides access to Microsoft OLE version 2
ORA_DE	Internal, do not use
ORA_FFI	Provides access to foreign functions
ORA_NLS	Provides information about the language environment
PECS	Provides performance-evaluation tools
STANDARD	PL/SQL built-in procedures and functions
STANDARD Extensions	ORACLE7 built-in procedures and functions to extend PL/SQL
STPROC	Internal, do not use
TEXT_IO	Provides file I/O
TOOL_ENV	Provides access to environment variables
TOOL_ERR	Provides error-handling subprograms, including MESSAGE
TOOL_RES	Provides access to strings in resource files
VBX	Provides access to VBX controls

TABLE 11-4. *Standard Packages in Developer/2000 Forms*

client-side programming language, it became necessary to have a way to store the code as file system objects that you could attach to your application.

Libraries work the same way for all the Developer/2000 products. You create a library as a separate module in any of the products or with the Procedure Builder. You then attach the library to any Developer/2000 module (form, menu, report, or display) to make all its components available to any of the objects in the module. You can also attach a library to a library module. You do not need to prefix names with the library name to use the components.

Creating a Library

To create program units (procedures, functions, package specifications, or package bodies) in a library, find the library module header in the Object Navigator and select it. Create a new library by clicking on the Create button, or open a previously saved library using the Open button. Select the Program Units heading under the library name and click on the Create button to create a program unit. You first see the New Program Unit dialog box (Figure 11-1), which lets you choose which kind of program unit to create (procedure, function, package specification, or body). When you make your choice and click OK, you see the standard PL/SQL editor with a template for the specific type of program unit, as shown here:

When you finish coding and compiling your unit, save it by saving the library module in the usual way with the Save button. Saving the library also sets the name of the library; you cannot change it in the Navigator directly. Make sure that you compile all the program units in the library; if you don't, modules using the library will have troubles. You can quickly check the status of the units by the presence or absence of special symbols on the unit names: an asterisk means uncompiled, and an at sign (@) means not saved to disk. Another strategy is to choose the File¦Compile All menu item with the library name selected, which ensures that either you compile all units or you see errors for ones that do not.

FIGURE 11-1. *The New Program Unit dialog box*

There are three kinds of library files:

- *PLL:* A file that contains both PL/SQL source and compiled code that you can execute; Developer/2000 generates this file when you save the library.

- *PLX:* A file with just the compiled code.

- *PLD:* A text file with just the PL/SQL source; you can use this file as the input to source-control software or as an input script of PL/SQL that you can include and compile.

To create a PLX file, *open* the library in the Procedure Builder and use the GENERATE command in the Interpreter to generate the library file:

```
.GENERATE LIBRARY <library> FILE [<directory>]<name>.PLX
```

To create a PLD file, *attach* the library in the Procedure Builder and use the EXPORT command in the Interpreter to generate the library text file:

```
.EXPORT LIBRARY <library> FILE [<directory>]<name>.PLD
```

For more information on the GENERATE and EXPORT commands, see the *Procedure Builder Developer's Guide* (Part Number A32485-1), Chapter 7.

Attaching and Using a Library

To attach a library, find the Attached Libraries node under the module to which you want to attach the library. Click on the Create button to see the Open File dialog box and choose the library you want to attach.

Clicking on Attach attaches the library as a read-only object. You cannot change anything in the library through this object. Instead, open the library under the library module heading and change it there.

When you attach a library to another module, that module can then refer to any component of the library without using the library name. The order of the libraries under the Attached Libraries header in your module is the search order for the name. Developer/2000 first looks for a program unit in the Program Units section of the module. If the name is not there, it looks in each attached library in order. You can thus override specific program units by positioning them either in the module's Program Units section or by positioning an overriding library ahead of another library. You can use this strategy to extend or adapt a library to a specific use, rather than having to rewrite or repackage the whole library.

Attaching a library to another library lets you build structured layers of library code that other modules can use with just a click of the mouse. You can also use this strategy to build extensions of other libraries by attaching the base library to the extending library and recoding some of the program units.

To use Developer/2000 variables (globals, system variables, parameters, items, or whatever), you have to use a subprogram parameter, a package variable, or indirection through the NAME_IN and COPY:

```
NAME_IN('Ledger.Amount');
NAME_IN('GLOBAL.SecurityLevel');
NAME_IN('SYSTEM.CURRENT_RECORD');
COPY(4.05, 'Ledger.Amount');
COPY('Secret', 'GLOBAL.SecurityLevel');
COPY('TRUE', 'SYSTEM.SUPRESS_WORKING');
```

> **NOTE**
> It is much better to use subprogram parameters to pass values than to refer to variables using NAME_IN or COPY. You use bind variable syntax (:Ledger.Amount, for example) to do this. When you take the NAME_IN/COPY approach, you are coupling the two parts of the system by a direct link from the middle of the code, never a good idea. Use subprograms and packages and parameters to move data in a structured, easily maintained way, and you will find that your libraries are much more reusable. Also, if you are writing code that is specific to a module and thus requires many references to module variables, you should probably move the code into the module Program Units section. This strategy gives you direct access to the variables. This code is not reusable, but with many module-specific references it probably is not reusable as a matter of design.

Combining what you have learned in this chapter with the basics of PL/SQL programming taught Chapter 10, gives you just about everything you need to know to develop very sophisticated applications with Developer/2000. The sophistication comes not so much from the whizzy things you can do on the screen, but from the many ways you can create a valuable application while building a set of reusable system components for future applications. By using the full set of features of PL/SQL, you simultaneously ensure that your applications can do what the user wants and that your code will serve you well in the future, increasing your productivity and the value you can deliver to your customers.

The next two chapters introduce the concepts you need to ensure that your components and applications do what they are supposed to do: testing and debugging.

CHAPTER 12

Pest Control

After the prototyping and design lessons of Part 2 and the chapters on programming, you now can design and build very complex, sophisticated applications. How do you know that they will do what your customers want? How can you predict how much you will need to spend to keep the application in the field?

As Talbot's Farms knows, pest control is seldom just a matter of applying large amounts of pesticides long after planting. The burgeoning market for organic produce is proving that preventing the bugs from taking hold is not only possible but the preferred approach to solving pest problems. This is a terrific metaphor for software development with Developer/2000.

The Best Offense

A software *failure* occurs when a program does something that it should not do or does not do something that it should do. A *fault* is an error in a program's code, design, or requirements that causes the program to fail. Faults, also known as *defects* or just plain *bugs,* can occur in any software object: requirements documents, designs, code, test scripts, installation systems, and any other part of the software development system. Your system can fail just as easily from a poorly defined requirement as from a poorly defined IF conditional in a trigger.

This chapter suggests ways of removing faults from your Developer/2000 application. You need not adopt all the suggestions to get good results, but the more you use, the better your results will be. You, personally, may not have the job title or experience to do everything this chapter suggests. If you are coding applications, you can do some of it and you can ask others why they are not doing the rest of it. There is no time like the present to start.

The process does not start with how to design tests as you might expect. It starts with reviews. Reviewing your requirements, designs, and code prevents problems, and testing finds ones you have let in. This section advocates learning the impact of several methods of assuring quality in an inside-out approach to building quality into your system. The next step is to learn defensive and offensive techniques that build protection into your system. Finally, you can dive into designing and building tests.

You can split testing into two basic camps: object and system testing.

Object testing (unit and integration testing) tests the objects of the system in isolation and as you integrate them into system components. The kind of object testing you do depends on the kind of object you are testing. Developer/2000 systems contain objects of wildly varying types, including forms, menus, reports, and displays; PL/SQL program units; and even third-generation program components as user exits. Each requires a different kind of testing.

System testing tests the system as a whole, with real data in a real environment. System testing in Developer/2000 is much like system testing for any other application, because this kind of testing treats the system as a black box.

A *regression test* redoes tests you have already done to verify that you have not broken something that worked in another version of the object or system. Regression testing applies to both object and system testing and usually requires some automation.

The final section of the chapter focuses on test automation. To automate testing, you build or buy frameworks that automate the testing job. This lets you productively run your tests over and over in regression tests at both the object and system levels. Automation can also ease the process of measuring how successful and complete your tests are.

NOTE
This chapter deals with the technical details of test modeling at a very high level. For more details, consult two comprehensive books by Boris Beizer on testing: *Software Testing Techniques, 2d ed.*, (Van Nostrand Reinhold, 1990) and *Black-Box Testing* (Wiley, 1995). These books give you a complete background in the mathematics and testing theory as well as the practical detail you need to build decent test models of your applications.

The Lineup

A police lineup lets witnesses identify the perpetrator of a crime. Software developers can use similar techniques to identify their own perpetrators: faults in requirements, designs, and code. The software development lineup is the review.

A *review* is a meeting with the objective of examining a software development object (a requirements document, a design, a code object) for possible flaws.

The nature of the review depends on the nature of the object. In requirements reviews, you use customer usability tests of prototypes and careful exploration of the details to determine whether your requirements reflect the true needs of the customer. In design reviews, you look at architectural cohesion and coupling, consistency, and completeness of architectural and low-level designs. In code reviews, you make sure that you can understand the code, you verify the design implementation, and you check to make sure that each object uses techniques likely to be correct and easily maintained over time.

In all reviews, you should look for conformance to any standards your organization applies to the reviewed object. In passing, I believe that you can overdo standards, particularly coding standards. You should standardize only things that you are willing to enforce, then enforce them. It helps if you can enforce them automatically with a program of some kind, though this is difficult with Developer/2000. One example of a useful standard is the naming convention you follow throughout your applications.

The specific techniques of reviewing are beyond the scope of this book. For more information, consult the extensive book by Daniel P. Freedman and Gerald M. Weinberg, *The Handbook of Walkthroughs, Inspections, and Technical Reviews, 3rd Ed.* (Dorset House, 1990).

Code reviews for Developer/2000 have one twist: how do you review the source code? Developer/2000 source code, as such, does not exist in the same way that you have source files for C or COBOL code. To review it, you must either do the analysis online, or you must use the internal documentation facilities in the Developer/2000 products to generate human-readable versions of the applications. The Forms and Reports products have a way to produce documentation for the modules that the product supports except for libraries and their program units. Graphics, unfortunately, does not.

To document a form or menu and all its objects, select the module in the Forms Designer Object Navigator, then choose the File ¦ Administration ¦ Forms Doc menu item. This runs a report that puts a .TXT file in the same directory as the FMB file and gives it the same filename. This text file lists all the objects that the form owns in the same order as in the Object Navigator. You can see all the properties, all the PL/SQL code in triggers and form program units, and all comments that you have put on the different objects.

NOTE
There is a menu item, Navigator ¦ Only Objects With PL/SQL, that hides all the objects that do not have any PL/SQL. This carries over into the documentation, so it can greatly reduce the amount of material in the report. Unfortunately, the code you put into a menu item as its command text does not print as part of this report. As a way around this problem, copy the command and paste it into the Comment for the menu item, which does print.

To document a report, select the report module and choose the File ¦ Administration ¦ Reports ¦ Portrait or File ¦ Administration ¦ Reports ¦ Landscape menu item. These items run a standard report (SRWDOCPB or SRWDOCLB, respectively) that documents the module you select. The landscape version (printing "sideways") usually gets more information onto a page, so the report is shorter.

You must have saved the report you are documenting to the database. If your report is in a file in the file system, you can use File ¦ Save As to save the file version into the database. To generate the report, you must connect to a database. Figure 12-1 shows the parameter form for the report. You can change the parameters to suppress different parts of the documentation: comments; PL/SQL; and report, data, layout, parameter, and procedure information. Figure 12-2 shows the report in the Reports previewer. It is also a good idea to print a sample report showing all the report features.

If these reports are not good enough for your reviews, your best strategy is to use the database storage facilities of Developer/2000 to create reports similar to SRWDOCPB. Because you have complete control, you can do anything you wish with these reports. You should start with the SRWDOCPB or SRWDOCLB report to familiarize yourself with the data models you require. You can also use SQL*Plus to examine the tables and their relationships, or you can look at the table installation scripts. When you have your report the way you want it, load the module into the database tables with File ¦ Save As, and run the report, supplying the name of the module as a parameter.

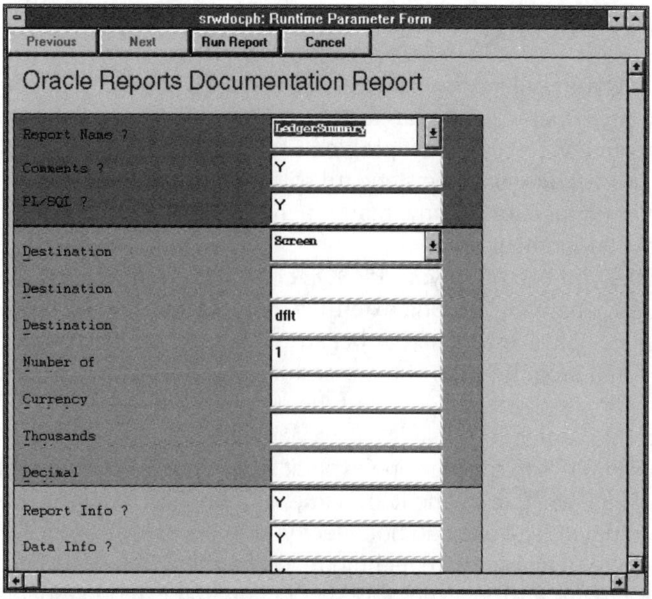

FIGURE 12-1. *Report documentation parameter form*

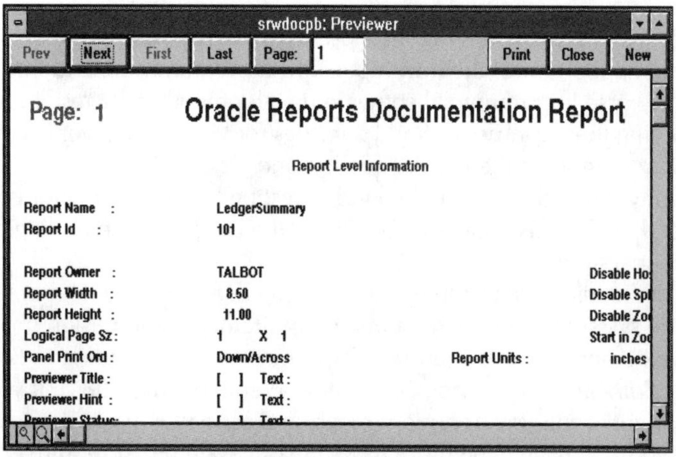

FIGURE 12-2. *Portrait report documentation for Ledger Summary report*

Defensive Driving

While reviewing your objects is vital to assuring quality, building quality into the code means doing whatever you can to make your code better. Some techniques are defensive in nature, warding off problems from external sources. Others are offensive in nature, going past the standard solutions to provide the best solution you can. This book mentions many, many such techniques in Developer/2000, as does the product documentation.

For example, you can build your PL/SQL code into subprograms and packages that you can test separately. Putting extensive, complex code into anonymous blocks in triggers makes testing harder because it ties the code to an event. If you have the code in a program unit, you can test the unit separately without the event occurring. You do, of course, have to test the event and trigger sequencing as part of your integration testing, but that is a separate issue.

Another example is to make scope explicit where possible. If you refer to an item in a block, always qualify the item name with the block name. This ensures that changes in different scopes do not affect your work.

As an example of an offensive technique, coding program units into libraries or database units creates a strong, reusable set of code that is independent of any one application. With adequate testing, this provides for extremely high-quality applications and for extremely high productivity through the reuse of the code. This is an offensive tact because, although it does prevent errors from occurring, it goes far beyond simple prevention to the direct provision of value.

Inside-Out Quality

In my experience, the word "testing" in most organizations usually refers to something that happens after the developers finish programming and freeze the code. What is worse is commercial software development's *beta test,* loosely defined as getting the customer to find your bugs for you. Worse yet is when software producers equate the words "quality" and "testing."

That is really too bad, because the kind of testing that goes on after code freeze, although useful, is the least efficient activity for the purpose: minimizing the costs of faults in your system.

This section focuses on a simple fact of life: it costs a good deal more to fix a problem in the system test phase than in the requirements and design phases of the software development life cycle (around four times more, according to Barry Boehm in his *Software Engineering Economics,* Prentice-Hall, 1981). If you do not do the requirements analysis or design stages, and instead go right into coding from prototyping, you will have even more flaws in your system that require costly fixes during system testing. Finding faults during reviews is dramatically cheaper than finding them after extensive test planning and coding.

There really is a better way of doing things. The iterative prototyping process distributes the different life cycle activities over time in the project, giving you the opportunity to reduce the cost of quality. Your focus should be on understanding and exploring requirements and on solid, reviewed designs and code. With that as the main focus, a secondary focus on defensive programming and object testing by the developer takes care of the rest. This is *inside-out quality:* creating quality during the inside of the development process rather than relying on adding it after development. If you *build* quality into your product by preventing problems, you will not depend on building inspectors or customers to find your problems, and you will spend a lot less money and effort finding and fixing problems.

Testing Objects

Developer/2000 consists almost entirely of objects: forms, blocks, items, triggers, program units, charts, displays, menus, reports, and many others. Therefore, testing objects is the same as testing your application—or is it? As with most things, the application as a system is a whole greater than the sum of its parts. You can test each object in the system by itself and still not have found all the possible failures—or even a majority of them. The distinction between a system and its components leads directly to the two different kinds of testing: testing objects versus testing systems. This section describes testing objects.

Object testing also can be separated into two kinds of testing: unit testing and integration testing. *Unit testing* is testing an object in isolation. *Integration testing* tests a component of the system comprising two or more objects and their interactions. Both kinds of object testing use the same models and techniques for testing.

Object Test Models, Cases, and Scripts

A *test model* is a relatively formal model of some aspect or part of your system, including the system as a whole. The test model differs from the other models of the system in its orientation to discovering a minimal set of test cases that adequately test your system. In fact, the criterion you use to evaluate your success depends entirely on the test model you use.

Programmers tend to think about testing as exercising the code. This test model leads directly to the success criterion of code coverage: the more lines of code you exercise, the better your test, with 100 percent being perfect. Unfortunately, this thinking derives from a serious misconception about the relationship of this criterion to the number of failures. More simply, *it does not work.* It does not generate test cases that you can reasonably expect to discover the failures.

The problem is that using code as a test model, and hence code coverage (statement coverage, line coverage, or whatever) as a test criterion, ignores what is important about the object while emphasizing irrelevancies. Code is a good model for code generation but a terrible one for test generation. To find an adequate number of failures, you need to use test models that reflect the *logic* and the *control and data flows* of your system directly without getting hung up in the code statements. Stepping through the code in the debugger, even if you see each statement execute once, tells you nothing about the conditions that prevent code from executing properly. It says little about the behavior of loops with conditional control or the possible variations on input data that cause calculations or control to fail.

The PECS performance evaluation collection services library that comes with Developer/2000 includes a line and object coverage tool that will tell you how many lines of PL/SQL or how many Forms objects you have executed or visited, respectively (see the *Forms Advanced Techniques Manual,* Part Number A32506-1, Appendix C). This can tell you whether your test cases are bad or really bad, but it cannot tell you whether your test cases are *good.* Only an adequate test model and full coverage of that model rather than lines of code will do that. For example, knowing a trigger has executed is interesting. If that trigger (and other triggers) call a subprogram, the statistics may show an execution of the subprogram, but it may not be for the trigger you want to test! For an adequate test, you might have to execute that subprogram 20 times, because it gets called under 20 different conditions by 10 different triggers.

Deciding Which Model To Use

Failure lurks in bad assumptions, misconceived control, and the erroneous flow of data through the object. There are several alternative test models, for example, for testing objects:

- *Transaction-flow:* A transaction-flow model structures your object as a life cycle, showing how you use the object in transactions with the software. A transaction in this sense is more than a database transaction, it can involve several such transactions. The flow may branch conditionally and loop. The individual test case is a single path through the network diagram that describes the transaction flow. The transaction-flow model does not assume any knowledge of the internal workings of the object; it just describes how it appears from the outside.

- *State-transition:* A state-transition model structures your object life cycle as a series of different states of the object and transitions between those states when events occur. The forms processes, with their item and record states and events, are a classic example of state-transition modeling. You can use this model quite effectively in testing Developer/2000 objects, but sometimes the states can get quite complex. A test case is a single path through the transition flow network diagram from object creation to object destruction. The state-transition model also assumes nothing about the internal workings of the object.

■ *Conditional:* A conditional model models the object and its behavior through a series of logical conditions that are *invariant* (do not change with the state or behavior of the object). Object-invariant conditions apply to the entire object; subprogram conditions apply to a particular trigger, procedure, or function. Object invariants state what must always be true about the object. Subprogram-invariants state what must always be true in the subprogram, such as input conditions, loop conditions, and output conditions. You can build conditional checks into your code, such as the Validate object-invariant checks in the Time24Package in Chapter 11. The test case is a single condition out of the set of conditions for the object.

■ *Control-flow:* A control-flow model represents the decision points in a procedural object (an object with PL/SQL or other procedural language constructs). You can also use a control-flow model to model the processes of forms, reports, and graphs in integration testing. For example, Chapter 6 shows the forms processes not as state-transition diagrams but as flow charts, as this leads to a better understanding of their nature.

■ *Data-flow:* A data-flow model is a control-flow model that represents both the decisions and the flow of data through those decisions, showing how data changes during control transitions.

You use different models for different kinds of objects. For most Developer/2000 objects, the conditional model is the most important model, followed closely by the state-transition and transaction-flow models. These models all apply to the external characteristics of an object. Control-flow and data-flow models are more appropriate for PL/SQL and other procedural code objects.

Developing Test Cases from the Model
Once you build a test model for an object, you can then develop the *test cases* from the model. The nature of the test case depends entirely on the type of test model. In a conditional model, a test case is a single condition; the test model consists of the set of such conditions. In a control-flow model, the test case is a single path through the control flow. A minimal criterion for testing completeness is to *cover* the test model: you should have test cases that exercise each condition or transition between two nodes in the control graph at least once. That is, if you draw a line over each transition when you execute it in a test case, a completely covered test model should have no transitions left to draw over.

Why is the test coverage criterion not simply to test all possible paths through the graph? Nothing simple about it. With potentially infinite combinations of data inputs, possibly infinite loops, and certain complexity surrounding combinations of different inputs, it is physically impossible to test all possible paths through a test model. For example, you can test the logical consistency of a conditional model, but you cannot possibly test all possible combinations of the data that the conditional model makes possible.

Turning a Test Case into a Test Script

The test case is thus a piece of the test model. You can then turn the test case into a test *script*, an implementation of the test case in a particular language. For example, to apply a condition to an object, you can encode the condition in a PL/SQL block expression, a format mask, or a list of values (LOV). To represent a control-flow path, you can code a sequence of inputs to the call to the procedure that forces it to take that path. To represent a state-transition path, you code a procedure that pushes the object through the indicated transitions.

This points up an aspect of testing that may not be obvious: you are doing it when you *program,* not just as a separate testing task. Field validation in forms, for example, is a form of conditional testing. In this case, it provides preventive behavior as well by preventing the user from entering data that will make the object fail. Building the full conditional model forces you to recognize what code you must provide for validation. It also tells you what logic must be checked separately because Developer/2000 does not provide a direct mechanism for applying that logic. With PL/SQL in triggers, there is very little you cannot do as part of validation processing (but you may not want to do runtime checks that cost a large amount of processing time). In any case, these are all test scripts.

A given test script can combine several test cases into a single script. If the database and application setup and cleanup activities are the same, and you can figure out a way to sequence the test cases, you can run through several test cases in a single script. This is purely a productivity issue, not a conceptual one.

The results of a TEST are the outputs of the test script. Outputs can range from a conditional TRUE or FALSE to data in database tables, depending on the nature of the object. For example, conditional testing of a PL/SQL block can result in an exception or in successful exit from the block. State-transition testing of a Forms block can result in data being inserted, updated, deleted, and queried from the database. Transaction-flow testing of a graphic with drill-down logic embedded in a form can result in graph screens with specific characteristics, and so on.

In object testing, you are less concerned with the overall processing of the system. Typically, that means that if your test involves database data, you do not necessarily care if the data is consistent with the system as a whole; leave that for system testing. In object testing, you focus on the output from a specific test on a specific object. This may require a special database setup with no integrity-checking constraints or triggers.

Domain Partitioning

Up to this point, testing has been a matter of adequately covering the right kind of test model. There is another aspect of test modeling, however, that can test beyond the standard coverage criterion.

Most Developer/2000 testing gets done by specifying the data to use as input to the object. Certain kinds of data lead to different test cases because they cause different processing. For example, depending on the value of an input parameter or a bind variable, a subprogram can branch into a conditional block. Depending on whether a particular condition occurs, the user can see a report line or not or can get an input validation error or not.

Beyond the direct effect on control branching and simple validation, input data can often cause different results depending on their values. A common class of faults reflects this. The *boundary condition* fault occurs when you define some condition that errs by treating a data value that should meet the condition as though it did not, or vice versa. For example, using greater than (>) rather than greater than or equal to (>=) is a common error that misses being correct by a single value.

A similar problem can occur in loops, where you loop through a certain number of records based on a condition but err by a single value in the statement of the condition. Worse, you can perform calculations inside the loop based on an error in the value (using the value rather than the value plus one, for example).

To find faults such as this, you must partition your input domain into clusters of data elements likely to cause failures. It is not enough, for example, to have one test case for each branch; you must also test the next value. For example, if a branch occurs for the condition of being greater than 0, you should test inputs of 1 and 0 to test the branch and values of 2 and –1 to test the boundary conditions. If a loop takes different actions depending on the loop counter, test input that leads to the different calculations rather than just testing the loop once. Testing the loop once is all that test model coverage requires, but it does not fully test the loop.

The partitions into which you break the inputs are *equivalence classes*. The input data in a particular equivalence class is the same with respect to its impact on the object's failure or success. That is, you can treat all the values as the same because they have the same effect on the object.

Equivalence classes permit you to reduce the number of test cases from the infinity of possible input data combinations to a few tests that represent the practical behavior of the object. If you extend your test model coverage by forming equivalence classes, you will get a set of test cases that will find most object failures. Remember, testing an object in isolation, or even a component made of several objects, does not test the behavior of the system as a whole. Again, that is why you also do system testing.

Testing SQL

Because PL/SQL and the Developer/2000 tools either generate SQL or parse the SQL you enter explicitly, you do not need to worry about testing the syntax of SQL statements. You do need to worry about testing the logic of the SQL.

The correct test model for SQL logic is probably the relational calculus and/or the relational algebra. SQL, at least in its ANSI 1989 form, does not map very well to the formal relational models, which makes using them for modeling SQL logic difficult. Until someone does the necessary theoretical work to turn this into an effective conditional test model for SQL, you will have to rely on more *ad hoc* ways to test your SQL logic.

There are several parts of a SQL statement that reflect control logic. Basing your test data on these SQL clauses is a good way to exercise your SQL logic.

- *Join condition:* Make sure the join logic does what it should, especially if it involves outer joins. There should be one row for each equivalence class of rows in each of the joined tables.

- *Nested subqueries with ANY, ALL, IN, and EXISTS:* Make sure the quantifier logic for these constructs does what it should. Test the nested SELECT separately to ensure its validity. There should be one test case for each equivalence class row that the nested SELECT returns.

- *Correlated subqueries:* Test any correlated subquery logic as you would a conditional loop. What are the possible inputs for the nested subquery? Does the subquery yield the correct results for each equivalence class of inputs?

- *IN with a list of values:* Make sure the values represent the correct enumeration of possibilities. There should be a test case for each value and at least one for a value that does not qualify.

- *GROUP BY and HAVING logic:* Make sure the grouping logic gives you the groups you want. Generate a test case for each potential equivalence class of groups. Test the HAVING condition by generating a test case for success and one for failure, and do the usual boundary condition test cases as well.

- *ORDER BY:* Generate a test case for equivalence classes of inputs that yield different ordering of rows.

- *CONNECT BY:* Generate a test model that represents the possible branching in the data. Test equivalence classes of inputs that yield different hierarchies of outputs. This is an ORACLE7 extension to ANSI SQL.

■ *DECODE:* Generate a test case for each of the argument pairs of this functional version of the IF-THEN-ELSE conditional statement. This is an ORACLE7 extension to ANSI SQL.

If you have platform portability requirements, you should test the SQL for database-specific constructs such as DECODE or CONNECT BY. If you can, run the SQL against several target database managers to validate the syntax as well as the logic.

Testing Systems

When you integrate your final component, you have a working system. If you are using the incremental, prototyping approach this book recommends, you reach this stage almost immediately. You continue to have a working system throughout the project. When do you start testing the application as a system?

Your admittedly subjective answer to this question is, when the system is *stable* enough to test. Your process should make clear when this happens by establishing a *baseline,* a configuration of system components that represents a stable, complete version of the system. The typical software development life cycle freezes the code, then declares an *alpha release* of the software. This is a baseline. At this point, you should have all components complete and working, with at least a draft of the system documentation. You then move through a series of test-fix iterations, rebaselining the system after each iteration, until the system is ready to release to customers. This testing process is the system test.

System testing is about finding the failures of the system as a whole rather than the failures of the parts. You should have tested the components thoroughly during the development phase before the baseline. The two key elements of system testing are validation and capability testing. *Validation* tests whether the system as a whole meets its requirements. *Capability testing* verifies that the implementation is capable of performing its required tasks in a real-world environment.

There is nothing special about system testing of Developer/2000 applications. They are applications like any other once you reach the system testing stage of the process. This section outlines the kinds of tests you apply during this phase, but you should consult standard books on system testing for detailed test methods.

Validation

Validation performs tests to ensure that the system as a whole does what you require of it. To do this kind of testing adequately, you must have a complete requirements specification of the product. There are many methods for developing such specifications, but without one, you cannot do serious validation testing. As with object testing, you need a test model. There are several candidates for this test model:

- *Functional specification:* A description of the functions of the system that systematically details, function by function, what the system should do. A test case is a path through the processes.

- *Object:* The object model is a description of the object structure of the system that details the things, or objects, that comprise the system. This model often includes an entity-relationship diagram or one of the more recent innovations in object and class diagramming. In a database application, the database schema usually reflects a good part of this object model, so the object model provides a good specification for the logical structure of the database. You thus need to validate the database schema against this requirements model. A test case is a set of objects that you can decompose from the overall model.

- *Documentation:* A popular way to represent the requirements for a system is as a version of the system documentation, including a User's Guide and a Reference Manual. A side benefit of this approach is that it makes the system documentation available early in the process: this is a prototyping approach. A test case is usually a section of the document.

- *State:* For the technically inclined, the state model lets you represent both the object structure and the behavior of a system with a series of state-transition diagrams or tables. This provides a strong, formal model that you can use as a system test model. You can then derive test cases and scripts from the model. A test case, as for state-transition testing at the object level, is a path through the state-transition network.

- *Use case:* Similar to transaction-flow models, the use case provides a series of scenarios for using the system. The use case model consists of the set of use cases that completely describes everything a set of actors can do in the system. A single use case may have the same conditional branches and loops of a transaction-flow diagram, and a test case by analogy is a single path through this network.

Whatever kind of requirements model you have, you build your system validation test in the same way you built your object tests. Analyze the test model to derive the test cases, then build test scripts that represent the test cases. For most system testing, you can use graphical user interface testing tools to automate the process (the next section gives details). You also need to build a reference database containing the expected results of the tests. When you run a test, you compare the actual results to this reference database to decide whether the test passed or failed.

You will usually find some gaps in the system where a requirement does not correspond to anything. You do not need a reference comparison to raise this missing feature as a fault in the implementation.

Capability Testing

If the requirements do not include them, capability testing must test such system capabilities as performance, ease of use, security, and maintainability. The focus of capability testing, however, is on interaction with the real world: stress and configuration testing.

Stress Testing

Stress testing ensures that the system responds well to real-world pressures on the system. This kind of testing requires a test model that identifies the stress points of a system. The obvious stress points in a database application are the simultaneous use of the system by multiple users, the size of the database tables on the server, and the size of the application data sets. Your test model must identify the nature and degree of stresses on the system. Each *stress boundary,* the point at which you define the system to be under stress, is a test case. You can develop test scripts for each test case to put the system under the indicated stress.

Configuration Testing

Configuration testing ensures that the system responds well to different, real-world configurations of software and hardware. It includes testing the installation procedures and the way the software and hardware configuration of the environment affects the system. Use equivalence-class partitioning to identify classes of configurations; this approach reduces the infinite number of possibilities to a reasonable number. For example, testing all the possible kinds of workstation hardware in combination with all the different network configurations and server setups is clearly not possible. You must identify in your configuration test model the set of equivalence classes that let you do a reasonable job of identifying failures of the system.

NOTE
Try to pick unusual setups that will lead to "unlikely" conditions rather than picking the usual ways to set up systems. The object is to make the system fail, not to make sure it works in standard situations.

Installation procedures, for some reason, tend to be outside the realm of requirements and formal system validation testing. For whatever reason, developers usually do not consider installation to be worthy of the full effort of development object testing. This book strongly recommends including the installation procedures and options in the requirements document as a full part of the system. Even if you do this, however, you must still test the system as a whole for installation problems that arise only in real-world situations. Your test model should identify the dependencies of the system on specific installation options. A test case is a particular configuration of installation options.

Automated Testing

Like most aspects of software development, there are great benefits to the full automation of testing, but the practical details are full of ambiguity. It would be wonderful if you could generate test models, test cases, and test scripts automatically from requirements and designs. Unfortunately, there is a long way to go before this becomes possible. For certain languages under certain conditions, you can generate test cases based on control-flow and other test models, but Developer/2000 and other such development systems generally do not have such tools available. Testing Developer/2000 is still a craft.

There are ways to automate parts of testing. You can certainly automate the maintenance of test documents and test results in a repository. You definitely want to automate conditional testing by putting the conditions right into the code as validation checks.

You can automate large portions of your PL/SQL test scripts by coding test *frameworks*: program units that are test scripts and programs that run test scripts. Your main test driver runs the drivers for individual test suites, each of which comprises a set of test-script procedures that implement one or more test cases. If your test scripts store their results in the test repository, which can be either database tables or flat files, you can also write program units to automate the comparison of actual results to expected results.

To automate system testing, you can use any of the several excellent graphical user interface (GUI) testing tools on the market. Some probably work better with Developer/2000 than others, but you can test the basic structures in your windows and menus through any of these tools. The idea is to work through a test script using the tool, recording your actions as you go. You can then store the resulting output file as a combination test script and expected results file. When you want to run the test again, you run the script and the tool tells you whether there are any differences between what happened before and what happened this time. Some tools provide a programming interface that you can use to create test scripts without having the baselined product available.

The real value of GUI testing tools is to automate regression testing rather than to automate new system tests. This compares well to using computer-assisted drawing tools in architecture and engineering. These tools do not save money in producing single-print, original drawings but in producing new versions of the originals, with changes and additions. Similarly, you will not save much time or money the first time through with a GUI testing tool. If you go through multiple versions of the system, each additional version and its regression test will put money in your pocket, saved from not having to repeat all your system tests manually.

This chapter has surveyed the ways you can assure the quality of your application. Testing and debugging (covered in the next chapter) are an important part of the equation, but adequate requirements exploration, design, and reviews should comprise the bulk of your quality effort. Prevent rather than cure the disease.

CHAPTER 13

Debugging

Having made your application fail through testing in Chapter 12, now you have to do something about it. Sometimes, the failure is obvious—you left out a field in a block, or you crossed an "i" somewhere that you should have dotted instead. But much of the time the cause of a failure—the *fault*—is not obvious, and you have to track it down. This tracking process is *debugging*, the art of solving a problem by finding and fixing a fault in the code.

Debugging is complementary to testing, though not exactly. You can find faults simply by inspecting your code, and that is a particularly effective way to debug. Testing combined with debugging is a powerful technique that lets you discover and fix problems early in the development process. If as a developer you test your objects thoroughly and use the techniques described in this chapter to find and fix the faults that cause the failures you run into, you will spend a lot less time in alpha and beta test doing debugging.

Using Developer/2000 to produce software applications removes large sources of faults that you might meet in standard programming. Pointer and memory allocation errors do not exist, and even SQL syntax errors do not happen. Your SQL gets parsed immediately, and you get immediate feedback on errors. That means that, if you learned to debug with another programming language, you will find that many of the specific techniques you learned are irrelevant to Developer/2000 applications. There is still quite a bit of classic debugging art that applies, however.

The Art of Debugging

Building test models, as the last chapter discussed, is a wonderful way to understand a piece of code—or a requirement or design component—thoroughly. As you will see in this section, understanding a piece of code is the essence of what you do when you are debugging. You will find that if you build object test models for the component objects in your application you will usually find many of the faults hiding in the component. You will find them, in fact, without running the tests or even without developing the test cases. The act of building the test model is often enough for a good developer to recognize logic and coding flaws in the object under test.

Some faults require more investigation, however. This usually happens because the fault involves something that is easy to overlook, something that is in more than one place or object, or something you base on a hidden assumption that is not a part of the test model you develop. That is when the art of debugging really kicks in.

The title of this section comes from a small book that is probably the best book in existence on testing and debugging software: Glenford Myers's *The Art of Software Testing* (Wiley, 1979). Despite its age and increasing obsolescence with respect to the technological and theoretical aspects of testing and debugging, this book provides a very practical introduction to its subject. No one who does software development for a living should continue doing it without reading this book. The rest of this section summarizes the points that Myers makes.

Locating Faults by Induction

The process of induction reasons from the parts to the whole (Figure 13-1). That is, using data about the failure, you narrow down the nature of the fault.

1. *Locate the relevant data about the failure.* Do not just say, "There's a problem" and start fixing things. Specify exactly how the failure occurs by observing how it occurs, showing how to make it occur reproducibly, and showing how to avoid the problem with similar but different test cases. Explore the context in which the failure occurs.

2. *Organize the data about the failure.* Induction proceeds by pattern analysis, and it is much easier to see the patterns and relationships in the data if the data are well organized. Myers has a table that shows what happens, where it happens, when it happens, and to what extent it happens versus the circumstances under which the failure does and does not occur. Organizing the events as a scenario can also be useful. Then, study the patterns of relationships that emerge from this data. One particularly effective way to do this is by *backtracking*: starting from a point where you have failed, work backward through the data about the process. Another possibility is to work through some additional test cases to see the patterns more clearly.

3. *Devise a hypothesis.* Having studied the relationships, propose one or more hypotheses about the fault. If you cannot devise a hypothesis that fits the facts, get more data.

4. *Prove the hypothesis.* Pick the hypothesis that seems the most likely, then prove that it is correct by showing, first, how it fits the known data, and second, how it works in the code.

5. *Fix the fault.* Change the code as your hypothesis suggests, then test the code again to prove that the fix does prevent the failure and that it does not cause any additional failures.

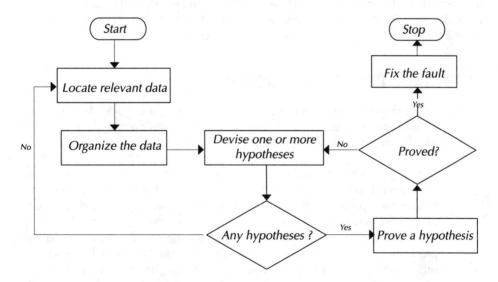

FIGURE 13-1.   *The inductive debugging process*

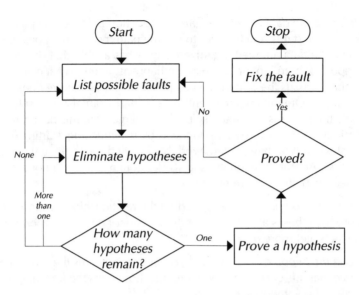

FIGURE 13-2. *The deductive debugging process*

You use induction when you have a set of data and a relatively poor understanding of how the program works and/or of the nature of the failure. Induction requires thorough data analysis and much time and effort to do well compared to the deductive approach in the next section.

Locating Faults by Deduction

The process of deduction reasons from the whole to the parts (Figure 13-2). That is, using your knowledge about the application and system, you deduce the nature of the fault by eliminating and refining hypotheses:

1. *List the possible faults that might cause the failure.* Brainstorm, preferably with other developers, the set of hypotheses about the fault that explain the failure. Even partial hypotheses are useful. There are some hypotheses that come from general programming theory, such as looking at recently changed code ("I only changed one thing, it can't possibly have caused the problem!"), code that is very complex ("I had to do it that way because otherwise it wouldn't have worked!"), or code that has a history of faults ("Not again!"). There are some hypotheses that come from programming practice, such as the boundary condition errors of Chapter 12 or the

standard misunderstandings of SQL constructs such as GROUP BY HAVING or outer joins ("Which one does the plus sign go on?").

2. *Eliminate hypotheses.* Analyze the data and its relationships. If you cannot eliminate all but one hypothesis, gather more data with an eye toward the remaining hypotheses. Often, working through some additional test cases works well. If you eliminate all the hypotheses, go back to brainstorming new hypotheses.

3. *Refine and prove the hypothesis.* Make the theory about the fault as specific as possible using the available data. What exactly is going on? Show how the refined hypothesis fits the known data and how it works in the code.

4. *Fix the fault.* Change the code as your hypothesis suggests, then test the code again to prove that the fix does prevent the failure and that it does not cause any additional failures.

You would use deduction when you have a good understanding of how the program works and of the nature of the failure. This good understanding lets you move right to a set of hypotheses. The key part of the method, however, is the elimination and refinement of hypotheses by data analysis. Skipping the data analysis will usually result in wild goose chases. You may think you know exactly what's happening, but then so did George Washington's doctors when they bled him to death. Check your data, then prove the hypothesis.

Locating Faults by Tracing

The *brute force* method of finding faults is to *trace* through the program, event by event, until you find something wrong. Most developers get a good, intuitive feel for what to look for during a debugging (that is, tracing) session. It should be clear, however, that this method is *much* less efficient than induction or deduction, largely because you do not *think* during the process. You can generate truly massive amounts of data to process, most of it irrelevant. And the larger the application, the harder it is to do: the technique simply does not scale well.

Of course, if you do not understand what is happening in the program and you do not understand the failure well enough, this may be the only approach to finding the fault. For Developer/2000 programs, this would apply only if you do not understand how Developer/2000 is processing. For example, if you do not understand the processes in Chapter 6, and you cannot reproduce the failure reliably enough to even start an induction process, then you might as well step through the debugger until something unusual happens. Lay in supplies, it will take awhile. If nothing else, the next time you will know how Developer/2000 works well enough to use deduction instead of brute force.

Fault Location Techniques

Here, in no particular order, are some thoughts about the practical details of induction and deduction.

- *Use your brain:* It may be your best programming asset.

- *Use your subconscious:* Let the problem rest awhile and do something else. Often you will have a flash of insight that will save you much grief.

- *Use your friends:* Talk to someone about the problem. You may find that talking about it lets you see a new hypothesis, or you may find your peer can develop a different hypothesis.

- *Avoid the debugger:* See the comment about using your brain.

- *Avoid banging on it:* Specifically, try not to change parts of the application at random to see what happens. This is worse than tracing because it disrupts the playing field, potentially by adding new failures.

Fixing Faults

There is a bit more to the process of fixing faults than just changing the code.

- While you are fixing the problem, look around the code.

- Make sure that you have fixed the entire problem. By implication, this means that you need to understand what the entire problem was. In other words, do not fix the fault until you understand completely how the application failed and the full ramifications of that failure. The inductive and deductive approaches to debugging are much more likely to give you a full understanding of a failure. Also, do not simply fix a symptom rather than the disease. Software faults are easier to cure than human faults.

- Make very sure that you have not broken something else. Especially as your applications get larger and/or more complex, the probability of inducing new failures gets quite high for each intervention. The best way to avoid doing this is with regression tests (see Chapter 12). These tests should demonstrate that everything works as it should. The next best way to do this is to inspect the code. In this case, you should inspect all code even indirectly related to the code you changed.

■ You should also study the pattern of faults in your code to learn from your mistakes. If your coding practices need to change to prevent certain faults, do it. If you find that certain kinds of faults seem to occur regularly in Developer/2000 code, put a standard in place to see if you can prevent them. If you find that certain kinds of failures are more frequent than others, focus your design efforts on ways to reduce those kinds of failures. An ounce of prevention....

Debugging Developer/2000 Objects

Having now thoroughly discredited the automated debugging tools as a method for debugging, the rest of the chapter tells you how to use these tools effectively. You should use these tools mainly in the hypothesis-proving stage of debugging.

The Developer/2000 environment lets you debug in several different ways. The built-in debugger lets you trace through your code and inspect virtually anything at will. See Chapter 21 of the *Forms Developer's Guide* (Part Number A32505-1) for a complete introduction to the debugger, and see also the *Procedure Builder Developer's Guide* (Part Number A32485-1) for details on the debugger, which is also available as the standalone Procedure Builder. Forms and Reports also let you debug using tracing facilities that tell you where you are in program execution.

The Debugger

The debugger lets you trace through the PL/SQL in your application using modern, interactive debugger techniques:

■ Interactive manipulation of breakpoints and triggers in the source code

■ Interactive inspection and manipulation of PL/SQL and variables

■ Inspection of the PL/SQL calling stack

■ Interactive execution of PL/SQL commands

Each tool sets up the application for the debugger in a different way.

The Forms Debugger
To use the debugger in a Forms application, you must generate your form and menu executable files using the debug option. Use Tools¦Options to display the Options dialog box, then set the Debug Mode option on. Whenever you generate your application, Forms embeds source code symbols in the application.

To run the debugger when you run your application, either run it from the Designer with the Debug Mode option set or use the F45RUN command line parameter DEBUG:

```
F45RUN workersk talbot/george debug=YES
```

The runtime system displays the debugger before loading the form to let you set any debugging actions (Figure 13-3). At this point, you can create a breakpoint in any trigger or program unit in the application, and you can create debugging triggers (triggers that fire on debugger events).

The top pane of the debugger shows the PL/SQL source from the currently executing block. This is the Source Pane. In Figure 13-3, this pane is blank because the debugger is not currently executing a block. You use this pane to set breakpoints, which exist only while you debug. The middle pane in Figure 13-3 is the Navigator Pane, which strongly resembles the Object Navigator but with fewer objects. This Navigator has a set of objects to use in runtime debugging, however, not the set of objects you see in the Object Navigator. You use this pane to inspect debug actions and variables (global, system, local) and parameters in the call stack. The lower pane is the Interpreter Pane, in which the commands you execute appear and which lets you execute commands by typing them in.

FIGURE 13-3. *The initial debugger window*

The Reports Debugger

Unlike Forms, the Reports debugger stores its debug actions in the report itself. In the Object Navigator in the Reports designer, you can see two headings: Debug Actions and Stack. The former stores breakpoints and trigger actions; the latter represents the call stack at runtime.

To create breakpoints, you invoke the Reports Designer debugger with the Tools¦Interpreter menu item. This displays a modeless, two-paned version of the debugger with the Source Pane and the Interpreter Pane (Figure 13-4). When you select a program unit or trigger in the Object Navigator, the Interpreter displays the PL/SQL code. You can then set breakpoints anywhere in the code (see the following section) that you can then save with the report. When you run the report, the runtime debugger pops up when you reach the breakpoint. This debugger is very similar to the one you see in Forms and includes the Navigator Pane. It acts as a modal dialog box in the report display.

NOTE
When you recompile program units, you need to reset any affected breakpoints to their new line numbers.

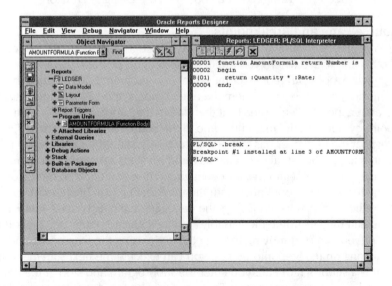

FIGURE 13-4.   *The Reports Interpreter*

The Graphics Debugger

Graphics works in much the same way as Reports. You start the modeless debugger in the Graphics Designer with the Tools⦙PL/SQL Interpreter menu item. See Chapter 14 of the *Graphics Developer's Guide* (Part Number A32482-1) for a complete discussion of the debugger in the context of graphics (although this material duplicates much of the material in the following sections and in the *Forms Developer's Guide).*

Most of your debugging work will be figuring out which option you got wrong in the display or charts, and the debugger is not going to help much with that. You "test" various option settings by running the display as a standalone graphic display; see the Chapter 5 graphics prototype for an example of this. By the time you integrate the display into a form or report, you should be confident in the internal consistency of the graphic.

If you get runtime errors in the display, you can use the debugger much as you would for a form or report. You can set breakpoints or debug triggers and inspect variables and parameters. Unless you have extensive use of PL/SQL in your displays, however, the debugger is not going to help much.

NOTE
If you correct program errors in the debugger and recompile there, you should choose the Edit⦙Synchronize Program Units menu item when you finish debugging. This synchronizes the changes in the debugger version of the code with the Designer versions.

The Source Pane and Breakpoints

You use the Source Pane, which displays the source as read-only text, to set breakpoints and to see where you are in the execution process. Figure 13-5 shows a debugging session with a breakpoint set in a subprogram body. Notice the B(01) in the left margin of the pane, where the line numbers appear. This indicates that there is a breakpoint (breakpoint 1) at that line in the subprogram. You can set the breakpoint by double-clicking on the line in the Source Pane. The arrow ("=>") indicates that the debugger has stopped execution just before executing that line.

When you see the initial debugger as Runform starts up, you enter a breakpoint at the place where you want to start debugging. Then you click on the Close button to start the form. Action continues until the form reaches the breakpoint you have set. When the form breaks, it displays the debugger again as you see it in Figure 13-5. You can then examine the variables in the Navigator Pane (see the following section), or you can start moving through the code using the Step commands.

By clicking on the Step Into button, you can execute the next statement. If that statement is a subprogram call, you enter the subprogram and stop at the first executable line of that subprogram. The Step Over button does the same thing but executes the subprogram and puts you on the next executable line after the

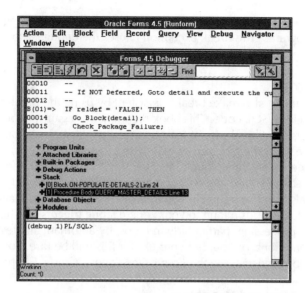

FIGURE 13-5. *The debugger in action at a breakpoint*

subprogram call. The Step Out Of button lets you continue executing until the current subprogram or block returns, then stops at the next executable line. By using these commands, you can navigate through the subprogram statement by statement, tracing your execution path. At any point, you can examine the values of any variables to see what is going on.

You can use the Go button to continue executing until the next break or until you exit the application. The Reset button exits the current debugging level and returns to the previous level; see the following section on the Interpreter Pane for details.

The other kind of debug action is a debug trigger. A debug trigger associates a PL/SQL block with a specific line of code in a program unit. The debugger fires the trigger when execution reaches that line. You can also set triggers to fire when the debugger takes control or at every PL/SQL source line. By raising the DEBUG.BREAK exception as part of the trigger, you can cause a break. This lets you set conditional breakpoints:

```
IF DEBUG.GETN('RELDEF') = TRUE THEN
   RAISE DEBUG.BREAK;
END IF;
```

In the trigger code, you access variables in the current scope using the GETN and SETN subprograms. The Break exception causes the debugger to break and display the current source line (the line that fired the debug trigger).

NOTE
You can also make breaks persistent by using the Break procedure in your PL/SQL code. This book recommends against debug triggers and persistent breaks for at least two reasons. First, you should be using breaks and the debugger mainly to prove a hypothesis, not to extensively trace your code. Second, if you forget it and leave the break in your code, a customer can suddenly fall into the debugger. This is unlikely to help you to provide a quality application; it actually adds a fault to your code. Debug triggers can help to speed up processing, particularly in loops, by automatically testing conditions for you, but your use for this will be rare. For details on debug triggers, see the *Forms Developer's Guide*, Chapter 21.

The Navigator Pane and Variables

The Navigator Pane lets you examine different kinds of variables. You can look at any item by navigating to it under the Modules heading. You can look at Global Variables, System Variables, and Command Parameters by navigating to them under those headings. The Stack heading provides the current state of the call stack for PL/SQL. This stack shows the hierarchy of PL/SQL blocks currently executing. In Figure 13-5, for example, the stack shows that the debugger is executing a trigger, ON-POPULATE-DETAILS, which in turn is calling a subprogram, QUERY_MASTER_DETAILS. Each item in this stack represents an executing scope that defines variables, and you can navigate to those variables (parameters and local variables) under the Stack items. Figure 13-6 shows the variables in the running subprogram, including the variable RELDEF in the IF statement at which execution has stopped. The Navigator Pane shows the current values of all variables; RELDEF, for example, is FALSE, so the IF statement condition is TRUE. You can also change these variables in the Navigator by selecting and entering the value directly after the equal sign.

NOTE
The Forms debugger does not currently support package body variables, and there is no way to inspect the values of these variables. Package body variables are those you declare in the declarations section of a package body. They are inaccessible outside the package, but all the subprogram bodies in the package and the package initialization code share these variables. See Chapter 11 for details.

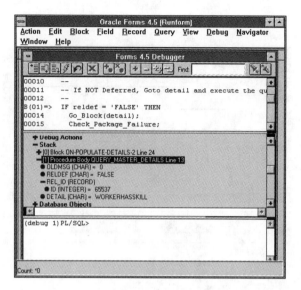

FIGURE 13-6.   *Examining procedure parameters and local variables*

You can also inspect the details of your debug actions through the breakpoint and trigger dialog boxes. Under the Debug Action heading, you can select any breakpoint or debug trigger and double-click on its icon to see the dialog boxes. For example, Figure 13-7 shows the Breakpoint dialog box for the breakpoint from the previous section. Using this dialog box, you can enable or disable the breakpoint with the Enabled check box. You can also enter some PL/SQL code as a trigger to execute whenever the break occurs.

The Interpreter Pane and Commands

The Interpreter Pane lets you enter the textual versions of the debugger commands such as Step Into or Go. You can also see the debugging level. The debugging level is the nesting level of the breaks in program execution. That is, you can break, step over a subprogram, and hit a break in the subprogram. This then establishes debugging level 2 in the Interpreter Pane. You can see the debugging level as a parenthesized expression in the Interpreter Pane command prompt, such as "(debug 1)PL/SQL>". This nesting of debugging levels gives you the ability to reset the debugger back to the previous debugging level, thus restarting your debugging session.

For a complete list of Interpreter debugger commands and their syntax, consult the online help for the debugger in the Forms Designer.

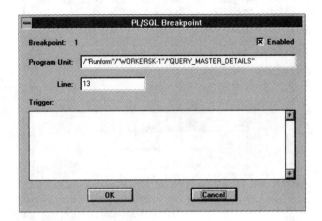

FIGURE 13-7. *The Breakpoint dialog box*

Tracing Forms

You can turn on special debugging messages when you run your application. Whenever an event occurs that causes a trigger to execute, the runtime system displays a message on the message line and an alert. When you click OK on the alert window, the application continues.

The debug message displays the name of the trigger and the name of the object that owns the trigger (form, block, or item). Figure 13-8 shows an example of a debugging message.

To display messages, add the DEBUG_MESSAGES parameter to the F45RUN command line:

```
F45RUN workersk talbot/george debug_messages=YES
```

NOTE
You will find very quickly that the caution given in the last section about massive amounts of data and long debugging time holds true when using debugging messages. Try it at least once to see what happens on a form with a reasonable number of triggers. This gives new meaning to the term "last resort."

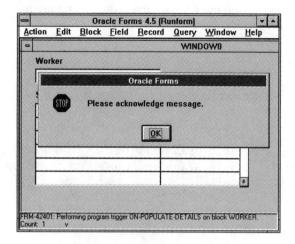

FIGURE 13-8.   *A Forms debugging message*

Tracing Reports

You can turn on report tracing with the Tools¦Trace menu item. Choosing this item displays the Trace Settings dialog box (Figure 13-9). This lets you check the statistics that you want the trace log to display.

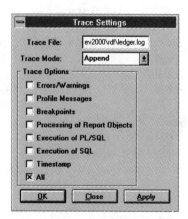

FIGURE 13-9.   *The Trace Settings dialog box*

This is the first part of the trace log for the Ledger Summary report that the full set of tracing options generates.

```
LOG :
        Logged onto server:
        Username: talbot


21:23:03   APP   (  Header
21:23:03   APP . (  Oracle Graphics Display   BOUGHTDISPLAY
21:23:29   APP . )  Oracle Graphics Display   BOUGHTDISPLAY
21:23:29   APP   )  Header
21:23:59   APP   (  Frame
21:23:59   APP . (  Text Boilerplate          B_2
21:23:59   APP . )  Text Boilerplate          B_2
21:23:59   APP . (  Text Boilerplate          B_1
21:23:59   APP . )  Text Boilerplate          B_1
21:23:59   APP . (  Text Field                F_2
21:23:59   APP . )  Text Field                F_2
21:23:59   APP . (  Text Field                F_1
21:23:59   APP . )  Text Field                F_1
21:23:59   APP   )  Frame
21:23:59   APP   (  Frame
21:23:59   APP . (  Frame                      M_PERSONBREAK_GRPFR
21:23:59   APP .. (  Frame                     M_LEDGERQUERY_HDR
21:23:59   APP ... (  Text Boilerplate          B_AMOUNT
21:23:59   APP ... )  Text Boilerplate          B_AMOUNT
21:23:59   APP ... (  Text Boilerplate          B_ITEM
21:23:59   APP ... )  Text Boilerplate          B_ITEM
21:23:59   APP ... (  Text Boilerplate          B_ACTIONDATE
21:23:59   APP ... )  Text Boilerplate          B_ACTIONDATE
21:24:00   APP .. )  Frame                      M_LEDGERQUERY_HDR
21:24:00   APP .. (  Repeating Frame            R_PERSONBREAK
21:24:00   APP ... (  Group                     PersonBreak   Local
Break:  0  Global Break:  0
21:24:00   APP .... (  Query                            LedgerQuery
21:24:00   SQL           EXECUTE QUERY : SELECT Person , ActionDate
, Item , Quantity , Rate FROM Ledger  ORDER BY 1 ASC , Person ,
ActionDate
21:24:00   APP .... )  Query                            LedgerQuery
21:24:00   PLS .... (  Function:         amountformula
21:24:00   PLS .... )  Function:         amountformula
21:24:00   APP ... )  Group                            PersonBreak
```

```
21:24:00  APP ... (  Text Field             F_PERSON
21:24:00  APP .... (  Database Column       Person
21:24:00  APP .... )  Database Column       Person
21:24:00  APP ... )  Text Field             F_PERSON
21:24:00  APP ... (  Frame                  M_LEDGERQUERY_GRPFR
21:24:00  APP .... (  Repeating Frame       R_LEDGERQUERY
21:24:00  APP ..... (  Group                G_LedgerQuery
Local Break:  0  Global Break:  0
21:24:00  APP ..... )  Group                G_LedgerQuery
21:24:00  APP ..... (  Text Field           F_AMOUNT
21:24:00  APP ...... (  Computed Column     Amount
21:24:00  APP ...... )  Computed Column     Amount
21:24:00  APP ..... )  Text Field           F_AMOUNT
21:24:00  APP .... (  Text Field            F_ITEM
21:24:00  APP ...... (  Database Column     Item
21:24:00  APP ...... )  Database Column     Item
21:24:00  APP ..... )  Text Field           F_ITEM
21:24:00  APP ..... (  Text Field           F_ACTIONDATE
21:24:00  APP ...... (  Database Column     ActionDate
21:24:00  APP ...... )  Database Column     ActionDate
21:24:00  APP ..... )  Text Field           F_ACTIONDATE
21:24:00  APP ..... (  Group                G_LedgerQuery
Local Break:  1  Global Break:  1
21:24:00  APP ...... (  Computed Column     Amount
21:24:00  APP ...... )  Computed Column     Amount
21:24:00  PLS ...... (  Function:           amountformula
21:24:00  PLS ...... )  Function:           amountformula
21:24:00  APP ..... )  Group                G_LedgerQuery
21:24:00  APP ..... (  Text Field           F_AMOUNT
21:24:00  APP ...... (  Computed Column     Amount
21:24:00  APP ...... )  Computed Column     Amount
```

The end of the log gives a summary profile of the report:

```
             +-------------------------------------+
             ¦ Oracle Reports Profiler statistics  ¦
             +-------------------------------------+


         TOTAL ELAPSED Time:     171.00 seconds

         Oracle Reports Time:    157.00 seconds (91.81% of
TOTAL)

                ORACLE Time:     14.00 seconds ( 8.18% of
TOTAL)
```

```
                    UPI:        6.00 seconds
                    SQL:        8.00 seconds

TOTAL CPU Time used by process: N/A
```

Tracing SQL and Client/Server Events

Although not strictly part of Developer/2000, there are two kinds of tracing that you may find useful under certain circumstances. Those circumstances are usually when you have no idea what is going on and you want to wade through enormous amounts of nearly useless material to figure it out. Unfortunately, this situation occurs more often than anyone would like to admit, so tracing tools at the client and server levels are still valuable, if time-consuming, tools of the application developer's trade. Again, the term "last resort" takes on new meaning.

SQL*Net Tracing on the Client

If you are using SQL*Net as your connection from the client to the server, you can use SQL*Net tracing. This produces a hexadecimal dump of all the events of which SQL*Net is aware. You can see exactly which characters you are sending to the server from the client, and perhaps this will be enough to identify your problem. This kind of trace is more useful for debugging third-generation programs, where you can create bizarre situations by overwriting memory locations or attaching mysterious unwanted characters to the ends of strings by accident. That is very hard to do in Developer/2000.

Turning on SQL*Net tracing differs between operating systems and versions of SQL*Net. Table 13-1 shows the different command sequences for setting up tracing.

NOTE
You should consult Oracle Corporation Technical Support for more information on using these techniques if the above description is not enough. The details are quite involved and are beyond the scope of this book. Also, these techniques are undocumented and can change at any time. Make sure you have enough disk space for the trace files, which can quickly grow very large (megabytes), and turn tracing off as soon as you get the trace information you need. Do not turn on tracing on a network basis, only locally (local variable setting or a local copy of SQLNET.ORA), or you will make your network administrator very unhappy as he or she struggles to figure out why there is no more disk space available on your system.

SQL*Net Version	Operating System	Commands
V1	Windows	Edit ORACLE.INI, putting in a line that reads OSNTDBUG=0xffff for TCP/IP or OSNDDBUG=0xffff for DECNET. This creates a file in your ORACLE home directory (ORAWIN, for example) with the trace information.
V1	UNIX	Set environment variable OSNTDBUG=0xffff for TCP/IP or OSNDDBUG=0xffff for DECNET; this prints debugging information on stderror, which you should redirect into a file using the 2> redirection command.
V1	VMS	Set the logical symbol OSNTDBUG to 0xffff for TCP/IP or OSNDDBUG=0xffff for DECNET; this prints debugging information on SYS$ERROR, which you should assign to a file.
V2	All	Set two parameters in the SQLNET.ORA file, TRACE_LEVEL_CLIENT (value 42) and TRACE_DIRECTORY_CLIENT (value is the directory in which you want to create the trace file); this writes a file called SQLNET.TRC in the directory you specify.

TABLE 13-1. *SQL*Net Tracing Setup*

SQL Tracing on the Server

On the server side, you can trace the SQL statements and their performance characteristics using SQL tracing.

In Forms, you turn on SQL tracing with the Statistics option (Tools⋮Options menu item, Runtime Options tab). In Reports, turn on tracing with an SRW procedure call in a Before-Parameter-Form trigger:

```
SRW.Do_SQL('ALTER SESSION SET SQL_TRACE TRUE');
```

In Graphics, use a similar call in an Open Trigger:

```
Do_SQL('ALTER SESSION SET SQL_TRACE TRUE');
```

You can also turn on tracing for every session by setting the _TRACE_FILES_PUBLIC parameter of the INIT.ORA file to TRUE, but you would not ordinarily want to do this; it is definitely overkill.

When you run your application with tracing on, the server produces an output trace file in a dump directory. You can identify this directory by running SQL*DBA and issuing the following command:

SHOW PARAMETER USER_DUMP_DEST

On Windows, this is likely to be \ORAWIN\RDBMS71\TRACE or something similar. Look in this directory for a file with extension .TRC and a unique identifier (process id or similar number), such as ORA18207.TRC. Running the BOUGHT.OGD Graphics application, for example, generates this trace file:

```
Dump file C:\ORAWIN\rdbms71\trace\ORA18207.TRC
Fri Nov 17 09:31:55 1995
ORACLE V7.1.4.1.0 - 90 day trial license.
To purchase a production license, call 1-800-492-9870(U.S only)
vsnsta=0
vsnsql=a vsnxtr=3
MS-WINDOWS Version 3.10
Fri Nov 17 09:31:55 1995

*** SESSION ID:(5.23)
=====================
PARSING IN CURSOR #1 len=32 dep=0 uid=10
ALTER SESSION SET SQL_TRACE TRUE
END OF STMT
EXEC #1:c=0,e=0,p=0,cr=0,cu=0,mis=1,r=0,dep=0,og=4
=====================
PARSING IN CURSOR #1 len=127 dep=0 uid=10
 SELECT Person "Person" , SUM ( Amount ) "Amount" FROM Ledger
WHERE Action IN ( 'Bought' , 'Paid' ) GROUP BY Person ORDER BY 2
END OF STMT
PARSE #1:c=0,e=0,p=0,cr=0,cu=0,mis=0,r=0,dep=0,og=4
EXEC #1:c=0,e=0,p=0,cr=0,cu=0,mis=0,r=0,dep=0,og=4
FETCH #1:c=0,e=0,p=0,cr=8,cu=3,mis=0,r=45,dep=0,og=4
STAT #1 id=1 cnt=45
STAT #1 id=2 cnt=184
STAT #1 id=3 cnt=225
```

```
Fri Nov 17 09:32:48 1995
XCTEND rlbk=0, rd_only=1
```

Although interesting, this file is somewhat hard to read. You can use the Oracle Toolkit profiler program (TKPROF) to format this trace into something you can easily work with. Figure 13-10 shows the TKPROF dialog box that appears when you run the profiler. Enter the name of the input TRC file and the name of an output file, which can be whatever you want. You should also enter the user name and password to see execution plans for queries.

Formatting the trace for the BOUGHT Graphics application yields this formatted trace file:

```
TKPROF: Release  - Production on Fri Nov 17 10:04:01 1995

Copyright (c) Oracle Corporation 1979, 1994.  All rights reserved.


****************************************************************************
count    = number of times OCI procedure was executed
cpu      = cpu time in seconds executing
elapsed  = elapsed time in seconds executing
disk     = number of physical reads of buffers from disk
query    = number of buffers gotten for consistent read
current  = number of buffers gotten in current mode (usually for update)
rows     = number of rows processed by the fetch or execute call
****************************************************************************
```

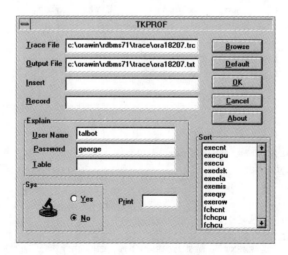

FIGURE 13-10. *The TKPROF dialog box for formatting SQL traces*

```
ALTER SESSION SET SQL_TRACE TRUE


call          count      cpu    elapsed     disk     query  current       rows
--------   --------   -------  ---------  --------  --------  -------  ----------
Parse             0     0.00       0.00         0         0        0           0
Execute           1     0.00       0.00         0         0        0           0
Fetch             0     0.00       0.00         0         0        0           0


--------   --------   --------  ---------  --------  --------  -------  ----------
total             1     0.00         00         0         0        0           0

Misses in library cache during parse: 0
Misses in library cache during execute: 1
Optimizer hint: CHOOSE
Parsing user id: 10   (TALBOT)
**************************************************************************
**

SELECT Person "Person" , SUM ( Amount ) "Amount"
FROM
 Ledger WHERE Action IN ( 'Bought' , 'Paid' ) GROUP BY Person ORDER BY 2


call          count      cpu    elapsed     disk     query  current       rows
--------    -------   --------  ---------  --------  --------  -------  ---------
Parse             1     0.00       0.00         0         0        0           0
Execute           1     0.00       0.00         0         0        0           0
Fetch             1     0.00       0.00         0         8        3          45


-------    -------   -------   ---------  --------  --------  -------  ---------
total             3     0.00       0.00         0         8        3          45

Misses in library cache during parse: 0
Optimizer hint: CHOOSE
Parsing user id: 10   (TALBOT)

Rows    Execution Plan
-------  ---------------------------------------------------------
      0   SELECT STATEMENT   OPTIMIZER HINT: CHOOSE
```

```
  45      SORT (ORDER BY)
 184        SORT (GROUP BY)
 225          TABLE ACCESS (FULL) OF 'LEDGER'
```

```
******************************************************************************

OVERALL TOTALS FOR ALL NON-RECURSIVE STATEMENTS

call        count      cpu    elapsed     disk    query  current       rows
--------    -------  -------  ---------  -------- -------- -------  ----------
Parse            1     0.00       0.00         0        0        0           0
Execute          2     0.00       0.00         0        0        0           0
Fetch            1     0.00       0.00         0        8        3          45

Misses in library cache during parse: 0
Misses in library cache during execute: 1

    2  user  SQL statements in session.
    0  internal SQL statements in session.
    2  SQL statements in session.
    1  statement EXPLAINed in this session.
******************************************************************************
Processed trace file: c:\orawin\rdbms71\trace\ora18207.trc
        1  session in tracefile.
        2  user  SQL statements in tracefile.
        0  internal SQL statements in tracefile.
        2  SQL statements in tracefile.
 12451842  unique SQL statements in tracefile.
        1  SQL statements EXPLAINed using schema:
              TALBOT.prof$plan_table
       26  lines in trace file.
```

NOTE
The statistics in the above example are all zero. You can turn on timing statistics by setting the TIMED_STATISTICS parameter of the INIT.ORA file to TRUE.

Part 3 has shown you how to use the sophisticated tools of Developer/2000 to code, test, and debug your final applications. Applying these tools methodically, you will create a system of high-quality, reusable code on which you can build many applications. The next part will help you move your application from the development environment to the real world, getting it into the hands of your customers and keeping it there by effective maintenance. It also shows you how to combine your applications with other software out there in the real world to leverage others' work in creating value with your own.

PART 4

Deploying Forms
with Other Tools

CHAPTER 14

Getting It Out There and Keeping It Out There

You have done your prototype, surveyed your users, redesigned and made secure your application, coded it, and tested and debugged it. What could possibly be left to do?

What happens after you finish doing your work on the application is arguably the critical part of the process—getting the application into the hands of its users and keeping it there. It is the difference between creating something for your own pleasure and education and producing a product.

Deploying Your Application

To *deploy* a software product is to distribute the product to its users. Deployment includes everything from packaging your software to installing it on the user's workstation or network.

Things to Worry About

To move a Developer/2000 application from your private working copy to a public application or product, you need to take some additional steps to *productize* your application:

- *User documentation:* You need to create a guide for the user that tells the application operator how to operate the application. This includes installation documentation.

- *Reference documentation:* You need to create a reference that describes each control in the application and the structure of the database.

- *Online documentation:* You need to create user and reference materials in an online help system or other online format that an operator can get to from within the application.

- *Training materials:* If the application is complex enough to require it, you should prepare training materials for the application. These can be online, computer-based training; video training; or training courses delivered in person.

- *Distribution media:* You need to create a system for installation on some kind of media, such as CD-ROMs or floppy disks. Alternatively, you can package the system for deployment over a network or even over a public network such as the Internet or one of the online service providers.

- *Marketing materials:* If you are selling the application as a product, you must create sales and marketing materials to publicize and sell your product.

The steps you take to productize your application depend entirely on the nature of the application. You could be building a tool for some friends, you could be building a system for in-house use in your company, or you could be building a product to sell to others. Each has its own unique requirements for deployment.

So, why worry about all this? All of this gets done somehow. However, if you think about it, there is quite a bit you can do to make the process easier if you understand what you or your company needs to do to deploy the product. You can design a product that is easy to deploy or hard to deploy, for example. You can make a product easy to document or hard to document, or you can leave the documentation process to the last minute to ensure it is of extremely poor quality. Thinking about the process as a system, a whole created of parts, can greatly increase the chance that your Developer/2000 application will wend its way into the world successfully and will stay where it is put.

Installation

The interface between you and your customer is the installation system of your product. This can be as simple as your walking around with a floppy disk to all the workstations and copying the disk onto them. It can be as sophisticated as creating a full installation system on CD-ROM or creating a tar tape with the appropriate files and directories.

Packaging Your Application

There are two dimensions that determine the scope of your effort in creating the installation system for your application: the degree of personal involvement in the installation process and the complexity of the installation process.

Usually, personal involvement directly relates to the nature of the application. Applications you yourself always install are typically personal or departmental tools or single-project applications. Corporate applications tend to require some personal involvement and some ability to turn it over to others. Applications the end user must install, with or without system engineering support (but certainly without your support) are usually products you sell to the end user.

The complexity of the installation process depends on several things. First, you may need to break the installation into *several parts*: client workstation versus server, several cooperating workstations, several distributed servers, and so on. Second, you may need to install portions of the package *conditionally*. That is, the user can choose to install only part of the package, or the installation process detects a specific configuration to determine which parts of the package to install, or it detects whether it is updating or newly installing, or whatever. Third, you may need to perform some kind of *processing* on the package: decompression, checking for files already present and newer, compiling, generating options files, or any number of creative ways to add complexity to the user's life.

If you have a product with no personal involvement in installation and with a relatively high degree of complexity, you should invest in a professional installation software package. These packages give you all the tools you need to make even the most complex installation look easy and professional to the end user (and to their managers, the ones who buy the product).

Otherwise, you just need to pay attention to the details to make sure you understand everything that needs doing and that you have everything you need in one place. One general rule for packaging is the oldest rule in the world: keep it simple. Install only the files the user needs. Do not clutter up the disk with compressed versions, 23 README files for different parts of the product, or 600 special icon bitmaps that the user can install to customize the application. Leave these on disk for special access.

Also, you must decide whether to ship source with your object files. This decision will usually depend on the nature of the contract between you and the user. If you need to protect users from their own mistakes, do not ship source. If you need to protect your proprietary rights to the system, do not ship source. If the user has no need or desire for source, do not ship source.

Here is a list of the Developer/2000 application components from the perspective of packaging. Table 14-1 tells you what components must ship as part of a package and what components are optional. You should carefully specify the purpose and nature of all the files in a README file or document you ship with the package.

There are also many miscellaneous types of files that you might package with the system, such as icons, bitmaps, sound files, video files, and so on.

You also need to consider what files to ship for an upgrade. You can ship a complete system, including all files, or you can ship just the changed files. If you take the latter approach, you will need to expand system testing to cover different configuration possibilities. You must ensure that the subset of files works for all the different, interesting configurations of your system.

NOTE
As a practical and legal matter, you may want to separate the ORACLE runtime code (F45RUN.EXE and so on) from your installation. Installing these things is a relatively complex business, and you should seriously consider using standard Oracle Corporation installation tools for these components of your system.

You can generate FMT and MMT form and menu source text files using the Forms Designer File¦Administration¦Convert menu item, which displays the Convert dialog box (Figure 14-1). To generate an FMT form source file, set the Type to Form, browse for the form file (FMB), and set the Direction field to Binary-to-Text. To generate an MMT menu source file, set the Type to Menu, browse for the menu file (MMB), and set the Direction field to Binary-to-Text.

File	Source or Object	Optional or Required	Comments
Application System			
INI	Source	Optional	Ship a model ORACLE.INI file with the application if you need to, or build one as part of your installation processing, that contains the paths and other variables the end user must set to run the application.
PRF	Source	Optional	Ship a model preferences file with the application or build one that contains the runtime options the system needs to run.
EXE	Code	Required	The ORACLE runtime executables, suitably licensed, and any executable tools you add; you can also require the user to install the runtimes separately.
DLL	Code	Required	The ORACLE runtime dynamic link libraries, suitably licensed, and any libraries your application system needs (user exits, foreign functions, and such); you can also require separate installation of these.
Forms			
FMB	Both	Possibly required	Contains all the Forms objects with both source and object format; only required if you do not ship the FMX file with object only.
FMX	Object	Possibly required	Contains the objects without source; only required if you do not ship the FMB file with both source and object code.
FMT	Source	Optional	Contains the ASCII text source for the form.

TABLE 14-1.   *File Components of Developer/2000*

File	Source or Object	Optional or Required	Comments
Menus			
MMB	Source	Possibly required	Contains the source and object code for the menu; only required if you do not ship the MMX file with object code only.
MMX	Object	Possibly required	Contains the object code only for the menu; only required if you do not ship the MMB file with both source and object code.
MMT	Source	Optional	Contains the ASCII text source for the menu
PL/SQL			
PLL	Both	Possibly required	Contains the source along with the object code; you need only ship this file if you want to ship both source and object and you do not ship the PLX file.
PLD	Source	Optional	Contains ASCII source code only in text file; must generate with Procedure Builder.
PLX	Object	Possibly required	Contains only the object code; you need only ship this file if you want to ship only object code or if you do not ship the PLL file; must generate with Procedure Builder or with F45GEN with the STRIP_SOURCE=YES option.
Reports			
RDF	Both	Possibly required	Contains source and object code for a report definition; required unless you ship the REP file that contains only the object code.
REP	Code	Possibly required	Contains object code for a report definition; required unless you ship the RDF file that contains both source and object code.
REX	Source	Optional	Contains ASCII source code in text format file; must generate with File ¦ Administration ¦ Convert menu item; use this format to create a portable report definition that installation can convert to a compiled RFD file for execution.

TABLE 14-1. *File Components of Developer/2000 (continued)*

File	Source or Object	Optional or Required	Comments
Graphics			
OGD	Both	Possibly required	Contains source and object code for a display definition; only required if you do not ship the object-only OGR file
OGR	Object	Possibly required	Contains object code for a display definition; only required if you do not ship the OGD file; must generate with File⁞Administration⁞Generate.

TABLE 14-1. *File Components of Developer/2000* (continued)

When you click Convert, the Designer produces a source text file for the form or menu.

NOTE
You can generate form and menu text-only files using the F45GEN command from the command line; use the SCRIPT=YES option, which tells the generator to generate a text script rather than object code.

You can generate REP files (report definitions in object-only format) in two ways in the Reports Designer. You can generate the file with File⁞Administration⁞ Generate, or you can covert the database or RFD version of the report definition to a REP version through File⁞Administration⁞Convert and the Convert dialog box

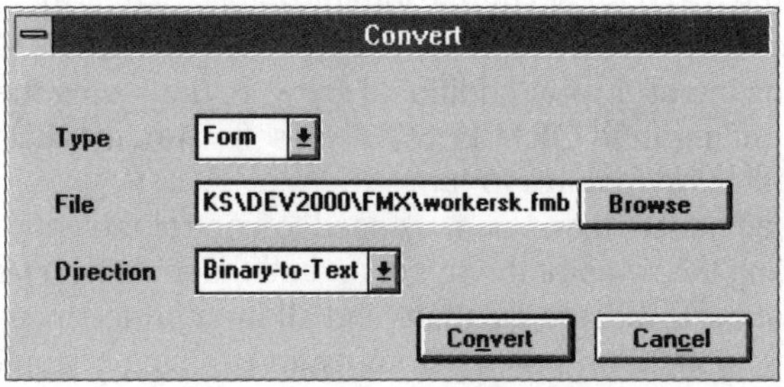

![Convert dialog box with Type set to Form, File field showing KS\DEV2000\FMX\workersk.fmb with Browse button, Direction set to Binary-to-Text, and Convert and Cancel buttons]

FIGURE 14-1. *The Convert dialog box for generating FMT and MMT files*

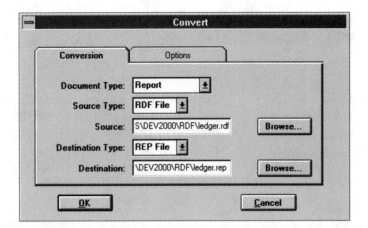

FIGURE 14-2. *The Convert dialog box for generating REP and REX files*

(Figure 14-2). Set the Source Type to RFD and browse for the report definition (RFD) file; set the Destination Type to REP. You can use the Convert dialog box to create REX files (report definitions in source-only text format) as well by selecting the Destination Type of REX instead of REP.

You can generate an OGR file (object code–only Graphics display) using the File¦Administration¦Generate menu item.

The Wonderful World of Client/Server Computing

Unless you want to spend massive amounts of money to develop a support organization, you should completely ignore the complexities of setting up the client/server environment for the user. This should be the job of the database administrator or system engineer at the user site, not of the application packaging and deployment system.

What you do need to do is to tell the user precisely what information he or she must obtain from the database or system administrator, such as the host connect string with the network file server and database server names. You should also be careful about telling the user what additional software (including the Developer/2000 runtimes and ORACLE SQL*Net software), in what specific versions, your application requires to run.

Under certain circumstances, you may need to control the entire architecture of the system, including the setup of the server and all that entails. If you do require this, go all the way: insist that the database and all its appurtenances belong completely to your application system. Do not allow mixing of application systems. If you do, you will almost certainly be stuck with the job of administering the whole mess, and mess it will be. You can try the legal route: simply deny any responsibility for anything and make the user sign it. Customers and end users tend not to like that.

The one exception to this rule is when you provide a clearly understood and demarcated way to extend your application system with additional applications, tables, and so on. But such extensions must be a logical part of your system, and you must take responsibility for supporting them to the extent of supporting the infrastructure that allows them.

Deployment

You can deploy your package in a number of different ways. Not so long ago, you just had to choose between different types of floppy disks or tapes, depending on the target operating system or systems.

Recently, the CD-ROM has been gaining favor, especially with large, commercial products such as ORACLE7 or Developer/2000. Whether it makes sense for you to get a CD-ROM mastering device (or to lease time on one) depends entirely on your circumstances.

Even more recently, the Internet and other online services and commercial bulletin boards have become a source for software packages. You connect to the appropriate server and ftp or otherwise download the package onto your workstation, and then install it. This is particularly popular for distributing low-cost software, free trial software, and upgrades. You could also use this mechanism effectively to distribute in-house applications if your corporate sites all connect to the Internet or to a central local- or wide-area network.

Most commercial installation products handle the creation of packages on all these different media. On floppies, for example, the system provides compression and packing of the files onto disks and the setup and processing of the compressed files as part of the installation process on the workstation. You can cheaply and easily package your files using a standard disk compression utility such as the ubiquitous PKZIP from PKWARE, Inc. Using larger-capacity media such as tapes, you can just dump your entire file hierarchy to tape and back again to a new workstation. The possibilities are endless.

Maintaining Your Application

Getting your application out into the world is the end of your project life cycle. In most cases, it is also the beginning of the next project life cycle: the maintenance project. Maintenance is the process of fixing problems in your application and extending the application with new features or data; in short, keeping the customer happy. You organize the maintenance of an application as a series of upgrades to the application. Each upgrade is a miniature project to produce an updated version of the application, and as such has its own project life cycle. You control the software during these projects with configuration management techniques to ensure that you understand how the application is changing. There does come a time, however, when it will be more productive to end the cycle, either because the needs the application serves no longer exist or because there is a better technology that can replace the application.

Failure and Fault Tracking

Chapters 12 and 13 (the testing and debugging chapters) distinguished carefully between faults and failures. Maintenance is where this distinction really begins to pay off.

Recall that a software *failure* occurs when a program does something that it should not do or does not do something that it should do. A *fault* is an error in a program's code, design, or requirements that causes the program to fail. Once your application is in the hands of its customers, this distinction lets you track what happens to it in a reasonable manner.

Your defect tracking system probably does not make this distinction, though it should. What you get from your customers are reports of *failures* of your application system, not faults. From a causal analysis of the failures, you determine the nature of the faults. If you confuse the two, you will always be dealing with apples and oranges in your maintenance efforts.

One sign of confusion, for example, is the common symptom of having to "link" defect reports because they are the same fault. If you track failures and faults, these so-called linked reports become multiple failures that refer to a single underlying cause or fault, which you determine by analyzing the cause of the failures. Measuring the number of failures can also inform you about the relative impact of the fault, giving you a way to prioritize faults other than just your own estimate of their importance. Measuring failures also gives you direct statistics on the quality of your product in the field, while measuring faults just tells you about the quality of your fault discovery process.

Another symptom of confusing failures and faults is an inability to distinguish easily between faults and "enhancement requests." An enhancement request is a failure that a fault did not cause. You address the failure by enhancing the application. You can prioritize such enhancements by their request rates.

When you fix a fault, you can determine the impact of that fix on the failure rate of your product. When you distribute upgrades to your application, you should include a list of the faults you have fixed, as well as a list of new features. You should give careful consideration to listing known failures of the product as well. That is, if you know the application fails in a certain way, even if you have not determined the fault that causes the failure, you can tell people about the failure and any ways of working around the problem.

Configuration Management

When you enter the maintenance life cycle of an application, it is vital to have the application under control of a configuration management system. If you have somehow managed to avoid configuration management or version control to this point, now is the time to bite the bullet. However, you should seriously consider version control at every step in your development process, including putting the requirements and design documents under version control.

Developer/2000 directly supports the PVCS configuration management system, a product of Intersolv. You use this system through the three items on the File¦Administration menu, Check-In, Check-Out, and Source Control Options. The various designers enable these menu items when you have installed PVCS on your system and put the following line into your ORACLE.INI file:

```
TVCCFG=C:\PVCS\PROJECT1\PROJECT1.CFG
```

The filename and path (C:\PVCS\PROJECT1\PROJECT1.CFG) are the filename and path of the configuration file for the project archive in which you want to store your application component versions.

This interface works by generating ASCII text for storing in the version control archive. You create the archive through the File¦Administration¦Source Control Options menu item and the Source Control Options dialog box, in which you specify the location and name of the archive directory.

The File¦Administration¦Check-In menu item displays the Check-In dialog box, which lets you check a module into the archive. The File¦Administration¦Check-Out menu item displays the Check-Out dialog box, which lets you check a module out of the archive. If you want to modify the module, you must check the Lock This File check box; otherwise, you get a read-only copy of the module file.

The configuration management life cycle within Developer/2000 proceeds as follows:

- Create the archive directory
- Check in initial versions of the modules
- Check out modules that you want to modify
- Check modified modules back into the archive with new version numbers

Using the windows of PVCS itself, you can manage the more sophisticated features of the configuration management system, such as declaring a release baseline across several modules. You can also generate difference reports using the File¦Administration¦Source Control Options menu item and Source Control

Options dialog box. Click on the Reporting Options button to see the Source Control Reporting dialog box. You can next specify two file versions to compare and then click on the Create Report button. This generates a report in a text file that compares the differences between the two files. You can look at this file in a text editor.

You can always use other configuration management systems, such as Source Integrity on Windows or rcs and sccs on UNIX, by exporting the text files into those systems, though you cannot check files in and out directly through Developer/2000. This slight disadvantage will not get in your way too much.

Version numbers can be arbitrarily complex in most configuration management systems. For most application software, a simple, two-part version number is sufficient: <Release>.<Version>. The <Release> number changes with major upgrades to the product, and the <Version> number changes with every upgrade. For example, 1.0 might be the initial release of the product. 1.5 might be the fifth minor upgrade. 2.3 might be the third minor release after the Release 2 major release. "Might be" describes all of these because you cannot count on this kind of simple logic with version numbers. There is Management involvement here. You will find all kinds of reasons to skip minor releases, to have parallel releases under two major release numbers, and a myriad of other confusing but perfectly reasonable (at least to the Marketing people) situations. All this will probably provide jobs for hundreds of archaeologists and historians in the year 3000 as they try to figure out our counting system for our primitive software organisms!

The Maintenance Release Life Cycle

It is very important to treat each maintenance release as a complete project. Your specification for the project should refer to the original specification. It should then add full descriptions of these kinds of modifications to the original specification:

- *Faults fixed* by changes to *external* features of the product (that is, features the user can see as opposed to internal PL/SQL or other changes not directly visible to the user except through a failure)

- *Enhancements*

- *Changes to installation and configuration files*, including bitmaps, sound files, and so on

Your design document should show any modifications to the original design documents. Your version number for source code should reflect the target release number.

As you move through your maintenance life cycle, you should carefully manage changes to the application through the change management system, checking files in and out to ensure that you overlook nothing. You should create object tests for the new and changed modules. You should run a regression system test to make sure that you have not broken something inadvertently, and you should add new system test cases as required by the changes and enhancements.

Product Euthanasia

At some point, you or your Marketing department must decide that enough is enough: that it is time to cast off the chains of the installed base and move ahead into the future. In other words, it is time to kill off your application. The business requirements of the application may have moved on with the rapid changes in the world. The technology may have changed enough so that you no longer can benefit from modifying the application system with Developer/2010 or whatever comes next. Oracle may merge with Microsoft; who knows. Things change.

The most important aspect of killing off your application is that you no longer need to continue maintaining it. That means you must have some way in your defect tracking system to say that a system has died and that you will not address the outstanding faults and failures of that system. Of course, these faults and failures could move into the next system, but your tracking must take that into account.

As well, you must terminate your configuration management control system. It is generally best to archive the archives in a way that you can easily retrieve them. Things may not have changed as much as you (or your Marketing department) thought.

This is also a good time to conduct the last rites for the application. Hold a review with everyone who has been involved with the product and discuss what went right and what went wrong with the product and its projects. This is an excellent time to learn something about your development process.

In this chapter, you have learned how to take the application from the development environment and put it into the real world. You have also learned some of the practical details of the process of keeping that application going in the real world. The next chapter continues the process of making your development process an *open system*, one that encourages communication with the environment, by showing you how to integrate Oracle and other external tools into your application, and even how to use database managers other than ORACLE7 to do your server work.

CHAPTER 15

You're Not Alone...

One brief stage in personal computer software history was the integrated application that could do everything: it worked as a spreadsheet, word processor, and database; allowed graphics and mail; and performed every other business function. The design limitations of this approach became apparent almost immediately. Marketers being marketers, no one threw in the towel, but several companies developed the application suite. Though many people do it, there are disadvantages in buying all your software from one company. You're buying one philosophy about how you should do business. These disadvantages have led to open systems.

An *open system* is one that permits the use of tools from different vendors. UNIX became the archetypal open system: there are many different UNIX operating systems that you can use interchangeably (well, reasonably so). Tool integration in the late 1980s started in the software tools market with the repository technology and tool integration architectures such as the Atherton Backplane that let programmers integrate multiple software tools into a coherent work process. Then came Dynamic Data Exchange (DDE) and Publish and Subscribe for PCs and Macintoshes, which let system designers communicate with other tools at runtime.

With the development of the Object Linking and Embedding (OLE) and its successor, OLE2, on the one hand, and the Common Object Request Broker Architecture (CORBA) on the other, the open systems movement is beginning to create software architectures that are open all the way down to the object level. Using these architectures, you can create objects and share their use among many applications and servers.

This chapter outlines some of the ways in which Developer/2000 gives you an open systems environment. You have now reached the stage of having your application out in the real world as a system. What does it take to open that system to the other systems already there? How can you create something that acts as part of a system community rather than just an island?

Integrating Oracle Products

The Developer/2000 tools can use one another as a first step toward integration of the outside world. You have seen such use in Chapter 5, in which your form and report prototypes used graphics prototypes. There are other possible combinations, such as displaying a report from within a graphics display. You could click on a pie chart slice and generate a report on the subject (although the technical details of drill-down activity like this are beyond the scope of this book).

This section gives you an overview of the basics of how to integrate the Developer/2000 products. You can refer to the individual manuals for each product for the details of the PL/SQL packages and how to use these packages in programming your applications.

Forms Integration Tools

The Forms component of Developer/2000 has the broadest array of tools for integrating other Developer/2000 products. You can run a report, a display, another form, or an ORACLE book document from PL/SQL code in a trigger. You can embed a chart in a block item, with all processing handled through the OG PL/SQL package.

Run_Product and Parameter Lists
The Run_Product built-in procedure is the mechanism in Developer/2000 Forms that lets you run other Oracle products. In Graphics, this procedure is part of the TOOLINT package, so you must add the package name to the procedure name: TOOLINT.Run_Product.

This is the syntax of the Run_Product built-in procedure:

```
Run_Product(<product>, <module>, <communication mode>,
            <execution mode>, <location>, <list>, <display>);
```

Table 15-1 shows the possible values and meanings of these seven parameters.

Parameter	Possible Values	Description
<product>	FORMS, REPORTS, GRAPHICS, BOOK	The ORACLE product to run: Forms, Reports, Graphics, or Book.
<module>	String	The name of the module or document to open when you run the product.
<communication mode>	SYNCHRONOUS, ASYNCHRONOUS	A synchronous call returns control to Forms after you exit the product you call; an asynchronous call returns control immediately, running the product you call in parallel.
<execution mode>	BATCH, RUNTIME	A batch product call runs a report or display in the background with no user interaction; a runtime product call runs the product in the foreground, allowing interaction; only Reports and Graphics can run in batch mode.
<location>	FILESYSTEM, DATABASE	This parameter tells the procedure where the module resides, in the file system or in the database.
<list>	Param_List object	The parameter list contains a set of parameters to pass to the product; you pass its name or its object id.
<display>	String	This is the name of the block chart item that will contain the display you are requesting from Graphics.

TABLE 15-1.   *Run_Product Parameters*

NOTE
You must use a SYNCHRONOUS communication mode when you pass a record group from the form to the product you are calling. You must use RUNTIME execution mode when calling a form or a book document. You use the display parameter only when the product is Graphics.

Parameter Lists and TOOLINT   Chapter 9 briefly discussed creating and using parameter lists with Run_Product to call a form from a form with your own parameters. This section gives you the complete details of using parameter lists.

There are two kinds of parameter, the text parameter and the data parameter. The text parameter lets you pass a string value for a named parameter, which can be a standard parameter in the called product, a user-defined parameter, a bind variable, or a lexical reference. A standard parameter name, bind variable, or lexical reference name must correspond to the exact name, such as DESTYPE or COPIES. A text parameter lets you pass any standard command-line parameter to the product you are calling. Any parameter that you could pass on the command line can be a text parameter.

The data parameter lets you pass the name of a Forms record group that contains the data records. You can pass data parameters to reports and graphics displays, but not to forms. If you pass a data parameter to a report, you can use it only in a master query, not in any child queries in the report data model.

To create a parameter list, you call the Create_Parameter_List built-in function, which returns a ParamList id. You then call the Add_Parameter built-in procedure for each parameter argument you want to add to the list. The actual list gets created in form memory and persists beyond the code block, so you need to create and add only once for the form instance. You do this by getting the id for the id variable, then testing whether it is null. Finally, you pass the ParamList id to the call to Run_Product.

```
DECLARE
  listID ParamList :=
    Get_Parameter_list('ReportArguments');
BEGIN
  IF ID_Null(listID) THEN  -- No list yet, create it
    listID := Create_Parameter_List('ReportArguments');
    Add_Parameter(listID, 'DESTYPE', TEXT_PARAMETER, 'PRINTER');
    Add_Parameter(listID, 'DESNAME', TEXT_PARAMETER, 'LPT2');
    Add_Parameter(listID, 'SkillQuery', DATA_PARAMETER,
    'SkillGroup');
  END IF;
```

```
Run_Product(REPORTS, 'Skills', SYNCHRONOUS, RUNTIME, FILESYSTEM,
    listID);
END;
```

Reports have no ability to pass parameters, but you can use the same procedures (Create_Parameter_List and Add_Parameter) in the ORACLE Graphics product as part of the Graphics TOOLINT package. This package gives you the ParamList data type and the procedures that use it. Unlike Forms, Graphics requires that you prefix the procedure and type names with the package name: TOOLINT.ParamList and TOOLINT.Add_Parameter, for example. Otherwise, the syntax is the same.

Graphics Logon Parameters   Graphics displays use data from either the database or from another data source that you specify. You can create a record group in a form, populate it with data from the database, then pass the record group to Graphics as a data parameter (see the preceding section). If you do this, you should also tell Graphics not to log on to the database, as this can use scarce resources and slow down your display unnecessarily. To do this, you must add a LOGON parameter to the Run_Product call, like this:

```
Add_Parameter(listID, 'LOGON', TEXT_PARAMETER, 'NO');
```

If you call another product from within Graphics, you can share your Graphics logon session by adding the logon information as the USERID parameter to the parameter list you create when you call the other product. See Chapter 16 of the *Graphics Developer's Guide* for a PL/SQL procedure that creates such a parameter list.

Chart Items and the OG Package

Chapter 5 has already shown you how to use the basic features of the OG package with chart items in a form. You use OG.Open and OG.Close in triggers to show a Graphics display. You can also use Run_Product to do this by supplying the name of the display item as the last argument to Run_Product:

```
Run_Product(GRAPHICS, 'sold.ogd', SYNCHRONOUS, BATCH, FILESYSTEM,
        NULL, 'control.sold_pie_chart');
```

After opening the display, you can use the OG.Refresh procedure to redisplay the Graphics display in the chart item, perhaps with a data parameter containing new data for the display.

```
OG.Refresh('sold.ogd', 'control.sold_pie_chart', listID);
```

The OG package also gives you two functions to get the character and number parameters in a Graphics display, GetCharParam and GetNumParam. You can use these functions to display parameter values from the Graphics display in form items, perhaps as captions or as further information about the display.

You can execute PL/SQL within the Graphics display by calling OG.Interpret, which invokes the PL/SQL interpreter on the string you pass. The interpreter executes the string as an anonymous block in the display scope. You can pass data into the Graphics display in this way to build complex, interactive Graphics displays. You can also use OG.MouseDown and OG.MouseUp to transmit mouse events from form mouse event triggers to the display. The corresponding mouse triggers in the display then take effect and do what the event requests. These facilities of the OG package permit you to build quite sophisticated, interactive forms with active, embedded graphics.

For details on all these subprograms and the use of the OG package in general, see Chapter 8 of the *Forms Advanced Techniques Manual* (Part Number A32506-1) and Chapter 16 of the *Graphics Developer's Guide* (Part Number A32482-1).

Graphics Displays in Reports

You saw in Chapter 5 how to embed a Graphics display in a report graphics item. You can have single-display items in the report header, or you can embed the graphics as items in any repeating group, causing the displays to repeat as well.

For a different situation, you can pass data to the Graphics display just as you can for Forms record groups, but the mechanism is very different from passing a data parameter in a Run_Product call. If you pass the data in from the report query, you can take filters and sorts into account, and you can improve report performance. With careful planning of the Graphics displays and their queries, you can reuse a single graphics display with different report queries. You can also parameterize the display query, but passing the actual data from the report is direct and fast.

Using the standard Oracle Graphics property sheet in the report, you can specify the Display Query on the O.G. Query tab. Figure 15-1 shows the O.G. Query tab replacing the standard query in the Bought display. You enter the name of the report query in the Display Query field, then select the report columns you want to map to the query's SELECT list. You then enter the display column names to complete the mapping process.

You might, for example, have a simple report that lists the summary amounts that Talbot's pays its workers. To generate this report, you code the following query:

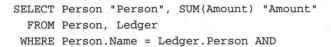

```
SELECT Person "Person", SUM(Amount) "Amount"
  FROM Person, Ledger
 WHERE Person.Name = Ledger.Person AND
```

```
        Person.Lodging IS NOT NULL AND
        Ledger.ActionType = 'Paid'
GROUP BY Person
ORDER BY 2
```

This query is similar to the query in the Bought display from Chapter 5. Instead of querying all bought ledger entries, however, it queries the entries "Paid" to a person with a lodging (that is, a "worker"). By entering the name of the display query (BoughtQuery) into the Display Query field and by selecting the Amount and Person columns, as in Figure 15-1, you can generate a report showing a pie chart of the breakdown of payments to workers without coding a new Graphics display.

Tool Integration

Tool integration is the facility of a software system to interact with other software systems as tools or components. Your application, for example, could call an external help tool to display application help, or it could embed a spreadsheet from a spreadsheet tool or a graphic from a graphic tool.

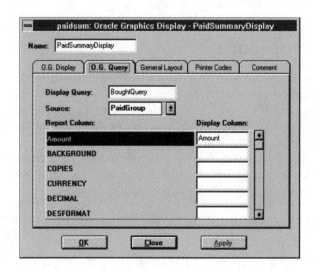

FIGURE 15-1.   *The O.G. Query tab in the Oracle Graphics property sheet*

There are several ways to integrate foreign tools into your application.

■ You can use the Host procedure in Forms to call a foreign executable program with parameters.

■ You can use the Object Linking and Embedding (OLE) architecture to link to or embed a component from a foreign tool running on your computer in your form, report, or display.

■ You can use VBX controls in Forms applications to enhance your user interface.

■ You can use Dynamic Data Exchange to communicate with other applications or tools running on your computer.

NOTE
Except for the Host procedure, all of these tool integration techniques apply only to the Windows 3.1 and Windows 95 platforms. If portability is an issue for the functionality you are trying to achieve, do not use these techniques.

The following sections provide only summaries of the extensive capabilities of the tool integration facilities of Developer/2000. For details, please consult the individual manuals as each section specifies.

The Host Procedure

The Host built-in procedure is an interface for executing operating system commands. Its single argument is a VARCHAR2 string variable that contains the command to execute. This string is exactly the same as though you had typed the command on the command line in DOS or UNIX or executed it with the Run dialog box in Windows.

As an example, you can use Host to call the Windows help system, which lets you specify a keyword topic to display (the -k argument). The following command displays the WORKERSK.HLP help file at the SkillLOV topic.

```
Host('winhelp -kSkillLOV c:\books\dev2000\help\workersk.hlp');
```

OLE

Object Linking and Embedding (OLE) is an architecture for tool integration that Microsoft gives you as part of the Windows platform. This architecture lets you link to or embed documents within other documents, where a document is a major application object of some kind. For example, Word documents, Excel spreadsheets, Excel macro sheets, and Visio drawings are all OLE documents.

The OLE Architecture

The OLE architecture divides the integrating tools into OLE servers and containers. A *server* is an application that creates and serves OLE objects in other applications. A *container* is an application that provides facilities for creation, manipulation, and storage of OLE objects. For example, Visio, a drawing application, is an OLE server that can create drawings in a container such as Microsoft Word or a Developer/2000 form.

An application can be both a server and a container. For example, Visio is also an OLE container that can store OLE objects such as Word documents or Excel spreadsheets in its drawings.

You can create objects in containers by either embedding them or linking them. *Embedding* an object means creating it and storing it in container storage, making the object accessible only to the container. *Linking* an object means creating the object in standard server storage (for example, a Visio file or a Word file) and linking to the object on demand. With a link, more than one container can contain the object. OLE containers also have a standard dialog box, Edit Links, that lets you manage the links to OLE objects in a container.

Guidelines for embedding versus linking are straightforward:

- When you need to *share* an object between containers, link to it.

- When you need to *conserve space* in the container storage, link to OLE objects.

- When you frequently need to *move* the OLE object around a network to different locations, embed the OLE object; otherwise, you need to modify the links constantly, as they contain the full path name of the linked object.

- When you want to *store* the OLE object in the database, embed it.

- Otherwise, flip a coin.

NOTE
Some applications have trouble managing large, embedded OLE objects in their container storage. Others have trouble with memory management, and particularly with system resources in Windows 3.1, when trying to link to and display OLE objects. You may have a configuration of tools that makes using OLE very difficult. You will need to experiment a good deal to find the right approach with a particular combination of tools.

You can display the OLE object in the container application either by displaying the object in a special field in a document window or by displaying an icon that represents the object. You activate a field-display object by clicking on it; you activate an icon object by double-clicking on it.

When you install an OLE server, you automatically register the server in the OLE *registration database.* Each server can handle one or more classes of OLE object (Word, for example, can handle the classes Word 6.0 Document and Word 6.0 Picture).

There are two ways to access an OLE object from within a container: in-place activation and external activation. *Activation* is the process of connecting to the server application and using its features to manipulate and display the OLE object.

In-place activation activates the object within the container application, which is only possible for embedded objects. When you activate an object in place, the object gets the user-interface focus and the server menu and toolbar replaces the container menu and toolbar, all within the container application. When you click outside the object, you deactivate the object.

External activation activates the object within the server application, displaying an instance of the server along with the container. When you close the object or exit the server, you update the object in the container. You can also update the object through a menu item or tool button whenever you wish.

OLE automation is the ability of an OLE server to provide a set of commands that a container can invoke. This provides for tighter integration of the OLE object into the container application. Usually, you use a macro language of some kind to issue the commands; but you can also do this through programming language extensions with certain tools, such as Visio.

OLE and Developer/2000

The Developer/2000 components have varying OLE capabilities.

Forms has the most extensive OLE *container* capabilities. Although you cannot make a Forms application an OLE server, you can embed or link to any kind of OLE object through the OLE container item. If you embed the object, you can store it in the database in a LONG RAW column. You can make the item part of a standard block that corresponds to a base table, or you can put the item in a control block and manage the display through triggers. You can initialize these fields by embedding or linking to an object in the Forms Designer. When you first display the item, it gets its default view from the initializing object, then replaces that from the database as you specify.

The Forms runtime program lets the user link to or embed an object at runtime and provides the standard OLE interface for managing objects and links. Forms also provides access to OLE automation through the PL/SQL library OLE2.PLL.

See Chapter 10 of the *Forms Advanced Techniques Manual* (Part Number A32506-1) for a complete description of the OLE2 features of Forms.

The Reports component offers more limited OLE container features befitting its more static approach to its job. You can have a column in your data model group object that corresponds to an OLE object you store in the database in a LONG RAW column. The Format property of the column is OLE2, and you must size the display field as appropriate for the object. You can also link to a file containing the object through a column containing the filename by setting the Read From File property for the column. You can activate the object in the Previewer, but you cannot change it using the server tools.

You can also create an OLE container field in the Layout editor as boilerplate. If you embed the object, you store it with the report definition. If you link to it, you store the link with the report definition. You can activate and change the object in the usual way through the Previewer.

See Chapter 16 of the *Reports Reference Manual* (Part Number A32489-1) and Chapter 7 of the *Building Reports Manual* (Part Number A32488-1) for details on using OLE 2 with reports.

Developer/2000 Graphics is an OLE server, but not a container. That is, you can link to or embed a display, but you cannot link to or embed other OLE objects in a display. As a server application, Graphics supports embedding or linking to a display from any OLE container. The Graphics server provides an image to the container based on the size you specified in the display, so you should size the container field using the same layout size. You can get the layout dimensions from the Layout Settings dialog box accessible through the View ┊ View Options ┊ Layout menu item.

You can also use OLE automation from the OLE container to manipulate the graphics. The Graphics server supplies the automation commands in Table 15-2.

See the *Graphics Reference Manual* (Part Number A32483-1), Chapter 7, and the *Graphics Developer's Guide* (Part Number A32482-1), Chapter 16, for details on using displays with OLE2.

VBX Controls

The Microsoft Visual Basic product introduced the Visual Basic (VBX) control. The VBX control is a special dynamic link library that provides standard events and properties for integrating visual controls into a user interface. There are many Microsoft and third-party VBX controls that you can use in your forms as VBX control items.

NOTE
VBX controls are not making the move to 32-bit operating systems such as Windows 95. The OLE Control (OCX) replaces the VBX control on those platforms.

Command	Arguments	Description
ClearQuery	Query name	Clears the Graphics query data
Connect	Connect string	Connects to a database
GetCharParam	Parameter name	Returns the value of a character parameter
Interpret	PL/SQL string	Interprets a PL/SQL block you pass as a string in the context of the Graphics runtime and its current display
MouseDown	X and Y positions	Sends a mouse down event to the display
MouseMove	X and Y positions	Sends a mouse move event to the display
MouseUp	X and Y positions	Sends a mouse up event to the display
SetRow	Query name, list of values	Adds a row of data to the named query as a series of values
Sync	None	Updates the container image to reflect the current status of the display in the Graphics server

TABLE 15-2. *Graphics OLE2 Automation Commands*

Here are just a few examples of available VBX controls:

- A calendar display with Gantt bars for blocks of time
- A Gantt chart display
- A grid with special properties (table display, spreadsheet, and so on)
- Special toolbars attached to objects
- Dials, sliders, thermometers, and other variable display options
- Special versions of standard dialog boxes such as File Open and Save
- Special field validation
- Special graphics displays
- Data compression dialog box
- Multimedia windows

You can thus use many speedy, flashy GUI features without having to program them in user exits or foreign functions. You can, for example, substitute a VBX control item for a text item to enable more sophisticated formatting or display.

You link the value of the VBX control value property to the item value through the name you enter into the VBX Control Value property in the item property sheet. The Forms Designer also maps many standard VBX control properties to their equivalent item properties, such as font or background color.

You can also refer to any valid VBX control property using the Get_Property and Put_Property subprograms of the VBX.PLL library.

To use a VBX control, you create a VBX control item using the VBX control button in the Layout editor. You then enter the absolute path for the control file and the particular control name in the VBX Control File and the VBX Control Name properties, respectively.

You use the When-Custom-Item-Event trigger attached to VBX control items to handle VBX events. Whenever the control raises an event, the trigger fires, and the system variable SYSTEM.Custom_Item_Event has the name of the event as a case-sensitive string. You then can program changes in values of the item in the trigger. You can access parameters for the event in the SYSTEM.Custom_Item_Event_Parameter variable.

You can build a list of parameters (a ParamList, as discussed in the section "Forms Integration Tools," earlier in this chapter) and raise a control event yourself using the Fire_Event procedure in the VBX package. You can also invoke a VBX method with the Invoke_Method_Property subprogram. For example, if a combo-box control has a method for adding items, you can use Invoke_Method_Property to invoke that method and add items to the list of values in the combo box.

DDE

Dynamic Data Exchange (DDE) is a slightly elderly, distant relative of OLE, but that relative is still alive, well, and working away on Microsoft Windows systems. DDE lets you import and export data from a form, making the form a DDE client. It also lets you execute commands on a server application. Using DDE, you can set up a link to another application called a *conversation* and send or receive data or send commands to the server using the conversation ID.

NOTE
You cannot automatically receive data change notices; DDE calls these events *advises*. You must check for changes to data and update the local copy of the data in PL/SQL code. Also, you cannot make a form a DDE server that responds to other applications' requests for data or execution of commands.

Table 15-3 shows the set of PL/SQL subprograms that the DDE package gives you.

Subprogram	Parameters	Description
App_Begin	Command, Mode	Starts up a DDE server application as a normal, minimized, or maximized application
App_End	AppID	Shuts down a DDE server you started with APP_BEGIN
App_Focus	AppID	Activates a DDE server, similar to clicking on the application window to give it the focus
Execute	ConvID, Command, Timeout	Executes a command in the server application, specifying a maximum length of time to wait for a response
GetFormatNum	Format String	Registers a data format name to establish an id to use in a POKE or REQUEST call
GetFormatStr	Format Number	Gets a string version of the format number from GETFORMATNUM
Initiate	Application, Topic	Opens a DDE conversation with a server application passing a specific topic, such as a filename; returns a conversation id
Poke	Conversation, Name, Data, Data Format, Timeout	Sends a data item by name in a conversation, specifying a maximum length of time to wait for a response
Request	Conversation, Name, Buffer, Data Format, Timeout	Requests a data value by name from a conversation, specifying a maximum time to wait for a response
Terminate	Conversation	Ends a conversation

TABLE 15-3. *DDE Package Subprograms*

There are a set of standard formats that the DDE package represents with a series of constants, which Table 15-4 details. You use these constants in the subprograms of Table 15-3 in the Data Format parameters.

Format Constant	Description
CF_BITMAP	A bitmap (BMP) file
CF_DIB	A bitmap with a special structure
CF_DIF	A data interchange format (DIF) file
CF_DSPBITMAP	A bitmap version of a proprietary format
CF_DSPMETAFILEPICT	A Windows Metafile version of a proprietary format
CF_DSPTEXT	A text version of a proprietary format
CF_METAFILEPICT	A Windows Metafile
CF_OEMTEXT	A null-terminated text string in an OEM character set
CF_OWNERDISPLAY	A format that the data's owner must display
CF_PALETTE	A color palette
CF_PENDATA	Windows Pen extension data
CF_RIFF	Data in Resource Interchange File format (RIFF)
CF_SYLK	Data in Microsoft Symbolic Link format (SYLK)
CF_TEXT	A null-terminated text string
CF_TIFF	Data in Tag Image File Format (TIFF)
CF_WAVE	Data in TIFF WAVE format describing a sound wave

TABLE 15-4.   *DDE Package Data Format Type Constants*

Using Other Database Managers with ODBC

The Open Data Base Connectivity (ODBC) standard is a de facto, standard application programming interface (API) for database managers. This API lets you write applications that you can move from one DBMS to another without rewriting or even recompiling your code. To use Developer/2000 with a DBMS other than ORACLE7, you need to know how it can access that DBMS through ODBC.

The Oracle Open Client Adapter (OCA) is an interface to ODBC that lets you make ODBC calls instead of ORACLE7 calls in Developer/2000. You access this software layer by using a special database logon string:

```
user_name/password@odbc:data_source
```

The user_name and password are the standard name and password for your database, and the data_source is the ODBC name for your database. By prefixing "odbc:" to the data_source, you tell Developer/2000 to use the OCA. You can also use an asterisk as the data_source, in which case ODBC prompts you with a list of the registered data sources on your machine.

To set up a data source, you use the ODBC Administrator or other database-vendor-supplied program. You should consult your database manager documentation or the ODBC driver documentation for details on setup.

NOTE
The OCA supports only specific data sources: Microsoft SQL Server, Microsoft Access, INFORMIX Online, SYBASE 4.9 and System 10, TANDEM NonStop SQL, and Rdb (versions 5.1 and 6.1). See the *Oracle Developer/2000 Installation Guide* (Part Number A32515-2), Appendix D, for details on driver support and restrictions. Other ODBC data sources may work, but Oracle Corporation does not support them.

You do not need to do very much to use Reports and Graphics applications with ODBC data sources. Forms applications, however, are another story. The rest of this section details what you must do to a form to get it to work with ODBC.

Oracle provides two property classes that do most of your work for you. You must change several properties of the form, its blocks, and its items in the Forms Designer. As a first step, open the form OCA_PROP.FMB you will find in OCA\ODBC10\DEMO under your main ORACLE directory (\ORAWIN\OCA\ ODBC10\DEMO\OCA_PROP.FMB for Windows, for example). Figure 15-2 shows the two property classes this form provides.

Copy these property classes into your form. You can alternatively create a reference to them if you wish.

Apply the OCA_Module_Property property class to the form module by double-clicking on the form in the Object Navigator to display its property sheet. Then select OCA_Module_Property from the drop-down list for the Class property, as shown in Figure 15-3. This sets one property, the Savepoint Mode property, which has the = next to it to indicate that it is inheriting from the property class. This prevents Forms from trying to create savepoints, which is an ORACLE7-specific feature.

Apply the OCA_Block_Property class to each base-table block in your form. This property class sets a series of Database group properties, as Figure 15-4 shows.

All the elements with = signs are relevant to ODBC processing. The Primary Key property and the Key Mode property relate to how Forms deals with checking primary key constraints. The Key Mode tells Forms to either use an ORACLE7 rowid as the key or to use the items in the block designated as primary key columns. The Updateable setting indicates the latter choice. The Records Buffered and Records Fetched properties and the Update Allowed and Update Changed Columns properties reflect values more appropriate for non-Oracle databases. The

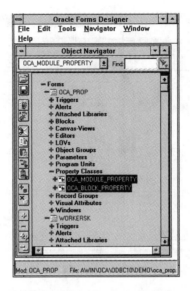

FIGURE 15-2. *OCA_PROP form and its property classes*

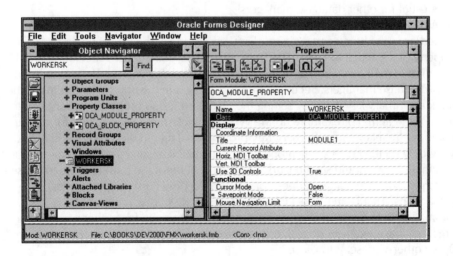

FIGURE 15-3. *OCA_Module_Property applied to form module*

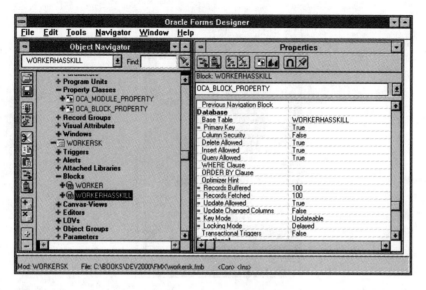

FIGURE 15-4. *OCA_Block_Property applied to block*

Locking Mode property, when set to Delayed, tells Forms to acquire locks when it tries to commit rather than when the operator modifies the item. This choice is more usual for other database managers.

After setting these property sheets, you also need to set a few additional properties in the block and its items. First, you must set the Column Security property of the block to False. The Column Security feature uses special ORACLE7 data dictionary information to do its processing, and this will not be available in other database managers. Second, you must designate the appropriate items in the block as primary key items by setting the Database group property Primary Key to True for the item. For example, in the Worker block in the WorkerSkill form, you would set the Name item Primary Key property to True. In the WorkerSkill block, you would set the Primary Key property for both the Name and the Skill items to True.

Finally, you should set the Cursor Mode property of the form module to Close if the target database manager does not support keeping cursors open across transactions. That is, in ORACLE7 a COMMIT or ROLLBACK does not automatically close open cursors, it just leaves them open for further work. If the target database manager does that too, leave the Cursor Mode property set to Open; otherwise, set it to Close.

Now, generate the form executable and you are ready to use the form with any ODBC-compliant database that OCA supports. You should carefully review the *Forms Advanced Techniques Manual* (Part Number A32506-1), Chapter 14, and the *Installation Guide* for the operating details for your particular target database managers. There are a fair number of restrictions on what your program units can and cannot do using ODBC and a particular database manager.

ORACLE Terminal for Key Assignments in Forms

The final topic of this chapter deals with a small but significant portion of the Developer/2000 Forms interface to the world. Oracle Terminal lets you change the keys you use to execute commands, both in the Designer and in the Runform program.

Developer/2000 Forms gets its key assignments from a resource file, such as the FMRUSW.RES file on Windows. The Oracle Terminal program lets you edit parts of that file to define a key binding. You can bind keys to application functions or to key triggers. This lets you modify the keyboard interface of your Forms applications to suit your needs. You can also modify the interface of the Designer to suit your own tastes.

When you run Oracle Terminal, it prompts you for a file. Find the resource file for Forms and click OK. On Windows, it is in the FORMS45 directory. If you try some other resource files, you will find these files do not have the right structure for use with Oracle Terminal. Terminal then displays the main terminal window (Figure 15-5). This window lets you set the product and device if the file defines multiple ones, which does not appear to be true for the current product. Click on the key-binding icon to edit the key bindings with the Key Binding Editor.

The Key Binding Editor displays a tree of key categories (Figure 15-6). Each of these categories contains a set of key bindings relating to a particular type of action. The intermediate categories (runform and design) have actions that apply to all situations in the product, such as Show Keys, Help, Cancel, and Exit. The leaf categories have actions that apply in specific situations.

To see the key bindings, double-click on the category circle. The Editor displays a table of bindings (Figure 15-7). This table shows the Action, such as [Next Block] or [Scroll Up], and the key to which it binds, such as Control+D or Shift+F9. You can have duplicate rows for an action, indicating that you get the action by pressing any of a group of keys. Each key for an action takes a separate row in the table.

To change a binding, find the action and change the key by typing over it. You can manipulate the rows with the Row buttons (Duplicate, Insert, and Delete Row). You can also enter the key by placing the cursor in the key field and clicking on Macro Mode. You can then enter the keys by pressing the actual keys rather than spelling out words such as "Control" and "Shift." Follow the instructions in the resulting dialog box for finishing up the macro recording.

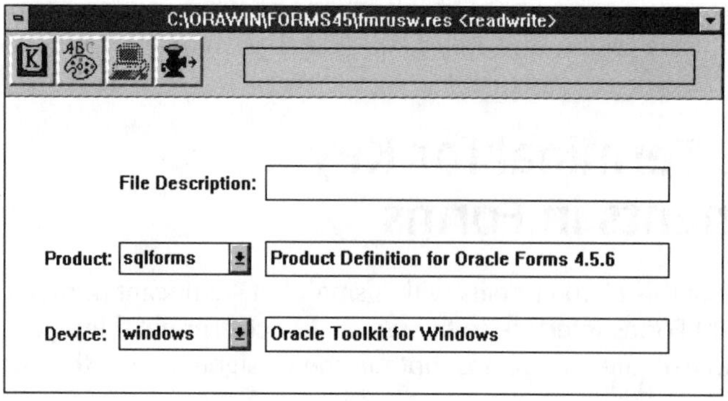

FIGURE 15-5. *The Oracle Terminal main window*

Setting up a key trigger is a bit more involved because you need to define the action. You do this at the top level, windows-sqlforms, in the Key Binding Editor. Double-click on the windows-sqlforms node. You see an empty action table. Click

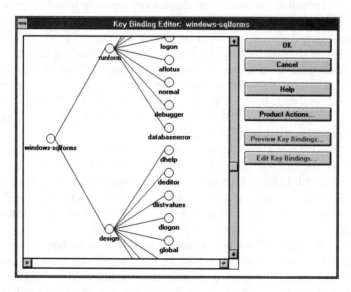

FIGURE 15-6. *The Key Binding Editor*

Action	Binding	
Clear Item	Control+u	
Clear Block	Shift+F5	
Edit	Control+e	
Search	Control+s	
Select	Return	
Clear Record	Shift+F4	
Delete Record	Shift+F6	
Duplicate Record	F4	
Insert Record	F6	
Duplicate Item	F3	
Return	Return	
Delete Backward	Backspace	
List of Values	F9	
Block Menu	F5	
Enter Query	F7	
Execute Query	F8	
Display Error	Shift+F1	

Key Binding Definition: normal

Buttons: OK, Cancel, Help, Duplicate Row, Insert Row, Delete Row, Macro Mode

FIGURE 15-7. *The Key bindings table*

on the Insert Row button to insert a row, then insert the action that corresponds to the key trigger (KEY-F3, for example, results in [User Defined Key 3]) and Code (85). Then enter the key binding just as you did previously.

Now click on the Product Actions button to invoke the Product Actions Editor, which is very similar to the Key Binding Editor graphically. Double-click on the sqlforms category to see the Product Action Definition window (Figure 15-8). Enter the action ([User Defined Key 3], for example), its corresponding numeric code (from 82 for key 0 through 91 for key 9), and a description to display in the list of key bindings. Click on OK to finish up.

When you finish defining bindings, click on OK to dismiss the Key Binding Editor and return to the main window. Save the key bindings, then click on the Generate button to generate a new resources file with the new bindings. Save again to complete the process.

Oracle Terminal provides a fitting end to this introduction to using Developer/2000. You have seen how to set up a life cycle for development. You have seen how to prototype your applications. You have seen how to take your design forward to a complete application. You have seen how to code, test, and debug that application. Finally, you have seen how to help that application to interact with the environment by deploying it, maintaining it, and connecting it to other software. The basis that this book gives you is just the beginning of discovering all the interesting things that Developer/2000 holds in store for you. Have fun!

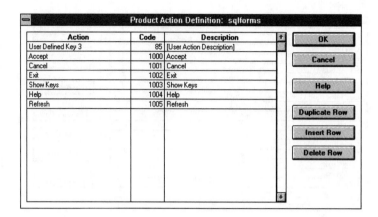

FIGURE 15-8. *The Product Actions Editor with key trigger action*

The Database

This appendix contains the full ORACLE7 SQL definition for the Talbot database. See Chapter 4 for an explanation of the different tables and for a full, graphical data model of the database showing the relationships between the tables.

You should use these commands logging onto a single ORACLE user, who needs CONNECT and RESOURCE privilege. You may want to add workspace constraints to the tables if you wish to closely control the size of the data, though this is not a very large database.

Dropping the Tables

The first set of SQL commands drops the tables and cluster, destroying any data in the database. These commands make sure you start with a clean example database.

```
DROP TABLE WorkerHasSkill;
DROP TABLE Skill;
DROP TABLE Ledger;
DROP TABLE Person;
DROP TABLE Lodging;
DROP CLUSTER WorkerAndSkill;
```

Creating the Physical and Logical Schemas

The following commands create the storage structures and schema (the physical and conceptual databases). The cluster holds the Person and Worker Has Skill tables, which share the name as key. The CREATE SCHEMA statement lets you create the tables in any order without worrying about the transitivity constraints imposed by the foreign key references. You should note that the authorization identifer, "Talbot" in the CREATE SCHEMA statement, corresponds to the user name of the account in which you want to create the schema. Because this book uses the TALBOT account, it uses TALBOT as the authorization identifier.

```
DROP SEQUENCE LedgerSequence;
CREATE SEQUENCE LedgerSequence /* sequence numbers for Ledger */;
CREATE SCHEMA AUTHORIZATION Talbot
CREATE TABLE Ledger (
LedgerID        INTEGER PRIMARY KEY,/* sequence number, primary key */
ActionDate      DATE,               /* when */
Action          VARCHAR(8),         /* bought, sold, paid, received */
Item            VARCHAR(30),        /* what */
Quantity        INTEGER,            /* how many */
QuantityType    VARCHAR(10),        /* type of quantity */
Rate            NUMERIC(9,2),       /* how much per quantity type  */
Amount          NUMERIC(9,2),       /* total amount = rate*quantity */
Person          VARCHAR(25) REFERENCES Person /* who */
)
CREATE TABLE Lodging (
Lodging         VARCHAR(15) PRIMARY KEY, /* short name for lodging */
LongName        VARCHAR(40),        /* complete name */
Manager         VARCHAR(25),        /* manager's name */
Address         VARCHAR(30)         /* address of the lodging */
)
CREATE TABLE Skill (
Skill           VARCHAR(25) PRIMARY KEY, /* name of a capability */
Description     VARCHAR(80)         /* description of the skill */
)
CREATE TABLE Person (
Name            VARCHAR(25) PRIMARY KEY,        /* worker's name */
Age             INTEGER,                /* age in years */
Lodging         VARCHAR(15) REFERENCES Lodging
                        /* reference to short name of lodging */
)
CREATE TABLE WorkerHasSkill (
Name            VARCHAR(25) REFERENCES Person, /* worker's name */
```

```
Skill         VARCHAR(25) REFERENCES Skill,  /* capability name */
Ability       VARCHAR(15),        /* how skilled is the worker? */
PRIMARY KEY (Name, Skill)
);
```

Creating the Data

The following INSERT statements build the actual database. You must load the tables in the following order so that you satisfy all the integrity constraints. For example, if you insert a Person with a Lodging without having already inserted the Lodging, you violate an integrity constraint.

The Lodging Table

```
INSERT INTO Lodging VALUES (
'Cranmer','Cranmer Retreat House','Thom Cranmer','Hill St., Berkeley');
INSERT INTO Lodging VALUES (
'Matts','Matts Long Bunk House','Roland Brandt','3 Mile Rd., Keene');
INSERT INTO Lodging VALUES (
'Mullers','Mullers Coed Lodging','Ken Muller','120 Main, Edmeston');
INSERT INTO Lodging VALUES (
'Papa King','Papa King Rooming','William King','127 Main, Edmeston');
INSERT INTO Lodging VALUES (
'Rose Hill','Rose Hill for Men','John Peletier','RFD 3, N. Edmeston');
INSERT INTO Lodging VALUES (
'Weitbrocht','Weitbrocht Rooming','Eunice Benson','320 Geneva, Keene');
```

The Skill Table

```
INSERT INTO Skill VALUES (
'Woodcutter','Mark And Fell Trees, Split, Stack, Haul');
INSERT INTO Skill VALUES (
'Combine Driver','Harness, Drive, Groom Horses, Adjust Blades');
INSERT INTO Skill VALUES (
'Smithy','Stack For Fire, Run Bellows, Cut, Shoe Horses');
INSERT INTO Skill VALUES (
'Grave Digger','Mark And Cut Sod, Dig, Shore, Fill, Resod');
INSERT INTO Skill VALUES (
'Discus','Harness, Drive, Groom Horses, Blade Depth');
INSERT INTO Skill VALUES (
'Work','General Unskilled labor');
```

The Person Table

```
INSERT INTO Person VALUES ('Bart Sarjeant', 22, 'Cranmer');
INSERT INTO Person VALUES ('Elbert Talbot', 43, 'Weitbrocht');
INSERT INTO Person VALUES ('Donald Rollo', 16, 'Matts');
INSERT INTO Person VALUES ('Jed Hopkins', 33, 'Matts');
INSERT INTO Person VALUES ('William Swing', 15, 'Cranmer');
INSERT INTO Person VALUES ('John Pearson', 27, 'Rose Hill');
INSERT INTO Person VALUES ('George Oscar', 41, 'Rose Hill');
INSERT INTO Person VALUES ('Kay And Palmer Wallbom', NULL, 'Rose Hill');
INSERT INTO Person VALUES ('Pat Lavay', 21, 'Rose Hill');
INSERT INTO Person VALUES ('Richard Koch And Brothers', NULL, 'Weitbrocht');
INSERT INTO Person VALUES ('Dick Jones', 18, 'Rose Hill');
INSERT INTO Person VALUES ('Adah Talbot', 23, 'Papa King');
INSERT INTO Person VALUES ('Roland Brandt', 35, 'Matts');
INSERT INTO Person VALUES ('Peter Lawson', 25, 'Cranmer');
INSERT INTO Person VALUES ('Victoria Lynn', 32, 'Mullers');
INSERT INTO Person VALUES ('Wilfred Lowell', 67, NULL);
INSERT INTO Person VALUES ('Helen Brandt', 15, NULL);
INSERT INTO Person VALUES ('Gerhardt Kentgen', 55, 'Papa King');
INSERT INTO Person VALUES ('Andrew Dye', 29, 'Rose Hill');
INSERT INTO Person VALUES ('Blacksmith', NULL, NULL);
INSERT INTO Person VALUES ('Boole And Jones', NULL, NULL);
INSERT INTO Person VALUES ('Dean Foreman', NULL, NULL);
INSERT INTO Person VALUES ('Dr. Carlstrom', NULL, NULL);
INSERT INTO Person VALUES ('Edward Johnson', NULL, NULL);
INSERT INTO Person VALUES ('Edythe Gammiere', NULL, NULL);
INSERT INTO Person VALUES ('Feed Store', NULL, NULL);
INSERT INTO Person VALUES ('Fred Fuller', NULL, NULL);
INSERT INTO Person VALUES ('Gary Kentgen', NULL, NULL);
INSERT INTO Person VALUES ('General Store', NULL, NULL);
INSERT INTO Person VALUES ('George August', NULL, NULL);
INSERT INTO Person VALUES ('George B. McCormick', NULL, NULL);
INSERT INTO Person VALUES ('Harold Schole', NULL, NULL);
INSERT INTO Person VALUES ('Henry Chase', NULL, NULL);
INSERT INTO Person VALUES ('Isaiah James', NULL, NULL);
INSERT INTO Person VALUES ('James Cole', NULL, NULL);
INSERT INTO Person VALUES ('Janice Talbot', NULL, NULL);
INSERT INTO Person VALUES ('John Austin', NULL, NULL);
INSERT INTO Person VALUES ('Lily Carlstrom', NULL, NULL);
INSERT INTO Person VALUES ('Livery', NULL, NULL);
INSERT INTO Person VALUES ('Manner Jewelers', NULL, NULL);
INSERT INTO Person VALUES ('Methodist Church', NULL, NULL);
INSERT INTO Person VALUES ('Mill', NULL, NULL);
INSERT INTO Person VALUES ('Morris Arnold', NULL, NULL);
INSERT INTO Person VALUES ('Palmer Wallbom', NULL, NULL);
INSERT INTO Person VALUES ('Phone Company', NULL, NULL);
INSERT INTO Person VALUES ('Post Office', NULL, NULL);
INSERT INTO Person VALUES ('Quarry', NULL, NULL);
INSERT INTO Person VALUES ('Robert James', NULL, NULL);
INSERT INTO Person VALUES ('Sam Dye', NULL, NULL);
INSERT INTO Person VALUES ('School', NULL, NULL);
INSERT INTO Person VALUES ('Underwood Bros', NULL, NULL);
INSERT INTO Person VALUES ('Verna Hardware', NULL, NULL);
```

The WorkerHasSkill Table

```
INSERT INTO WorkerHasSkill VALUES ('Dick Jones','Smithy','Excellent');
INSERT INTO WorkerHasSkill VALUES ('John Pearson','Combine Driver',NULL);
INSERT INTO WorkerHasSkill VALUES ('John Pearson','Smithy','Average');
INSERT INTO WorkerHasSkill VALUES ('Helen Brandt','Combine Driver','Very Fast');
INSERT INTO WorkerHasSkill VALUES ('John Pearson','Woodcutter','Good');
INSERT INTO WorkerHasSkill VALUES ('Victoria Lynn','Smithy','Precise');
INSERT INTO WorkerHasSkill VALUES ('Adah Talbot','Work','Good');
INSERT INTO WorkerHasSkill VALUES ('Wilfred Lowell','Work','Average');
INSERT INTO WorkerHasSkill VALUES ('Elbert Talbot','Discus','Slow');
INSERT INTO WorkerHasSkill VALUES ('Wilfred Lowell','Discus','Average');
```

The Ledger Table

```
INSERT INTO Ledger VALUES (LedgerSequence.NEXTVAL,
'01-APR-01','Paid','Plowing',1,'Day',3,3,'Richard Koch And Brothers');
INSERT INTO Ledger VALUES (LedgerSequence.NEXTVAL,
'02-MAY-01','Paid','Work',1,'Day',1,1,'Dick Jones');
INSERT INTO Ledger VALUES (LedgerSequence.NEXTVAL,
'03-JUN-01','Paid','Work',1,'Day',1,1,'Elbert Talbot');
INSERT INTO Ledger VALUES (LedgerSequence.NEXTVAL,
'04-JAN-01','Paid','Work',1,'Day',1,1,'Gerhardt Kentgen');
INSERT INTO Ledger VALUES (LedgerSequence.NEXTVAL,
'04-FEB-01','Paid','Work',.5,'Day',1,.5,'Elbert Talbot');
INSERT INTO Ledger VALUES (LedgerSequence.NEXTVAL,
'05-APR-01','Paid','Work',1,'Day',1,1,'Dick Jones');
INSERT INTO Ledger VALUES (LedgerSequence.NEXTVAL,
'06-AUG-01','Paid','Plowing',1,'Day',1.8,1.8,'Victoria Lynn');
INSERT INTO Ledger VALUES (LedgerSequence.NEXTVAL,
'07-OCT-01','Paid','Plowing',.5,'Day',3,1.5,'Richard Koch And Brothers');
INSERT INTO Ledger VALUES (LedgerSequence.NEXTVAL,
'09-SEP-01','Paid','Work',1,'Day',1,1,'Adah Talbot');
INSERT INTO Ledger VALUES (LedgerSequence.NEXTVAL,
'09-OCT-01','Paid','Work',.5,'Day',1.25,.63,'Donald Rollo');
INSERT INTO Ledger VALUES (LedgerSequence.NEXTVAL,
'10-NOV-01','Paid','Work',1,'Day',1.25,.63,'John Pearson');
INSERT INTO Ledger VALUES (LedgerSequence.NEXTVAL,
'10-AUG-01','Paid','Work',1,'Day',1,1,'Helen Brandt');
INSERT INTO Ledger VALUES (LedgerSequence.NEXTVAL,
'11-AUG-01','Paid','Work',1,'Day',2,2,'Helen Brandt');
INSERT INTO Ledger VALUES (LedgerSequence.NEXTVAL,
'11-SEP-01','Paid','Work',1,'Day',.75,.75,'Roland Brandt');
INSERT INTO Ledger VALUES (LedgerSequence.NEXTVAL,
'12-DEC-01','Paid','Work',1,'Day',1,1,'Bart Sarjeant');
INSERT INTO Ledger VALUES (LedgerSequence.NEXTVAL,
'12-JAN-01','Paid','Work',1,'Day',1,1,'George Oscar');
INSERT INTO Ledger VALUES (LedgerSequence.NEXTVAL,
'13-JUN-01','Paid','Work',1,'Day',1,1,'Peter Lawson');
INSERT INTO Ledger VALUES (LedgerSequence.NEXTVAL,
'14-JUL-01','Paid','Work',1,'Day',1.2,1.2,'Wilfred Lowell');
```

```
INSERT INTO Ledger VALUES (LedgerSequence.NEXTVAL,
'15-JUL-01','Paid','Work',1,'Day',2.25,2.25,'Kay And Palmer Wallbom');
INSERT INTO Ledger VALUES (LedgerSequence.NEXTVAL,
'03-OCT-01','Sold','Boot Between Horses',1,'Each',12.5,12.5,'Gary Kentgen');
INSERT INTO Ledger VALUES (LedgerSequence.NEXTVAL,
'01-NOV-01','Bought','Calf',2,'Each',2,4,'Gary Kentgen');
INSERT INTO Ledger VALUES (LedgerSequence.NEXTVAL,
'02-NOV-01','Bought','Mare',1,'Each',5,5,'James Cole');
INSERT INTO Ledger VALUES (LedgerSequence.NEXTVAL,
'03-NOV-01','Bought','Pig',1,'Each',2,2,'Andrew Dye');
INSERT INTO Ledger VALUES (LedgerSequence.NEXTVAL,
'04-NOV-01','Bought','Hay',1,'Wagon',5,5,'Andrew Dye');
INSERT INTO Ledger VALUES (LedgerSequence.NEXTVAL,
'05-NOV-01','Bought','Hay',4,'Wagon',5,20,'Andrew Dye');
INSERT INTO Ledger VALUES (LedgerSequence.NEXTVAL,
'05-NOV-01','Bought','Line',1,'Set',.75,.75,'Andrew Dye');
INSERT INTO Ledger VALUES (LedgerSequence.NEXTVAL,
'06-NOV-01','Bought','Colt',2,'Each',4.5,9,'Andrew Dye');
INSERT INTO Ledger VALUES (LedgerSequence.NEXTVAL,
'06-AUG-01','Paid','Plowing',2,'Day',2,4,'Andrew Dye');
INSERT INTO Ledger VALUES (LedgerSequence.NEXTVAL,
'07-NOV-01','Paid','Sawed Wood',1,'Day',.5,.5,'Andrew Dye');
INSERT INTO Ledger VALUES (LedgerSequence.NEXTVAL,
'09-NOV-01','Bought','Colt',1,'Each',10,10,'Andrew Dye');
INSERT INTO Ledger VALUES (LedgerSequence.NEXTVAL,
'10-NOV-01','Sold','Hefer',1,'Each',28,28,'Pat Lavay');
INSERT INTO Ledger VALUES (LedgerSequence.NEXTVAL,
'11-NOV-01','Sold','Boot Between Horses',1,'Each',6,6,'Pat Lavay');
INSERT INTO Ledger VALUES (LedgerSequence.NEXTVAL,
'11-NOV-01','Sold','Butter',1,'Pound',.15,.15,'Pat Lavay');
INSERT INTO Ledger VALUES (LedgerSequence.NEXTVAL,
'12-NOV-01','Paid','Work',2,'Day',.75,1.5,'Pat Lavay');
INSERT INTO Ledger VALUES (LedgerSequence.NEXTVAL,
'13-NOV-01','Paid','Cut Logs',.5,'Day',.5,.25,'Pat Lavay');
INSERT INTO Ledger VALUES (LedgerSequence.NEXTVAL,
'13-NOV-01','Paid','Drawed Logs',1.5,'Day',.5,.75,'Pat Lavay');
INSERT INTO Ledger VALUES (LedgerSequence.NEXTVAL,
'13-DEC-01','Paid','Sawed Wood',1,'Day',.5,.5,'Pat Lavay');
INSERT INTO Ledger VALUES (LedgerSequence.NEXTVAL,
'14-NOV-01','Sold','Hefer',1,'Each',35,35,'Morris Arnold');
INSERT INTO Ledger VALUES (LedgerSequence.NEXTVAL,
'15-NOV-01','Sold','Beef',37,'Pound',.04,1.48,'Fred Fuller');
INSERT INTO Ledger VALUES (LedgerSequence.NEXTVAL,
'16-NOV-01','Sold','Butter',5,'Pound',.16,.8,'Victoria Lynn');
INSERT INTO Ledger VALUES (LedgerSequence.NEXTVAL,
'18-NOV-01','Sold','Butter',6,'Pound',.16,.96,'John Pearson');
INSERT INTO Ledger VALUES (LedgerSequence.NEXTVAL,
'20-NOV-01','Sold','Heifer',1,'Each',30,30,'Palmer Wallbom');
INSERT INTO Ledger VALUES (LedgerSequence.NEXTVAL,
'21-NOV-01','Sold','Beef',116,'Pound',.06,6.96,'Roland Brandt');
INSERT INTO Ledger VALUES (LedgerSequence.NEXTVAL,
'22-NOV-01','Sold','Beef',118,'Pound',.06,7.08,'Gerhardt Kentgen');
INSERT INTO Ledger VALUES (LedgerSequence.NEXTVAL,
'01-DEC-01','Bought','Beef',138,'Pound',.05,6.9,'Victoria Lynn');
INSERT INTO Ledger VALUES (LedgerSequence.NEXTVAL,
```

```
'01-DEC-01','Bought','Beef',130,'Pound',.06,7.8,'George B. McCormick');
INSERT INTO Ledger VALUES (LedgerSequence.NEXTVAL,
'03-DEC-01','Bought','Beef',130,'Pound',.05,6.5,'Peter Lawson');
INSERT INTO Ledger VALUES (LedgerSequence.NEXTVAL,
'03-DEC-01','Bought','Beef',125,'Pound',.06,7.5,'Helen Brandt');
INSERT INTO Ledger VALUES (LedgerSequence.NEXTVAL,
'05-DEC-01','Bought','Beef',140,'Pound',.05,7,'Robert James');
INSERT INTO Ledger VALUES (LedgerSequence.NEXTVAL,
'05-DEC-01','Bought','Beef',145,'Pound',.05,7.25,'Isaiah James');
INSERT INTO Ledger VALUES (LedgerSequence.NEXTVAL,
'07-DEC-01','Bought','Horse',1,'Each',30,30,'George August');
INSERT INTO Ledger VALUES (LedgerSequence.NEXTVAL,
'07-DEC-01','Bought','Reaper/Binder',1,'Each',47.5,47.5,'Janice Talbot');
INSERT INTO Ledger VALUES (LedgerSequence.NEXTVAL,
'03-JAN-01','Bought','Hominy',1,'Bushel',1.25,1.25,'General Store');
INSERT INTO Ledger VALUES (LedgerSequence.NEXTVAL,
'09-JAN-01','Bought','Lice Killer',1,'Each',.5,.5,'General Store');
INSERT INTO Ledger VALUES (LedgerSequence.NEXTVAL,
'11-JAN-01','Bought','Mending Brace',1,'Each',.15,.15,'General Store');
INSERT INTO Ledger VALUES (LedgerSequence.NEXTVAL,
'11-JAN-01','Bought','Stove Blacking',1,'Each',.05,.05,'General Store');
INSERT INTO Ledger VALUES (LedgerSequence.NEXTVAL,
'13-JAN-01','Bought','Grinding Bat',10,'Each',.03,.3,'General Store');
INSERT INTO Ledger VALUES (LedgerSequence.NEXTVAL,
'14-JAN-01','Sold','Beef Hide',1,'Each',5.46,5.46,'General Store');
INSERT INTO Ledger VALUES (LedgerSequence.NEXTVAL,
'14-JAN-01','Sold','Cheese Flat',13,'Each',3.15,40.95,'General Store');
INSERT INTO Ledger VALUES (LedgerSequence.NEXTVAL,
'14-JAN-01','Bought','Lantern Globe',1,'Each',.1,.1,'General Store');
INSERT INTO Ledger VALUES (LedgerSequence.NEXTVAL,
'15-JAN-01','Bought','Stamp For Letter',1,'Each',.02,.02,'Post Office');
INSERT INTO Ledger VALUES (LedgerSequence.NEXTVAL,
'15-JAN-01','Bought','Stocking',2,'Pair',.15,.3,'General Store');
INSERT INTO Ledger VALUES (LedgerSequence.NEXTVAL,
'16-JAN-01','Bought','Oil',4,'Gallon',.1,.4,'General Store');
INSERT INTO Ledger VALUES (LedgerSequence.NEXTVAL,
'16-JAN-01','Bought','Sugar',25,'Pound',.07,1.75,'General Store');
INSERT INTO Ledger VALUES (LedgerSequence.NEXTVAL,
'16-JAN-01','Bought','Molasses',1,'Gallon',.6,.6,'General Store');
INSERT INTO Ledger VALUES (LedgerSequence.NEXTVAL,
'16-JAN-01','Bought','Card Of Thanks',1,'Each',.3,.3,'General Store');
INSERT INTO Ledger VALUES (LedgerSequence.NEXTVAL,
'17-JAN-01','Bought','Horse Shodding',1,'Each',.85,.85,'Livery');
INSERT INTO Ledger VALUES (LedgerSequence.NEXTVAL,
'17-JAN-01','Bought','Corn',230,'Pound',.01,2.3,'Feed Store');
INSERT INTO Ledger VALUES (LedgerSequence.NEXTVAL,
'18-JAN-01','Bought','Corn Meal',213,'Pound',.01,2.13,'Feed Store');
INSERT INTO Ledger VALUES (LedgerSequence.NEXTVAL,
'18-JAN-01','Bought','Paper',50,'Sheets',.01,.5,'General Store');
INSERT INTO Ledger VALUES (LedgerSequence.NEXTVAL,
'18-JAN-01','Bought','Coffee',1,'Pound',.3,.3,'General Store');
INSERT INTO Ledger VALUES (LedgerSequence.NEXTVAL,
'18-JAN-01','Bought','Seeded Raisins',1,'Pound',.12,.12,'General Store');
INSERT INTO Ledger VALUES (LedgerSequence.NEXTVAL,
'18-JAN-01','Bought','Cotton Stocking',3,'Pair',.08,.24,'General Store');
```

```
INSERT INTO Ledger VALUES (LedgerSequence.NEXTVAL,
'19-JAN-01','Bought','Cotton Stocking',3,'Pair',.08,.24,'General Store');
INSERT INTO Ledger VALUES (LedgerSequence.NEXTVAL,
'19-JAN-01','Bought','Grinding Bat',24,'Each',.03,.72,'General Store');
INSERT INTO Ledger VALUES (LedgerSequence.NEXTVAL,
'19-JAN-01','Bought','Telephone Call',1,'Each',.15,.15,'Phone Company');
INSERT INTO Ledger VALUES (LedgerSequence.NEXTVAL,
'19-JAN-01','Bought','Tea',.5,'Pound',.5,.25,'General Store');
INSERT INTO Ledger VALUES (LedgerSequence.NEXTVAL,
'19-JAN-01','Bought','Hat',1,'Each',.1,.1,'General Store');
INSERT INTO Ledger VALUES (LedgerSequence.NEXTVAL,
'19-JAN-01','Bought','Salt Peter',1,'Each',.08,.08,'General Store');
INSERT INTO Ledger VALUES (LedgerSequence.NEXTVAL,
'19-JAN-01','Bought','Envelopes',6,'Each',.02,.12,'General Store');
INSERT INTO Ledger VALUES (LedgerSequence.NEXTVAL,
'19-JAN-01','Bought','Creoal',2,'Qaurt',.37,.74,'General Store');
INSERT INTO Ledger VALUES (LedgerSequence.NEXTVAL,
'23-JAN-01','Sold','Wood',1,'Cord',2,2,'Methodist Church');
INSERT INTO Ledger VALUES (LedgerSequence.NEXTVAL,
'24-JAN-01','Bought','Schooling',1,'Each',1,1,'School');
INSERT INTO Ledger VALUES (LedgerSequence.NEXTVAL,
'24-JAN-01','Bought','Hominy',186,'Each',.01,1.86,'General Store');
INSERT INTO Ledger VALUES (LedgerSequence.NEXTVAL,
'28-JAN-01','Bought','Grinding',1,'Each',.9,.9,'Mill');
INSERT INTO Ledger VALUES (LedgerSequence.NEXTVAL,
'28-JAN-01','Bought','Popcorn',5,'Pound',.04,.2,'General Store');
INSERT INTO Ledger VALUES (LedgerSequence.NEXTVAL,
'02-FEB-01','Bought','Sulpher',5,'Pound',.25,1.25,'General Store');
INSERT INTO Ledger VALUES (LedgerSequence.NEXTVAL,
'03-FEB-01','Bought','Oil',4,'Gallon',.13,.52,'General Store');
INSERT INTO Ledger VALUES (LedgerSequence.NEXTVAL,
'03-FEB-01','Bought','Swamp Root',1,'Each',.75,.75,'General Store');
INSERT INTO Ledger VALUES (LedgerSequence.NEXTVAL,
'04-FEB-01','Bought','Shoeing Ned',1,'Each',.5,.5,'Blacksmith');
INSERT INTO Ledger VALUES (LedgerSequence.NEXTVAL,
'04-FEB-01','Bought','Grinding',1,'Each',.47,.47,'Mill');
INSERT INTO Ledger VALUES (LedgerSequence.NEXTVAL,
'05-FEB-01','Bought','Pills',1,'Each',.25,.25,'General Store');
INSERT INTO Ledger VALUES (LedgerSequence.NEXTVAL,
'07-FEB-01','Bought','Thread',2,'Each',.05,.1,'General Store');
INSERT INTO Ledger VALUES (LedgerSequence.NEXTVAL,
'08-FEB-01','Bought','Shirts',2,'Each',.5,1,'General Store');
INSERT INTO Ledger VALUES (LedgerSequence.NEXTVAL,
'10-FEB-01','Sold','Butter',9,'Pound',.25,2.25,'General Store');
INSERT INTO Ledger VALUES (LedgerSequence.NEXTVAL,
'18-FEB-01','Bought','Horse Medison',1,'Each',.13,.13,'General Store');
INSERT INTO Ledger VALUES (LedgerSequence.NEXTVAL,
'18-FEB-01','Bought','Elbo Stove Pipe',1,'Each',.15,.15,'General Store');
INSERT INTO Ledger VALUES (LedgerSequence.NEXTVAL,
'18-FEB-01','Sold','Calf',1,'Each',4,4,'Lily Carlstrom');
INSERT INTO Ledger VALUES (LedgerSequence.NEXTVAL,
'25-FEB-01','Sold','Butter',21,'Pound',.25,5.25,'General Store');
INSERT INTO Ledger VALUES (LedgerSequence.NEXTVAL,
'28-FEB-01','Bought','Swamp Root',1,'Each',.75,.75,'General Store');
INSERT INTO Ledger VALUES (LedgerSequence.NEXTVAL,
```

```
'28-FEB-01','Bought','Liver Pills',1,'Each',.2,.2,'General Store');
INSERT INTO Ledger VALUES (LedgerSequence.NEXTVAL,
'28-FEB-01','Sold','Butter',3,'Pound',.25,.75,'Helen Brandt');
INSERT INTO Ledger VALUES (LedgerSequence.NEXTVAL,
'01-APR-01','Bought','Grinding',1,'Each',.45,.45,'Mill');
INSERT INTO Ledger VALUES (LedgerSequence.NEXTVAL,
'06-MAR-01','Bought','Medison For Indigestion',1,'Each',.4,.4,'Dr. Carlstrom');
INSERT INTO Ledger VALUES (LedgerSequence.NEXTVAL,
'06-JUN-01','Bought','Breading Powder',1,'Each',.9,.9,'Mill');
INSERT INTO Ledger VALUES (LedgerSequence.NEXTVAL,
'06-MAR-01','Bought','Pants',1,'Pair',.75,.75,'General Store');
INSERT INTO Ledger VALUES (LedgerSequence.NEXTVAL,
'07-APR-01','Bought','Hominy',200,'Pound',.01,2,'Mill');
INSERT INTO Ledger VALUES (LedgerSequence.NEXTVAL,
'08-MAR-01','Bought','Tobacco For Lice',1,'Each',.25,.25,'Mill');
INSERT INTO Ledger VALUES (LedgerSequence.NEXTVAL,
'07-MAR-01','Bought','Shoeing',1,'Each',.35,.35,'Blacksmith');
INSERT INTO Ledger VALUES (LedgerSequence.NEXTVAL,
'07-APR-01','Bought','Pins',1,'Each',.05,.05,'General Store');
INSERT INTO Ledger VALUES (LedgerSequence.NEXTVAL,
'07-MAR-01','Bought','Mail Box',1,'Each',1,1,'Post Office');
INSERT INTO Ledger VALUES (LedgerSequence.NEXTVAL,
'10-MAR-01','Bought','Stove Pipe Thimbles',2,'Each',.5,1,'Verna Hardware');
INSERT INTO Ledger VALUES (LedgerSequence.NEXTVAL,
'13-MAR-01','Bought','Thermometer',1,'Each',.15,.15,'General Store');
INSERT INTO Ledger VALUES (LedgerSequence.NEXTVAL,
'14-MAR-01','Bought','Lot In Cemetery No. 80',1,'Each',25,25,
'Methodist Church');
INSERT INTO Ledger VALUES (LedgerSequence.NEXTVAL,
'14-MAR-01','Paid','Digging Of Grave',1,'Each',3,3,'Jed Hopkins');
INSERT INTO Ledger VALUES (LedgerSequence.NEXTVAL,
'16-APR-01','Bought','Grinding',1,'Each',.16,.16,'Mill');
INSERT INTO Ledger VALUES (LedgerSequence.NEXTVAL,
'16-MAR-01','Bought','Grinding',1,'Each',.16,.16,'Mill');
INSERT INTO Ledger VALUES (LedgerSequence.NEXTVAL,
'23-MAR-01','Bought','Cloth For Dress Lining',2,'Yard',.27,.54,
'General Store');
INSERT INTO Ledger VALUES (LedgerSequence.NEXTVAL,
'18-AUG-01','Bought','SYRUP Thermometer',1,'Each',1,1,'General Store');
INSERT INTO Ledger VALUES (LedgerSequence.NEXTVAL,
'25-MAR-01','Bought','Boots For Shirley',1,'Pair',2.5,2.5,'General Store');
INSERT INTO Ledger VALUES (LedgerSequence.NEXTVAL,
'27-APR-01','Bought','Syrup Cans',2,'Dozen',1.07,2.14,'Verna Hardware');
INSERT INTO Ledger VALUES (LedgerSequence.NEXTVAL,
'22-MAR-01','Bought','Milk Cans',2,'Each',2.5,5,'Verna Hardware');
INSERT INTO Ledger VALUES (LedgerSequence.NEXTVAL,
'23-APR-01','Bought','Dubble Strainer',1,'Each',.95,.95,'Verna Hardware');
INSERT INTO Ledger VALUES (LedgerSequence.NEXTVAL,
'25-JUN-01','Bought','Milk Stirrer',1,'Each',.25,.25,'Verna Hardware');
INSERT INTO Ledger VALUES (LedgerSequence.NEXTVAL,
'27-MAR-01','Bought','Hominy',77,'Pound',.01,.77,'Mill');
INSERT INTO Ledger VALUES (LedgerSequence.NEXTVAL,
'28-APR-01','Bought','Corn',104,'Pound',.01,1.04,'Mill');
INSERT INTO Ledger VALUES (LedgerSequence.NEXTVAL,
'06-APR-01','Bought','Funeral',1,'Each',3.19,3.19,'Underwood Bros');
```

```
INSERT INTO Ledger VALUES (LedgerSequence.NEXTVAL,
'30-APR-01','Bought','Brush',1,'Each',.05,.05,'General Store');
INSERT INTO Ledger VALUES (LedgerSequence.NEXTVAL,
'30-APR-01','Bought','Sand',5,'Bushel',.03,.15,'Quarry');
INSERT INTO Ledger VALUES (LedgerSequence.NEXTVAL,
'31-MAR-01','Sold','Molasses',3,'Gallon',1,3,'Harold Schole');
INSERT INTO Ledger VALUES (LedgerSequence.NEXTVAL,
'28-MAR-01','Sold','Molasses',1,'Gallon',1,1,'Gerhardt Kentgen');
INSERT INTO Ledger VALUES (LedgerSequence.NEXTVAL,
'30-MAR-01','Bought','Fixing Shirleys Watch',1,'Each',.25,.25,
'Manner Jewelers');
INSERT INTO Ledger VALUES (LedgerSequence.NEXTVAL,
'04-APR-01','Sold','Butter',9,'Pound',.23,2.07,'Harold Schole');
INSERT INTO Ledger VALUES (LedgerSequence.NEXTVAL,
'05-APR-01','Bought','Soda',1,'Each',.05,.05,'General Store');
INSERT INTO Ledger VALUES (LedgerSequence.NEXTVAL,
'05-MAR-01','Bought','Telephone Call',1,'Each',.2,.2,'Phone Company');
INSERT INTO Ledger VALUES (LedgerSequence.NEXTVAL,
'06-APR-01','Bought','Gloves',1,'Pair',.25,.25,'General Store');
INSERT INTO Ledger VALUES (LedgerSequence.NEXTVAL,
'06-APR-01','Bought','Shoes For Shirley',1,'Pair',2,2,'General Store');
INSERT INTO Ledger VALUES (LedgerSequence.NEXTVAL,
'09-APR-01','Bought','Peanuts',1,'Each',.05,.05,'General Store');
INSERT INTO Ledger VALUES (LedgerSequence.NEXTVAL,
'11-APR-01','Bought','Bran',300,'Pound',.01,3,'General Store');
INSERT INTO Ledger VALUES (LedgerSequence.NEXTVAL,
'15-APR-01','Bought','Shoeing',2,'Each',.3,.6,'Blacksmith');
INSERT INTO Ledger VALUES (LedgerSequence.NEXTVAL,
'17-APR-01','Bought','Hominy',173,'Pound',.01,1.73,'General Store');
INSERT INTO Ledger VALUES (LedgerSequence.NEXTVAL,
'17-APR-01','Bought','Bran',450,'Pound',.01,4.5,'General Store');
INSERT INTO Ledger VALUES (LedgerSequence.NEXTVAL,
'17-APR-01','Bought','Calf Meal',110,'Pound',.01,1.1,'General Store');
INSERT INTO Ledger VALUES (LedgerSequence.NEXTVAL,
'22-APR-01','Bought','Hominy',454,'Pound',.01,4.54,'General Store');
INSERT INTO Ledger VALUES (LedgerSequence.NEXTVAL,
'22-APR-01','Bought','Bran',300,'Pound',.01,3,'General Store');
INSERT INTO Ledger VALUES (LedgerSequence.NEXTVAL,
'22-APR-01','Sold','Calf',1,'Each',1,1,'Pat Lavay');
INSERT INTO Ledger VALUES (LedgerSequence.NEXTVAL,
'25-APR-01','Bought','Calf Meal',100,'Each',.01,1,'General Store');
INSERT INTO Ledger VALUES (LedgerSequence.NEXTVAL,
'27-APR-01','Bought','Shoeing Ned',1,'Each',.5,.5,'Blacksmith');
INSERT INTO Ledger VALUES (LedgerSequence.NEXTVAL,
'07-JUN-01','Received','Breaking Colt',1,'Each',5,5,'Sam Dye');
INSERT INTO Ledger VALUES (LedgerSequence.NEXTVAL,
'07-JUN-01','Received','Keeping Colt',1,'Each',4,4,'Sam Dye');
INSERT INTO Ledger VALUES (LedgerSequence.NEXTVAL,
'17-JUN-01','Bought','School Tax',1,'Each',6.56,6.56,'School');
INSERT INTO Ledger VALUES (LedgerSequence.NEXTVAL,
'17-JUN-01','Received','Threshing',2,'Day',1,2,'Henry Chase');
INSERT INTO Ledger VALUES (LedgerSequence.NEXTVAL,
'18-JUN-01','Paid','Threshing',.5,'Day',1,.5,'William Swing');
INSERT INTO Ledger VALUES (LedgerSequence.NEXTVAL,
'18-JUN-01','Bought','Sheep',22,'Each',.87,19.14,'Boole And Jones');
```

```
INSERT INTO Ledger VALUES (LedgerSequence.NEXTVAL,
'15-MAR-01','Sold','Potatoes',5,'Bushel',.25,1.25,'General Store');
INSERT INTO Ledger VALUES (LedgerSequence.NEXTVAL,
'15-MAR-01','Sold','Cow',2,'Each',33,66,'Sam Dye');
INSERT INTO Ledger VALUES (LedgerSequence.NEXTVAL,
'15-MAR-01','Received','Boot Between Horses',1,'Each',10,10,'Adah Talbot');
INSERT INTO Ledger VALUES (LedgerSequence.NEXTVAL,
'18-MAR-01','Sold','Wagon',1,'Each',5,5,'Adah Talbot');
INSERT INTO Ledger VALUES (LedgerSequence.NEXTVAL,
'04-APR-01','Sold','Harnes',1,'Each',2,2,'Adah Talbot');
INSERT INTO Ledger VALUES (LedgerSequence.NEXTVAL,
'16-APR-01','Sold','Cow',3,'Each',30,90,'George B. McCormick');
INSERT INTO Ledger VALUES (LedgerSequence.NEXTVAL,
'09-JUN-01','Bought','Use Of Pasture',1,'Each',10,10,'George B. McCormick');
INSERT INTO Ledger VALUES (LedgerSequence.NEXTVAL,
'28-JUN-01','Bought','Sheep And Bull',1,'Lot',97.88,97.88,'Edward Johnson');
INSERT INTO Ledger VALUES (LedgerSequence.NEXTVAL,
'03-JUL-01','Sold','Heifer',1,'Each',35,35,'Sam Dye');
INSERT INTO Ledger VALUES (LedgerSequence.NEXTVAL,
'18-MAY-01','Bought','Middlings',180,'Pound',.01,1.8,'Dean Foreman');
INSERT INTO Ledger VALUES (LedgerSequence.NEXTVAL,
'20-MAY-01','Bought','Middlings',450,'Pound',.01,4.5,'George Oscar');
INSERT INTO Ledger VALUES (LedgerSequence.NEXTVAL,
'22-MAY-01','Bought','Middlings',640,'Pound',.01,6.4,'Edythe Gammiere');
INSERT INTO Ledger VALUES (LedgerSequence.NEXTVAL,
'23-MAY-01','Bought','Middlings',110,'Pound',.01,1.1,'John Austin');
INSERT INTO Ledger VALUES (LedgerSequence.NEXTVAL,
'28-MAY-01','Bought','Comb',1,'Each',.07,.07,'General Store');
INSERT INTO Ledger VALUES (LedgerSequence.NEXTVAL,
'29-MAY-01','Bought','Buttons',1,'Each',.1,.1,'General Store');
INSERT INTO Ledger VALUES (LedgerSequence.NEXTVAL,
'05-JUL-01','Bought','Beans',6,'Pound',.03,.18,'General Store');
INSERT INTO Ledger VALUES (LedgerSequence.NEXTVAL,
'29-MAY-01','Bought','Raisons',3,'Pound',.08,.24,'General Store');
INSERT INTO Ledger VALUES (LedgerSequence.NEXTVAL,
'29-MAY-01','Bought','Cheese',3,'Pound',.09,.27,'General Store');
INSERT INTO Ledger VALUES (LedgerSequence.NEXTVAL,
'04-JUN-01','Bought','Beer',1,'Each',.2,.2,'General Store');
INSERT INTO Ledger VALUES (LedgerSequence.NEXTVAL,
'04-JUN-01','Bought','Cough Syrup',1,'Each',.25,.25,'General Store');
INSERT INTO Ledger VALUES (LedgerSequence.NEXTVAL,
'26-JUN-01','Bought','Shoe String',2,'Pair',.04,.08,'General Store');
INSERT INTO Ledger VALUES (LedgerSequence.NEXTVAL,
'26-JUN-01','Bought','Close Pins',1,'Each',.05,.05,'General Store');
INSERT INTO Ledger VALUES (LedgerSequence.NEXTVAL,
'26-JUN-01','Bought','Close Brush',1,'Each',.1,.1,'General Store');
INSERT INTO Ledger VALUES (LedgerSequence.NEXTVAL,
'06-MAR-01','Sold','Eggs',14,'Dozen',.12,1.68,'General Store');
INSERT INTO Ledger VALUES (LedgerSequence.NEXTVAL,
'06-MAR-01','Sold','Hens',12,'Each',.5,6,'General Store');
INSERT INTO Ledger VALUES (LedgerSequence.NEXTVAL,
'15-APR-01','Sold','Eggs',13,'Dozen',.1,1.3,'General Store');
INSERT INTO Ledger VALUES (LedgerSequence.NEXTVAL,
'27-APR-01','Paid','Plowing',1,'Day',3,3,'Richard Koch And Brothers');
INSERT INTO Ledger VALUES (LedgerSequence.NEXTVAL,
```

```
'16-APR-01','Paid','Plowing',1,'Day',3,3,'Richard Koch And Brothers');
INSERT INTO Ledger VALUES (LedgerSequence.NEXTVAL,
'17-DEC-01','Paid','Sawing',1,'Day',.75,.75,'Dick Jones');
INSERT INTO Ledger VALUES (LedgerSequence.NEXTVAL,
'28-JUL-01','Paid','Sawing',1,'Day',.75,.75,'Dick Jones');
INSERT INTO Ledger VALUES (LedgerSequence.NEXTVAL,
'18-AUG-01','Paid','Weeding',1,'Day',.9,.9,'Elbert Talbot');
INSERT INTO Ledger VALUES (LedgerSequence.NEXTVAL,
'29-SEP-01','Paid','Work',1,'Day',1,1,'Gerhardt Kentgen');
INSERT INTO Ledger VALUES (LedgerSequence.NEXTVAL,
'19-JAN-01','Paid','Work',1,'Day',1,1,'Gerhardt Kentgen');
INSERT INTO Ledger VALUES (LedgerSequence.NEXTVAL,
'30-JAN-01','Paid','Work',.5,'Day',1,.5,'Elbert Talbot');
INSERT INTO Ledger VALUES (LedgerSequence.NEXTVAL,
'28-FEB-01','Paid','Work',1,'Day',1,1,'Elbert Talbot');
INSERT INTO Ledger VALUES (LedgerSequence.NEXTVAL,
'20-MAR-01','Paid','Work',1,'Day',1,1,'Dick Jones');
INSERT INTO Ledger VALUES (LedgerSequence.NEXTVAL,
'21-JUL-01','Paid','Work',1,'Day',1,1,'Victoria Lynn');
INSERT INTO Ledger VALUES (LedgerSequence.NEXTVAL,
'22-OCT-01','Paid','Plowing',1,'Day',1.8,1.8,'Dick Jones');
INSERT INTO Ledger VALUES (LedgerSequence.NEXTVAL,
'23-SEP-01','Paid','Discus',.5,'Day',3,1.5,'Richard Koch And Brothers');
INSERT INTO Ledger VALUES (LedgerSequence.NEXTVAL,
'22-AUG-01','Paid','Sawing',1,'Day',1,1,'Peter Lawson');
INSERT INTO Ledger VALUES (LedgerSequence.NEXTVAL,
'23-AUG-01','Paid','Sawing',1,'Day',1,1,'Peter Lawson');
INSERT INTO Ledger VALUES (LedgerSequence.NEXTVAL,
'24-MAY-01','Paid','Work',1,'Day',1.2,1.2,'Wilfred Lowell');
INSERT INTO Ledger VALUES (LedgerSequence.NEXTVAL,
'11-MAY-01','Paid','Work',1,'Day',1.2,1.2,'Wilfred Lowell');
INSERT INTO Ledger VALUES (LedgerSequence.NEXTVAL,
'26-JUN-01','Paid','Painting',1,'Day',1.75,1.75,'Kay And Palmer Wallbom');
INSERT INTO Ledger VALUES (LedgerSequence.NEXTVAL,
'02-JUL-01','Bought','Middlings',220,'Pound',.01,2.2,'Edythe Gammiere');
INSERT INTO Ledger VALUES (LedgerSequence.NEXTVAL,
'03-JUL-01','Bought','Pig',1,'Each',3,3,'John Austin');
INSERT INTO Ledger VALUES (LedgerSequence.NEXTVAL,
'08-JUL-01','Bought','Cheese',1,'Pound',.09,.09,'General Store');
INSERT INTO Ledger VALUES (LedgerSequence.NEXTVAL,
'09-JUL-01','Bought','Beer',1,'Each',.2,.2,'General Store');
INSERT INTO Ledger VALUES (LedgerSequence.NEXTVAL,
'02-AUG-01','Bought','Milk Cans',3,'Each',2.5,7.5,'General Store');
INSERT INTO Ledger VALUES (LedgerSequence.NEXTVAL,
'05-AUG-01','Bought','Hominy',120,'Pound',.01,1.2,'General Store');
INSERT INTO Ledger VALUES (LedgerSequence.NEXTVAL,
'08-AUG-01','Bought','Brush',1,'Each',.06,.06,'General Store');
INSERT INTO Ledger VALUES (LedgerSequence.NEXTVAL,
'12-AUG-01','Bought','Corn',90,'Pound',.01,.9,'General Store');
INSERT INTO Ledger VALUES (LedgerSequence.NEXTVAL,
'25-MAR-01','Sold','Molasses',5,'Gallon',1,5,'Sam Dye');
INSERT INTO Ledger VALUES (LedgerSequence.NEXTVAL,
'29-AUG-01','Sold','Butter',5,'Pound',.23,1.15,'Gerhardt Kentgen');
INSERT INTO Ledger VALUES (LedgerSequence.NEXTVAL,
'06-SEP-01','Bought','Telephone Call',1,'Each',.2,.2,'Phone Company');
```

```
NSERT INTO Ledger VALUES (LedgerSequence.NEXTVAL,
'09-SEP-01','Bought','Peanuts',1,'Each',.05,.05,'General Store');
INSERT INTO Ledger VALUES (LedgerSequence.NEXTVAL,
'12-SEP-01','Bought','Bran',170,'Pound',.01,1.7,'General Store');
INSERT INTO Ledger VALUES (LedgerSequence.NEXTVAL,
'13-SEP-01','Bought','Shoeing',4,'Each',.3,1.2,'Blacksmith');
INSERT INTO Ledger VALUES (LedgerSequence.NEXTVAL,
'15-SEP-01','Bought','Hominy',144,'Pound',.01,1.44,'General Store');
INSERT INTO Ledger VALUES (LedgerSequence.NEXTVAL,
'20-APR-01','Bought','Bran',370,'Pound',.01,3.7,'General Store');
INSERT INTO Ledger VALUES (LedgerSequence.NEXTVAL,
'17-JUL-01','Bought','Calf Meal',90,'Pound',.01,.9,'General Store');
INSERT INTO Ledger VALUES (LedgerSequence.NEXTVAL,
'20-JUL-01','Bought','Hominy',300,'Pound',.01,3,'General Store');
INSERT INTO Ledger VALUES (LedgerSequence.NEXTVAL,
'25-JUL-01','Sold','Calf',1,'Each',1,1,'Sam Dye');
INSERT INTO Ledger VALUES (LedgerSequence.NEXTVAL,
'19-SEP-01','Bought','Bran',100,'Pound',.01,1,'General Store');
INSERT INTO Ledger VALUES (LedgerSequence.NEXTVAL,
'23-SEP-01','Bought','Calf Meal',110,'Pound',.01,1.1,'General Store');
INSERT INTO Ledger VALUES (LedgerSequence.NEXTVAL,
'25-SEP-01','Bought','Hominy',80,'Pound',.01,.8,'General Store');
INSERT INTO Ledger VALUES (LedgerSequence.NEXTVAL,
'07-OCT-01','Paid','Work',1,'Day',1,1,'Jed Hopkins');
INSERT INTO Ledger VALUES (LedgerSequence.NEXTVAL,
'12-OCT-01','Bought','Sheep',12,'Each',.9,10.8,'Boole And Jones');
INSERT INTO Ledger VALUES (LedgerSequence.NEXTVAL,
'15-OCT-01','Sold','BEEF',935,'Pound',.03,28.05,'General Store');
INSERT INTO Ledger VALUES (LedgerSequence.NEXTVAL,
'18-OCT-01','Received','Boot Between Horses',1,'Each',10,10,'Adah Talbot');
INSERT INTO Ledger VALUES (LedgerSequence.NEXTVAL,
'12-OCT-01','Sold','Heifer',1,'Each',35,35,'George B. McCormick');
```

APPENDIX B

Translation Tools

If you are in the situation of having to distribute your Developer/2000 applications to customers who require the application to operate using a language different from the native language of the application, read this appendix.

As a rule of thumb, you are always going to be better off if you make linguistic portability a requirement for the application from the beginning. The world has gotten drastically smaller in the 1990s, and the next century promises to squeeze it even more. If you start out believing you will have to support applications in Norwegian, Russian, Arabic, and even Kanji, you are likely to design an application that can accommodate these languages, however diverse their requirements.

There are three areas you need to understand to facilitate translation of your Developer/2000 applications into different languages:

- National Language Support (NLS)
- Layout Design
- String Translation

National Language Support in ORACLE7

ORACLE7 provides an extensive facility for dealing with linguistic differences that it calls National Language Support (NLS). See the discussion of this facility in the *ORACLE7 Database Administrator's Guide,* Appendix C, "National Language Support." If you are going to work with multiple character sets and languages, you should start by reading that appendix, because you definitely need to know what ORACLE7 does for you.

Briefly, NLS provides support for these linguistic issues:

- Text and character sets for different languages stored in the database

- Messages from ORACLE7 and the runtime programs in different languages

- Format masks defaulting to appropriate formats for different languages

- Sorting or *collation* sequences for different alphabets used with relational operators in SQL expressions and in ORDER BY clauses

- Bidirectional formatting of displayed items in forms, reports, and graphs

By "support," ORACLE7 in this case means handling everything transparently. As an application developer, you do nothing except to tell ORACLE7 what language and territory you wish to use; it takes care of everything else. You specify the language with the NLS_LANG environment variable in ORACLE.INI. See the *ORACLE Developer/2000 Installation Guide for Windows* (or the manual for your operating system), Appendix B, "The ORACLE.INI File," for details.

The NLS facility, while useful, departs in a major way from the direction set by the American National Standards Institute (ANSI) SQL 1992 standard. That standard defines a completely different way of handling character sets and collation sequences. This renders the future of NLS a bit uncertain.

You can use the ALTER SESSION statement (an ORACLE7 SQL extension to the ANSI standard) to change any of the parameters for NLS. If you wish, you can exercise a fine level of control over language support. This book advises you to go lightly with this, both because the NLS facility does not conform to the emerging ANSI standard and because with this kind of feature you are generally better off accepting the defaults. You can endlessly tweak and fix and investigate to get the behavior just right for Libyan Arabic, or you can go with the flow....

Another place for going with the flow is to use default format masks. All of the Developer/2000 products use format masks to format number and date data. Various examples in this book recommend setting the format masks to specific values for dates, numbers, and monetary values. If you are going to provide language-independent applications, ignore this advice. Use the default format masks. NLS automatically uses the right mask for the language you specify in NLS_LANG. If you use an explicit format, you lose this automatic handling. You then must code around everything, which can get unsurprisingly tedious.

There are some specific format mask characters you can use that ORACLE7 interprets correctly using NLS:

C	The international currency symbol
L	The local currency symbol
D	The decimal separator in numbers
G	The thousands separator in numbers

L999G999D00, for example, is an internationally portable version of $999,999.99. NLS also interprets various date components in local versions, such as the names of months or days of the week. See the Forms, Reports, and Graphs documentation on format masks for details.

There is a special case you must watch for: PL/SQL expressions. If you use date constants in PL/SQL for any reason, wrap them in a TO_DATE function to make sure that PL/SQL handles them correctly. For example, here is a language-dependent expression:

```
:Ledger.ActionDate := '1/1/01';
```

This is language dependent because PL/SQL converts the string using the standard "American" format mask, 'dd-MON-yy', regardless of the current language. Instead, you should use this kind of code:

```
:Ledger.ActionDate := to_date('01/01/01', 'DD/MM/YY');
```

Layout Design

The key issue in layout design is precisely the same issue that you have in windowing system portability. You have to accommodate different sizes for objects at different times. With a windowing system, buttons are different sizes, as are default fonts. Some buttons have double lines around them on one system and none on another.

With different languages, there are several layout issues:

- The size of text strings varies with the translated string length.

- The size of formatted strings (format mask territory) varies with the language.

- The size of "widgets," the various graphical objects you display on screen that include text, such as radio buttons, varies with the language.

- The location of labels varies with the size of the fields they label, which in turn depends on language.

Oracle recommends a rule-of-thumb value of 30 percent expansion room for all these cases. If you can, you should develop the original application in the language that takes up the most room.

Also, you should design your screen, report, and graph layout for linguistic portability. Use less boilerplate; this static material will get in the way when you need to expand fields, and every bit of text you add will require translation. Do not clutter the boilerplate with graphics that will interfere with expansion. Arrange the fields so that different languages will look reasonable, even if the reading direction is the reverse of the language in which you develop the application.

String Translation

Any application you develop is going to have a lot of strings. To minimize string translation, you should use as few strings as possible in boilerplate. For example, for applications that need to be internationally portable, do not put a lot of text directions for use into the boilerplate. Put it in the database and display it in a display-only field.

There are two kinds of strings to worry about in Developer/2000 applications:

- Boilerplate text, including labels and titles
- String constants and variables in PL/SQL procedures

Boilerplate Text

Boilerplate text is any text in your forms, reports, or graphics that you type in through an editor rather than fill in from the database. The designer saves this text in various formats in your application files (or in the database if you save the application there).

Translation of boilerplate text is a matter of finding the text and translating it to the language or languages in which you wish it to appear. There are at least a couple of ways to approach the problem. First, you can make one application file (form, report, graphic) for each language. Second, you can replace the boilerplate with display fields and fill them in from the database, using special PL/SQL code to figure out the correct language and data location. This book recommends the former approach. Though slightly more tedious, maintaining the application data is a lot easier than maintaining the relatively complex code you would have to add to your applications.

There is a separate product called the ORACLE Translation Manager utility facilities in the NLS*WorkBench for translating application boilerplate. This product can make your life substantially easier when translating applications.

Again, limiting the amount of such text is a good strategy for international applications.

PL/SQL Strings

At various times, your PL/SQL code is going to display error, warning, or advisory messages through alerts or other mechanisms, such as display fields. Often, you will construct these messages by concatenating automatically generated strings. If you want an internationally portable application, you have to take measures to make sure these strings appear in the right language. You can code them dynamically to check the current language and respond correctly, but there are better ways to achieve the same results.

The most effective method centralizes your string handling in a PL/SQL library (see Chapter 12 for details). You can code simple, constant messages with message number lookups, or you can develop specific functions that take parameterized input and produce an appropriate message. You build one library for each language you want to support; each library contains the same set of functions. When you install your system, you use the FORMS45_PATH, REPORTS25_PATH, and GRAPHICS25_PATH environment variables to point to the language directory in which your translated library resides. You can even switch languages by resetting this path. When you load a form, report, or graph, the runtime program looks for the attached libraries in the directories in the path. It loads the first version it finds. When your application calls one of the string functions, PL/SQL calls the one defined for the current language. Thus, all you need to do is to make sure that the correct directory is first in the path.

Using NLS in ORACLE7 gets you a long way toward linguistic portability in your applications because it makes many of the character set issues you face transparent: it just works. With careful screen layout and rigorous string management in your applications, you are well on the way to having applications that will work around the world.

Index

R

S

U

V

W

X

Y

Z

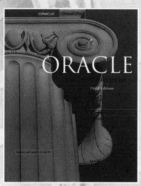

ORDER BOOKS DIRECTLY FROM OSBORNE/McGRAW-HILL

For a complete catalog of Osborne's books, call 510-549-6600 or write to us at 2600 Tenth Street, Berkeley, CA 94710

☎ Call Toll-Free, *24 hours a day, 7 days a week, in the U.S.A. and Canada*
U.S.A.: 1-800-822-8158   **Canada: 1-800-565-5758**

✉ Mail *in the U.S.A. to:*
McGraw-Hill, Inc.
Customer Service Dept.
P.O. Box 547
Blacklick, OH 43004

Canada
McGraw-Hill Ryerson
Customer Service
300 Water Street
Whitby, Ontario L1N 9B6

📠 Fax *in the U.S.A. to:*
1-614-759-3644

Canada
1-800-463-5885

orders@mcgraw-hill.ca

SHIP TO:

Name _____

Company _____

Address _____

City / State / Zip _____

Daytime Telephone *(We'll contact you if there's a question about your order.)*

ISBN #	BOOK TITLE	Quantity	Price	Total
0-07-88				
0-07-88				
0-07-88				
0-07-88				
0-07-88				
0-07088				
0-07-88				
0-07-88				
0-07-88				
0-07-88				
0-07-88				
0-07-88				
0-07-88				
0-07-88				

Shipping & Handling Charge from Chart Below	
Subtotal	
Please Add Applicable State & Local Sales Tax	
TOTAL	

Shipping & Handling Charges

Order Amount	U.S.	Outside U.S.
$15.00 - $24.99	$4.00	$6.00
$25.00 - $49.99	$5.00	$7.00
$50.00 - $74.99	$6.00	$8.00
$75.00 - and up	$7.00	$9.00
$100 - and up	$8.00	$10.00

Occasionally we allow other selected companies to use our mailing list. If you would prefer that we not include you in these extra mailings, please check here: ❏

METHOD OF PAYMENT

❏ Check or money order enclosed (payable to Osborne/McGraw-Hill)

❏ AMERICAN EXPRESS   ❏ DISCOVER   ❏ MasterCard   ❏ VISA

Account No. [ ][ ][ ][ ][ ][ ][ ][ ][ ][ ][ ][ ][ ][ ][ ][ ]

Expiration Date _____

Signature _____

In a hurry? Call 1-800-822-8158 anytime, day or night, or visit your local bookstore.

Thank you for your order   Code BC640SL

Disc Warranty

WARNING: BEFORE OPENING THE DISC PACKAGE, CAREFULLY READ THE TERMS AND CONDITIONS OF THE FOLLOWING CD-ROM WARRANTY.

Limited Warranty

Osborne/**McGraw-Hill** warrants the physical compact disc enclosed herein to be free of defects in materials and workmanship for a period of sixty days from the purchase date. If Osborne/**McGraw-Hill** receives a defective disc along with written notification within the warranty period of defects in materials or workmanship, and such notification is determined by Osborne/**McGraw-Hill** to be correct, Osborne/**McGraw-Hill** will replace the defective disc.

Osborne/**McGraw-Hill**
2600 Tenth Street
Berkeley, CA 94710

The entire and exclusive liability and remedy for breach of this Limited Warranty shall be limited to replacement of the defective disc, and shall not include or extend to any claim for or right to cover any other damages, including but not limited to, loss of profit, data, or use of the software, or special, incidental, or consequential damages or other similar claims, even if Osborne/**McGraw-Hill** has been specifically advised of the possibility of such damages. In no event will Osborne/**McGraw-Hill**'s liability for any damages to you or any other person ever exceed the lower of the suggested list price or actual price paid for the license to use the software, regardless of any form of the claim.

OSBORNE, A DIVISION OF McGRAW-HILL, INC., SPECIFICALLY DISCLAIMS ALL OTHER WARRANTIES, EXPRESSED OR IMPLIED, INCLUDING BUT NOT LIMITED TO, ANY IMPLIED WARRANTY OF MERCHANTABILITY OR FITNESS FOR A PARTICULAR PURPOSE. Specifically, Osborne/**McGraw-Hill** makes no representation or warranty that the software is fit for any particular purpose, and any implied warranty of merchantability is limited to the sixty-day duration of the Limited Warranty covering the physical disc only (and not the software), and is otherwise expressly and specifically disclaimed.

This limited warranty gives you specific legal rights; you may have others which may vary from state to state. Some states do not allow the exclusion of incidental or consequential damages, or the limitation on how long an implied warranty lasts, so some of the above may not apply to you.

This agreement constitutes the entire agreement between the parties relating to use of the Product. The terms of any purchase order shall have no effect on the terms of this Agreement. Failure of Osborne/**McGraw-Hill** to insist at any time on strict compliance with this Agreement shall not constitute a waiver of any rights under this Agreement. This Agreement shall be construed and governed in accordance with the laws of New York. If any provision of this Agreement is held to be contrary to law, that provision will be enforced to the maximum extent permissible, and the remaining provisions will remain in force and effect.

Personal Developer/2000™
Trial Products for Software Developers

Learn for yourself why Developer/2000 is the world's hottest client/server development tool—another best-seller from Oracle.

This exciting new CD contains the latest in Oracle's database, development, and end-user tools, as well as an interactive multimedia presentation and a comprehensive Designer/2000 presentation.

See for yourself. This CD contains full-feature copies of:

Personal Oracle7
Oracle Developer/2000 (Release 1.2)
Oracle Discoverer/2000 (Release 1.2)
SQL*Plus
SQL*Net
Intersolv DataDirect Drivers
and more

Installation   To install products from this CD-ROM, insert into your Windows CD-ROM drive, and type:

d:\setup.exe

This will create a program group. To run the application, double-click on the Oracle icon.

We recommend that you install the products from the interactive presentation. However, if you wish to install the products manually, please follow the instructions in the readme file on the CD:

d:\readme.txt

Support   These products are provided for you to evaluate on a trial basis free of charge. No support is provided by Oracle or Osborne/McGraw-Hill for this trial. We recommend you use the Oracle Forum on CompuServe or the Internet—both forums are monitored by Oracle personnel as well as a group of independent consultants.

In addition, please visit Oracle's World Wide Web site for up-to-the-minute information:

http://www.oracle.com

About this Trial CD   This trial CD is for Windows 3.x only. Oracle's development tools are available on all popular "GUI's" and leading computing environments.

For further details, or to place your order in the USA, please dial **1-800-ORACLE1.** In all other countries, please contact your local Oracle representative.

This trial software may be used for 90 days from the date of acquiring it. It may not be used for production applications. You are not entitled to use this software after 90 days without purchasing it.

SEE DISC WARRANTY ON PREVIOUS PAGE